Cohen-Rosenthal,
  Edward.

Mutual gains.

$24.95

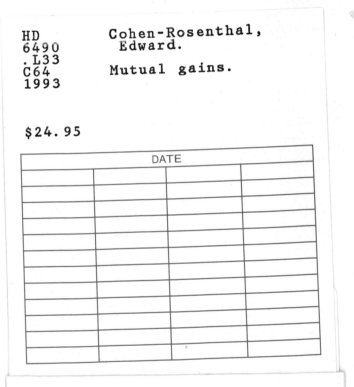

DATE			

MUTUAL GAINS

A Guide to Union-Management Cooperation

Second Edition, Revised

Edward Cohen-Rosenthal
and Cynthia E. Burton

ILR Press
Ithaca, New York

Copyright © 1993 by Cornell University

Library of Congress Cataloging-in-Publication Data

Cohen-Rosenthal, Edward.
Mutual gains: a guide to union-management cooperation / Edward
Cohen-Rosenthal and Cynthia E. Burton. — 2nd ed., rev.
p.   cm.
Includes bibliographical references and index.
ISBN 0-87546-312-6 (pbk.: alk. paper)
1. Labor-management committees—United States.   2. Industrial
relations—United States.   I. Burton, Cynthia E.   II. Title.
HD6490.L33C64   1993
331'.01'12—dc20   93-11918

First ILR Press edition 1993
Originally published in 1987 by Praeger Publishers

Copies may be ordered through bookstores or directly from

ILR Press
School of Industrial and Labor Relations
Cornell University
Ithaca, NY 14853–3901

Printed on acid-free paper in the United States of America
5 4 3 2 1

Contents

Preface

Much has changed in the world and industrial relations since we began to write the first edition of *Mutual Gains* in 1985. At that time quality circles were the rage and unions were under direct attack in the aftermath of the firing of more than eleven thousand striking air traffic controllers. The full impact of international competition had still not been felt. The domestic auto industry was at its lowest ebb, and it seemed that the Japanese could do no wrong. In the first edition we wrote about Eastern Airlines, which in a short span went from a promising example of cooperative labor-management relations to a debacle. Union-management cooperation seemed to be on the verge of becoming an anomaly. We wrote about employee participation in communist countries as one example of an approach to participation; but the Iron Curtain has since come down. What has emerged over the last eight years has been a broadened concern for democracy around the world, a reawakening of community spirit to counter the me-ism of the 1980s, a broadened consciousness of ecological hazards and possibilities, and a deeper understanding of the role of quality in designing and sustaining markets. Yet, as we sat down to write the second edition of this book, it was comforting to see that the basic ideas and approaches still hold up. What has not changed is the basic notion that unions and employers should seek out their common interests and build on them.

We used the first edition of this text with thousands of managers and unionists around the world. For this edition, we have added many new techniques unions and management can use together, from strategic scanning to environmental committees. We have included a full chapter on quality issues, which have taken on a new prominence since we first wrote our book.

What is alarming about each new fad that sweeps American industry is how short our memories are and how little we learn from what works and what doesn't. Writing the chapter on quality was difficult because, although it contained many new concepts, we also drew on much that had come before. The same was true of the material on self-directed work teams. Those who have followed our prescriptions for a carefully thought out process that builds programmatic strength while recognizing the political nature of each party have developed excellent programs with sterling results. They stand above the fads and the labels.

The underlying message of our book is more important today than ever. For managers, success does not come from dictating compliance but from seeking to achieve common goals with all employees. For unionists, the clock cannot be turned back to the days when unions got their way; the way forward is to challenge employers to manage better in ways that lead to greater employment security and higher incomes. For neither party is there any real choice. A workplace devoid of unions or with useless unions is a danger to a democracy. Without an internal gadfly to press for improved performance and sharing of the rewards through higher incomes, the economy suffers.

Both parties have opportunities to provide leadership that can lead to prosperity and better work lives. This is not the time to be defensive or to explain away cooperation as if it were a sign of weakness. Rather, it is time to embrace cooperation as a common strategy. What we need is broader and more effective union-management cooperative efforts in which unions don't shy away from full involvement and managers look to develop expansive partnerships.

Introduction

Union-management cooperation seems at some level almost paradoxical. After all, aren't managers and unionists supposed to be at odds and fighting all the time? It doesn't have to be that way; at the very least, it doesn't have to be that way all the time. Unions and management can cooperate on broad issues and still maintain their integrity and advocacy positions. Many issues and concerns form the basis for joint action while respecting different perspectives.

This book is about why and how to cooperate in ways that lead to mutual gains for both the union and management. We contend that the union-management relationship is not as adversarial as it might seem in theory, but rarely do the parties fully tap the beneficial possibilities of their relationship.

We believe in a system of industrial organization that balances the interests of management and unions. In the spirit of union-management cooperation, our goal is win-win. We are both pro-union and pro-management.

We feel that society, employees, and employers are best served when there is union representation at the workplace. We recognize that not everyone will agree with this assessment. Some feel that unions are an unnecessary anachronism in dealing with today's challenges. We are less sanguine about disposing of democracy and checks and balances to blind trust and questionable expertise. Some view unionization in the workplace as an evil to be avoided at all costs. They object to "third parties" interfering with the prerogatives of management. For us, a union is not a third party but an instrument of the workers. The international union with which they are affiliated is no more an outsider than are managers at higher corporate levels. The vehemence of antiunion opposition underscores the need for a modifying force in the work force. We do not believe that either side, union or management, holds any moral superiority or claim to rectitude. The union is far from perfect in practice, and management too rarely applies the principles taught in business schools. Our preference for unionism is based on our personal experience and values as well as our professional judgment.

With this orientation laid bare, we do not provide extended rationalizations of the benefits of unionization or make caveats about its effectiveness. Nor do we describe how the ideas put forth in this book could be applied in a nonunion setting. We leave that elaboration for others. Nor do we naively believe that all situations can be positive, that conflicts do not occur, or that confrontation does not create caution. Our hope is to find affirmative options that hold possibilities for the growth of everyone involved.

The aim of this book is twofold. The first goal is to uncover the breadth of application of union-management cooperation. Covering so much territory and linking areas that have never before been tied together in one volume raises the danger of covering issues too lightly. But our primary aim is to paint a broad picture of union-management cooperation from its roots in collective bargaining to ventures for the future.

The second goal of this book is to demonstrate that union-management cooperation is not just a theory but a viable, practical alternative. Our writing is the result of direct experience in working with a wide range of employers and unions to make cooperation real. This experience helps us ensure that our prescriptions are workable.

This book is not an in-depth guide to every cooperative activity. Rather it is intended to help labor and management think about cooperation. Few readers will need to read the entire book. The contents and index provide a way to identify quickly what you need to read.

Part I provides a broad overview of the basis for union-management cooperation. It examines definitions of cooperation and the particular perspectives of both the union and management. The history of union-management cooperation is presented to provide a perspective on where the approach comes from and its successes and limitations.

Part II provides a panorama of the possibilities for cooperation. Starting from the basic agreement, it works its way outward. New ways to apply the principles of negotiation and to handle grievances are discussed. A variety of ways to set up labor-management committees and worker participation in management are also outlined. Finally, a consideration of marketing, product development, and investments illustrates ways to build together for the future based on an expanding revenue base. The second edition outlines how quality can be a unifying banner for broad improvement strategies.

Part III discusses how to implement a joint program. A clear lesson of cooperative efforts is that although flexibility is needed, there are right ways and wrong ways to apply the principles of cooperation in practice. Important questions and structures are discussed concerning getting started, planning, design, training, governance, management, communications, monitoring, and evaluation. Though particular applications may vary, these areas need to be addressed in each and every cooperative effort. This section is not a cookbook or a how-to-do-it manual but a comprehensive overview of the major factors and considerations that need to be taken into account.

Part IV examines the connection between money and cooperation. Financial rewards and the ways to structure pay to encourage cooperation and workplace change is a critical and often overlooked area. The potential role of collective bargaining and profit sharing is addressed. Various individual and group incentive systems are outlined, including pay for knowledge and pay for performance. The pros and cons of gain-sharing and employee stock ownership plans are highlighted. Good pay alone is not enough to create a good workplace, and participation alone is not sufficient either. Linked together in some fashion, however, they can be strong influences in creating an overall better quality of work life.

Acknowledgments

W e want to thank William Batt, Robert Cole, Barry Cornwell, Harvey Samo, Susan Schurman, and John Simmons for their help in reviewing the original manuscript and for their valuable comments. Special thanks are due to Roy Rosenthal for preparing the graphics for both editions. We appreciate the willingness of the editors at Praeger to publish the original version in 1987, when "mutual gains" was a passing reference. Fran Benson, director of the ILR Press, recognized early that this book would be a significant contribution to practitioners in the field. She has stuck with and supported us over the several years and hurdles it has taken to bring out a revised edition. Erica Fox and Patty Peltekos have helped immeasurably in making the second edition more focused.

We particularly want to extend our appreciation to our families—Raymond, Laura, Ellen, Janna, Mollie, and Jacob—for their forebearance and assistance in helping to make this book possible. They have dealt with our absences more than they should have, as we have gone from location to location to help organizations put to use the prescriptions of this book.

Our sincere appreciation is due to those colleagues and organizations that have helped us by trying new methods and stretching in new directions. We dedicate this book to those who make our work worthwhile: the working women and men, at all levels in the organizations we have worked with, who recognize that it is better to struggle together than to battle against each other. We have learned from them and drawn on their strength and inspiration.

Part I. Union and Management Perspectives on Cooperation

1. What Is Union-Management Cooperation?

U nion-management cooperation as a concept is really very simple. It is that unions and management can identify at least one goal in common that they can work toward together—and can find ways to accomplish that goal jointly.

From this idea cooperation gets more involved. The union and management may have one goal or many goals in common. Union-management cooperation can address a broad range of issues in the workplace, from the handling of tools to strategic planning. It can take a wide variety of forms and structures, including labor-management committees, quality improvement teams, and self-managing work groups. It can take place at all levels, from the shop floor to the boardroom. Union-management cooperation is an affirmation of the leadership in both the union and management with the goal of seeking better ways of working and new avenues to success.

In some ways, it is easier to describe what union-management cooperation is *not*.

It is not a denial of the identity of either party. Too many descriptions portray union-management cooperation as if they were describing the Bobbsey twins hand-in-hand off on a picnic. Cooperation does not imply turning managers into unionists or unionists into managers. This results

in a weak and confusing muddle. In real union-management cooperation, each party is clear about its interests and whom it represents. They
work together because they believe it is in their own best interests, not
merely out of altruism. Management has a responsibility to stockholders
in the private sector and to taxpayers in the public sector.The union has
an obligation to represent workers' interests. Not only is it acceptable to
have clearly separate identities, but the differences in perspective are a
source of strength to any joint effort.

What we are talking about in this book is a hard-nosed version of
cooperation. It may involve cooperating with people you don't trust—or
even like. Managers and union leaders do it because it is in their own
interests. The starting point for cooperation is mutual respect and
common interest. That's it. Trust comes later as each party exhibits trustworthy behavior. We are able to cooperate when assertion of our own
interests is not confused with deprecating others. People cooperate best
when they recognize that their own interests are frequently diminished
the more the other party is undercut. Unions are there to *promote workers'
interests*—not to fight management. The managers' role is to *promote
shareholders' interests*—not to engage in ideological combat with unions.
You can have mutual gains.

To be interest-based does not imply that there cannot be trust or
goodwill between the parties. There can be. Trust makes cooperative
programs between labor and management better. It is, however, not a
precondition of cooperation. When organizations and people have positive experiences working together, they may even come to like and trust
one another. Trust is a wonderful secondary *outcome* of cooperation. But
expecting trust upfront not only is unrealistic, it can block its possibility
if expecting it prevents doing anything together that could build trust in
the long term.

It is not the absence of conflict. To some, cooperation evokes millennial
visions. The image of the big happy family is used to epitomize the happy,
tranquil workplace. But bucolic notions of the family are a 1950s television fantasy and are an inappropriate metaphor for the workplace. Real
families fight and have lots of problems. Notions of familism at work
ignore its roots in paternalistic company towns. Harmony at home and at
the workplace both come from respect for each person and open communication. We welcome workplaces with a sense of community and caring.
But when analogies to families are used to smooth over conflicts, invade
privacy, or divert focused attention from work that needs to get done, the
analogies are harmful.

For unionists, allusions to a conflict-free workplace are difficult to
swallow. Many unions were born out of conflict. Considering conflict
illegitimate calls into question the legitimacy of the union. Theoretically,

conflict could be eliminated if we all thought alike: management and the union, every department, every employee. But in real life, all organizations and interpersonal relations experience some conflict. Conflict brings out divergent opinions and perspectives. It sparks creativity and change. It is not only inevitable but desirable. This is why unilateral programs that suppress differences lack the vitality of a union-management effort.

The question is how much conflict there is and how it is handled, not whether it exists. Conflict continues to exist in organizations even after implementing successful, broad-ranging union-management cooperation efforts. What should be different is how that conflict is managed and the ways it is creatively channeled to achieve common goals. In the real world, cooperation harnesses the positive aspects of difference and conflict.

It is not laissez-faire or a sweetheart deal. Laissez-faire describes a hands-off or distant relationship. Union-management cooperation is not each side doing its own thing or leaving one another alone. It is joint, deliberate, and structured. Cooperative approaches often involve highly complex, intricate sets of social and organizational relationships and boundaries. Cooperation implies that the two parties care enough about issues in common that they are willing to work together on them. A cooperative environment is not one in which neither party bothers the other; it is one in which each bothers to bother constructively.

During the 1950s an insidious distortion of union-management cooperation occurred in many industries as they colluded on wages and prices. For example, the construction industry is now paying the price of sweetheart arrangements in which both parties denied entry to contractors and craftspeople to protect their own access to lucrative markets and jobs. It was such shortsighted exclusionary practices that sowed the seeds for the decline of the unionized construction industry. The parties are now hard at work trying to make up for their shortsightedness.

Deregulation and competitive forces made cozy, self-serving relationships counterproductive and heightened the need for new forms of joint partnership to address market pressures. In the post–World War II period, it was easy to pass along wage increases to the consumer. Growth and rising real wages made this feasible. In today's competitive global marketplace such agreements border on suicide. The only way to increase profitability and standards of living is to increase productivity significantly and expand markets through a common commitment to and broad involvement in enhancing quality.

It is not limited to one kind of workplace. Cooperation between labor and management is not limited to manufacturing. It is found in all industries and in workplaces of all sizes. Teachers and administrators are learning together how to improve education through site-based decision making in the schools. Construction contractors and building trades leaders along with construction users have developed expansive programs such as BUILT-RITE in Philadelphia, in which the parties participate in projects together at the job site and explore communitywide solutions to construction bottlenecks. In the public sector at the federal level, the Internal Revenue Service and the National Treasury Employees Union jointly sponsor broad quality programs. At state and local levels, public sector unions and managers have joined hands to improve the quality of public service. In hospitals, labor and management have worked together to improve career opportunities for hospital workers and patient care for those they serve. In retail trades, some unions and managers have established programs targeted at customer service and have opened new stores such as Super Fresh in the Delaware Valley. Railroad workers from twenty-three local unions along with Conrail management developed labor-management forums, quality circles, and concept teams that contributed greatly to the turnaround of that company. In the high-tech telephone industry, the Communications Workers of America (CWA), International Brotherhood of Electrical Workers (IBEW), and management have evolved a process of employee involvement. Public utilities have developed new compacts with their unions for improved performance. These are but a few examples.[1]

Cooperative programs have taken hold throughout industry in almost every location, have used a broad range of approaches, and have addressed an array of topics. This diversity demonstrates clearly one of the premises of this book—there is no one way to design a cooperative program; the contours of each particular labor and management situation determine its characteristics. The breadth of application is not always matched by its spread in the industry, staying power, or quality. But the diversity of forms of cooperation makes clear that creativity in the union-management relationship is more important than the effectiveness of any one technique.

It is not the domain of any one country. Many in America believe that the concepts of quality and cooperation are Japanese imports. Although impressive examples of Japanese union-management cooperation to improve quality have spurred changes worldwide, this is far too simplistic an analysis. Cooperation is a global phenomenon.

The situation in Japan is much more varied than the caricature that is often painted. Quality techniques and quality circles are important, but so are union-management consultation efforts. A joint consultation system at various levels of the company involves the union broadly. This system makes a difference. The export trade sector, which is heavily unionized, is the most productive part of Japan. Other sectors, such as services, retail, and the government, are not very productive at all and have few of the productivity structures found in parts of manufacturing.

Japanese unions contain a mix of militant left-wingers and those willing to enter into more cozy relationships. According to a study by the Asian Productivity Organization, about half of all Japanese workers describe labor-management relations as class warfare, and indeed there is a great deal of conflict within Japanese society.[2] The enterprise affiliation in Japan is probably not much different than that of most unions in the United States. When one looks at the total picture, it becomes clear that cultural stereotypes of the Japanese are hollow and an excuse for those unwilling to devote the hard thought and work that the Japanese have. Neither Japan-bashing nor fawning over Japan are called for. In truth, through common action and smart management, Japan has gone from a low-quality pretender to the dominant force in world trade with a sterling reputation for the quality of its products. Union-management cooperation has helped it make this change.

There is an alternative model found in Europe and especially in Scandinavia to the Japanese system of lean production. After World War II, the Allied forces in Germany instituted a system of codetermination, guaranteeing employees a voice in corporate decisions. Actually, works councils, in companies with more than five employees, were developed before World War I. Their current powers are extensive. Management is required to consult with them on all social matters, including operation of the enterprise, leave arrangements, pay plans, job and bonus rights, welfare services, health and safety, the organization of work, vocational training, hiring, firing, discipline, promotion, and transfer. In case of a dispute with the works council, decisions are taken to independent arbitration. Although all employees, not just union members, may be elected to works councils, most members are unionists. Given the economic success of Germany, it is obvious that union participation on the whole has been a contributor to its success.[3]

The participation of unions is extensive and guaranteed by law in all Scandinavian countries. Through board-level representation, works councils, and other forms of industrial democracy, unions are broadly involved. Most managers when surveyed on how well these structures work point to the positive contributions they make.

In Australia, sweeping new reforms are being introduced with the active involvement and leadership of the country's union movement. These have led to improvements in productivity, new industrial relations practices, the consolidation of trade unions, new skills and career ladders, and the introduction of new technology.[4]

Sometimes it is assumed that cooperative union-management activities occur only in advanced industrialized countries. Not so.[5] As early as

1924, India had a Colonial Labour Law establishing employee councils. This was extended during the 1950s after independence. The Indian constitution guarantees employee participation in management decisions. Tata Iron and Steel is one of the premier examples of successful cooperation in the world. In Israel, the huge Histadrut sector of union-owned enterprises has worker representation on its board of directors and has had joint productivity committees since the earliest days of the country. In Africa, Tanzanian workplaces have extensive requirements for worker and community representation, and successful quality of work life programs have been established. The International Labour Organisation has documented the existence of joint mechanisms in scores of countries in Africa, Asia, and Latin America.[6] Not all are successful, but clearly worker participation is an international phenomenon not linked to any one country or culture.

It is not an answer to all ills. Union-management cooperation is not a salve for all that ails a company or agency. When promoted as a miracle cure, it is oversold. The truth is that management is not always right *and* the union is not always right. But they will be more right if they work together than if they work apart. Cooperation alone does not guarantee good results. It cannot control such outside forces as economic swings, political upheavals, or natural disasters. But it can help the parties adjust better and faster to these conditions. As a *process* it can provide a better *way* to get things done. Good judgment and the quality of information remain very important. Cooperation is not a panacea, but it is a better way to generate solutions and higher commitment.

The Real World of Labor Relations

The popular conception of union-management relations evokes images of dueling gunfighters in the Old West. This picture is encouraged by the media, which focus their reports on conflicts and strikes. The real world is very different. Lost days due to strikes are about .0004 percent of time in large firms, as documented by the Bureau of Labor Statistics in 1991.[7] About 10 percent of all employees submit a grievance each year, and about 1 percent of these reach arbitration, according to estimates of the American Arbitration Association. To turn these figures around, 99.9996 percent of the time union members are on the job, 90 percent file no grievances and 99 percent of the grievances get resolved internally. In more than 90 percent of contract negotiations, the parties come to agreement without a mediator.

To be sure, there are locations where the labor-management relationship is terrible and little if anything is shared. And in many places, cooperation may not be as extensive as it should be or labor agreements may not be totally satisfying. Nonetheless, the degree of clash and conflict in the workplace is overstated. For every Phelps Dodge or Eastern Airlines that is unable to reach agreement, there are tens of thousands of companies in which agreements are reached. The adversarial side of labor relations is literally the tail that wags the dog.

Given that the parties come to agreement so often, one might reasonably ask, Why not leave them alone? Because this record of success suggests greater possibilities for a more proactive, even more cooperative relationship. It is extremely important for workers, employers, and the general society to find ways to improve the process on the way to agreement and to magnify the beneficial outcomes of cooperation.

Although adversarial situations are the exception in the labor-management relationship, they are still very important. The ability to take an adversarial posture creates critical boundary conditions that often encourage more cooperation and agreement. The threat of a strike or a lockout can help the parties come to a compromise. The ability to file a grievance minimizes violations of the contract and provides protections of due process for the membership—even if the members don't use the option. The right of management to say no to unreasonable demands or to resist intimidation is also important. The right to strike, even if unexercised, provides a sense of power and self-determination to the union. Finally, there are times when cooperation is not possible and confrontation is called for. Cooperation does not mean capitulation to a one-sided deal. Each side has limits that cannot be crossed. When these limits are violated, each side has to stand up and fight.

Yet the possibilities for real cooperation have not been adequately tested. Too often the parties are frozen in adversarial postures when a cooperative approach could work. In many cases, the efforts at cooperation are too timid or too limited. In the absence of effective cooperation, adversarial strategies look inviting. War is always more promising in the abstract. Meanwhile, confrontation and padlocked gates take their toll on the lives of employees, union leaders, and managers. Someone may win, but at what cost? Usually, the prospects for joint construction are better than the prospect of mutual destruction.

Is Union-Management Cooperation a Process or a Program?

We want to address head-on the most common question, whether cooperation needs to be expressed in programmatic initiatives. When it comes time to translate union-management cooperation from theory into practice, there are many difficult choices. To some, union-management cooperation is a state of mind in which the principals in the relationship have trust and respect, characterized by their ability to talk to one another. Some are reluctant to concretize that relationship into a specific set of activities for fear it will ruin the magic of their relationship. Others stay away from establishing programs, saying that programs have a beginning and an end and theirs has no end point. Some proponents of cooperation shy away from formal programs and measuring results since the "process" is most important to them.

Frankly, we couldn't disagree more. In our opinion, the argument between process or program is dilatory when the real question is what should be accomplished and how. Certainly, we value good interpersonal relationships and general feelings of goodwill between management and the union. But those parties who stop at an attitudinal interpretation of cooperation at best are squandering the possibilities to turn their common commitment into specific outcomes that will be of mutual gain. At worst, they are papering over differences that will ultimately erode the facade of cooperation. We believe that union-management cooperation has to take concrete form in activities and programs not because we advocate any particular approach but because action, not passive acceptance, is the avenue for cooperation. Union-management cooperation is best served when it is well conceived and well managed. In short, we propose the common sense dictum, "Find what you can do together, and do it!"

A Framework for Union-Management Cooperation

The best way to visualize the union-management situation is as overlapping interests, as in figure 1.1. Some unionists focus solely on the differences, asserting that workers have nothing in common with their bosses and that their goals never intersect. They believe that all management is indeed manipulation, cynically pulling on the strings of workers and their union dupes. According to this view, it is therefore best that they keep their interests as separate as possible to avoid misunderstanding which side they are on.

By contrast, organizational development theorists only see the overlap. They envision a blissful identity of interests between the parties; everyone is going in the same direction and shares a common culture. They see all people as just people who happen to work somewhere. They discount any differences of interests or hierarchy and believe that good managers are totally aligned with their employees' concerns. Their conception is that the two circles in figure 1.1 totally overlap.

In our opinion, both views are naive. Union and management interests will never be identical since at a fundamental level employers want more for providing executive compensation, dividends, and investments, while

Figure 1.1. Overlapping Goals of Employers and Unions

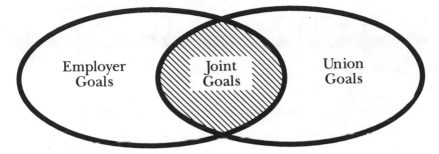

workers want higher wages, benefits, and the best working conditions. There is nothing wrong with these different orientations, and in fact they can help each party succeed. Both commonality and difference occur in all situations. The degree of overlap determines the degree of cooperation. Too often the parties refuse to work with their counterpart because they are afraid that the other party's gains will come out of their own hide or will be larger. Instead, the parties should focus on maximally attaining their own goals with integrity, including ways that require or can be enhanced by cooperation between them. Union members elect officers to get them more, not less. They get less when an aversion to cooperation leaves potential gains on the table. Stockholders want higher dividends and should have little patience when matters of ego interfere with higher levels of performance.

About forty years ago, Frederick Harbison and John R. Coleman of the University of Chicago laid out an excellent broad model of labor-management relations (figure 1.2). Using field research, they examined union-management agreements and divided them into three categories: armed truce, working harmony, and union-management cooperation. We have added an initial category of confrontation. Their definitions of these terms are particularly instructive since they bring together organizational change and industrial relations practices. Armed truce is defined as follows:

1. A feeling on the part of management that unions and collective bargaining are at best necessary evils in modern industrial society.
2. A conviction on the part of the labor leadership involved that the union's main job is to challenge and protest managerial actions.
3. Basic disagreement between the parties over the appropriate scope of collective bargaining and the matters which should be subject to joint determination.

Figure 1.2. Continuum of Labor-Management Relations

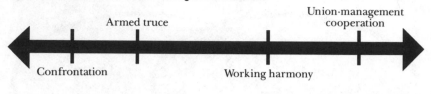

Based on Harbison and Coleman, *Goals and Strategy in Collective Bargaining* (New York: Harper and Brothers, 1951).

4. Rivalry between management and the union for the loyalty of workers.

5. A frank admission on the part of both parties that settlements of major differences in collective bargaining are made on the basis of the relative power positions of the company vis a vis the union.

6. A mutual desire to work out an orderly method of containing conflict and compromising differences by living together under the terms of a collective bargaining contract.[8]

The best that can be said about this type of relationship, predominant in the 1950s and now, is that there isn't open warfare. Management sticks to its interpretation of the letter of the agreement, and the union uses the agreement as the sole foundation for a relationship. The organizations involved come to agreement over the contract, thereby avoiding strikes, but only after adversarial posturing. The attitudes of the union and management feed off each other. Management believes that the union exists because of bad management. The union agrees and tries to point this out as often as it can. The reductio ad absurdum of this argument is that absolutely terrible management is great for the union. It doesn't work out that way.

The next category, working harmony, is quite different and describes the labor relations in many organizations. Harbison and Coleman define it as follows:

1. A genuine acceptance of collective bargaining on management's part based on a conviction that the union is an asset as well as a liability in running the business.

2. A conviction on the union's part that attainment of its objectives is dependent in large measure on the continued prosperity and well-being of the company with which it bargains.

3. An awareness by both parties that, although their objectives are in conflict in important areas, it is possible to make compromises which allows each side to feel that it is advancing its interests thereby.

4. The retention by management of the sole responsibility for the carrying out of the core functions in running the business, while the union confines its activities to vigilant policing of managerial actions and to removing certain obstructions which lie in the path of efficient production.
5. A tendency continually to broaden the scope of matters subject to joint discussion and negotiation.
6. A recognition by each party of the complexities of the internal problems of the other coupled with a willingness to help in solving some of the thorny issues involved.[9]

Organizations with working harmony are characterized by the use of labor-management committees, quality circles or action teams, joint study teams, and other parallel and limited cooperative activities. They recognize interdependence but guard institutional autonomy.

The final level, union-management cooperation, is the hardest to achieve and is found in the fewest organizations. Cooperation is described in these terms:

1. A conviction on the part of management that the union as an institution is both willing and able to organize cooperative activity among employees to achieve lower costs and increased efficiency.
2. A willingness on the part of the company to share some vital managerial functions with the representatives of the union.
3. An eagerness on the union's part to be a production-boosting agency in return for tangible and intangible benefits for the union and its members.
4. A resulting relationship in which the parties assume joint responsibility for solving production problems and eliminating obstacles interfering with greater efficiency.
5. Outward manifestations of mutual trust and respect coupled with expressed confidence that the partnership of union and management "pays off" for both parties involved.[10]

This forty-year-old definition describes accurately the union-management cooperation being attempted today at the Saturn project between General Motors and the United Automobile Workers of America (UAW), and at the Shell-Sarnia plant with the Energy and Chemical Workers Union of Canada. Originally it was meant to describe relations at the American Velvet Corporation in Stonington, Connecticut, which developed a program in 1939 with the Clothing Workers union that incorporated the union into production planning and resulted in gainsharing payouts. This program is still ongoing today.

The wisdom of this model is not in how the categories can be used to label any one company or union but how the model defines areas for improvement in the labor-management relationship. In this book, our goal is to describe how employers and unions can move from having an armed truce to establishing working harmony and union-management cooperation.

History of Union-Management Cooperation

Union-management cooperation is almost as old as union-management conflict. Initially, there may have been struggle and conflict over union representation, but employers and unions have always had limited choices—continued conflict or cooperation for mutual gain. An increased incidence of union-management cooperation is often described as a sea change in management culture, indicative of a new peaceful age in industrial relations. The historical record shows instead that waves of increased union-management cooperation have often been associated with national and economic crises.

Though there were earlier attempts, the shop committee, developed before World War I, is most clearly the ancestor of U.S. union-management cooperation and employee participation developments today. Similar joint committees, called Whitley Committees or works councils, were established in Europe at the beginning of the century. A shop committee is "a form of organization for collective dealing by means of joint committees, composed of an equal number of representatives of both employees and the employer."[1] Soon after the United States entered World War I, the need for full production and domestic labor peace catapulted the theories of workplace cooperation into government action. The shop committee was one of the key components of this effort. During the war years, 225 plans were established by the National War Labor Board (NWLB) with the support of President Woodrow Wilson.

As a patriotic act, the American Federation of Labor (AFL) endorsed the shop committee concept and urged union involvement. Many of the committees were in nonunion settings, however, and set up as alternatives to unions for the purposes of dispute resolution and employee involvement. Though some unions were involved, the shop committees became anathema to many in organized labor because of this preventive use. William Leavitt Stoddard, administrator of the NWLB, supported the unequivocal right of employees to form unions. He addressed the position of shop committees as follows:

> On the surface . . . the shop committee is neither a union nor a non-union scheme. It is primarily a method of organizing the employees of a given plant

with the employers for the purpose of bringing about efficiency and better working conditions. The character of this organization is in several respects different than trade union organization. One important respect is that the organization is *dual* or *joint* and that it is based on the theory of cooperation rather than the theory of competition or conflict.[12]

Immediately after the war, many employers abandoned their shop committees and employee representation plans, which came back even stronger during the 1920s. The number of workers covered by shop committees climbed from 319,000 in 1919 to 1.5 million in 1924 in more than 800 firms, including Goodyear, International Harvester, Procter & Gamble, Commonwealth Edison, Armour, and Youngstown Sheet and Tube. Again, many companies introduced plans to stave off union organization.

The union movement responded with its own initiative by expanding on its previous positive experience with endorsing cooperation. Recognizing collective bargaining with an independent trade union as a prerequisite, the AFL at its 1926 convention declared: "Conflict and arbitrary management are poor production policies. Conference and cooperation lead to united work efforts. . . . Workers and management are reciprocally dependent. This is obviously a relationship which calls for cooperation that is to all intents and purposes a real partnership in a work undertaking." For the next fifteen years the AFL developed an alliance with the Taylor Society, marrying due process, union participation, and industrial science. Though the founder of scientific management, Frederick Winslow Taylor, had little patience for unions, his followers learned the value unions bring to creating a better workplace.

The biggest success story of this period was at the B&O Railroad. Cooperation later spread to many railroads in North America, and representatives from other countries came to study its success. The initiative for the B&O plan came from the International Association of Machinists (IAM). Later, a similar program was proposed by management for the Canadian National Railroad. The B&O project began in 1924 as an experiment in the Glenwood shops outside Pittsburgh. It proved so successful that joint shop committees were established throughout the railroad and a system-level committee was established. This program lasted until the early 1960s. The first fifteen years of the program resulted in more than thirty-one thousand suggestions for improvement, of which almost 90 percent were accepted. The improved service and morale on the B&O enabled it to survive the Depression in far better shape than its competitors. The Railway Employees Department of the AFL described the B&O Plan in this way:

> Union-management cooperation is not a weapon. Instead it is a tool, a tool to be used by us jointly for mutual welfare. . . . The second big lesson to be

learned from our performance of our cooperative policy to date is that our unions in particular and organized labor in general are capable of being as potent a force making for better industrial performance and for a richer life than any of the other factors composing our society today.[13]

The philosophy of Otto S. Beyer, the consulting engineer credited with designing the program, is instructive. In a lecture at Harvard University in 1928, he said:

I am not thinking of industrial plants whose personnel is made up of submissive, apathetic, timorous workers, or where the management is not troubled with "labor problems"; where in other words, it has its own sweet way. My conception is of a situation where labor and management are consciously, definitely and systematically working together for mutual benefit and public service. It goes beyond the mere peaceful settlement of wage questions and the orderly adjustment of grievances. It includes more than the protective relationship, often really nothing more than an armed truce, which frequently prevails under the conventional form of collective bargaining. I maintain that industrial relations are on a better basis when the employees, individually and collectively, are quite definitely stimulated to help the management in the solution of its problems, and the employers take a similar attitude toward the labor force, each striving to improve the conduct of their industry and willing to share the gains which result. In other words, better industrial relations, in order to deserve the name, must make not only for peace, but also for progress—progress for the worker as well as for the employer and the consumer.[14]

As the danger of fascism rose in Europe and the Pacific, discussion of union-management cooperation and industrial democracy reached new heights. The Murray Plan, put forward by Philip Murray, the president of the Congress of Industrial Organizations (CIO), proposed joint union-management involvement from the shop floor to the industry level. Though it was rejected by employers' associations, the plan generated intense discussions. They were early versions of today's industrial policy debates.

In 1942, *Dynamics of Industrial Democracy* was published by Clinton Golden and Harold Ruttenberg, two veterans of the Steel Workers Organizing Committee (SWOC). They articulated a theory of cooperation in which workers and their unions would be deeply involved in the production process. They worked with Joseph Scanlon, a local SWOC leader, to develop new participative practices and a financial reward system that came to be known as the Scanlon Plan. Seeing a new age of industrial relations, Golden and Ruttenberg predicted:

We believe that American industry is on the threshold of a new era in human relations—the greatest period in union-management relations. The turmoil and strife of the last decade have merely reflected the transitional character of the relations between workers and management. Out of this transitional period is emerging a new capacity on the part of those in industry. Regardless of their different positions, in point of view of responsibility and authority to work together as a unit—literally with a singleness of purpose and action for the attainment of a common objective. . . . The increasing extension of democratic methods into industry will lead to fuller production and employment and toward increasing the stature, well-being, dignity and happiness of the individual worker.[15]

Though only for a short time, their prediction was correct. A new labor-management relationship emerged during the war years. With the escalation of World War II, President Franklin D. Roosevelt established the War Production Board (WPB) to ensure maximum production. It promoted labor-management production committees throughout American industry, which were endorsed by the AFL, the CIO, the Chamber of Commerce, and the National Association of Manufacturers. In all, about fifty-thousand production committees were formed, covering more than 7 million workers, including most of the large defense contractors. The targets of cooperation varied: conservation of materials, transportation, absenteeism, care of tools and equipment, productivity, quality control, and training.

After the war, the labor-management climate worsened significantly. Without wartime pressures and with the return of servicemen to the work force (and the exit of Rosie the Riveters), tensions increased and strikes broke out. Management rights clauses and union security agreements became commonplace, demarcating separate lines of authority and recognition. At the same time, the Americans who were living abroad and rebuilding war-torn economies helped institute codetermination systems in Germany and a strong version of union-management consultation systems in Japan. At home, union-management cooperation fell by the wayside.

Several important studies urged continuation of union-management cooperation and employee participation. In 1949, the Twentieth Century Fund convened a distinguished panel from management, government, labor, and universities who urged that labor and management should be "partners in production." The National Planning Association, a private organization, conducted investigations over a seven-year period of the practice of industrial peace. It identified nine conditions necessary for it to exist[16]:

1. There is a full acceptance by management of the collective bargaining process and of unionism as an institution. The company considers a strong union an asset to management.

2. The union fully accepts private ownership and operation of the industry; it recognizes the welfare of its members depends upon the successful operation of the business.
3. The union is strong, responsible and democratic.
4. The company stays out of the union's internal affairs; it does not seek to alienate the workers' allegiance to their union.
5. Mutual trust and confidence exist between the parties. There have been no serious ideological incompatibilities.
6. Neither party to bargaining has adopted a legalistic approach to the solution of problems in the relationship.
7. Negotiations are problem-centered—more time is spent on day-to-day problems than on defining abstract principles.
8. There is widespread union-management consultation and highly developed information sharing.
9. Grievances are settled promptly, in the local plant whenever possible. There is flexibility and informality within the procedure.

The twenty-two-day wildcat strike in 1972 by a predominantly young work force at GM's Lordstown, Ohio, facility dramatically illustrated that the workplace was not immune from the strains of a society facing challenges to authority and a demand for real change. The UAW, led by Irving Bluestone, demanded to be a part of GM's organizational development interventions affecting union members.[17] In retrospect, the 1973 GM agreement may have been the symbolic event that reopened the era of union-management cooperation. Also in 1973, the U.S. Department of Health, Education, and Welfare study *Work in America* generated intense discussion of worker alienation and the need for new forms of work organization. European quality of work life (QWL) and democratization activities fostered excitement about possibilities for a new workplace and a new role for industrial democracy. During the 1970s, joint experiments took place in unionized American workplaces in manufacturing, wood products, hospitals, and the public sector. Though most were not long-term successes, these efforts provided important lessons about the value and practice of cooperation.

By the end of the 1970s there was again a tremendous growth of interest in and activity involving cooperation. The overall difficult economic climate called for new responses, and union-management cooperation was once again a significant tool. Competition from the Japanese sparked the emergence of quality circles in both union and nonunion workplaces. Quality and customer responsive strategies came to the fore. Cooperation was rediscovered as a way to increase the viability of the unionized sector, competitiveness, and worker satisfaction.

This historical perspective makes it clear that today's forms of cooperation and participation are not all that new. If workers have yearned for participation from the beginning of this century, then claims that there is a "new breed" of worker are not accurate. If previous efforts took aim at automation, calls for urgency because of the latest technology seem somewhat old hat. Understanding that earlier prophets talked about new ages in industrial relations and cultural shifts in management style should make us think twice about the validity of such claims today. On the one hand, it is comforting to know that union-management cooperation has been espoused for nearly a century. On the other hand, it is disconcerting that so many of the programs of the past are now artifacts. What happened to them?

Cooperative programs aren't permanent. To the best of our knowledge, the longest-running U.S. cooperative program is at the American Velvet Company, mentioned above, which has lasted since 1939. Few have lasted that long. Structured programs last far longer than informal programs based on the personal relationship between the union and management leaders. At some point, management or the union usually loses patience with cooperation and resorts to confrontation, or the people involved and/or their business environment changes substantially. Frequently, cooperative programs fail to keep pace with internal changes. Long-term success isn't natural; it is a function of hard work and constant renewal.

Macroeconomic forces play a major role in the longevity and incidence of cooperative programs. Many programs started during World War I were hurt by the depression of 1921. Many others established during the 1920s were decimated by the Great Depression. Local union-management cooperation programs can't stop large-scale industrial restructuring in the economy or dramatic shifts in consumer behavior. Major changes in the work force and the end of national crises also seem to have negative effects. After both world wars, cooperative programs fell by the wayside when the soldiers returned to the factories more used to conflict than cooperation. The sense of national emergency had passed and pent-up demand exploded.

Conversely, cooperation increases when there are strong competitive pressures on the economy. When there is an excess of supply over demand, the partners are more motivated to work together. Pressured by outside forces, management looks to the union for help. Without it, they often mistake good fortune for good management. Unions seek cooperation more when there is general acceptance by employers of their legitimate role and they feel squeezed by unemployment and competition from nonunion shops.

Larger social forces also have their impact. It is no coincidence that participative programs and pressures for women's and minority rights and work force participation increased simultaneously during the 1920s, World War II, and more recent decades. Political scandals such as Teapot Dome and Watergate reduce confidence in closed approaches to decision making and increase interest in expanded participation.

Historically, there has been a contest between joint union-management programs and management-initiated avenues for participation. Employers seem to be perpetually searching for a mechanism that will make a union unnecessary. Many unionists fear the dangers of these company programs. But a longer-term view reveals that unilateral management programs do not last. They either fold because of a lack of sustained interest or inadvertently fuel unionization by showing that collective action is important in achieving lasting improvements in working conditions. Many of the nonunion programs started during World War I were in companies that were later unionized, such as Westinghouse, Bethlehem Steel, and International Harvester. The highly touted employee representation plans run by the steel industry provided the framework for the Steel Workers' Organizing Committee (now the United Steelworkers of America). In the telephone industry, the Communications Workers of America arose out of an association of company unions demanding greater independence. More recently, in the Electromation, Inc., case, the National Labor Relations Board ruled against a unilateral participation program in which employees were selected by management to discuss compensation, hours and working conditions. The International Brotherhood of Teamsters won the election.

Most organizations that have introduced union-management cooperation have not paid attention to history. The participants tend to review recent experiences and to extrapolate from them in an effort to achieve better industrial relations in the future. Their short-term vision ignores the ongoing challenges of maintaining vital union-management cooperation. A longer view of history teaches that union-management cooperation has been a valuable tool in many industries and at many times. Cooperation alone cannot solve the economic and social problems that employers and unions face, but it can definitely make things better.

Emerging Trends in Industrial Relations

The 1980s brought new insight into union-management relationships in the United States. Traditional patterns no longer made sense for unions or for management. Union membership continued to decline as a percentage of the labor force, and declining global competitiveness and standards of living were forcing a rethinking of the way American organizations and the people within them work.

In 1986, leading industrial relations scholars Thomas A. Kochan, Harry C. Katz, and Robert B. McKersie reported that a fundamental transformation was occurring in industrial relations. They described significant changes both on the shop floor and at strategic levels, two arenas that had not responded well to traditional collective bargaining efforts. They suggested that to have an impact on competitiveness, action was required at the shop-floor, collective bargaining, and strategic levels: "Only when the innovations at all three levels are linked together in an integrated fashion do unions and employers appear able to introduce the complete range of changes and sustain their commitment to innovations that both close the competitive gap and recapture the innovative position in industrial relations."[18]

The Collective Bargaining Forum, a private group of corporate and union leaders, has crafted a new compact for labor and management that sets a positive tone for the future. Under the direction of Malcolm Lovell, the group has explored the relationship between a union's commitment to the competitiveness of an enterprise and management planning for employment security. The group's position is summarized in the following statement:

> We recognize that there are both some enduring differences and broad areas of mutual concern in the interests of workers and employers. We understand that labor and management do not always share completely joint goals. However, in today's world it is essential that labor and management actively pursue opportunities for advancing their common interests. Given the intensity of international competition, failure to identify ways to work together effectively means that neither party will achieve its goals or fulfill its functions. Thus, both parties must fully respect and respond to the basic needs of the other.[19]

There is an emerging consensus that new forms of union-management cooperation are required for both management and unions. This book describes how cooperation can be achieved with integrity and addresses new forms of work reorganization and employee involvement, new uses of collective bargaining, and areas for broad strategic involvement in creating successful businesses and agencies.

Conclusion

Union-management cooperation institutionalizes the common aspirations of the two parties to achieve a better future and the best possible relationship. Union-management cooperation will not occur in all places, at all times, and in all ways. Cooperative approaches do not guarantee industrial utopias or wonderful workplaces. The basis for any union-management cooperation is simply *respect* between the two parties. Cooperation then engages the principal parties in their common struggle for significant betterment. Joint efforts can thus result in important and tangible improvements for all concerned.

In traditional adversarial labor relations, the union is often a drag on flexibility and change. In a cooperative environment, the union and management work together to achieve positive change. They look together for operational, market, product, technological, and human resource answers to the questions of how jointly to achieve success. A union and management can do almost anything they set out to do when they summon their imaginations and are dedicated to having the highest-quality cooperation to match their commitment to the highest-quality products and services.

2. The Union's Decision to Cooperate

Entering into a cooperative venture requires judgment. Each party has to determine what it means for itself. For the union, the primary questions center on what cooperation will mean for the membership and what it will mean for the union as an organization both in the short and long term. Some unions decide that cooperation is not for them or that their situation makes it impossible. Other mainstream trade unionists, however, from Samuel Gompers to Lane Kirkland, have carefully examined the issues and chosen to try to make cooperation work to mutual advantage while warning against deceptive advertising on unilateral versions.[1] In 1919, Gompers wrote: "Industry, like government, can only exist by the cooperation of all. . . . Every edifice, every product of human toil is the creation of the cooperation of all the people. In this cooperation, it is the right of all to have a voice and to share in an equitable proportion of the fruits of these collective enterprises."[2] Kirkland, president of the AFL-CIO, said in 1985:

> The element of difference—of conflict if you will—enters of course when we're negotiating a collective agreement or when we're engaged in an effort to organize a group of employees. Once a trade union is accepted as a negotiating partner, once collective bargaining exists, once a contract is in force, then

there are numerous opportunities for a cooperative rather than a competitive or adversarial approach to a whole range of issues that affect the well-being of the firm and of the industry. And we are more than willing—we're anxious—to pursue those efforts.[5]

Unions around the world have also pursued cooperation for broader ideological reasons, as a way to empower workers and their institutions to shape their lives at work. Joint approaches to management of the enterprise can increase the solidarity of the membership, provide longer-term employment and membership, and contribute to the health of members, communities, and countries. Very often discussions of cooperative activities focus only on the organizational change and impact on the employer. But if the effort is truly joint, the union as an organization will also be affected profoundly. In a joint effort, the union must also be empowered and improved.

Impact on Contract Negotiation   The collective bargaining relationship as articulated in a written contract forms the foundation for any cooperative project. The contract establishes basic boundaries for the cooperation. The contract both responds to and structures the industrial relations and the operational environment. Collective bargaining as a process cannot be divorced from the cooperative proceedings. Directly or indirectly, the contract lays out the mandate or framework of the cooperative effort or describes the gainsharing plan. It sanctions cooperation.

In the Relations by Objectives (RBO) program of the Federal Mediation and Conciliation Service, difficulties in the labor-management contractual relationship are generally the springboard for examining cooperation. In most QWL and cooperative programs, however, contract negotiations per se are held apart from the cooperative activities. As a general rule, when the cooperative or participative approach does not work, the parties retain the right to bring any issues to the bargaining table and to settle them through that process. The contract retains its binding nature, subject to normal procedures for renegotiation.

Although they help reduce the probability of strikes, cooperative activities are no guarantee of contract agreement. In fact, unions in companies with notable cooperative programs, such as the CWA and the IBEW at AT&T and NYNEX and the Newspaper Guild at the *Minneapolis Star-Tribune*, have struck over economic issues after good joint programs were in place. These examples demonstrate that it is possible to have a mix of cooperative and adversarial postures.

The more conflict-ridden the relationship, the more difficult are contract negotiating sessions. If each side creates buffer zones to protect against incursions of the other, then there is less to give and take. If the employer manages poorly, then the union seeks more work rules for protection. If the coffer is low because of poor management, then the membership can get less. Both in terms of what is available and the nature of the relationship, cooperative union-management relations can yield better contract negotiations. In places with highly developed cooperation, bargaining sessions become joint problem-solving and strategic planning sessions. Within the union, new cooperative approaches can lead to new practices. In win-win bargaining, the union gathers interests not demands. At the Saturn plant, UAW officials interviewed every member for forty-five minutes before negotiating their first local contract to get full participation and a wide range of ideas.

Impact on Contract Administration   A similar relationship exists between cooperation and contract administration. The right to file a grievance remains intact. The duty of fair representation remains in place.

For several reasons, a cooperative working relationship makes contract administration easier. First, the parties are looking for areas of agreement, not opportunities to draw the line. Second, there is less retaliation in a cooperative environment, making grievances less frequent and easier to settle. Third, grievances related to communications breakdowns fall off dramatically. In the early 1980s when the Tarrytown, New York, General Motors plant started a QWL process with the UAW, the number of grievances went from twenty per week to three per month. But even in workplaces with model cooperation, grievances almost never disappear completely, which illustrates that even reasonable persons can have different perspectives and that an effective grievance procedure is always necessary. Decisions on grievances are important ways that the contract takes on clearer definition.

Because of the decline in the total number of formal grievances in cooperative workplaces, those on the docket get faster and more complete attention. There are fewer arbitration and labor board appeals, which saves considerable resources that the union can better use elsewhere. Often, union officials file fewer formal grievances. Because of their broader contact with the membership, they are just as busy (if not more so) helping solve their members' problems.

Some argue that the effectiveness of a union is measured by how many grievances can be filed. This is wrong; effectiveness is measured by how many grievances are *resolved*. No member thinks his or her union is effective when it takes a long time to get a claim resolved or if legitimate beefs are traded off. In a cooperative work environment, the representational role of the union is retained but energy is expended on a broader range of approaches to resolution.

Impact on Membership Service   Many union members and outside ob-
servers have the impression that unions are for the alleged 10 percent of
employees who are "troublemakers." This is way off the mark, because
union-won wages and benefits are for everyone. In the day-to-day life of
an agreement, the truth is that a disproportionate share of time *is* spent
dealing with the chronic problem employee or the frequent griever. But
the daily workplace concerns of the other 90 percent of the work force are
also important to the union. A large proportion of the membership has
few run-ins with management and files few if any grievances. Too often
they become disaffected from the union.

Especially in "right-to-work" states, servicing all employees is critical
to maximizing membership. Many strategies can be used to broaden the
membership base outside the workplace, including holding social events
and providing services in the legal, health, education, community service, and consumer areas. The union can also promote opportunities in
the workplace for the majority of workers who want to do a good job and
see the employer prosper but feel frustrated when they see that reality
falls far short of possibility. Contact with the membership and notions of
service can be expanded through programs, including cooperative activities, that improve work life.

Impact on Union Politics   Cooperation can have a mixed impact on union
politics. If members are not clear about what they are getting out of a
cooperative program, or if the process is hidden, the union leadership
can become open to charges of selling out or of being in bed with
management. Further, dissident caucuses ideologically opposed to cooperation are likely to attempt to make any cooperative effort an issue.

If handled correctly, however, cooperative programs can be a decided
plus for the union leadership. In fact, the turnover rate among leaders of
unions with good participation programs is far lower than in unions in
traditional adversarial settings. One reason is the perception by a broad
segment of the membership that they are getting something out of the
union's advocacy. In many programs, the union leadership learns new
skills, which helps improve their performance. They may gain new insight into how to plan and manage union affairs. They may learn how to
run meetings with less emphasis on ritual and Roberts' Rules of Order
and more on clear agendas and broader involvement and problem solving.
The results can be increased attendance at union meetings and greater
participation in union events. Successful programs fully acknowledge
the union's political structure, and the joint process strengthens it. When
a parallel system is set up to keep union politics at arm's length, the result
is likely to be nasty and often losing battles between participants in the
joint program and the existing power structure.

Impact on the Union as an Organization A cooperative project involves organizational change. Too often the sole focus is on changes in the employer. But if it is truly a joint process, it must also have a positive impact on the union. Many cooperative projects serve to change the structure, problem-solving abilities, and communications capabilities of the employer. New structures may be necessary in the union to cope with its added responsibilities.

Unions can use the problem-solving approaches generally used in cooperative programs to analyze the problems they face. One trade unionist in Rhode Island set up a "quality circle" in the local labor council to identify answers to the political problems it was facing. Some unions are applying quality techniques to better service members. More open communication and better listening can help the union perform its job better. Unions at all levels need to ask themselves the same question posed to employers: "How can we do our job better?" The quality of work life for union leadership and staff also needs to be considered. Learning new approaches for improving organizational competence can only help.

Charles C. Heckscher of Rutgers University and formerly of the Communications Workers of America has argued that the new forms of industrial relations and employee involvement are reflected in new forms of unionism, which are more associational. According to Heckscher, the union's processes in a more associational model become more participative, member-sensitive, and flexible in organizational and representational structure.[4]

The fundamental workplace goals of the union remain the same as always in a cooperative program: better working conditions and increased dignity on the job. The basic structure of elected representation also remains the same. What changes as a result of involvement is the tone and content of the work unions do and the degree of communication among the various levels within the union.

Requirements for Labor Education Traditional labor studies are even more necessary for unions engaged in cooperative efforts than for adversarial locals. Trade unionists should know their history to understand that cooperation has often come after years of struggle. They need to understand labor laws to make sure they are fully discharging their responsibilities. They need to know how to prepare for and conduct negotiations and how to handle grievances to ensure that they are not leaving their flanks open to charges of negligence. They need to understand the broader social agenda of the labor movement so that internal cooperation does not lead to insularity from larger issues in the economy and the society or indifference to the difficulties of others.

There are also new skills that need to be learned.[5] Labor education should address the particularities of negotiation and grievance administration in a cooperative environment. Labor history needs to take into account the history of union involvement in cooperation so that there is a sense of pride in previous union efforts and a clear perspective on the present. Problem-solving skills and the administration of joint union-management initiatives can also be taught.

Benefits and Risks of Cooperation for Unions

Rarely is any decision in the workplace unalloyed; there are good points and bad points in any situation.[6] The precise mixture will vary from union to union and from location to location. The relative benefits and risks need to be weighed for any cooperative activity. We discuss below some of the critical risks and benefits. The risks can be minimized and the benefits maximized if thought is given to how to deal with them.

There are a series of possible pitfalls. We start with the initial premise that the union must maintain its clear identity as the representative of the workers. If the union becomes an apologist for management or simply a prod for productivity, then it loses its authority as the workers' representative. This diminishes its effectiveness as a union and paradoxically makes it less useful to management. Involvement in joint activities should not be a preamble to softness in negotiations over traditional collective bargaining matters such as wages and benefits. If the union allows communication to go directly to the membership without the union's involvement and acknowledgment of its role, then there is a danger of weakening union allegiance among the work force. Most people prefer cooperation to confrontation, and perception of the union as blocking positive activity can cause membership estrangement and resentment.

There has been a long history in unions of developing uniform rules to combat capriciousness in treatment and to encourage solidarity among workers in an industry. Some unionists are concerned that participative programs lead to unequal treatment of employees, thereby contradicting this practice. There are other pitfalls to watch for, including political splits, violations of the contract, job loss resulting from increased productivity, speedups, downgrading of jobs, or loss of comparability in an industry.

Clearly, many things can go wrong with a cooperative effort. If simple machines can go on the blink, how many more possibilities are there for problems in complicated human relationships testing out new ground? Yet each of the items mentioned has remedies and preventive steps that can be taken. These are discussed in part III.

There are also many potential benefits for the union. Some of these derive from the process directly, such as increased access to information and prenotification of changes in work arrangements and technology. Additional input can also help management avoid errors or decisions that would hurt the union membership.

As discussed earlier, other benefits result from the increase in membership representation. In almost all programs, the number of grievances goes down, sometimes dramatically. Members find that their concerns are resolved more quickly and more fully. In a number of cases, including the team-based system developed by the Energy and Chemical Workers Union in Sarnia, Ontario, attendance at union meetings has gone up after instituting a participation program.[7]

Of course, there are a variety of other ways that a successful program better assists union members. Work satisfaction may increase. The union may be able to address a broader range of personal concerns. Membership education and skill levels may increase. Stress caused by poor supervision or unnecessary barriers to doing a good job may be reduced. Finally, better communication with co-workers may result.

The increased visibility of the union in a joint project helps its image both internally and externally. The membership sees the union taking the lead in innovation and advocating important issues other than just compensation justice. A cooperative spirit aimed at improving customer service and quality can also win applause in the industry and the public.

A final set of benefits has to do with the broad impact of cooperative programs on improving bottom-line performance. There may be more money for higher wages and benefits, for modernization and expansion, or for health and safety improvements, among many possibilities. And funds are increased not through the loss of jobs but by expanding the market and cutting nonpersonnel costs. The improved condition of the employer may result in ensuring that jobs are not lost because of uncompetitiveness. Sometimes joint projects result in more jobs.

How to Avoid Co-optation

The biggest union fear of a cooperative program is often co-optation. The union worries whether fancy management programs or slick consultants will be used to render the union toothless and impotent. There is a real distinction, however, between getting along and going along.

First, and most important, the union must keep its own interests in mind in the development and maintenance of a joint effort. A union should not become engaged in a joint program to "do management a favor" or because "we had no choice." It should be involved because the program is helping it meet *its own* important objectives. Too often, the union does not think through alternatives and negotiate more acceptable options to the programs management has presented. If management is unwilling to engage in a give-and-take on the development and design of the program, then it has no interest in cooperating.

Second, the program should be equal and truly joint. If the union is a junior partner, it will generally become a high-profile partner in blame and a silent partner in success. If the union has little access to information about a program and is separated from the levers of power over it, the program could become problematic. In some cases, union leaders let a program begin but want nothing to do with it. They reason that if the employer runs it, then they will not get blamed. Unfortunately, this hear-no-evil, see-no-evil, do-no-evil posture has the opposite effect. The membership demands to know why the union was not on top of the program and why it allowed it to be established in the first place. If the union participates equally in all aspects of the program, then it can assert itself with confidence.

Third, the union must be knowledgeable about cooperative programs and the proper ways to design them. Co-optation can result if there is ignorance. By allowing management to provide *all* the information, do *all* the planning and design, and set the *whole* framework, the union abdicates its responsibility. Some managers may need to learn about joint programs; the union should be in a position to teach them.

Fourth, the union must participate in the evaluation of the program. An evaluation assesses whether the program did what it was supposed to do and its other effects. Unless there is joint involvement in this process, it may be hard to tell whether the union has been co-opted. The results should document a balance of benefits for management and the employees. If there has been little benefit to the employees, then the program needs to be changed to redress the balance or discontinued. Unions should keep in mind that good cooperative programs are ones that they have worked hard for and on, not ones in which they have acquiesced to management. They are an extension of union advocacy, not sellouts.

Over the last decade there has been vigorous debate in union circles on the wisdom of engaging in cooperative programs. At one end of the debate are those who oppose any involvement and suggest using joint programs as avenues to embarrass employers. *Labor Notes* authors Mike Parker and Jane Slaughter, for example, have identified many programs that are shams or attempts to manipulate workers.[8] Cooperative programs run counter to the "us versus them" ideology they believe is required for militant unionism. Unfortunately, many managers have provided this line of argument with much ammunition, for many programs are indeed one-sided and poorly run. Yet, this siren call to traditional unionism makes little sense. That managers make mistakes—

frequently—is not a reason not to be involved in cooperative programs but one of the prime reasons why unions need to be involved—to provide workers a voice to point out when things are wrong. If managers did everything right (a logical impossibility), there would be little need for unions or for that matter for a myriad of management and social services organizations provide. Unions are necessary to represent employees' interests even when management is good.

Anger that management acts in management's interests in joint programs is displaced. The revelation is not that management acts in management's interests. The bigger question is why labor is not more forcefully representing its own interests. Rather than protecting classification systems often used to divide workers and foster discrimination, unions should move beyond just saying no and affirmatively describe their vision of a more desirable workplace. Management does everything it can to protect its own interests. But simply because management says it has awarded generous pay increases is no reason to refuse increases won through negotiation. Similarly, Guillermo Grenier of Florida International University has pointed out how some managers have used participation for union avoidance or union busting.[9] The record shows that it has worked effectively as a tactic for union avoidance. But rather than rail against involvement, which most workers want, the union role should be to challenge management-dominated approaches to involve workers more. In organizing, a union never suggests a rollback on wages; why suggest a rollback on participation? In a struggle between unilateral management involvement schemes and joint processes, the more pressing need is for unions to create excellent models to show nonunion workers that participation is better and more secure with union representation.

Other critics, such as Andy Banks and Jack Metzger, have recognized the attractiveness and impact of participation and have argued for union-led participation to contain management contact with union members and manipulation of their ideas.[10] They suggest that the union set up its own system of participation and negotiate with management about what it gets. This is an effective tactic when management refuses to provide unions with a genuine role. It makes little sense, however, when true cooperative possibilities appear. Such restrictions can lead to restricted resources and flows of information, diversionary tactics by employers, and limited implementation. Further, it puts the union in the position of passing judgment on its own members' ideas, which fosters division in the name of maintaining solidarity.

Critics of cooperation and participation provide a valuable service. They introduce reasonable skepticism about what can be accomplished. They remind us of how often good intentions go awry and thus help advance theory and implementation. But when criticism plays on the fears of unions and wards unions away from true opportunities, then the membership loses. We have seen more than one occasion when leaders got spooked by horror stories of participative efforts when they could have established such efforts to advance union interests.

To avoid co-optation, the union has to take the initiative; it has to develop militant cooperation. Australian commentator John Mathews identifies the challenge clearly:

> Workers and their unions have traditionally stood back from work organiza-
> tion issues, seeing them as the employer's responsibility. They have also
> adopted a hostile and defensive attitude to technological change, seeing it
> primarily as a job killer. This is a wholly understandable attitude, given the
> costs that workers have expected to bear through two hundred years of
> unregulated change since the beginning of industrialization.
>
> However, in the less authoritarian, more participative and democratic
> workplace that is emerging, these attitudes inherited from the past will no
> longer be appropriate. Workers and their unions now face the challenge of
> developing a new strategy of intervention, oriented towards a broad concep-
> tion of a future economy and social system. Meeting the challenge will require
> members of unions to radically revise their attitudes to questions of technol-
> ogy, work organization, skills formation and industrial relations. Defensive
> attitudes will have to be transformed into the promotion of a certain kind of
> technology, entailing a certain kind of work organization and pattern of skills
> formation, shaped in turn by a certain kind of industrial relations and wages
> system. It is a shift from antagonism to protagonism.[11]

What If the Decision Is No?

Samuel Gompers presented the basic dictum of the labor movement almost a century ago—"more." The union's job is to obtain more for its members than workers could achieve acting alone. Of course, this applies to benefits, wages, and time off, but Gompers also meant "more" to apply to the quality of life in society and the quality of work life. Workers want more democracy and more say on the job. They want their work to be as positive an experience as possible. And they do not like it when their union seems to stand in the way.

When the union says no to cooperating, it had better be because management has refused to go along with proposals that provided more say and more security in the relationship. In workplaces with bad labor-management relationships, many workers can be mobilized to oppose involvement. But this is only if the program is clearly a unilateral man-agement program and can be shown to be counter to workers' interests or an employer ruse to undercut the union or manipulate employees.

When the union is opposed to a cooperative program, it better be able to stop it dead in its tracks. If this is not the case, then many workers will sign on to the program and there will be little the union will be able to do to stop it. A negative stance splits many in the work force from the union and creates tremendous problems.

The union may be forced to say no to particular proposals that do not include important safeguards or do not go far enough. When this is the case, the union, rather than being seen as opposed to change, involvement, and improvements in the workplace, will be seen as the champion of participation. The union's decision to say no should be reasoned and principled, and the leadership should be confident that the overwhelming majority of the membership will stand together once the union's decision is communicated to the membership.

Yes or no, adversarial or cooperative, the union should strive to represent all of its members in the best way possible. All unions use multiple strategies to advance the concerns of the membership. Some approaches are adversarial, some political, some based on internal activities, and some cooperative. If real cooperation is possible, seek it, mold it, and use it.

3. Management's Decision to Cooperate

Management has responsibility for the success of the organization as a whole. In the private sector, management must make the company or operation as profitable as possible to fulfill its obligations to stockholders. In the public sector, management must make the organization as effective as possible to meet the needs and expectations of citizens and their legislative authorities. Management's partner in the workplace is the union. This partnership can be effective or ineffective, positive or negative. Regardless of the quality of the partnership, the union is management's partner, and the character, health, and strength of this partnership are major factors in the success of the organization.

Why Should Management Cooperate with the Union?

A responsible management uses every asset and avenue it can to maximize the success of the organization. When the union is willing to commit to the success of the enterprise by working cooperatively, then management should pursue this opportunity vigorously. For managers, cooperation has little to do with being enlightened or progressive—it has to do with being smart.

The basic question for managers should be, "Why shouldn't management cooperate with the union?" In the unionized workplace, cooperation is built into the human dynamics of the organization. Regardless of the adversarial nature of the relationship or conflict that may develop, management and the union have to get along to work together. Decertifications occur in a very small percentage of contracts, and fighting the union at every step is a costly proposition.

We do not expect most managers to be ecstatic about working with unions. But in workplaces with union representation, managers have an obligation to work with unions in the best possible way they can. Managers may wish they had no union or different leadership. But they also wish they had better customers, more reliable suppliers, improved technology, more rapid transportation, and a host of other things. Management's job is to obtain the best possible return on assets. The union can be treated as an asset. The notion of cooperation expressed in this book has little to do with soppy notions of concern, though we do believe that trust and concern for the other party does emerge from the cooperative process. Given the cold realities of the business world, cooperation makes sound business sense.

Furthermore, union-management cooperation in its participatory forms is an extension of the management principle of delegating responsibility. Problems and solutions are turned over to those who deal with them most directly, thereby freeing managers to handle other problems and responsibilities.

Management should take the initiative in seeking union-management cooperation, thus affirming its overall responsibility for leadership in the workplace. The improvements and gains that result will directly enhance not only organizational performance but also management's own quality of work life. In certain situations, some managers may feel that cooperating with the union means giving in to "the other side." Cooperation does not require either management or the union to give in. Managers are not expected to betray members of their management team. In fact, management furthers its goals and objectives through successful cooperation, which in turn results in more effective, stronger management.

Flexibility is a central management imperative. Organizations must be able to respond to rapid change in virtually all areas. Maximizing flexibility is a strategy for managing change. Top management especially is concerned about the implications of the hierarchical management structure for the present and the future. In many organizations, this hierarchy is more attentive to maintaining itself than functioning effectively. Furthermore, the hierarchical form may not be a good fit for functioning in a rapidly and continuously changing workplace and market. Intelligent management seeks new ways both to manage generally and to manage organizational change specifically.

To keep up with changes in the marketplace and changes in technology, management is moving away from the old bureaucratic, status quo mentality into an entrepreneurial, change-oriented mentality. The search for management approaches that complement this new orientation has led to innovations within management, such as matrix management, vertical slice task forces, and a wide array of team-building strategies. These changes make it even more feasible to pursue union-management cooperation. In fact, these changes often stimulate management to pursue a partnership with the union.

What Are the Risks and Benefits of Cooperative Efforts?

Any worthwhile endeavor has risks and benefits, and union-management cooperation is no exception. Experience demonstrates that real benefits can result from the effort, but not without some significant risks.

Union-management cooperative efforts can fall short of their goals and objectives or can fail outright. If this happens, management probably will not be able to justify the investment, which in turn will reflect badly on managerial performance. Since managers are judged by their results, concern about success is central. Management can minimize this risk by working with the union from the beginning to set realistic goals and objectives for their effort and lay out a feasible design and plan. Risk of failure can also be reduced by adopting a joint monitoring and evaluation process. In this way, problems can be identified early and solved before they threaten the cooperative activities and their future. Furthermore, by using a joint process for staying on top of what is happening, management shares responsibility with the union for ensuring the program's success.

Cooperation can upset the balance of power within management, within the union, or between management and the union. Management represents the exercise of power in an organization through the allocation of resources and rewards. Fear of the loss of power can lead some managers to balk at sharing power with employees, the union, or rival managers. But this notion of power is flawed. When power is power *over* rather than power to *accomplish*, the organization as a whole suffers. The arrogant use of power always comes back to haunt those who abuse it. Managers can also use their position and expertise in an organization to help align people and galvanize resources to get things done well. In cooperative programs, managers can increase their power by developing alliances with employees in their areas, the union, suppliers, customers, and other managers. Under these conditions, participation is empowering, and both the organization and the cooperating parties become more powerful.

Finally, sometimes a cooperative effort disrupts parts of an organization's operations. When training is part of the cooperative effort, participants will have to be freed up to attend. Further, many efforts involve a variety of meetings that have to be fit into preexisting work schedules. At times, such meetings disrupt operations or at least require creative scheduling and personnel assignments. Organizations that have experienced such disruptions believe that any negative effects were far outweighed by the benefits. Realistic planning will help ensure that new cooperative activities fit into the management organization, the union organization, and the workplace as a whole. Effective union-management cooperation is integrated into managerial goals, plans, structures, and operations.

Cooperation means change, and change needs to be managed. To prepare for cooperation, management must have a realistic sense of what is involved, the degree of difficulty, the connection between union-management cooperation and organizational change, the risks involved, and strategies for eliminating or minimizing those risks. Then management will have confronted effectively the initial challenge of cooperating with the union.

There are indeed many benefits management can reap from cooperative programs. Few organizations realize all of them, and those they get, usually come with hard work and constant attention. The benefits to management of union-management cooperation are well described by the Federal Mediation and Conciliation Service as follows:

1. A forum to review budget considerations, complaints and other management concerns. This forum enables employees to see their role in problems that concern management and gain a better understanding of management's position on issues.
2. An opportunity for advance discussion of operational problems, planning and scheduling and other matters that have a potential impact on employee work schedules, overtime schedules, layoffs, recalls, temporary transfers or new job opportunities. Since new proposals unilaterally initiated by management without employee input are frequently resisted by employees, labor-management committees provide a forum for resolving such resistance before it arises.
3. An open channel of communication to establish rapport with the union. Day-to-day labor relations problems such as grievances are not discussed so as to avoid getting bogged down in small issues.
4. An opportunity to respond to the ideas, suggestions and complaints of employees. This demonstrates to the union and employees that management is sincerely interested in improving the workplace.

5. A means of communicating with employees through their own elected leaders.[1]

Union-management cooperation in its many forms involves employees in decision making that affects their jobs and provides an outlet for employers to express concern for employees. In this way, it motivates employees to perform well in their jobs. Motivating employees is a management goal around which there is often confusion and controversy. Usually managers think they have to do something *to* or *for employees* to motivate them. Union-management cooperation provides a vehicle for working *with employees* in new ways. In turn, employees become self-motivated. A 1979 Gallup poll conducted by the U.S. Chamber of Commerce found that "the overwhelming majority [of employees] believe that if they are more involved in making decisions that affect their job, they would work harder and do better."[2]

Union-management cooperation can have a very positive impact on the collective bargaining process in both contract negotiations and contract administration. Labor negotiations can be conducted more effectively because the union-management relationship is better. Both management and the union improve their skills in problem solving, communications, planning, and group process through involvement in cooperative activities. They, in turn, apply these skills during contract negotiations. Day-to-day contract administration becomes more problem-solving and problem-preventing oriented as a result of the cooperation in other areas, thereby saving management time and money by reducing time and energy spent on contract administration. Resources traditionally used for contract negotiations and administration can then be redirected into cooperative problem solving and problem prevention. All of these benefits make management more effective and managers' jobs easier.

What Are the Payoffs of Cooperation to Management?

Successful union-management cooperation can result in significant immediate and long-term payoffs to management. The six most significant payoffs that relate directly to overall management goals and objectives are covered below.

Higher Profitability Improved profitability is one of the major returns management can realize from union-management cooperation. Cooperation helps management improve both the cost containment and the revenue generation sides of the profit picture. Most joint problem-solving efforts initially address cost containment issues. This is particularly true in cases in which the motivation for cooperation is concern for the economic health and survival of the organization. When the cooperative effort extends to the shop-floor level of the organization, problem solving is usually oriented to "working smarter, not harder." Employees focus on cutting waste, reducing bottlenecks, and making overall operations run more smoothly. All of these changes result in reduced costs. For management, having more "members of the team" focused on keeping costs in line is a real bonus.

That participation positively affects the bottom line is supported by data from a survey conducted during 1983–84 and reported in *Personnel*. For the survey, 850 U.S. industrial companies were randomly selected from the *Value Line Investors Survey* and *Moody's Industrials*. These companies were asked to complete a questionnaire on the extent of their participatory activities and the state of labor relations in their companies. The participatory measures drawn from the questionnaire data were then compared with the following financial measures: financial strength, stock price stability, price-growth persistence, earning predictability, sales per share, cash flow per share, earnings per share, average annual price-earnings ratio, average annual earnings yield, net profit margin, net worth, percentage earned total capital, and percentage earned net worth.

"Overall, the study clearly showed that the more participatory the firm, the higher the level of financial and behavioral success. Both the published financial ratings and the state of internal labor relations reported were more favorable for participatory firms." The author went on to discuss the implications for management:

> These results indicate that participatory management in the United States increases profitability to a significant extent—according to the Value Line financial indicators. Participatory management also helps create good industrial relations to some extent; this is reflected in some positive association between participation and the behavioral indicators. If these overall trends are typical, then it may be that a further competitive advantage can be achieved by intensifying participative efforts, both in participative and nonparticipative organizations.[3]

Union-management cooperation clearly can improve profitability. This result alone should compel management to consider a partnership with its union counterparts.

Improved Management Effectiveness   Another payoff from union-management cooperation is improved management effectiveness. This comes about in several ways. First, cooperative programs generally attack organizational bottlenecks and thereby improve operations. Second, broader communications channels are developed as part of the cooperative effort, which enhance management effectiveness. Management uses these channels to keep employees at all levels informed about the status of and challenges for the organization and to receive ideas for improvements. Third, effective management means obtaining the necessary resources and facilitating the completion of work. Union-management cooperation opens avenues for pursuing these twin goals.

The joint union-management process also leads to more technical assistance and support for management in the running of the company or organization. Union officials and employees at all levels are more willing to share their valuable expertise with a cooperative management. The truism that the people doing the work generally know how to do it best applies here. When there is cooperation these people are more available to work with management to ensure an effective operation.

One of the key indicators of management effectiveness is quality. Quality improvement has often been a goal of union-management cooperation in both the private and public sectors. Union members usually have important insights into how quality can be maintained. To operate most efficiently, systems such as statistical quality control and zero defects require the full cooperation of the work force. Quality can be a critical component in overall competitiveness and a source of pride.

Recent studies by Joel Cutcher-Gershenfeld of activities at the Xerox Corporation with the Amalgamated Clothing and Textile Workers Union demonstrated the connection between quality and better working relationships as well as the strong link between cooperation and better financial results. The researchers studied twenty-five work areas within Xerox's primary manufacturing complex in Rochester, New York, looking for patterns of interaction in labor-management relations. The question asked was, "Is there a connection between the financial performance of a work unit and the labor relations within it?" The researchers classified for each of the twenty-five work units the predominant form of labor-management interaction as traditional, transitional, or transformational based on its performance against six economic performance measures: cost performance (i.e., prime overhead rate); quality performance (i.e., worker hours lost to scrap and defects per worker); schedule performance (i.e., delivery variance); and productivity (i.e., productivity variance and net return to direct hours worked). The study clearly showed that work units with transitional and transformational patterns of labor-management interaction had higher levels of economic and quality performance than those with traditional labor-management relations.[4]

Some research seems to indicate that the industrial relations climate may be even more important than participation in bringing about strong financial performance.[5]

In many programs, managers acquire a set of new and/or strengthened skills useful not only to them in the cooperative effort but in the exercise of day-to-day functions. These skills are in the areas of planning, communications, group leadership, the running of meetings, problem solving, and conflict resolution. Some organizations therefore assign their managers to the cooperative effort as part of their career development.

Managers with whom we have worked in cooperative programs have reported that they have applied what they learned through the cooperative effort in executing their assigned management responsibilities. Even something as simple as learning to use a written agenda and a flip chart at meetings can contribute significantly to managerial effectiveness. One manager said that adopting these two simple techniques changed his daily staff meetings from "morning beatings" into "morning meetings."

Many managers feel assaulted on all sides by market pressures, a variety of demands from within their organizations, and the accusation that management failure is at the root of all the problems in American companies and organizations. Union-management cooperation is an avenue for enhancing management effectiveness that provides individual managers with additional resources and broadened support to meet their challenges better.

Increased Organizational Flexibility   Increased organizational flexibility is another payoff for management. Managers and supervisors learn new ways to work together as they participate in the cooperative effort. Probably the most important learning in this regard is that people at different levels and functions within management all have something valuable to contribute. One operations vice president expressed it to us this way: "I never thought personnel could contribute anything worthwhile to operations until we worked together on this [labor-management cooperative] program." The traditional isolation within management by function and/or level is often broken down as a result of the program. New bases for real teamwork are established as a result of management working together on the cooperative effort. Management as a group thus becomes more flexible within its own ranks.

Furthermore, increased organizational flexibility results through experiments with different ways to structure the work, such as vertical slice task forces, autonomous work groups and self-directed work teams, business or work teams, and the like. Increased organizational flexibility within management specifically and within the broader workplace enables management to adopt more innovative approaches. These in turn broaden the skill base and responses available to adjust to changes in service or product requirements, resources, and technology.

Improved Working Environment   Management may also find that the working environment improves as a result of union-management cooperation. Too often quality of work life improvements have focused solely on hourly employees. Supervisors and managers deserve and need work life improvements as well. More positive working relationships with other managers and supervisors as well as with union officials and hourly employees develop out of cooperative efforts. By addressing joint problems and challenges through the cooperative effort, management may be freer to tackle problems solely within its realm. Managers at all levels can move away from being "Mr. Fix-its," "referees," or "police officers" to being coordinators and planners. These improvements can relieve managers of some of their more significant sources of stress.

Further, the older, more traditional forms of managing have often led to a "lone ranger" approach that can lead to burnout, a variety of stress-related diseases, such as heart disease and hypertension, and family and marital difficulties. Any manager with an "I can/have to do everything myself" attitude toward his or her work is destined for personal and probably organizational difficulties. Union-management cooperation provides managers with additional problem-solving capacity and an improved working environment.

Managers who are active in a cooperative effort can be more proactive and less reactive in their management activities. Such managers gain a greater sense of being in control, even though they are sharing more responsibility. They provide organizational leadership rather than just heroically fighting organizational brush fires. They can truly demonstrate their skill at managing and stop functioning just as organizational caretakers.

Finally, cooperative efforts usually result in improved union-management relations and thus ease or prevent many traditional labor relations headaches and nightmares. These improvements are usually particularly noticeable to first-line supervisors, who often feel as if they serve on the front lines of management. First-line supervisors who are involved in cooperative efforts almost unanimously report a shift in the attitudes and behavior of the people who work for them—a shift from sometimes working for but never working with their supervisors to working together in a spirit of real teamwork. By contrast, when supervisors are unilaterally given the order to establish self-directed work teams, stress skyrockets.

Enhanced Productivity   Enhanced productivity can also result from successful union-management cooperation. Through joint problem solving, work procedures and processes become more efficient and therefore workers become more productive. Many of the principles for fostering a successful productivity improvement effort are the same as those for developing a successful cooperative effort. These include involving employees in problem solving and decision making regarding their work and work environment; involving the union from the beginning of the effort; fostering more open communications, particularly regarding organizational goals, objectives, and performance; and providing training and education opportunities in support of personal growth and development.

Much research supports the connection between employee participation and productivity improvement. In 1975, Suresh Srivastra and his associates surveyed more than two thousand literature references on worker participation experiences in the United States to determine whether participative efforts improve productivity. Their literature included empirical studies, field studies, and correlational studies. Eighty percent of the studies reported a positive impact on productivity from participation. The authors therefore concluded that there was a positive relationship between participation and productivity enhancement.[6]

Another study conducted in 1977 by Raymond Katzell and his associates at New York University analyzed 103 worker participation experiments in the United States between 1971 and 1975. Again, more than 80 percent resulted in favorable effects on one or more aspects of productivity.[7]

More recent literature continues to report a perception of higher productivity, but quantitative studies often show mixed results.[8] Frequently, studies do not correct for the kind of union involvement in the process and lump participation programs in unionized firms together without looking at the quality and level of the participation. Those who work inside joint programs know that the quality of the work that goes into these programs shows up in the quality of the outcomes.

The employee involvement program at the Sharonville, Ohio, Ford Motor Company plant with the UAW provides an excellent example of a program in which productivity improved as a result of union-management cooperation. In a typical manufacturing zone, in which all six production departments were involved in the employee involvement (EI) effort, management reported a 22 percent improvement in direct labor efficiencies. To obtain this improvement, only 2.5 percent of production time was diverted to EI activities.[9] Such an improvement is not unusual for successful union-management efforts of this type.

In general, the empirical evidence supports a common-sense assertion that organizations are more productive when people are working together rather than battling and when their common focus is on organizational improvement. Not all joint programs lead to high gains in productivity. When the focus is on other measures or when there is difficulty in the relationship, these gains may not show up as strongly or last as long.

Stronger Market Profile   The last return to management from union-management cooperation considered here is a stronger market profile. The cooperative effort can address revenue generation as an area of common interest. Activities undertaken in this regard can include joint customer service programs, joint marketing efforts, and new business and product development. In the auto industry, both General Motors and Ford Motor Company have profiled their involvement in union-management cooperation in their print and electronic media advertising. General Motors did this in its ads, saying "GM Is People." Ford Motor Company's ads stated "Quality Is Job One." In both cases, the ads are describing joint quality of working life and employee involvement programs and the positive results for potential car buyers from such programs.

Another company that built a stronger market profile through the use of joint marketing teams was the Milwaukee Road Railroad. The use of such teams grew out of a systemwide cooperative effort that involved the use of labor-management committees and quality circles throughout the property. These efforts built up the value of the previously bankrupt railroad, which enhanced its sale value when it was sold to the Soo Line. Both managers and bargaining unit employers, who had exchanged portions of their compensation for stock, benefited handsomely. Union Pacific and local unions conducted a similar effort to build business on short lines in the Midwest. Finally, a nationwide promotional campaign undertaken by the jointly trusteed International Masonry Institute designed to promote the use of brick and block by the construction industry benefited contractors as much if not more than it did the union.

Conclusion

In summary, union-management cooperation presents a real challenge to management—and a real opportunity. Though there are real risks to cooperation, these risks can be minimized or managed within the cooperative effort itself. The benefits and payoffs to management are far more significant. At a minimum, these benefits and payoffs should stimulate management to consider carefully the advisability of cooperation with the union and seek to find the broadest possible areas for cooperative activity.

In some situations the union will decline to participate. Rather than seeing a rejection as a final no to joint involvement, management should remain open to the possibility that the union will reconsider and join in fully at a later date. It may take a while before sincerity is appreciated or the relationship is improved. Once the union is committed to a joint effort, management should carefully and consistently pursue cooperation with the union. Joint involvement can transform the labor-management connection from a wrestling match to a joint commitment to success.

Part II. Guide to Approaches to Union-Management Cooperation

4. Reorienting the Roots: Collective Bargaining and Grievance Procedures as Problem-Solving Tools

Collective bargaining is the primary mechanism in North America whereby union-management cooperation is sanctioned and the quality of work life is improved. At its root, collective bargaining means that *both* parties reach an agreement they can live with. The contract sets out mutual obligations and understandings. It often provides the language that sets into motion the other more elaborate forms of union-management cooperation discussed in this section. Whether the cooperation is truculent or reluctant, cautious or extensive, this mutual agreement provides the common ground of the relationship. Since wages, hours, and working conditions help determine the quality of working life, all collective bargaining agreements are quality of working life documents and their implementation a QWL program.[1] The particulars may vary, but the objectives of the contract to improve the lot of the worker and to help order human resources management are constant. Despite these common features, approaches to collective bargaining can run the gamut from harshly adversarial to strategic joint problem solving.

A sensible analysis shows that consistent and long-term adversarial bargaining is self-defeating. If management consistently "wins" in negotiations by limiting wage and benefit levels, it will have difficulty attracting and retaining employees, who will fare better at other locations. If employees feel they have been had, they will respond with poor service, low productivity, and inferior quality. Short-term, contract-to-contract labor relations is as effective a management strategy as dividend-to-dividend financial planning. It can show splashy immediate results, but it can erode the long-term viability and growth potential of the employer.

For labor, the spoils of victory can also be short-lived. Winning compensation gains that far outstrip those in the industry can lead to competitive disadvantages, thereby inhibiting long-term income and spurring job loss. Likewise, work-rule agreements that unnecessarily reduce flexibility and productivity can provide short-term protection but long-term problems in adjusting to change and competition. The alternative for both parties is to seek win-win solutions that benefit both parties.

Most collective bargaining does not follow the prescriptions outlined in this chapter. Most bargaining is distributional—in other words, it is focused on how the pie will be divided. Compensation, investments, and returns to shareholders all are legitimate demands, but the balance among them needs to be addressed, and finding solutions is often difficult. This chapter does not discuss traditional distributional bargaining over wages and hours. Nor does it cover arbitration or mediation extensively, which are also industrial peacemaking tools. Many texts address these issues. Nor do we discuss intimidation, feints, tradeoffs, good guy–bad guy ploys, histrionics, and other games people play in negotiations. Instead, we will focus on more creative ways to improve the basic bargaining relationship and to adopt negotiating strategies that are anticipatory and problem solving. Our primary concern here is achieving a new perspective on the bargaining process.

The place to begin the search for cooperative possibilities is the collective bargaining relationship. This chapter discusses negotiations, joint visioning, contract administration, and hiring and separations as the basics of any relationship. Chapter 5 identifies many specific ways labor-management committees can be used. Chapter 6 takes a fresh look at organizational structures, and chapter 7 considers very broad-ranging and advanced forms of cooperation aimed at growth. Chapter 8 ties many of these approaches together in a discussion of quality programs, which have become a way of thinking about organizational change. Unions and management can consider any one or a combination of these approaches to cooperation.

Moving from a Conflictual to a Cooperative Framework

Some union-management relationships are characterized as conflictual. Excellent work has been done on how to move the parties in these relationships from warfare to openness to joint cooperative activities.

What follows is a description of several processes that work. From the center of a struggle, the relationship often feels despairing, but relationships can change for the better.

The Relations by Objectives (RBO) process of the Federal Mediation and Conciliation Service (FMCS) provides a model of how to use the collective bargaining relationship as a springboard for the formation of joint labor-management committees and other cooperative activities. Developed in 1975 and first used with the Georgia Pacific Corporation and the United Paperworkers International Union, the FMCS has initiated hundreds of RBO programs to help overcome union-management difficulties arising out of very difficult negotiations or bitter strikes. Programs have also been implemented in Canada with great success.

According to the FMCS, RBO

> is utilized in those situations where the labor-management relationship has deteriorated to an unacceptable level and the leadership at the top becomes committed to rescuing it. It is basically a conflict resolution process in which the RBO group, generally comprised of representatives of all levels of management and the union, is guided through their own intensive analysis of their present hostile relationship, the setting of mutually acceptable objectives to improve that relationship, and the planning of action steps and a timetable to meet those objectives. (Internal memo)

The RBO process has six steps, initiated in three- to four-day intensive sessions of twelve to fourteen hours each day with twenty to forty people. The first step is that the union and management each separately analyzes the relationship. Each group lists what participants believe each party should do to improve the relationship. Most of the discussion centers on operational issues in the organization. In the second step a joint meeting is held where the lists are shared, clarified, and discussed. The parties are often surprised by the degree of overlap. This leads into the third step, in which they agree on a single list of goals for improvement. During the fourth step the group breaks down into smaller union-management teams to discuss action steps on the goals identified. The fifth step is that the teams report back to their union and management groups about what they discussed and the proposals they wish to put forward. The sixth and final step is that they come together to review the action items and agree on a course of action. The joint initiative that emerges from this process is maintained in an ongoing way in an action plan and a joint committee. Sometimes the mediator assists with follow-up, and he or she may chair the joint committee.

The strength of the RBO approach is not only that it recognizes industrial relations issues but also that it focuses on developing concrete solutions. Management and union negotiators feel comfortable working

with mediators who are well versed on the collective bargaining relationship. The FMCS has been very pleased with the success of the RBO
program and points to both improvements in the labor-management
relationship and in the operations of the companies involved. John J.
Popular, who developed the initial program for the FMCS, trumpets
impressive results that have emerged from this process, including better
communication between the union and management, reductions in the
number of grievances, and strong operational improvements. He says,
"As a catalyst for improving attitudes at all levels, RBO is the starting
point for long-range cooperative efforts to enhance employee participation and improve productivity and quality."[2]

For more intense conflict, a more psychologically oriented process
might be followed, but this should be undertaken only with highly
competent facilitation. After World War II, the National Training Laboratories pioneered intergroup laboratories on conflict resolution. Based on
this experience, Robert R. Blake and Jane S. Mouton tested a conflict
resolution model that helped set the tone for cooperation. The basis for
their approach is rooted in behavioral science theory about intergroup
relations. It seeks to treat symptoms of intergroup pathology as one would
a medical illness. The idea is to recognize union and management
disputes as symptoms of a pathology in the problem-solving area, diagnose the causes that produce the symptoms, and treat the causes directly,
rather than deal with symptoms only.[3]

The union-management intergroup laboratory seeks to expose root
problems in the relationship. The basis for the approach is that "the
union-management situation, in particular, is very prone to becoming an
intensely hostile, win-lose relationship; although its general purpose
should be a problem solving one. During [the] next two days [of the
laboratory] what we [the management, union, and consultants] wish to
explore are problems that are blocking the relationship—to identify
them, and, if possible, to plan constructive steps for their elimination."[4]

The focus is on understanding the character and nature of the relationship, not on resolving concrete issues directly. Blake and Mouton prescribe
a process in which the participants develop self-images and images of the
other party, share and discuss these perceptions and their implications,
diagnose their current relationship, consolidate understanding on key
issues and points of friction, and wind up with plans for the next steps in
the resolution of commonly perceived problems. This kind of intense
analysis may be necessary for dealing with deeply rooted and intensely
personal conflict between the union and management.

Almost twenty years after they developed their conflict resolution
laboratories, Blake and Mouton came up with a version that in many ways
synthesizes the two approaches described above.[5] In a four-day session,

Figure 4.1. Distorted Communications

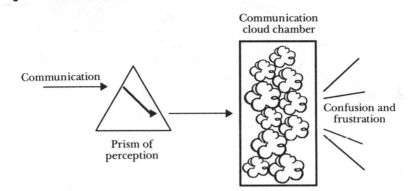

the parties switch back and forth between separate and joint sessions. They start by describing the characteristics of a sound relationship, then open up about their actual relationship, examine the gap between the two, and develop specific plans about how to move more toward the ideal relationship. At each stage, the parties formulate their thoughts in separate sessions, present them to the whole group for clarification and discussion, and, when appropriate, develop joint statements.

We have modified the Blake and Mouton model still further over the past few years with outstanding success. We have found that when communications between and within the parties are refracted, even good messages are not heard correctly (fig. 4.1). Some proponents of cooperation prefer to plow ahead on a technique or content and let the relationship issues get resolved obliquely. We have tried that approach and find it less effective than assuring that there is clear communication in the beginning and encouraging the relationship to be a positive contributor to change rather than a nagging drag on performance. Our model has been applied not only with organizations that had serious problems but with participants who recognized that a sound relationship is a key component in maintaining and growing success (fig. 4.2).

The parties begin by separately identifying their ideal relationship. As part of this process, they are prompted by the following five questions:

1. What kind of labor-management relationship would help you meet your own responsibilities?
2. In the normal course of labor relations, how should we work together?
3. How can the labor-management relationship contribute to the best operation of the organization now and in the future?
4. How should people involved in this relationship treat one another?
5. What can the other party reasonably expect of you?

Figure 4.2. Force Field of Union-Management Relations

Best possible union-management relationship

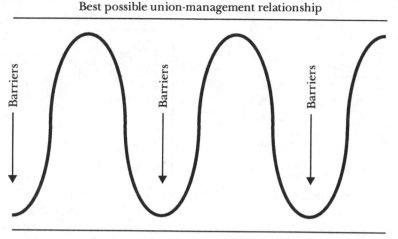

Current union-management relationship

Our experience has been that developing internal consensus within management and labor is more difficult than developing consensus between the groups. The common presumption is of agreement within the parties. Not so; the range and bitterness of internal disagreements may be more pronounced inside than between the groups. Such lack of internal cohesion is often read as confusion or inconsistency by the other party. This process encourages an open exploration of thoughts, feelings, and options privately by management and the union first. Participants first expand their notions of what is possible in the relationship. The parties then develop a common list based on the overlap between their two ideal lists as well as areas on one party's list that the other finds acceptable. We find that this approach produces goals that are simultaneously broader and more specific than those generated during traditional joint brainstorming. The items included are ones on which there is broad consensus, not simply pabulum accommodation. There are always items that are not agreed on. Facing up to the reality of differences helps ensure the integrity of the process. The result is an agreement that spotlights commonality and engenders hope in the future.

Rather than have a free-for-all as the Blake and Mouton model prescribes, we have used a "when-then" feedback format that provides insight into the current situation while avoiding personality conflicts. Learning how to give feedback helps enhance the opportunity to move forward by getting important issues and feelings out in the open. Each group separately examines questions such as the following: What situations cause the most difficulty in performing your job? What situations make you angry or upset with the other party? What behaviors do you find counter-productive or wasteful? What situations make you most pleased, or what behaviors do you find most welcome? Based on the candid and often strongly felt feedback given in the mixed-group session, each group comes to understand its current relationship. Participants also learn to give constructive feedback.

After brainstorming the barriers between the ideal and the real in mixed groups, the parties know where they want to go, what the current situation is, and what is blocking progress. At this point, we ask the union and management groups to identify separately their institutional interest in moving forward and unilateral actions that would help the relationship progress. This step enables the groups to communicate after the session in a way that connects to their constituencies. Making uncondi-tional commitments to improve the relationship helps both parties dem-onstrate trustworthy behaviors that are also in their own interest. Offering unilateral commitment shows real commitment and not evi-dence of a cat-and-mouse game. The parties then develop strategies together based on what they can do jointly. The overall process provides a way to ensure institutional integrity, clear the air, and generate specific action steps both unilaterally and jointly. It opens new pathways in relationships that were bad and those that can be better.

Joint Strategic Collective Bargaining

There are basically two approaches to cooperative bargaining: strate-gic and problem-solving. The strategic approach looks to the future as the relevant period when the agreement will be applied,[6] whereas the problem-solving approach looks to resolve difficulties that have occurred in the past or that currently face the parties. The strategic approach is the broader framework. It creates a community of interest vital to healthy cooperative relationships. Its advantage over the problem-solving ap-proach is its more positive emphasis and that it enables the parties to formulate more comprehensive and anticipatory agreements. The advan-tage of the problem-solving approach is that it enables the parties to choose a manageable number of commonly perceived difficulties to work on or to back into broader or more difficult problem areas more delicately. Both approaches go beyond traditional forms of collective bargaining that are often incremental and reactive to particular de-mands placed on the table.

To engage in strategic bargaining, the parties have to make a long-term commitment to one another. They become, in effect, partners in produc-tion. In doing so, the parties accept two fundamental strategic objectives:

(1) the long-term success of the employer either as a business or governmental agency and (2) the permanent presence of the union as an agent for the employees to maintain employment and improve working conditions. Strategic bargaining is representative of Harbison and Coleman's highest form of relationship, union-management cooperation.

A strategic approach to collective bargaining may be used to complement other strategic decision making by management and the union or it may be a catalyst for strategic decision making overall. This approach would seem to have great potential in the public sector, where employees make a long-term commitment to public service in their agencies but usually cannot bargain directly on issues such as wages, benefits, and hours. Too often public sector bargaining gets mired in the pettiest of issues, rather than opening up a space for exploring common commitments. By envisioning common strategic goals, civil employees could become the measuring rod for collective bargaining.

Joint Strategic Scanning

The first step in joint approaches to strategic analysis is to conduct a *joint strategic scan* of the environment. This grounds discussion in the real business or organizational environment. The union and management should review past trends, current status and future projections of the market (including the competition), product and service, financial resources, natural and other input resources, technology, and human resources. Environmental analysis of political, economic, regulatory, and social trends is also very important. The partners should draw on a variety of sources of data, including planning information available from the employer or industry association. Some international and local unions have done strategic planning and, if this is the case, the findings should be incorporated into the scan. Local universities or planning agencies can also be a source of information. Most of the technical information is usually provided by management.

Union-management teams should collect and analyze the data. By learning together the answers to the critical questions identified by the parties, the data of each party will be more respected and more accurate and complete. One approach is for the teams to conduct a series of scenarios ranging from probable to possible. The teams then brainstorm possible questions related to each category of the scan, identify possible sources of information, gather and analyze the data, and draw conclusions to share with others in management and the union.

In some organizations we have worked with, strategic scans were done independent of bargaining. One plant conducted a round of scanning with top leadership that included bringing in experts from corporate headquarters, the union, and the community to learn together about challenges to the future. They then cascaded the scan through the organization, including first-line supervisors and stewards, to establish an in-depth understanding of the need for change. Platitudes on the need for change were replaced with real insight. In this case, scanning alone had tremendous impact on their relationship and ability to handle change together. In every case, the joint approach led to adjustments and new insights into management's previous planning.

The union and management can take the scanning process further by generating a list of joint objectives. These might include such areas of common interest as producing the highest-quality product and service, wage and benefit stability, employment security, wise use of new technology, and market and product diversification and expansion. At this stage, the aim is to arrive at an overall definition of their common enterprise based on the previous analysis. These common strategic goals need to be further specified into concrete objectives and functional strategies for the operations of the work organization, the nature of the collective bargaining relationship, and the development of employees. Many of these goals will not be realizable within the term of one labor agreement. But at some point an agreement that moves in the direction of meeting the common goals needs to be reached.

Collective bargaining proposals should be evaluated based on whether they meet long-term joint strategic goals and objectives, not whether they provide short-term satisfaction of current demands. The current contract can also be assessed for the degree to which it supports common strategic objectives. Finally, it is important that the partners develop a concrete plan for implementing their objectives and engage in ongoing monitoring to check that the plans are being followed, whether the strategic objectives are being met, and whether the objectives require rethinking.

Clearly, strategic bargaining is more difficult if not impossible in settings where there are animosities in the relationship that block simple understanding. This strategy may provide a way, however, to frame the issues in broader, more positive terms. Strategic scanning or bargaining does not predict the future with precision or guarantee outcomes, but it does provide a common purpose that can help inform decisions and provide direction. Rather than tumbling and fumbling into the future, the parties strategically position themselves together in the very best way they can. In short, they are bargaining for the future.

Joint Visioning

There are several other tools management and unions can use to help create a better future. We have recently applied a visioning process in a paper mill that was performing very well and where the work force had good wages, benefits, and employment security.[7] A problem-centered approach in this environment would lead to only marginal change. There was strong interest, however, among management and the union leadership in examining possibilities for significant change to maintain and improve their position.

Joint visioning is a way for management and unions to create the best possible future together. The parties articulate what their future can or should be, communicate that vision throughout the organization, and develop supporting behaviors and strategies to make the vision real (see fig. 4.1). Broad involvement, input, and commitment are characteristic of a joint visioning process. The approach is holistic and comprehensive in that it looks at the business or agency multidimensionally and at a broad range of possibilities for the future.

Before articulating their vision, the parties make important decisions about the time frame and how data will be collected to inform their decision making. Possible methods include strategic scanning, soliciting information from experts, polling employees, and benchmarking. If appropriate, the parties seek to align their vision with the vision or purpose of the employer or union at higher levels.

The level of specificity in the vision needs to fit the level of the organization involved. In some cases, partners have developed specific vision statements by examining subcategories such as customers; technology; union-management relations; environment, community, and family; safety and the work environment; how people work together; people development; and operations and finances. Focusing on these subcategories helps ground the vision in concrete aspirations, not the vacuous pabulum that characterizes most vision statements.[8] The vision becomes a hologram that has dimension, not a flat, cheerleading chant.

Union and management leadership take the first stab at drafting the vision statement, for that is the role of leadership. They help answer the question that most employees have: where are we going? But the leadership's vision statement is only a first step. Employees at *all* levels provide input on the draft statement by commenting in small group meetings on whether it is understandable, connected to real concerns, and motivating. This process builds commitment and demonstrates joint union-management leadership.

Turning vision into reality means translating the vision statement into specific, observable behaviors expressed in organizational, team, and individual practices. These behaviors must be clearly connected to the vision statement. They must describe the vision in action and be generated by those who will be involved in the behavioral change or application. Natural work groups are asked to describe behaviors that fit the vision but that are also realistic, desirable, and within their control. They should describe what they would hear, see, or do when the vision is occurring. They then decide what to do—and do it!

Some organizations have developed organizationwide key behaviors to reinforce best practice and have encouraged work units to reach a consensus on a manageable list of priority behaviors that the group will emphasize. All of the ideas generated provide an extensive library of possible approaches throughout the organization. The behavioral focus moves the effort beyond fingerpointing and wish lists to concrete actions that support the overall vision.

In any organization, there are barriers to making a vision real. The leadership as well as the employees need to be involved in identifying these barriers. Strategies tailored to the organization and its vision can then be developed at organizational and team levels to help eliminate or reduce the barriers.

The vision statement should not be simply a plaque placed on the wall. It must be constantly reviewed to ensure that the statement remains relevant and motivating. It also must be continuously tracked to see whether the vision has become reality. The degree of realization can be measured by surveying the organization regularly to audit implementation of the vision both in the organization as a whole and in its various parts. A survey can measure how important the various elements are to each employee and each employee's assessment of how often each element occurs. This audit, using the language of the vision statement and the behaviors of those in the organization, identifies areas requiring additional attention or new strategies. It also creates a baseline for measuring realization of the vision both to celebrate accomplishment and target specific areas for action. Taking aim at the top items where the gap between importance and occurrence are greatest helps the organization focus on key levers for change. Further, employees must review the vision statement and associated behaviors periodically to move on to new challenges. The data-based link between auditing the vision and behaviors brings insight and ensures attention to the process. The dynamics of the process, which involves leadership and all members of the organization engaging in a dialogue on where the organization should go and how, infuse the organization with a sense of common purpose and provide a compass for decisions made by the organization and each of its members.

A similar process was undertaken in Norway in a large company that rooted its new vision in a garden metaphor. They engaged all levels of the work force in elaborating on their image and what it meant for their work. Marjorie Parker writes about the experience: "Visions are rooted in reality but focused on the future. Visions enable us to explore possibilities. While vision directs us towards the future, it is experienced in the present." She talks about the critical role of the union's involvement, including its participation in the planning and organizing of all the phases of the effort and its willingness to back the process in the face of some resistance. Some claim that visioning is for the privileged and the prophets. Parker speaks well to its broad possibilities: "Any group of people can create a shared vision. Any challenge can be the focus of shared vision."[9]

Search Conferences

Another process that has been used successfully in work reorganization and union-management settings is the search conference. The search conference is a participatory methodology that enables groups to grapple with issues and set future directions. It "generates co-operative and purposeful activity in groups that finds its typical expression in participatory planning. . . . Others emphasize the contribution that the search conference can make in values clarification, in problemsolving or in conflict resolution."[10] Searches can help broaden perspective and build commitment, especially when there are a number of diverse constituencies. They provide a valuable way to include different perspectives within a union, such as maintenance and production, as well as within management, including engineering, accounting, and supervision. They have frequently been used in Australia, Europe, and North America as tools in work redesign as well as community development.[11]

A search conference is guided by a search conference manager over the course of two or more days. The search manager meets with the participants individually or in small groups ahead of time to design the search questions and to ensure understanding of the process. Participants should include representatives of all of the key interest groups involved in the issue. A search usually involves fifteen to sixty people, although some have been much larger. They are generally held off-site to create a "social island" to encourage freedom to think.

After an initial overview of the process, there are a series of breakout sessions followed by plenary sessions. A typical search conference begins with an examination of the past, maps the current environment, then moves to envisioning an ideal future. The last step focuses on action steps to move toward the ideal future.

Marvin Weisbord discusses the use of search conferences in building community and new solutions: "Search conferences excite, engage, produce new insights and build a sense of common values and purpose. We base the future search on three assumptions: 1) Change is so rapid that we need more, not less face to face discussion to make intelligent strategic decisions. . . . 2) Successful strategies—for quality in goods and services, lower costs, more satisfying ways of working—come from envisioning preferred futures. Problem-solving old dilemmas doesn't work under fast changing conditions. . . . 3) People will commit to plans they have helped develop."[12]

Though search conferences can be exciting forums for consensus, they require a skilled manager who can draw out issues from the group and deploy alternative routes to action plans based on the group's direction. For some, search conferences are exhilarating; for others, they are frustrating. For organizations that have used them well, they have always uncovered new possibilities and paths for action.

Integrative Collective Bargaining

In the past few years, the win-win approach to bargaining has become much more popular, and it has been used successfully in both the private and public sectors. The International Brotherhood of Electrical Workers trained all its staff in this technique, often with management counterparts. Though we are seeing many new applications, the general concept has been used for many years. In 1965, Richard Walton and Robert McKersie outlined a model of collective bargaining that analyzed not the topics of bargaining but its process. These divided roughly into two basic kinds of bargaining: distributive and integrative. The first is most familiar: "The joint decision process for resolving conflicts of interest is *distributive bargaining*. The term itself refers to the activity of dividing limited resources. It occurs in situations in which one party wins what the other party loses."[13] Distributional bargaining means that a fixed sum is divided up for such matters as wages, benefits, profits, and hours.

But not all collective bargaining is win-lose. Each labor-management negotiation also consists of a considerable amount of *integrative bargaining*. Integrative bargaining is of two types: "In the first, one (or more) possible resolution(s) of the agenda item by itself offers both parties a gain in absolute terms over their respective positions in the status quo; for such a resolution neither party experiences any loss."[14] The second type occurs when the parties are trying to find the "maximum mutual utility function"—the best possible alternative, even though it might be the least worst or not have a similar value to both sides. When bargaining issues are posed as problems, there is integrative potential for their solution. When issues need to be adjudicated, a compromise is the best they can do. Concerns such as absenteeism, job security, flexibility, job classifications, productivity, safety, job satisfaction, benefit cost containment, overtime, and other issues can be battlegrounds when posed as distributive dilemmas and opportunities for joint resolution when an integrative framework is employed.

Figure 4.3. Three Approaches to Collective Bargaining

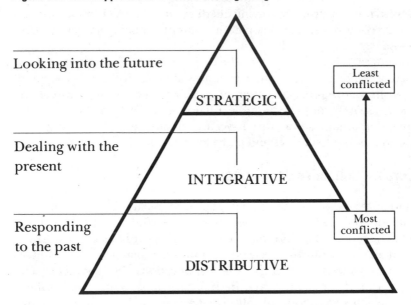

Looking into the future

STRATEGIC

Least conflicted

Dealing with the present

INTEGRATIVE

Responding to the past

Most conflicted

DISTRIBUTIVE

There are three steps in the Walton-McKersie integrative bargaining problem-solving model:

"Step one involves a maximum exchange of information about the problems perceived by each party in order that these problems be clearly identified and defined in their essentials."[15] Initially, the parties need to identify a topic as having integrative potential. In the process of learning about and discussing the issue, the problem will be more clearly clarified or may even be redefined by the parties. Specificity about the problem is important.

The second step "assumes alternative courses of action (potential solutions) are not immediately apparent but rather have to be discovered or invented. It also assumes that the full consequences of a course of action are again not obvious; instead they have to be inferred from an analysis of all the facts available."[16] In this step, the parties generate the maximum number and range of alternative solutions to the problem.

The third step involves assessing the various alternatives to see which best serves the interests of both parties. Some options may be better for certain parties than others. The best balance of benefits has to be found to be able to move ahead with that alternative. To engage in integrative bargaining, the parties must be willing to explore openly alternative solutions to commonly agreed-upon problems. The process is aided when participants have access to information that helps increase their understanding of the problems and assess alternative solutions. Based on an empirical study, Lane Tracy and Richard Peterson identified the key elements for successful integrative bargaining:

> Problem solving is more likely to succeed when both sides explore subjects informally and non-committally during the regular bargaining session and when both take a farsighted view. From the union point of view, problem solving is also aided by both sides discussing their feelings about a problem and the cause of it, as well as by management's ability to state issues clearly and specifically. Management negotiators further relate success in problem solving to exploration of subjects outside of the regular bargaining sessions and to an absence of criticism from the union negotiators.[17]

For example, statements made while brainstorming in integrative bargaining cannot be used as weapons if and when the parties switch to distributive bargaining. The freedom to test alternatives without negative consequences is important. Walton and McKersie are clear that although a minimum level of trust and openness is needed, there does not have to be a totally harmonious relationship for integrative bargaining to work well. There does not have to be trust or a good relationship for integrative bargaining to result in better agreements, but having a good relationship does help.

During the 1950s in the steel industry, integrative bargaining was applied in an interesting way in joint study teams that met prior to negotiations to examine particular issues of common concern. The Human Relations Commission in the steel industry provided a model for these efforts. The ground rules going into the sessions were "freedom to advance an idea without committing one's self to accept it in the last analysis, ability to change position frequently, and freedom to make a proposal without consulting the parent organization."[18] Other joint study teams were set up on such issues as training, subcontracting, wage incentives, medical care, and sabbatical leaves.[19]

Usually, bargaining contains a mix of distributive and integrative functions. Knowing when to be in which mode is not always easy since the styles appear very different. One can start by roping off some areas of mutual concern for testing the integrative model. These can gradually be expanded to more areas of common concern. Some groups have applied the model to the whole collective bargaining agreement and then identified certain issues as distributive when an integrative approach did not work. One can also engage in hard distributive bargaining and still use integrative bargaining approaches. If the parties are open to it, integrative solutions may surface while they try to sort out seemingly intractable distributive issues.

Framing Win-Win Bargaining

Fundamentally, collective bargaining is a problem-solving exercise. Each party comes to the table with a set of problems it wants to resolve. On management's side, these could be overall compensation costs, flexibility in operation, absenteeism, and a host of other issues. The union may be concerned about such matters as rising living costs, job security, career mobility, and fair treatment in the workplace. In traditional bargaining, these issues get placed on the table in the form of proposals and counterproposals or demands. A fair compromise is attempted, but both parties seek to distribute the benefits as closely as possible to their own bottom lines.

Integrative bargaining as described in the previous section is a way to engage in problem solving when the focus is on the problem at hand, not simply the specific proposals. A good example of the use of this approach occurred during bargaining between Ford and the UAW in 1982. Ernest J. Savoie, director of the Ford Labor Relations Planning and Employment Office, reports:

> When the negotiators came to the 1982 table, they came in a problem resolution mode and they came with a demonstrated, highly visible set of successful local experiences [employee involvement programs]. The value of this was more and more evident as the negotiations progressed. There was full, upfront problem exploration without the posturing that is sometimes a part of more traditional bargaining.[20]

The agreement resulted in an integrated web of approaches, including improved employee involvement language, "Mutual Growth Forums," an extensive joint employee development and training program, pilot projects for lifetime job security, profit sharing, and assistance to displaced workers.

The precise manner in which to conduct win-win negotiations is concisely and clearly outlined by Roger Fisher and William Ury from the Harvard Negotiation Project.[21] They developed four basic principles, working in a wide range of fields from international conflict to commercial negotiations. Their approach is particularly relevant to union-management relations because, like it or not, the parties are so reciprocally dependent. The labor force makes profitability possible; profitability makes a fair standard of living achievable. Unlike negotiating for a new car, where most people can shop around, labor and management usually have more limited choices. So, if the parties are going to be together awhile, the smartest solution is to collaborate on finding mutually advantageous solutions, not knocking the other party down.

Fisher and Ury's four basic principles for general negotiations are very applicable to the union-management setting.

1. *"Separate the people from the problem."* They suggest being hard on the problems and soft on the people. In collective bargaining negotiations, the bargainers are agents for interests beyond their own. The manager has an obligation to maintain the most flexibility for management and to cap the cost of an agreement. The union committee has an obligation to the membership to obtain the best possible overall compensation, job security, and working conditions. When either bargainer overpersonalizes the positions, agreement is much harder to reach. The issues become personal honor and not problem resolution. At the same time, bargainers deserve to be treated with dignity and respect. In collective bargaining, the two parties need to deal with one another after the negotiation of the agreement. It is therefore important to pay attention to maintaining a long-term, positive relationship by separating the specific issues of disagreement from personal antagonism. Paradoxically, the best relationships are formed when there is hard attention to the content of the issues on the table.

Fisher and Ury identify key behaviors that should help the parties manage their relationship during negotiations. These include imagining oneself in the other's shoes, not blaming the other side for one's problems, discussing one another's perceptions, and phrasing proposals so they are consistent with one's counterpart's values. When both parties participate actively in the exploratory process, greater commitment to arriving at workable solutions can be developed. The parties should also exercise good communication skills.

The key to a mature and problem-solving union-management relationship is to recognize that at times the other side will need to let off steam and that actions are not always consistent. There are going to be times when the relationship will be frustrating because of mood swings or because the parties are boxed in by the situation. Sometimes not everyone on the other team will keep commitments. The parties need to roll with the punches and keep focused on solving the problems at hand and maintaining ongoing understanding.

2. *"Focus on interests, not positions."* Each side comes to the bargaining table with legitimate interests. In most cases, there are multiple interests and not all have equal weight. Each side may agree on some interests and not on others. But almost never is there total opposition of interests. The parties should openly acknowledge the interests of the other side. Openness about one's own interests uncovers many areas of common interest. In some situations, the interests may be very different but complementary, such as increased productivity and increased wages. This builds the framework for agreement.

Negotiators should be sensitive to the other party's interests. This is in their self-interest, for unless the other side's interests can be addressed, there can be no agreement to proceed with meeting one's own interests. It also makes good political sense to focus on interests. When the union leadership stirs up the membership to expect demands to posture for the negotiation, it is a letdown when a compromise is reached. The same is true for managers who have unrealistic targets. By demonstrating to their constituencies how the results will meet *their* interests, the negotiators help ensure that their constituencies view the negotiations as a success.

3. *"Invent options for mutual gain."* Fisher and Ury identify four areas that inhibit the generation of options: "(1) premature judgment; (2) searching for the single answer; (3) the assumption of a fixed pie; and (4) thinking that solving [the other party's] problem is their problem."[22] The parties need to be creative so as to arrive at a variety of solutions to difficult problems. Ask "what if?" and try each option on for size. Rarely is there a simple, single, either/or choice.

When brainstorming alternative solutions to a problem does not generate answers, try to reframe the issue by putting it into a different context or making hypothetical modifications in basic assumptions. Though reframing does not always help solve the immediate problem, it may stimulate the creative juices necessary to break conceptual deadlocks on the conception of the problem. Sometimes it helps to break the problem up into its constituent causes or parts and to try solving the parts.

Helping the other side solve a problem may open up room for the other side to solve one of your problems. For example, the statement that the employer cannot pay comparable industry wages poses a problem, not a position. Discussion can focus on cost cutting, marketing, better management, or other alternatives to determine if solutions are available. The same might be true for work rules. A work rule is one way to address a particular problem. In most cases, there may be many ways to address each problem other than the specific approach placed on the table or past accommodations.

4. *"Insist on using objective criteria."* When negotiations become based on the relative muscle of the union and management, then problem solving breaks down. One side may win, but there are substantial indirect costs. Before agreeing to specific proposals, there must be some agreement on the common criteria for acceptance. These may include standards of cost, fairness, reciprocity, professional standards, prevailing rates and conditions, scientific measurements, precedents, equity, legality, effectiveness, efficiency, verifiability, and/or other mutually agreeable measuring rods. Fisher and Ury suggest that the parties "(1) frame each issue as a joint search for objective criteria; (2) reason and be open to reason as to which standards are most appropriate and how they should be applied;

and (3) never yield to pressure, only principle."[23] By arguing on merit and common criteria, the parties can be assured that they are talking the same language and are evaluating the proposals jointly in a common framework. The strategic bargaining approach uses a common data base and joint strategic goals to establish common criteria. In the application of win-win negotiations, the item most often ignored is common criteria. It is precisely the power of common criteria that moved us to suggest the strategic approach.

Employing an integrative method of negotiation enables the parties to meet their individual interests by giving full rein to the joint exploration of acceptable alternatives. Both the union and management retain the right to assert their interests and to withhold agreement until they feel they are sufficiently met. Each party is clear on its best alternative to a negotiated agreement (BATNA), which helps ensure that the results advance the interests of all parties. This method helps enhance the long-term relationship while opening up options for the resolution of pressing issues faced by both sides. In this way, the negotiation session is not just a test of will or matter of slicing the baby in half through compromise but a search for solutions that will maximally benefit all concerned.

Hundreds of organizations have now experimented with win-win, integrative, or, as some call it, "mutual gains" bargaining. The results have almost always been an improvement over past bargaining practices.

Grievance Handling as a Management Diagnostic Tool

In traditional contract administration and grievance handling, each side has a wins and losses tote board. Often lost in the counting is the merit of each grievance. Grievances should not be opportunities for the employer to assert that management is right all the time; nor should they be a forum for the union to beat up on the employer. Rather, the grievance procedure should give definition to the contract and provide an avenue for continuous clarification and discussion of the mutual relationship.

Right or wrong, grievances tell a lot about an organization. The grievance procedure can, with proper record keeping and imagination, register the heartbeat of an organization and provide clues for improvement. The most important part of the process is understanding why the grievance was filed and reviewing patterns of grievances to determine what the organization as a whole should do. In some cases, a party may be technically correct, but the grievance is a symptom of a deeper problem. Ongoing squabbles over overtime, for example, require attention not only to the particular cases but to planning to avoid the need for overtime.

Rather than hide from the issues, the union and management should face and address them.

Arthur A. Sloane and Fred Witney, in a basic text on labor relations, point out:

> Depending on the attitude of the company and the union, the grievance procedure can also be used for functions other than the settlement of complaints arising under the labor agreement. Many parties, for example, use the grievance machinery to prevent grievances from arising as well as to dispose of employee, union and employer complaints. Major grievances are viewed here as symptomatic of underlying problems, and attempts are jointly made to dispose of these problems to prevent their future recurrence. In other cases, the parties may utilize the scheduled grievance meeting time, after the grievance itself has been dealt with, to explore ways of improving their general relationship and also as an avenue of bilateral communication on matters of interest to both institutions.[24]

Grievances can relate to any one or a combination of the following factors[25]:

1. *Interpersonal communications.* Many grievances result from a lack of effective communications between a supervisor and an employee. They represent a communications breakdown in which the grievance procedure and discipline become a substitute for discussion between the parties. In many cases, the situation has already deteriorated to the point where the parties think that talking to one another is a waste of time.

2. *Factual communication.* Grievances can also represent a misunderstanding of the factual basis of a contract or company procedures. In some instances there may be a genuine difference in interpretation. In other cases, the factual basis of the contract may not have been explained well enough to current or new employees.

3. *Discrimination.* Perceived or actual discrimination in the workplace on the basis of sex, race, religion, national origin, sexual orientation, or physical handicap can lead to the filing of grievances. A desire for fairness underlies many grievances.

4. *Employee problems.* In many grievance cases that deal with absenteeism, tardiness, or erratic behavior, the employees involved have serious personal problems, such as alcohol and drug abuse, marital difficulties, and/or depression. They may also have other health-related problems that affect their performance in the workplace. These problems are each employee's, and they need to be dealt with firmly and sensitively.

5. *Management problems.* Some grievances relate to work flow, work pace, production standards, job descriptions, tools, and the structure of work. These problems are not always as obvious as they seem. Poor structuring of work can cause stress, which can result in grievances that

appear more personal in nature. In reality, health and safety grievances relate to the operation of the enterprise.

6. *Union problems.* Grievances can result because of internal union politics. They can be a form of grandstanding by individuals seeking election or a way to embarrass a faction within the union. Such grievances should provide the impetus for serious thought and effort at conflict resolution and expanded membership participation within the union.

7. *Mobility.* Grievances related to seniority, promotion, training, performance appraisals, transfer, and job assignments all involve mobility. The positive face of mobility is career advancement and income potential, whereas on the negative is worry about the nature of future assignments and arbitrary use of assignments for punishment.

8. *Income.* Disputes over wage adjustments caused by job changes, incentive payments, differentials, overtime, benefits payments, and other matters regarding financial payments relate to overall income concerns and frequently are matters for dispute. Sometimes the underlying issue is the notification schedule or changes in work requirements.

9. *Time.* Issues concerning time are another major source of grievances, and these include vacation, overtime, excused time, scheduling, lateness, absenteeism, and similar issues. The parties should examine whether rigid start times are necessary, for example, or whether the employee has other personal problems.

10. *Job security.* These cases involve the frequently grieved matters of suspension, dismissal, and other disciplinary actions. In some situations, these cases are required by the duty of fair representation incumbent on the union. Sometimes they result from bumping rights or confusion or manipulation concerning seniority assignments.

11. *Work environment.* These cases involve the amenities of work, such as parking, use of the cafeteria and bathrooms, and other services and functions that are not a direct part of the work process but are connected to it.

Some grievances fall into more than one category. You may want to create other categories or combine several. Looking at which category grievances fall into may help in identifying areas in which overall action is needed. Each party should categorize the grievances as it sees fit. A comparison of both parties' lists will reveal the degree of difference in opinion and common judgment. If there is a difference of opinion on the basic categories that cannot be resolved, then this difference should be respected and the traditional course of adversarial contract administration take its course. Likewise, if there are areas in which both parties see a need for action, this can provide the basis for joint discussion, problem resolution, solution analysis, and activity. Each party may also attempt unilateral solutions to deal with the basic causes of the grievances.

By doing reviews quarterly, the parties can monitor developments in the organization and highlight emerging problem areas or underline areas of improvement. Engaging in this joint process will help reduce the irritants and underlying conditions that increase the number of grievances. It can also open up communications between the parties.

The American Society for Personnel Administration's handbook on grievances wisely states:

> A grievance is one of the products of an employee-supervisor relationship. The existence of a grievance does not necessarily mean that the relationship has broken down. Actually the grievance may mean the relationship is healthy. An employee expression of dissatisfaction through the grievance procedure may be more beneficial to the organization than if he bears his grievance silently for a long time. . . . No action should be taken in the area of prevention of grievances until a complete analysis of the organization's problems is made. . . . Grievances are a product of the behavioral structure of the organization, and a formula for their prevention must be developed within that behavioral structure.[26]

Grievance Handling as a Joint Problem-Solving Session

For particular grievances, the issue is who is right and who is wrong. Charges have been filed, and they must be decided. We do not address here the due process issues of grievance handling; these are covered in most texts on labor and industrial relations. When exploring variations on the normal theme, the parties have to be careful to protect due process and fair and full representation.

The first step in ensuring good application of the grievance process is to make sure that all the parties know what they are doing. In a number of cases, management and the union have conducted joint classes to explain the contract and the procedure. The International Union of Electrical Workers (IUE) and General Electric Company have had good success with joint orientation sessions. Supervisors and stewards may have differences of interpretation that each side can explain. The belief in one's interpretation may not change, but awareness of the other party's perspective may influence how disputes are handled. Ensuring a common understanding of the grievance procedure and the contract is a foundation for better working relationships by showing respect for the contract.

We have recently worked with many groups of supervisors and stewards that wanted to develop a better understanding of their relationship and improve their communications skills. This effort did not in any way change the institutional responsibilities of the supervisor and steward. Rather, it provided them with an expanded set of tools to communicate and act on their concerns. Supervisors and stewards do not like grievance systems in which the first step is a brief way station up the ladder. Empowering them to analyze and solve problems at their level both demonstrates respect for their role and reduces significantly the costs for both parties of contract administration.

In addition to reviewing the general patterns of grievances, unions and managers should first approach each individual grievance as a problem-solving challenge. Good problem solving requires a cycle of problem identification, data collection, data analysis, the development of alternative solutions, the development of a plan for the best alternative, and evaluation of the results. By phrasing an issue as a common problem, union leaders and managers can use an individual claim to trigger a common search for effective solutions, not as matters of winning or losing.

The key to this process is to define the problem adequately. The item first stated may not be the major problem and may in fact obscure the fundamental disagreement or "iceberg grievance." It helps if both parties can view the situation or incident from the perspective of the other party. The step most critical to effective win-win grievance processing is the development of alternative solutions. The remedies suggested by the two parties in the initial petition may not be the only ones; there may be more integrative solutions. Look at at least three alternatives. To complete the process, the situation should be evaluated to ensure that it does not recur. Appreciation should be expressed to those who helped resolve the problem.

Another approach to handling grievances that has gained increasing popularity is *grievance mediation*. It has been used extensively by Southern Bell and the Communications Workers of America, the Chicago Transit Authority and the Amalgamated Transit Union, Aircraft Gear and the IAM, and in school systems. Some proponents see grievance mediation not as just an improved mediation technique but as a bridge to broader cooperation and involvement. Stephen B. Goldberg and William P. Hobgood state, "If the movement toward more participative worker-management relations is to be successful in unionized firms, it is likely that the traditional collective bargaining process will be modified to accommodate the demands of the employee involvement program."[27] Other practitioners have insightfully noted that

the problem solving nature of mediation may facilitate the resolution of a number of grievances or related issues at one time and illuminate hidden causes of dissatisfaction that, if left to fester, could provide the spawning ground not only for new grievances but also for the deterioration in the parties' basic relationship. . . . Grievance mediation is particularly relevant in an economy that requires timely problem resolution for efficiency's sake. In addition to helping parties to deal with immediate challenges, effective grievance mediation has the significant policy by-product of improving labor-management relationships."[28]

Grievance mediators use all the tools in the contract administration phase that a mediator deploys in contract negotiations. Sometimes grievance mediators work with both parties separately and serve as go-betweens as the parties explore the issues and alternatives. They may use techniques such as those described by Fisher and Ury to teach an interest-based approach to win-win problem resolution. The parties can still progress the issue to arbitration without prejudice if they are unsatisfied. Some mediators will draft a written advisory opinion on what they think the outcome of arbitration will be to guide the parties on whether to escalate the issue.

Mediation approaches to resolving significant disputes have been shown to be quite successful. About 85 percent of all disputes in which mediation was used were settled before arbitration.[29] Mediation dramatically reduces the costs of arbitration and increases the speed with which decisions are made. But more important than the efficiency of the grievance machinery, both management and the union report more satisfactory results and better relationships.

Many, if not most, grievances can be dealt with effectively by adopting a system for the analysis of their occurrence and a problem-solving approach to resolution of particular grievances. This approach can lead to improved organizational performance and enhanced employee satisfaction and can save substantial time and money. Rather than the bane of organizations, grievances can be important warning signals and reminders of the need for organizational change.

Joint Orientation Sessions for New Hires

One way to demonstrate cooperative behavior and increase awareness of cooperative activities is to conduct joint orientation sessions for new hires. These orientations will differ depending on the nature of the union and the employer. They can be conducted for employees who work for many employers, such as building tradespersons, and for those who work for one employer.

Some unions and managements also cooperate on hiring. Responding to a union taunt in a discipline hearing that management had hired the employee, the Bakery, Confectionery and Tobacco Workers International Union and a tobacco company decided to screen new hires jointly. The hiring decision is still management's, but the union has input.

In workplaces where union membership is a condition of employment after an initial trial period, it is a show of good faith for a union representative, as part of the orientation session, to explain the history, role, and structure of the union, how dues dollars are used, and how new employees can get involved in or use the union. The contract and the grievance procedures should also be explained. It is particularly important to let new employees know how they can participate in the union, including how they can put forward proposals for bargaining, ratify the contract, and file grievances if necessary. In organizations without a union or agency shop provision, there is nothing preventing the employer from inviting the union to make a presentation. Doing so can go a long way in creating a good union-management relationship. Extending such an invitation demonstrates convincingly that the employer wants to find ways to work with the union and will not attempt to sabotage the union's relationship with its members.

Without exercising censorship, both parties should be aware of the other's presentation. This avoids worries, uncomfortable situations, and open conflict. Ideally, the new hire orientation should be used as an opportunity for cooperation and both the union and management work up an outline of what new employees should know and conduct the session jointly. A joint presentation will probably be more complete, credible, balanced, and moderate than separately held sessions. If the union and management are working together on joint initiatives, the orientation session is a good time to let new employees know that there are areas of common concern the parties are addressing.

A union that has contracts with many employers, such as in the building trades or the performing arts, can provide the locus for an orientation. It can invite a range of employers to come together to present information to new members and employees about their practices. The union can describe the benefits members receive, how the union relates to the various employers, members' rights under the contract, and ways to participate in the union.

Joint Meetings for Preretirement and Layoffs

The flip side of joint activities for hiring is joint activities preparatory to separations other than for discipline. The most positive address preretirement. After an employee's long period of service and membership in the union, the union and management can help ease his or her way into retirement. One of the best ways this can be done is to institute a voluntary cutback in hours before an employee reaches retirement age. This allows for a gradual transition to retirement without the shock of a sudden separation from co-workers and routines maintained over many years.

Preretirement education about financial planning, health issues, legal concerns, consumer education, employment after retirement, volunteer work, leisure activities, continuing education opportunities, and other critical issues is increasingly essential in our society.[30] Joint activities provide an opportunity to describe fully the pension benefits that employees will receive from the employer or the union. The union can inform retirees about ways that they can stay active in the union through the increasing number of retirees' clubs. Studies of union retirees by the National Institute for Work and Learning have documented the wide range of interests of retirees and their strong desire to remain connected to their unions.[31]

Properly approached, retirement can be a point of entry into other engaging activities; ignored, it can be traumatic. The time to consider retirement issues is not immediately before retirement but at least five to ten years earlier so that adequate planning can take place. Preretirement programs can be sponsored, designed, and even presented by the union and management together.

More difficult are the times when there is separation from the employer because of layoffs or plant closings. Although each party may do everything it can to avoid layoffs and ensure the survival of the organization, this is not always possible.[32] Employees need to hear clearly what the situation is, what recall rights they have, how to apply for unemployment benefits, what social services are available in the area, and other information that will help them cope realistically and as well as possible. In Canada, for example, joint activities aided by the government help employees deal with the difficulties that can arise from layoffs.[33]

The most sensible approach is to recognize shifts in the economy and figure out what to do ahead of time. Massive shifts from military to domestic production, for example, require forethought and planning. The Swedes and Japanese showed this is possible when they helped transform industries in decline into new production sites and helped workers find new jobs. When the aluminum industry was shut down in Japan because of energy considerations, new jobs arose in their place; in Sweden, a car factory was erected on the site of an old shutdown shipyard.

When there is a plant closing, the union and management have a responsibility to those who have lost their jobs to help by providing them with all the information mentioned above as well as employment counseling and health-care information.[34] The euphemism "dislocated" generally means out of work and out of luck. In some cases, the employees may be eligible for Trade Adjustment Assistance, which can help with retraining and relocation. The union may want to establish an ongoing support group for workers dealing with the pain of unemployment and the frustrations of looking for new work while trying to support themselves and their families. The union and management need to marshal all the resources available in the community to aid the disemployed adequately. Helping workers, families, and communities is a shared responsibility of labor and management in times of economic crisis.

Conclusion

The collective bargaining relationship provides the basis for cooperation. Likewise, the union-management relationship can serve to catalyze the partners to create a compelling common vision of the future. Contract negotiations and the relationship, approached cooperatively and creatively, can provide opportunities for strategic planning or to solve problems jointly. Similarly, contract administration, especially the grievance procedure, can be used to diagnose overall problems in the workplace and to assess the union-management relationship, as well as for specific problem solving. Finally, hiring and separation can provide opportunities to demonstrate cooperation. The collective bargaining relationship and the contract can also be the basis for other mechanisms of cooperation, described in the following chapters.

Collective bargaining has always been a dynamic arrangement for dialogue, the signaling of commitment, and action between management and the union. Its creative possibilities can be the foundation for a wide range of cooperative approaches that can enhance the lives of working people and the success of their employers.

5. Building Linking Structures:
Labor-Management Committees

Far and away the most common forum for union-management cooperation is the labor-management committee. Joint committees serve as a bridge between collective bargaining and joint problem solving. Labor-management committees are composed of representatives of management and representatives of the union who meet to deal with mutually agreed-upon topics. Sometimes these committees are called for in the contract, and probably as often they are not. They may be general committees whose purpose is to maintain open communications between the union and management, or they may be oriented toward specific topics such as health and safety or training. There are few issues that have not been the subject of a labor-management committee somewhere.

In general, labor-management committees are appendages to existing structures used for communication and problem solving. Occasionally, they have decision-making authority. In appraising why these committees are so common in the United States, two professors of management observed: "First, labor-management committees offer a less radical, more gradual departure from traditional American patterns of industrial relations in that they leave intact the separate perspectives, interests and capabilities of both management and organized labor. Second, the mechanics of labor-management committees are already available and have been utilized successfully for many years."[1] Usually, they co-exist with other structures. Joint committees are used both in traditional organizations and as part of high-involvement team-based systems.

Labor-management committees have a long history. The shop committees of the early part of the century were among the earliest versions. More than fifty thousand general labor-management committees were established in the United States during World War II. Also at that time, Canadians started using joint committees on a large scale. Intermittently, the Canadian government promoted labor-management committees as a voluntary approach to joint consultation and workplace improvement.

Labor-management committees come into existence in several ways. Often, they arise out of the collective bargaining arena because an issue is clearly of common interest and of an ongoing nature. Committees also emerge during collective bargaining as a way of dealing with nonstrikable issues not resolved during the bargaining sessions. Hence, a committee may be empowered to deal with an issue after the acceptance of a contract. Some "committees" are proposed as window dressing when there is no resolution of an issue on the table but a constituency requires a show of some action on the item. A committee can also be proposed and constituted at any time if either party suggests that one be formed. Sometimes committees are formed when representatives of the other party are added to an already-established unilateral committee.

Labor-management committees also operate at area and industry levels. Area labor-management committees composed of representatives of many employers and unions have been formed in many parts of the United States, forging partnerships for economic development in cities, counties, and states. They often have ties to the local government. In some cases, they work with local employers and unions to develop labor-management committees on-site. The Jamestown (New York) Labor-Management Committee was one of the earliest and most successful area committees that helped turn around a depressed area through community-based and site-specific cooperative efforts.[2] In several industries, such as retail food, men's clothing, and masonry, national-level industry committees have helped with modernization efforts and labor relations. At the national level in the United States, the Collective Bargaining Forum provides a venue for the discussion of common issues, as does a national union-management group convened by former Secretary of Labor John Dunlop. Although these are very valuable and interesting approaches to union-management cooperation, this chapter focuses more on the particular employer-union relationship.

Labor-management committees have a mixed record of accomplishment. They can be excellent and provide a real forum for common analysis and decision making. In practice, however, many committees never meet their potential, and too frequently committees agreed to in contracts never meet on a regular basis. They often wither away when the person most interested in the issue leaves or becomes concerned with other issues. Members of labor-management committees rarely receive training on how to manage a committee or on how to engage in joint problem solving, and sometimes the results provide evidence of this lack of skill. Resources are not often allocated specifically for the work of the committee, and they must scavenge to meet their needs.

The effectiveness of a labor-management committee varies depending on the caliber and level of the people involved, the resources and training available to the committee, and the commitment the organization involved has to the topic being addressed. Admittedly, few employees find the prospect of another committee energizing or innovative. But well-run committees although mundane in form can spark innovation and inject energy into their organizations.

General-Purpose Labor-Management Committees

As a starting point for union-management cooperation, some organizations have set regular meetings during the term of the contract for the purpose of facilitating ongoing general communication between management and union representatives. They may meet as infrequently as twice a year or as frequently as once a month. Typically, the agenda is largely informational. Management informs the union of operational results of the period since they last met and major initiatives that are planned for the future. The union shares information and concerns of a general nature that it has learned from the membership. There is some discussion of the issues presented but little in-depth or ongoing problem solving. Open communication is a building block of any successful cooperative effort and these meetings serve a valuable function by providing an avenue for discussion. They are a good idea even as part of more extensive joint efforts.

Some organizations have adapted the labor-management committee concept for dealing with quality of work life (QWL) initiatives. When all employees in a work area cannot be on a team or problem-solving group, representatives sometimes form a general labor-management committee. In the RBO program discussed in chapter 4, there is a general committee at the top. There may also be several layers of labor-management committees at the departmental or divisional level for the purposes of general communication and problem solving. Some advocates of labor-management committees have added problem-solving responsibilities to general informational labor-management committees.[3] Most QWL programs are governed by a labor-management committee, and some lower-level problem-solving groups are in fact labor-management committees. One of the most successful labor-management programs in the public sector emerged from weekly labor-management meetings at the New York City Sanitation Department.[4] The committee built the trust to proceed, and it then tackled important operational issues, which resulted in major savings and improvements in the work environment.

The Federal Mediation and Conciliation Service provides "Ten Summary Points for an Effective Labor-Management Committee" applicable to most such committees.[5]

1. Both parties share mutual interests in the long-term survival and success of the enterprise and the community, even though they may have conflicting goals in other matters.

2. Both sides want to make the labor-management committee work and have realistic expectations of what it can accomplish. Participation in regular sessions symbolizes this commitment, which is known throughout the organization.

3. Labor members of the joint committee are believed and trusted by the rank and file; management members have sufficient status and authority.

4. Maximum voluntary participation is encouraged; employees, including supervisors, are kept informed and involved in matters considered by the labor-management committee and have opportunities to express their views on its recommendations.

5. The joint committees do not take up matters that infringe on the rights of either party as established under the collective bargaining agreement or the grievance procedure.

6. Job security is recognized as a basic to the program's success.

7. The parties have a mature, open relationship. Each is willing to listen to the other side. Both agree to concentrate on finding answers to problems at hand and discovering opportunities for collaborating.

8. The joint committees are promptly informed about the status of their recommendations. If they are not, the committees lose interest and stop operating.

9. Numerous channels of communication are encouraged and an atmosphere of mutual respect prevails. However, communications must be accompanied by substantive recommendations.

10. New ideas are encouraged and their value weighed objectively. Concrete problems of interest to both management and labor must be pursued by the committee if it is to function productively.

General labor-management committees can provide an umbrella for cooperative efforts for the organization as a whole or for specific labor-management committees as described below, or supplement other organizational change initiatives.

Health and Safety Committees

Joint health and safety committees are the most common and most important specific labor-management committee. According to a nationwide study, 75.8 percent of workers believe that they should have a complete say or a lot of say on health and safety.[6] This is higher than for any other category of workplace concern.

In 1971–75, at least a third of all collective bargaining contracts contained language calling for health and safety committees, covering more than 3.2 million workers and 41 percent of all employees in the surveyed group.[7] By 1986, according to the Bureau of National Affairs, 49 percent of all contracts called for such committees. Sixty-two percent of manufacturing contracts included provisions for these committees, compared to 27 percent of nonmanufacturing contracts.[8] Many more joint health and safety committees exist, though they are not specifically mentioned in agreements. There may be well over 150,000 in the United States alone.

Health and safety committees usually range in size from six to sixteen members, often split equally between the union and management. But despite the good work done by many of these committees, the potential of health and safety committees has barely been tapped. A minimal number of these committees receive training on health and safety matters, for example, or how to operate effectively.

In 1992, the province of Ontario began to certify more than 100,000 management and employee health and safety representatives, who will help aid their mandated health and safety labor-management committees. Management and union representatives developed the curriculum in cooperation with the government.

Kevin Sweeney, who developed safety-based labor-management committees for the American Center for Quality of Work Life, observes:

> Cooperative labor management committees generate a body of very precise information that had been previously unavailable. Consequently management is in a better position to see health and safety as a real cost factor. Such information provides a greater incentive to engage in proactive problem solving and forecasting. From the perspective of labor, the committee's most immediate benefit is labor's involvement in the decisions that affect the welfare of every employee. Those on the job are afforded a mechanism contributing to the solution of problems and the improvement of their work

environment. Their jobs will become safer, less stressful, easier to perform and more rewarding.[9]

A joint health and safety committee can undertake a wide variety of activities, including making periodic inspections, accompanying safety inspectors, red-tagging dangerous areas, providing safety and health education, screening for hazards, analyzing accidents and chemical spills, reviewing and promoting personal protective equipment, and providing publicity and communication activities. Some committees have the authority to shut down unsafe machinery. The committee may review and analyze employer records to determine areas of frequent or serious problems and conduct safety audits to identify difficult areas that need more in-depth problem solving. Prevention techniques can include a review of new machinery from a health and safety perspective as well as assessments of the potential health hazards of chemicals being introduced into the work area. Finally, right-to-know legislation can provide an opportunity to expand the education of all employees on workplace hazards and what to do about them. To be effective, however, the committee needs to be knowledgeable about federal, state, and local regulations on health and safety and receive ongoing thorough training, especially in the areas of hazardous chemicals and evacuation procedures.

Joint health and safety action is common in Sweden, where considerable funds are available for research, education, and intervention. Swedish joint committees have extensive power, including the right to veto any plans for new machines, materials, or work processes for health and safety reasons; decide how to spend their company's health and safety budget; approve the selection of the company doctor, nurse, safety engineer, or industrial hygienist; review all corporate medical records; shut down any dangerous operations; and decide how much time the joint committees need to do their work.[10]

In a study of joint committees in New York State, Thomas A. Kochan, Lee Dyer, and David Lipsky identified critical problems in making joint committees work. One problem was maintaining continuity over the long term: committees tended to wither away and lose effectiveness. The researchers identified the key to countering this as continued rank-and-file involvement in the committee's actions. Another major problem was "buffering the committee from the collective bargaining process."[11]

What does a truly empowered committee look like? It has a clearly defined mandate from top management and union leadership. More than likely key decision-makers will serve on the committee. It has the influence to persuade production managers to stop work when a safety hazard has been detected. It has a budget so that it need not be dependent on other departments whose resources are already being stretched. Its presence and activities are widely publicized throughout the organization through a variety of communications mechanisms such as newsletters, safety reps and incentive programs. It has a track record for quick response to employee complaints. Its members are highly visible as they perform regular plant audits and elicit employee input. It has the information it needs to be able to determine how much its efforts are producing results.[12]

Health and safety committees are an important joint initiative. They are relevant in almost all industries and work environments, in manufacturing, transportation, building and construction, and offices. They can mesh well with management safety and health efforts carried on independently in accordance with responsibility and liability in this area. They can also complement union health and safety committees. Joint committees are not a substitute for adequate government regulation of health and safety since monitoring is still necessary, but joint efforts sincerely approached can reduce the need for inspections and government intervention.

Analyses of joint labor-management health and safety committees have documented their impact. The Business Roundtable found that there was a 40 percent reduction in injuries and a 20 percent increase in productivity in construction firms that had cooperative safety and health programs. Two programs saved their companies a total of $44 million, returning $44 for every dollar spent on the program. In addition, there were substantial indirect benefits, including increased morale, lower workers' compensation costs, less lost time because of injuries, decreased property damage, and fewer legal claims.[13] In other settings, there have been clear indications that committees increase the awareness of hazards and the importance of safety.

A far more difficult area to assess is the value of cooperative health and safety committees in health promotion. Health and safety committees should monitor health with as much dedication as they address safety, especially with the increased costs of health care. To control the escalating costs of health coverage, employers and unions both need to consider ways to reduce utilization. Their common point of interest is health promotion.

Other than changing national health-care policy, two viable strategies can be pursued to help reduce health problems: confront organizational contributors to these problems and help individuals and their families live more healthfully. On an organizational level, it is critical to conduct extensive, data-based analyses of work processes and chemical use to ensure that they are not contributing to long-term health problems. For example, carpal tunnel syndrome is a major health ailment that develops over many years as a result of regular, ingrained work processes. Dust and other particulates in the air can cause long-term respiratory ailments.

Finally, high stress can contribute to whether or not a person gets heart disease. This link has been well documented by Robert Karasek and Tores Theorell, an American-Swedish research team:

> If the models of work organization that we use everyday are so clearly connected to stress development, then we may be in the process of creating even more stressful environments—now on a global scale—that are totally incompatible with human physiological capabilities. . . . Unless many present models of economic and production organization are changed, the future will see not only a progressively poorer trade-off of health for productivity but many situations in which both are needlessly lost.[14]

Paying attention to ergonomics, the fit between people and technology, is one way to make the work environment more conducive to good health.

We discuss ways to increase wellness among employees and their families in the section on employee assistance later in this chapter. Wellness programs have a significant effect on health-care cost containment. The use of chemicals at the workplace and the abuse of smoking and drugs can be a deadly combination, for example. Rather than letting health-care cost containment become an arena for combat, labor and management should review their coverages, negotiate better arrangements with providers, and introduce practices that reduce costs while maintaining high standards of medical care.[15] The example set by AT&T, the CWA, and the IBEW, which jointly examined options for containing health-care costs while retaining premium services, illustrates that joint action is possible. Wasteful practices do not contribute to health. By contrast, an emphasis on appropriate diagnosis and treatment with strong incentives for prevention can result in healthier workers and lower health costs.

The State and Local Government Labor-Management Committee noted that "labor-management health care cost containment efforts are more effective in constraining costs than unilateral employer cost containment initiatives that have been implemented without union involvement."[16] Costs rose 5.8 percent faster in unilateral efforts than in joint programs. The committee sees union involvement as helping to contain costs and improve quality in the following four ways:

- pooling bargaining power in relation to insurance companies, hospitals, and doctors, labor and management can implement plan changes, encourage more cost-effective forms of care, negotiate reduced rates and cut administrative costs.
- monitoring employee health costs, utilization rates, and the impact of plan changes. Labor and management can make informed changes in plan design and then hold insurers and providers accountable to implement these changes.

- providing employees with information about physician and hospital practice patterns, alternatives to expensive care, and good health practices, labor and management can demand better, more cost-effective health care services.
- implementing wellness and other health education programs, labor and management can practice preventive medicine which is the most effective long term cost containment and quality strategy.[17]

Labor and management can work together in ways that significantly improve the health of workers. Health improvements pay off not only in quality of life but in productivity and reduced costs.

Joint Training Committees

Perhaps the second most common and most taken-for-granted kind of joint union-management committee is involved in joint training for apprentices. In 1978, more than 500,000 people were enrolled in joint apprenticeship programs in the United States. These programs are especially common in the construction and building trades. Joint apprenticeship programs are also found in many other parts of the private and public sectors, however, ranging from tool machining to the health-care professions.

The mutual interest in apprenticeship is easy to explain. The employer wants well-trained, competent crafts or tradespersons. The union builds its claim for better wages on the higher skill levels in its ranks. Further, both the employer and the union bring to the committee real-world experience on what is actually needed on the job. Former U.S. Secretary of Labor Ray Marshall has repeatedly noted that apprenticeship is a way to connect education and work: "On-the-job training and apprenticeship systems are important skill development processes, and are most successful when conducted jointly by labor and management."[18] One function of joint training committees is to make sure that graduates of apprenticeship programs will have the skills necessary to compete in the five to ten years after they complete these programs. Members of these committees should ensure that apprentices have a general knowledge of their industry and the union and have the competencies needed to perform high-quality work in their craft. Committee members may also require training on the latest developments in their field and how to guide instructional programs.

Apprenticeship alone is not enough, however, to maintain a competitive, well-trained work force. Procedures, tools, machinery, materials, regulations, and other matters that affect employees change constantly. Thus, another function of a joint training committee is to inventory workers' skills, assess recent changes, and determine future needs so as to establish an effective continuing education program. The International Union of Operating Engineers and the Sheet Metal Workers' International Association and their contractors have connected apprentices and journeypersons to apprenticeship programs for college credit, leading in some cases to associate's and bachelor's degrees. Committees can also maintain a training record for journeypersons by tracking their continuing education and certifying new areas of specialized competency. The Los Angeles tile setters, for example, established a master craftsperson category based on superior training and experience. By cooperating on a regional basis, committees can also provide skills in highly specialized areas not supportable on the local level.

The need for ongoing employee training and retraining is not restricted to the traditional industries where apprenticeships are common. Additional skills are essential in all areas of modern employment. Employees who do not receive continuing education are like funds that are not put in the bank; their value goes down over time. Every job requires a set of initial skills and ongoing skills development to maintain and expand employees' capabilities. Joint training committees can be used in any environment to help in the identification of training needs as well as to assist in the design, delivery, and evaluation of training. Conducting training in a joint manner can enhance the effectiveness of training conducted by the employer and augment the skills and increase the employability of employees.

Joint training committees are greatly needed to ensure comprehensiveness and responsiveness in ongoing learning. They are gaining in popularity as American businesses face up to skill shortages and literacy problems. International experience has shown that union-management training, especially for new technology, can enhance organizational performance and employment security.[19]

In the last decade, there has been an exciting development in union-management education and training in the auto industry and similar activity in the telecommunications and steel industries. In 1983, the CWA and the telephone companies negotiated to establish Joint Training Advisory Boards designed to develop, promote, evaluate, and modify personal and career development training and relocation training for laid-off employees. Subsequently, the CWA and the IBEW and AT&T developed the Alliance for Employee Growth and Development to provide extensive educational assistance to current employees and those whose jobs have been affected by downsizing and new technology. In 1982, the UAW negotiated with General Motors, Ford, and Chrysler to set up a fund that is now based on a dime-an-hour contribution (and up to $5 for each overtime hour based on total overtime ratios) to help pay for training and retraining current and laid-off employees. These programs are administered jointly at the national level, but each local plant has a Joint Skill Development and Training Committee responsible for maintaining local funds and activities. The United Steelworkers of America has negotiated a large program to assist employees in basic steel. In the public sector, massive programs have been developed in New York City with District Council 37 of the American Federation of State, County and Municipal Employees; District 65 of the United Auto Workers; and with hospital unions to help in career advancement and a wide range of educational services. Taken together, labor-management educational initiatives represent the largest source of new funds, and in many ways of new energy, in adult and higher education.

A study reviewing these programs concluded: "Joint training initiatives are among the furthest reaching changes in industrial relations. Joint training promises to help address the realities of dislocation and permanent layoff, while assisting active workers in facing the changes caused by new technology, global competition, and new business practices. From a management perspective, joint training would help workers adjust to the shorter product cycles, shifts in the way production is organized, higher standards of quality, and increased pressure on cost."[20] The authors note that joint programs have some characteristics that make them different from unilateral initiatives by management: they provide broader career mobility; they attract broader participation of blue- and pink-collar workers; they have broader input from employees, who help in program design; and they address a wider range of educational and support needs.

The Ford-UAW program has been particularly active. In addition to a wide range of services for dislocated workers, the program offers workers an extensive range of services, including life/education planning, basic skills enhancement, prepaid tuition aid in any subject, on-site educational activities, counseling programs, retirement planning, and noncredit personal development programs. The national staff of the program, drawn from both management and the union, assists eighty-five local committees, which develop and screen proposals for activities. The program is explicitly designed to complement other joint UAW-Ford programs, such as health and safety education. According to the directors of the joint program:

> The Employee Development and Training Program is one of the more extensive joint efforts underway between Ford and the UAW. Because of these joint efforts . . . , UAW-represented Ford-hourly workers have more opportunities than ever before to become involved in decisions affecting their work; their job satisfaction has grown; they are upgrading their skills; and they have the chance to undertake a wide variety of projects of their own choosing. In

addition, because of the joint actions of Ford and the UAW, Ford product quality has improved, operating styles are changing, information is widely shared, and the working environments in Ford plants have generally improved.[21]

Similar joint programs are in place at General Motors and Chrysler.

In Australia, the labor movement views skills formation as a cornerstone of industrial restructuring. Australians see skills formation, new technology, changes in industrial relations, and new work organization as closely interrelated; changes in one area need to be reflected in the other three to be truly effective. The Australian Council of Trade Unions (ACTU) has declared that "Australia must produce a workforce characterized by both high level technical and intellectual skills such as problem setting and solving, analytic ability, initiative, effective communication, creativity and decision making. The workforce must have the ability to adapt to frequent changes in work organization and technology."[22] The ACTU sees this continuous process as guided by local labor-management committees with decision-making authority for designing training. Some Australian labor contracts have negotiated at least 5 percent of work time for education for all workers, and career ladders are contractually negotiated to ensure that all workers develop competency and income mobility.

Negotiated tuition assistance programs, affecting millions of workers, are another area in which joint training committees can play a role. Currently, hundreds of millions of dollars of negotiated funds are left untapped. Typically less than 5 percent of the eligible work force takes advantage of tuition assistance, and those who have the least education are least likely to participate. Joint action by the union and management could reverse this trend and in some cases is already reversing it. The National Institute for Work and Learning points out, "In recent years, employers and unions have found innovative ways to build skill development, career development, and succession planning programs combining both in-house training and employee-initiated learning using tuition assistance. . . . Joint responsibilities is a key concept in effective use of tuition assistance plans."[23] The Council for Adult and Experiential Learning (CAEL) has developed a number of innovative ways to encourage "returning to learning" through labor-management joint ventures.[24] And Mountain Bell and the telephone unions have sponsored very successful joint pathways to learning throughout fourteen western states that increased use of tuition assistance to a dramatic 20 percent.

A series of innovative labor-management approaches to increasing literacy have been developed in the United States and Canada with impetus from national workplace literacy initiatives in each country. These programs provide opportunities to improve the level of skills at the workplace and thereby make it more productive while empowering workers with the skills they need to better participate at home and in their unions and communities.[25]

A wide range of techniques are used by labor-management groups to improve literacy, including on-site classes, classes at union halls, tutorials, computer-aided instruction, and videos. In some cases, literacy is being designed into apprenticeship or on-the-job training. Joint union-management literacy programs have greater credibility than unilateral programs with union members and offer a clear channel for integration at the workplace.

Critical questions in literacy programs are defining literacy and the objectives of the program. The American Society for Training and Development's broad definition of literacy covers not only reading, writing, and computation but also such skills as listening, oral communication, creative thinking, problem solving, negotiation, goal setting, teamwork, interpersonal skills, and how to learn.[26] Some have urged "learning audits" in which current skills are measured against employer needs and a plan is developed to fill the gaps. Others have argued strongly against this caulking notion of skill development and have suggested that workplace literacy should be part of a strategy to reexamine work organization and increase overall skill. Anthony Sarmiento, of the AFL-CIO Education Department, states: "As we seek to raise the basic skills of the workforce, it is important for policy makers to recognize that workplace literacy programs can support the path toward either low wages or high skills. Depending on who's involved, which program goals are selected, and what planning process is followed, a workplace literacy program can maintain outdated workplaces or foster high performance workplace structures."[27]

Education—skill-based, linked to basic literacy, or further education— is an important area for common effort, whether it stands alone or is integrated with other organizational changes. There is a critical connection between education and work reorganization. In the prestigious report *America's Choice: High Skills or Low Wages!* this line is highlighted.[28] Higher skills can lead to higher quality and performance, but without a new work organization the potential talent is never realized. To survive as a worker in the new workplace requires a broader range of skills than ever before. Meeting the challenge of making the workplace a "learning organization" can help both individuals and organizations grow and improve.

Employee Assistance and Wellness Committees

Every workplace should consider having a joint employee assistance program. One of the fastest growing employee-oriented programs in the 1980s, employee assistance programs (EAPs) make a lot of sense for both management and labor. At the very least, they provide a way to help troubled employees, especially those with alcohol and substance abuse problems. When more broadly considered, EAPs can provide an extensive variety of services, including family counseling, financial advice, stress management, legal assistance, weight loss counseling, and smoking control. Some EAPs focus on health prevention and include diet, exercise, and lifestyle programs. Some joint EAPs have designed and installed exercise facilities on company premises. EAPs can also help in AIDS education and advocate for a broad understanding of employees infected by HIV. EAPs can be a major part of an overall strategy to develop healthful lifestyles among employees and their families as part of a health-cost containment effort.

The connection between work and family has been the focus of EAPs and/or of separate joint committees. Companies and unions are becoming more aware of their responsibility to help all employees—men and women—manage child-care and elder-care issues, balance responsibilities at home, and acknowledge the link between stress in the family and work performance. EAPs can be a major comfort to employees whose family members are in personal crisis. They can establish on-site support groups for employees confronting difficult issues or link employees to groups in the community. Such family-friendly policies lead not only to improved work performance but also employee retention.[29]

The initial impetus for the formation of many recent EAPs has been the requirements of the Drug Free Workplace Act. To comply with the act, many companies have contracted for services from EAP firms. Many such programs are pasted together, however, and have no thoughtful labor-management guidance at all. Alcoholism and drug abuse adversely affect the workplace in many very important ways. They lead to increased absenteeism, turnover, discipline, poor quality, higher accident rates, lower productivity, and a host of other problems. They increase tensions between supervisors and employees and among employees themselves. Abusers provide dilemmas for the union, which has a legal and moral obligation to defend members against workplace charges, although the underlying problem may be substance abuse. By joining together, the union and management have greater resources and credibility in dealing compassionately and effectively with the broadest range of employees. When the issue of EAPs gets framed around drug testing, there is great possibility for union-management conflict regarding civil liberties issues, but when a preventive and rehabilitative approach is taken, EAPs provide a marvelous opportunity for joint activity.

On the one hand, the workplace has an obligation to deal forthrightly with the consequences of an abuser's behavior at work and to insist that standards be maintained. On the other hand, the human dimension must be taken into account, as well as the investment the employer has made in the employee. Every effort should be made to provide troubled employees with the assistance they need to deal appropriately with their problems. This can range from sponsoring workshops to counseling and support groups in the work area to enrollment in detoxification and withdrawal programs. By working sensitively and sensibly with these employees, real progress can be made. Ignoring the problem or handling it incorrectly can lead to greater workplace disruptions and increased human tragedy.

Labor-management committees in the employee assistance area have some very important challenges. EAPs need to be especially well planned and organized.[30] For some employees, they provide a lifeline, and the programs should be as strong as possible. In most programs, internal employees trained to be sensitive to employee problems are used to generate referrals to specialists (usually external) in the various areas addressed by the EAP. Often these include detoxification centers, community mental health programs, legal clinics, and physicians.

There are also many independent EAP providers. These professionals should be accessible, community-based, and as cost-effective as possible. Control over the program should remain inside the work organization with the committee and its joint coordinators. Although advice from professionals should be taken seriously, turning the program over to "professionals" would in most cases be harmful to the program's credibility and effectiveness.

Joint EAP programs can be very successful. Operation REDBLOCK, an EAP conducted by the railroads and their unions, focuses on public safety issues on the railroads. The United Paperworkers International Union (UPIU) has been especially active in promoting joint efforts to confront alcohol and drug abuse. Frank P. Burger, director of this program, says:

> Employee assistance professionals are engaged in an education process designed to change the way supervisors, union stewards and employees are accustomed to thinking and behaving. Three major goals come quickly to mind: 1) unhesitant referral of troubled employees by supervisors, 2) assurance that aftercare plans are followed and 3) full integration of the employee assistance program into the culture of the workplace. . . . At first blush, the idea of a strong joint committee may sound corny (another committee—oh brother!). But the effort of a strong joint committee can have a lot to do with accomplishing all three of the goals mentioned.[31]

The UPIU is clear on the union's role in constructive confrontation. In their EAP materials they state: "If an employee's job performance deteriorates to a clearly unacceptable level, the union will work in cooperation with management to advise the employee of his or her options: a) to advise the worker in a confidential, non-threatening environment of the availability of these crucial treatment services; b) to encourage the worker to accept the needed service; c) and finally to make it clear to the employee of the somber and predictable consequences of failing to improve his or her job performance." The goal is to involve the union early in a cooperative search to help the individual but to allow no wiggle room for those who deny their addiction to alcohol or drugs.

In addition, the EAP committee should support training for management and union leadership at all levels on how to make a referral (or use the services themselves). It is most important to build teamwork between first-line supervisors and shop stewards so that they will recognize and handle problems appropriately in their work areas. The composition of the EAP committee should be broad and may include several employees who understand dependency and recovery from their own experience.

Confidentiality is an essential element of a successful EAP, though defining and maintaining it is difficult.[32] It must be ironclad, or few will participate in the program.

The union-management committee will want to monitor the EAP carefully to make sure that it adequately addresses the full range of needs in the workplace, that provider agencies are effective and responsive, and that all levels of employees are being reached. Visits to provider agencies are one way to learn how well services are being provided.

Employee assistance programs are important efforts toward improving the quality of work life.[33] Most QWL advocates believe that improved work environments will reduce alienation and hence personal trauma and that new work structures will empower those who have been locked out. Theoretically, the improved work environment should lead to improved personal health.[34] The real world is not utopian, however, and there remains the need even in the best workplaces to help individuals cope with their personal problems and the tensions of the larger world. At the same time, EAPs should not be apologists for poor work environments. Information about recurring "personal" issues in the workplace may provide important clues about the need for organizational change, health hazards, or ways the work structure exacerbates personal difficulties. The interplay between work and personal issues is most evident among those doing shift work. The strain placed on families and the physiology of workers on rotating shifts is real. Third-shift workers tend to have higher incidences of drug and alcohol abuse. The dark of the night may provide a haven for individuals with abuse problems, but the isolation of graveyard shifts can also magnify or perhaps cause these problems. EAPs can provide an important complement to an overall effort at organizational change. Standing alone, they can be an important first step in union-management cooperation and a vital service to many employees.

Environmental and Energy Conservation Committees

Energy and natural resources fuel the production process and represent a natural area in which the union and management can work together on cost reduction and productivity. At the local level, the energy and resource issue is a quadruple win-win issue. If energy and resources are saved, then the work process is less costly to manage; there are more resources available for other items, including compensation; the country benefits because there is less reliance on external energy sources; and the global ecosystem suffers less disruption and depletion of resources. In addition, reducing the use of natural resources increases geopolitical and economic stability. The decades ahead herald much greater environmental consciousness among consumers, employees, and employers. Labor and management can exercise good judgment concerning their own interests and model proper stewardship of the earth's resources by being proactive on environmental concerns.

Fascinated by the possibilities in the environmental area, we conducted extensive research in conjunction with the University of Michigan in which we compared employee participation and union-management cooperation in resource conservation in the United States and Japan.[35] The research revealed that greater participation was clearly linked to higher savings. The strongest relationship existed when there was an energy conservation committee and an employee involvement program. The research showed that there was no area of technical, natural or energy resource, or organizational improvement over which employees did not have at least some input. These findings would probably apply to any technically oriented joint effort. Based on the research, conservation committees would probably be most effective if they followed these suggestions:[36]

1. If appropriate, have both establishment level and corporate or agency level energy conservation committees.
2. Aim for high levels of coordination between ECCs (Energy Conservation Committees), other establishment conservation activities, and the employee involvement program(s).
3. Create well defined and established broad authority of the ECC "to plan on a regular basis", "to monitor and evaluate programs", "to make final decisions", and "to implement on a regular basis".
4. Deliberately determine the composition and size of the committee based on its authority, making sure to have necessary functions or departments represented, necessary levels of management represented, and a large enough committee to have all of the relevant representatives.

5. Acquire and make available resources to the ECC's work, including a budget as well as engineering, computers and research and development assistance. Training is helpful for the committee in both energy conservation techniques and social process (for example, meeting facilitation and management).
6. The ECC should choose a wide array of activities to involve other employees in its work. Activities should include monitoring and evaluating conservation programs and considering both new technologies and machinery as well as new work processes or designs.

Japanese workers have been involved in conservation more extensively and over a longer period of time than workers in the United States. Yet the Japanese continue to report significant savings via employee involvement, demonstrating that conservation is an ongoing challenge and can harvest long-term yields. Because of the length and breadth of their experience, they tend to be more involved in cogeneration, alternative fuels, and other more frontier areas of conservation. In Japan, union members take part in two-thirds of the conservation committees.

There have also been interesting cooperative conservation ventures in the United States. The Maryland Department of Health and Mental Hygiene, for example, included its union in an innovative effort targeted at conservation inside state mental health institutions and the homes of employees and patients.[37] The Sheet Metal Workers' International Association works with contractors to promote, install, and guarantee solar energy equipment to commercial, governmental, and residential properties. As this and other examples illustrate, new energy and environmental policies at the workplace can generate new jobs and market opportunities.[38]

Unions and management can also cooperate in efforts to deploy both technical and organizational measures to improve resource use. In many situations, technical, engineering, or machine-based solutions represent the extent of the conservation strategies considered. Technical solutions require human cooperation to identify, implement, and then use that technology effectively. Industrial and energy engineering can be very helpful in providing technical insight, but because workers have an intimate knowledge of their work processes and environment, they can often identify other possibilities and solutions. Committees should therefore consider ways to train and empower employees to conduct basic energy and resource audits in their work areas and to monitor use patterns. Resources and energy may not be the largest part of a budget, but it is essential that they be managed wisely and efficiently.

The greening of the corporation calls for new cooperation between unions and management.[39] Consumers and union members are much more ecologically aware and want to be part of the solution of environmental problems. This includes being more involved in recycling efforts, process flow analyses to identify areas where waste and effluents can be reduced or reused, decisions about packaging, ensuring efficient use of fleet vehicles, and a host of other areas. Organizations need to monitor their effect on air, water, and land quality. A total quality perspective includes writing value statements on environmental impact and recognizing that the work process runs from extraction to processing all the way to final disposal or reuse. Environmental action also contributes to health and safety since employees are the first to pay the price of environmental disasters and often have the highest level of exposure.

If labor and management do not cooperate in the area of conservation, they are much more liable to have to deal with government and community pressures that could affect them negatively. The General Secretary of the International Confederation of Free Trade Unions, John Vanderveken, has declared: "Many workers are exposed to the twin evils of dangerous workplace conditions and an unacceptable environment outside the workplace. Workers are also often well informed regarding practicable solutions for particular problems—though they are frequently ignored when they attempt to suggest improvements. And all workers have a vested interest in ensuring the continuing health of the planet."[40]

Managers are also acutely aware of the need for action. Two Canadian businesspersons, Patrick Carson and Julia Moulden, assert: "One of the benefits of the corporate greening process can be an improved relationship with your unionized employees. . . . Unions are developing their own environmental agendas; make sure that you develop a comprehensive course of action that encourages a team spirit."[41] Labor and management might want to establish environmental committees with a broad mission of investigating ways to alter workplace systems and behaviors that are contributing to pollution.

An ecological consciousness will pervade the market, work force, and workplace of the future. Unions and management can go well beyond responding to pressure and regulation and view environmental improvement as an opportunity to improve work processes and attract new markets.

Technology Committees

In today's workplace, there is a shift from the Fordist paradigm, predicated on routinization, to a post-Fordist orientation, centered on flexible, value-added technology. New technology holds the possibility of being a topic of great conflict, great cooperation, or a mixture of both. Not cooperating on new technology can create a lose-lose situation.

Management has reduced utilization of the new equipment or approach and generally has to trade costly provisions in staffing, time, and wages to win union acceptance. In a worst-case scenario, the union may be forced to negotiate concessions with little room or time to maneuver and have to settle for the least loss to the membership.

Few in labor are Luddites who want to smash their machines. Consequently, the serious difficulties of introducing new technology have been addressed by unions throughout the world and throughout their histories.[42] Unions often have great attachments to technology since it provides a basis for their members' skills and craft. Likewise, productivity improvements and market possibilities opened by new technology can lead to an increased standard of living and greater job security since technology is a critical component of a firm's competitiveness. A study of union responses to technological change found that union objections had to do primarily with the lack of planning for the consequences of the change, rather than with the particular technology.[43] Some unions such as the IAM have developed comprehensive blueprints concerning technological change, including a call for technology stewards.[44]

The terminology associated with new technology can be daunting for many unionists (and, for that matter, for nontechnical managers, such as those in industrial relations) and may limit the quality of the involvement. Both management and labor need to learn a common language to be able to talk about technology intelligently as well as approach it from an overall strategic perspective. Both management and labor run the risk of segmenting technology into departments of R&D or technology stewards. Their attempts to focus resources and limit conflict within the organization on technology issues paradoxically sets up competition between different departments or union functions. Technical resources need to be broadly connected throughout both organizations.

The process of working together on technological change is unrelated to the particular technology being introduced.[45] Whether it is new computerization, fiberoptics, VDTs, scanners, numerically controlled machinery, CAD-CAM, robotics, biotechnical advances, or other technologies, the specific technology is important only insofar as it affects the training needs of a joint committee and the related recommendations that emerge from the common effort. The areas for involvement and the process of joint problem solving remain largely the same.

The first step in working together on technological change should not occur after new machinery is installed. The two parties must work together from the very beginning, when the basic objectives for the new technology are being formed. Cooperation around the new technology must be an important strategic objective of both parties. It must be remembered that technology is a tool toward some end and that the choices of that end are determined by people. Shoshana Zuboff insightfully illustrates this concept when she describes the future use of information technology and the importance of participation and union involvement.[46] One choice is to use technology to automate jobs, which leads to deskilling and displacement. The other path is to "informate," which empowers workers to use technology more creatively and in ways that enhance community at work. Common agreement is possible when the discussion centers on how to reduce hazards and accidents, improve feedback to the operator, increase quality, make the work flow more sensible, reduce stress, and other benefits. Strong disagreement can emerge around such issues as the risks of reductions in employment, overall pay and skill requirements, health and safety, and external monitoring. If the new technology will prompt major job changes, then the consequences need to be addressed early on through retraining, reassignment, or the approaches to growth described in chapter 7.

After determining the objectives, the next step is to design the new technology jointly. There are usually several design options for any technology that meets the basic objectives of the organization involved. Because of their emphasis on flexibility, new technologies expand rather than contract the options to be considered. John Mathews, an Australian with a keen insight into new technology, notes: "Programmability is the key to *flexibility*; and it is flexibility that gives computerised systems such a boost in *productivity*. . . . Different designs can have radically different implications."[47] Hence, choosing a design does not have to mean sacrificing human needs for performance requirements.

Ergonomic concerns about the fit between the operators and the machinery are relevant in the design stage. Just as cost, technical feasibility, and a series of other operational issues should be weighed as part of making design decisions, so too there must be an awareness of the potential impact of design decisions on employment, relocation, health and safety, bargaining unit changes, skills, income, job qualifications, career advancement, job control, job pressures, and job satisfaction.[48] Rarely is any decision without pluses and minuses, but it is best if the human resources and industrial relations consequences of technology design decisions are examined upfront and early. The goal is always to achieve the best mix. Knowing that there was serious joint effort given to meeting human needs and performance requirements can mean there are far fewer concerns later on.

Very often, costly modifications have to be made in the workplace to compensate for design omissions. A number of employers have thus begun to involve workers in meeting with vendors to ensure a good fit between operator needs and performance and vendor specifications. For major purchases, some companies have sent joint union-management teams to examine applications of the machinery at other plants or to the manufacturer.

Another area for cooperation is the implementation of the new technology. Employers frequently recognize the need for input from the work force at this stage only because the first effort to put the technology in place did not work well. Implementation implies not only the physical startup and adaptation of the particular technology to the rest of the mechanical and operational process but also the development and delivery of training for operators.

New technology is inextricably linked to new work organization. General Motors proved that massive investments in hardware mean little if human systems are not changed. As Mathews writes: "Although the new computerised technologies of manufacturing are critical to the increases achieved in productivity and flexibility, the changes *are not technology driven*. The critical factors that always emerge are the capacities of skilled workers to utilise the new technologies to their full productive potential. Skill enhancement and new productive forms of work organization, conjoined within a favourable industrial relations environment, remain the keys to unlock the potential of the new manufacturing technologies."[49]

The final area for joint involvement is in the evaluation of the technology against the initial objectives. The work force provides an important source of information about how effective the technological change has been and what implications resulting from the changes still need to be considered. The evaluation should measure the impact of the technology on both operational effectiveness and the quality of work life. These findings can be used in determining the need for equipment upgrades, future purchases, or additional training.

Bert Painter, a Canadian consultant, reviewed labor-management efforts in the United States and Canada that focused on new technology and identified within a broad strategic framework of support the following factors as among those critical to skill-based technology:[50]

- software and hardware which give workers a degree of control or choice in the pace or method of work
- software which provides workers with immediate access to information for diagnosis of problems or for operational decision-making
- hardware which provides workers with safe and easy access to equipment for repairs and operation

Painter suggests continuous technical training and an ongoing commitment to social skills development. He emphasizes the importance of developing engineer-worker interaction, which improves the maintenance consciousness of engineers, respect for the information and skills each brings, and connects technical resources more closely to shop-floor concerns.

Richard Walton provides an overview of the possibilities in joint efforts for technological change:

> The potential benefits of labor-management planning and problem solving in relation to new work technology include the better utilization of basic technology because of attention to economic and social effects; stronger labor and management institutions; and greater employee voice. In addition, the mutuality/participation system is expected to be *more inventive* in developing new solutions to both old and new problems; more *adaptive* to changing conditions; and more productive of a *higher level of commitment* to solutions on the part of employees, unions and management.[51]

Benchmarking and Cost Study Teams

Recently we have seen the development of joint labor-management teams or committees specifically designed to measure and improve the competitiveness of an enterprise. Benchmarking has received attention as a way to measure the performance of one's own organization against the best standards in the marketplace. A precursor to benchmarking involved the use of joint cost study teams to help save jobs in a beleaguered industry.[52] Perhaps the best example was the Xerox–Amalgamated Clothing and Textile Workers' effort, begun in the early 1980s. When Xerox received the Baldrige Award for quality, it reflected more than a decade of joint commitment to world-class standards and continuous improvement.

Pressed by declining market share and foreign competition in the late 1970s, employees in several parts of the flagship Rochester, New York, Xerox facility had been under the gun to compete effectively or lose their jobs. Labor proposed the formation of cost study teams, and management agreed to the joint effort. A team in the wire harness department pioneered the effort by looking at direct material, space utilization, production standards and methods, quality systems, machine depreciation, stabilization of staff, organizational structure, tooling, maintenance, training, indirect labor, and allocations. At the end of six months, the team identified twelve ways to save $3.7 million. Cost study teams then became a part of the union-management cooperative and total quality structure at Xerox.

Programs for Employment and Workplace Systems (PEWS) at Cornell University worked with managers and workers in developing cost study teams as a way to fight to retain jobs. Sally Klingel and Ann Martin state, "In cost study teams, union members work together with management to find ways to restructure production to achieve cost savings so as to restore the competitive strength of the threatened operation."[53] They identify as critical to success top-level sanction, joint participation, access to information, adequate time, specific dollar targets set at the outset, agreement to proceed before commitments to outsource or shut down operations, and a way to evaluate success. Training in group processes and problem analysis techniques also help.

Benchmarking has become a standard part of total quality efforts. Usually it is a unilateral management activity, but a number of organizations have found great value in doing it jointly. David Kearns, chief executive of Xerox, defines benchmarking as "a continuous process of measuring products, services and practices against the toughest competitors or those companies recognized as industry leaders."[54] Each organization requires a tailored approach that reflects its character and industry. Most experiences have been with technical areas, but human resources is a fertile area to benchmark.

Robert C. Camp outlines a process that begins with the identification of what needs to be benchmarked. This phase provides an opportunity to explore jointly areas of common concern, including the conduct of labor relations. The process proceeds to the *analysis phase*, during which other organizations are reviewed; an *integration phase*, when internal goals and targets for change are established; and finally the *action phase*, when specific approaches are developed to meet or beat the benchmarking goals. The process is iterative, one of searching for continuous improvement.

Since benchmarking focuses on external measuring rods, labor has been concerned about being whipsawed in comparison with nonunion facilities, especially on human resource questions. Benchmarking should be clearly aimed not only at improving operational performance but also making the organization the best place to work. One way the union can be involved is on visits to benchmarking sites. Since benchmarking continuously poses the question why not be the best, it should help organizations raise their sights. Since it provides clear criteria and data on how to improve practices, it can lead to desirable change. If it broadly involves unions and employees in this search, it can be empowering and provide a basis for solid strategic bargaining. But when benchmarking leads to mimicry of other companies and the selection of benchmarking partners and criteria are slanted, it can steer an organization off course. Used as a spur to improvement, innovation, and involvement, benchmarking can be an effective joint strategy to pursue.

Joint Community Involvement

We have listed joint community service drives last because of the limited nature of the engagement. Nonetheless, they can be an important joint initiative. When labor and management cannot agree on internal joint projects, working to help those in need in the community presents a forum for experimenting with joint initiatives. For example, the labor movement and employers have been active in their support of the United Way, the Red Cross,[55] and other charitable organizations. Throughout the country almost four hundred labor liaisons connected to the AFL-CIO Department of Community Services work with community organizations and provide direct service to union members and their families.[56] They are valuable sources of information on ways to cooperate in the community interest.

The United Way recognizes that the best campaigns inside a workplace are those in which the union and management cooperate; both parties jointly take leadership roles in explaining to employees the local recipient agencies of the United Way and the ways they help their communities. One of the very early efforts highlighted by the United Way was in 1967 at the Chevrolet Shell Division of General Motors with the UAW.[57] As a result of joint effort, support, and explanation, the average contribution per employee was more than 250 percent higher than during unilateral campaigns. Joint meetings were held with employees to explain the United Way campaign, and publicity and communications were handled jointly. Management enthusiasm and encouragement can help create a climate of giving, and the union official can point to the close relationship between union community service programs and United Way agencies.

Fund drives are only one way to work together on community service. Both parties could jointly adopt a school and provide a balanced perspective on the labor-management relationship. They could aid in blood donations or disaster relief, help at food banks or shelters for the poor, care for the elderly, clean up environmental eyesores, or become involved in big brother and big sister programs or a host of other programs. What is needed is the will to work together in service to the broader community. Community service is especially important in towns dominated by a few unionized industries. For the company, community service demonstrates good corporate citizenship; for the union, it enhances its community image through the services or funds that are provided.

Conclusion

Labor-management committees come in all sizes and descriptions and deal with almost any topic. General committees provide open-ended forums for the exchange of information or, if desired, joint problem solving. When they are well run, they can have a strong impact on organizational performance and industrial relations. The adaptability of labor-management committees, however, should not be a precursor to lax implementation. The members should understand well their particular concerns and the process of accomplishing their objectives through a committee.

Committees can address general communication and problems inside organizations and/or help in the larger community. When working inside, their issues can range from specific workplace problems such as absenteeism, fire safety, job design, and contract bidding to any other issue. The possibilities span the production process, from resource use to total quality to technology. They can also contribute directly to the welfare of employees while having strong organizational impacts via employee assistance programs, education and training initiatives, and health and safety efforts. The particular application of labor-management committees depends on the imagination of the partners and their common desire to use a common forum effectively.

6. Developing New Organizational Structures: Quality Circles to Sociotechnical Redesign

At some point form followed function in the design of workplaces. Yet the functions, vexingly, refuse to stand pat. To serve a changing external environment and shifting demands inside an organization, new forms of work organization need to evolve. Unions and management often find themselves in situations in which the traditional structure does not respond to, or may be the cause of, significant problems. This chapter discusses a variety of possible work arrangements. We hold that no form of organizational structure is a given. Instead, the union and management as partners need to exercise choice and judgment in the construction and maintenance of organizational structures.

Traditional Structures

The attachment managers and unionists have to particular organizational structures is amazing. The current structure provides mooring against the winds of organizational change and a safe harbor from a stormy external environment. Managers receive status from their positions in the organizational structure. Their positions tell them to whom they report and for whom they are responsible. By referring to the current structure, most managers can determine where they have come from and where they could go. Organizational structures create boundaries that others parallel or below cannot cross without permission. Paradoxically, many managers tend to view structural adjustment below them as the way to confront change and structural adjustment above them as a way to alter power. Structural adjustment becomes an all-purpose cure-all even when the real issues are performance and the quality of relationships. The most dreaded part of any managerial change at the top is reorganization. Often this solves one set of problems while creating another perplexing set. Further, the transition can inhibit productivity while unsettling the lives of employees. Managers need to distinguish between situations that call for structural change and those that do not. It is easy to mandate reorganization but difficult to make it work.

We have been surprised at the tenacity with which unionists also hold on to an organizational framework. If one brought together unionists working within a variety of organizational structures, each would argue vehemently the merits of the basic structure in which he or she worked while criticizing its application. Frankly, often the most positive point about the current system is that it is the devil people know. Over the years, workers have been able to figure out what could go wrong and how to work with it or avoid it to their best advantage. Workers' responses become institutionalized in the rules, practices, contractual job classifications, bidding rights, and other forms of accommodation at their work site. In doing so, they are accepting management's assumptions about how work should be organized. These assumptions may not be accurate, may not have been examined in light of other alternatives, and may have a negative impact on the union membership. Many unions resist team-oriented work settings, however, not because they are "bad" but because they upset the uneasy balance provided by more routinized and familiar operations. Unionists resisted segmented work approaches when management introduced them. This observation should lead individual unions to consider being less reactive to management's initiatives and more proactive in proposing organizational styles appropriate to their work environments and that better accommodate their members' needs.

The resistance to new organizational approaches illustrates not only the obvious, that people resist change in any organization, but also several other powerful organizational truths. The organization of work codifies power in work organizations and provides the medium through which relationships are built and maintained. When the work organization is changed, managers become concerned about where they will end up, the erosion of their influence, and the impact on their career paths. Unions become concerned that the change will bring abuses of power and erode solidarity and connection among the membership. These are all legitimate concerns. In a cooperative union-management relationship, these concerns are made public and are addressed head-on. Many mechanisms for their resolution are considered. It is the power of organizational structures that they can energize or stymie joint efforts at organizational change.

A traditional approach to the organization of work may indeed be the most appropriate, but the excuse that it is traditional is not enough. It must be appropriate. Management and unions should examine the range of alternatives, from a top-down hierarchy, to parallel structures, to an egalitarian redesign, to bottom-up organizational styles, to a combination of several approaches.

Before choosing a work structure, the parties must answer the following questions: Is this work organization most appropriate for addressing our market conditions and customers (in the public sector, "customers" are the people and groups served by the agency)? Does this structure promote the greatest efficiency in the use of resources? Does it ensure high-quality standards and organizational effectiveness? Does available technology impose contours for the work organization or open up new opportunities? How can the individual development of employees be fostered? How can the health and safety of employees and customers be ensured? How can the development of workplace community and teamwork be best incorporated? This chapter explores some of the possibilities in work force organization, ranging from minimal add-ons such as quality circles to radical sociotechnical revisions.

Quality Circles and Employee Participation Groups

Quality circles became very popular in the United States in the early 1980s. As recently as 1979, only a few companies had them, but by 1983 the International Association of Quality Circles estimated that there were more than 135,000 in more than eight thousand locations in the United States. Initially found in manufacturing, quality circles spread to all kinds of workplaces, including in the public and service sectors.[1] By the end of the decade, however, patience ran out on quality circles as a quick fix for America's industrial ills and it became clear that the expectations heaped on quality circles were greater than their capacity to deliver. The term has recently been derided in many settings.[2] Yet, when we examine the structure of many so called quality programs, we see quality circles redux. Quality circles and other similar groups of employees who meet regularly to solve problems do have value; the question is how to use them as part of an overall cooperative strategy.

A quality circle (QC) is an ongoing work site problem-solving group composed of five to fifteen employees from a common work area who analyze problems in their area and propose solutions to management. Members of the circles are provided with specific training on problem identification, problem analysis, and solution development. Usually circles meet once a week for an hour led by a first-line supervisor. Facilitators are trained to assist the various circles, and the program is often overseen by a senior-level steering committee. In joint union-management programs, the steering committee, often with equal representation from both parties, directs the program.

Quality circles do not challenge managerial authority and responsibility but provide a valuable extra tool to managers astute enough to welcome the input. The devotion of about 3 percent of the workweek to reflection and action on improving the other 97 percent of the time is a minimum essential for sound management. Nor do quality circles change the structure of work organization.

Many involvement programs are called quality circles even though they do not operate at the shop-floor or office level. A basic tenet of quality circles is that they encompass a common work area. Many work areas do not have enough people who are related by task or even by location to form a traditional quality circle. Although problem-solving groups may be formed in these areas, they represent a different form of employee participation known as cross-functional teams. At the same time, programs that go by other names, such as employee involvement groups and employee participation groups (EPG) or quality improvement teams (QIT), in reality are often quality circles.

The idea for quality circles came to flower in Japan, although there are major differences between the Japanese and the American versions. The highly successful Japanese experience arose out of the teachings of W. Edwards Deming and Joseph M. Juran, both American quality control experts. The Japanese were motivated by the necessity for quality improvement in their export industries. Under the leadership of the Japanese Union of Scientists and Engineers, training in the techniques of quality control was given to first-line supervisors and then to other employees via circles that dealt primarily with quality and productivity issues.[3]

The American versions have a distinct organizational development slant and place far less emphasis on quality control issues. Quality of work life concerns and attention to the group process are emphasized. Most Japanese circles meet on their own time, whereas American groups generally meet during working hours. The continuing, successful application of quality circles in Japan and the abandonment of the concept in America says more about differences in the long-term views of managers in the two countries than about the merits of quality circles themselves.

Unions are split regarding quality circles. Since most are operated unilaterally by management or are management-dominated, some unions have rejected the label and/or the practice. They are concerned that circles will deal with collective bargaining issues and divert solutions to problems away from the union winning via the contract or grievance procedure.[4] Some view QCs as too narrow in scope because they do not deal with broad organizational policy. They worry about how to keep tabs on what is happening within the circles, given the limited resources available to unions. Some unions see quality circles as union-busting techniques or speedup gimmicks—and they have been used in this manner in some locations. The United Electrical, Radio, and Machine Workers, an independent union, resolved that UE continue to oppose quality circles and other "phony participation schemes devised by management." Several other unions, such as the International Association of Machinists; the Oil, Chemical, and Atomic Workers International Union; and the American Postal Workers Union, have taken a hard line nationally against any involvement.

Many more unions (and some locals with national opposition), however, have become involved in successful joint quality circle programs.[5] In these versions, the union is an equal partner.[6] It has equal representation on the steering committee, equal numbers of facilitators, and sometimes co-leads the circles. Conrail and the Milwaukee Road railroads have had very successful circles in which all the members were unionists, a union member was the leader (part of a supervisors' union), and there was a union facilitator. One such circle came up with a return of $750,000 on its first project!

As an example of a more positive position, the International Union of Electronic, Electrical, Technical, Salaried and Machine Workers, affiliated with the AFL-CIO, adopted the following position:[7]

1. The IUE go on record in support of the concept of quality circles and encourage union participation where the union feels such participation is in the best interests of its membership and where it is determined and assured that management has made an equal commitment to the mutual goals of such a program.
2. Where quality circles are considered, that the Union insist that it be a part of the planning, development, implementation and evaluation process.
3. Local unions should make certain that Quality Circles do not in any way infringe on the collective bargaining process or on matters and conditions covered by the collective bargaining agreement.

Owen Bieber, president of the UAW, notes that although the quality circle "does not solve all problems and it does not change the grim noninspiring nature of many factory and office jobs . . . it does make things better." He concludes: "It is quite apparent that properly constituted, quality circles is a methodology by which unions can greatly enhance the furtherance of worker democracy at the worker's place of employment."[8]

Today's challenge for quality circles and employee participation groups is how to sustain them. Research by Susan Albers Mohrman and Gerald E. Ledford, Jr., at the University of Southern California has identified some critical elements:[9] (1) participation groups must include or have access to the necessary skills and knowledge to address problems systematically; (2) formalized procedures enhance the effectiveness of the group; (3) participation groups should be integrated horizontally and vertically with the rest of the organization; and (4) the groups should be a regular part of the organization rather than special or extra activities. Their finding that design has a major impact on effectiveness should be a spur for organizations to look beyond labels and concentrate on the design features that lead to lasting success.

Quality circles and other employee participation groups can harness the positive problem-solving potential of shop-floor or office-level employees and often do lead to impressive gains in performance and productivity. The combination of specific training and the use of small group dynamics results in an exceedingly powerful tool. This approach is best suited to dealing with changing terms and conditions of work and how work is done, not to broad issues of organizational change or major policy decisions. Although quality circles can be a valuable way to develop shop-floor problem solving, they should not be the total response in an effort to further cooperation, participation, or organizational change— but then again neither should any other strategy.

Parallel Organizational Structures

Another approach to organizational change that does not replace the traditional system is to develop parallel organizational structures. Unlike a more informal change, parallel structures become an explicit and planned part of the organizational fabric. Teams are established from various parts of the organization to address current and future institutional challenges. It is management aided by a complement of broadly and creatively engaged task forces.

Sometimes organization charts get in the way of organizational effectiveness. Functional divisions of authority and responsibility too often become ossified into rigid boundaries that may not meet the current and future needs of the organization. According to Barry A. Stein and Rosabeth Moss Kanter:

> The parallel structure . . . provides a means for managing change and providing flexibility and responsiveness. It is a source of opportunity and power above

and beyond the (limited) sources that exist in the bureaucratic structure, and one that in particular is important for people in positions least characterized by those properties. It is thus a structural mechanism for building high quality of work life and environmental responsiveness *permanently* into an otherwise bureaucratic organization.[10]

Dale Zand describes the "collateral organization" in similar terms and views the overlaid structure as the one best suited to dealing with diffuse problems and circumstances since it results in higher-quality, faster, and more creative solutions.[11] The collateral organization provides organizational choice to those managing change regarding the appropriate forum for resolving pressing issues.

What makes parallel structures work is that they provide a forum for a combination of perspectives. Such perspective in an organization is often defined by position in the hierarchy. Yet a diversity of perspectives is often needed to solve cross-disciplinary and cross-departmental challenges. The parallel approach implies that all people in an organization can contribute regardless of job title and that they can meet as equals in the parallel setting. At the same time, it acknowledges differences in authority in the traditional sphere and does not seek to replace the traditional hierarchy. The outputs of the parallel system are inputs to the formal organization, and a test of its success is the degree of acceptance inside the traditional structure. The traditional hierarchy provides for the maintenance of the system and fulfills the functions of control and continuity. Stein and Kanter state: "The main task of the parallel organization is the continued reexamination of routines, exploration of new options and the development of new tools, procedures and approaches. It seeks to institutionalize change."[12]

Another similar approach to organizational change creates permanent fluidity in the structure through the development of *matrix management.* Where the parallel organization provides structures for dealing flexibly with selective *issues,* a matrix provides an overall flexible framework for dealing primarily with *task management.* In traditional management structures, each employee has one boss to whom he or she reports. In a matrix structure, each employee has more than one, usually two, a functional supervisor and a task/product/program group supervisor. Matrix management can range from essentially a set of parallel structures overlaid on the traditional system to advanced matrix organization in which most of the organization is configured in a matrix model.

Matrix management was born in the aerospace industry during the 1950s but has been introduced successfully in a wide range of organizations. It typically affects only the top part of the organizational hierarchy, and employees at lower levels may not even be aware of its existence.

Matrix organizations work best when more than one critical function in the organization needs to be integrated, when the organization deals with complex and interdependent tasks, and when the organization is large enough to have a variety of functional subspecialties that could be assigned to matrix teams, thus affording an economy of scale.

The most important features of matrix management are the teamwork and planning among the different functions in the organization. Teamwork provides new energy and imagination and reduces delays in access to functional specialties. Planning enhances clarity on what is to be done by whom and when. There is sometimes confusion that team management means an anarchistic approach to management. In fact, team approaches require greater planning and understanding because less is taken for granted by virtue of position.

There is no reason that a union could not be included as a partner in a parallel structure, though its role has not been clearly defined in the literature or in examples of this approach. Since the union is centrally connected to issues of power, opportunity, and perspective in an organization, it should have intimate connections with the construction and implementation of parallel arrangements. The union provides perspectives that would be very valuable for these deliberations. It could be involved either as an equal, as in union-management task forces (described below), or as a member of matrix and parallel teams. Very few organizations use a matrix approach for the whole organization and therefore few include bargaining unit members in the matrix configuration.

For the union, operating in a matrix environment could be difficult because of the dual or shifting lines of authority. Agreement might need to be reached with several centers of authority. In situations in which bargaining unit members are involved in the matrix, this would have an impact on job descriptions, wages, grievance systems, career paths, and transfer issues.

Union-Management Task Forces

A union-management task force differs from a labor-management committee, discussed in the previous chapter. Whereas a labor-management committee has an ongoing life related to a specific subject area, task forces are meshed with the principles of matrix and parallel organizational structures by their impermanence and attachment to innovation and function. A union-management task force is a flexible structure designed to meet jointly perceived changing needs. Though task forces can be used in organizations that adopt the matrix style of management, they can also be part of other ongoing union-management cooperative activities.

Task forces, chaired jointly by representatives of the union and management, draw members from throughout the organization to help solve problems facing more than one unit, to plan for impending changes, and/or to consider new opportunities. Task forces work best when the union and management recognize that they could use additional expertise or perspectives on an issue or when they are considering a topic affecting a broad cross-section of the work force.

Task forces should be constituted by union and management decision makers. They should determine its mission, time frame, resources, and membership. The length of time a task force exists and how long it meets vary depending on the scope of the task or the pressure for results. In any case, the parameters should be specified ahead of time. The decision makers to whom the task force reports is also determined based on the mission and composition of the group.[13]

Three types of union-management task forces seem most appropriate: problem solving, planning, and ad hoc. *Problem-solving task forces* are rather straightforward. They address issues of broad concern in the organization and seek to come up with solutions to the problems encountered. One task force at a location we worked with took on the question of employee turnover and surveyed previous employees to find out their reasons for leaving. It then devised solutions to the major problems it addressed. Another looked at sanitation problems and constructed appropriate charts outlining steps workers could take to clean up their areas.

A *planning task force* assesses upcoming events or changes. Using this approach can help normally scheduled changes or new initiatives be better accepted and integrated by the work force. Another type of planning task force examines new ideas or opportunities that the organization might undertake. Most organizations are rife with ideas for new opportunities but there is precious little opportunity to develop them. Too often, joint union-management activities just react to the negatives or problems of their situation. Planning task forces seek to be anticipatory and explore the affirmative. For example, one task force we helped facilitate looked at how incentive programs for new sales could boost income.

Both problem-solving and planning task forces require that participants have some training, but some issues or topics simply do not require in-depth analysis. The issue may be communication with a particular group of employees, for example, and call for only a session or two to address the issue. Thus, *ad hoc task forces*, short-term cooperative efforts, may be formed. They should not be overused because more in-depth approaches have a deeper impact on an organization.

A task force is a way to involve employees from various levels of an organization in problem solving and planning. Sometimes the fact that people are brought together is more important than the specific outcomes of their work. The important point is that they feel included and empowered. Task forces provide flexibility to the union and management partners insofar as a union-management committee can handle more activities by chairing several joint task forces than by working together on all the projects. Task forces can be an important way to generate involvement and results early in a larger process to demonstrate progress toward cooperation and organizational change.

Sociotechnical Redesign

Sociotechnical approaches to work impel management and the union to look deeply at how work is conducted and to offer new ways to structure the work. At one level, sociotechnical systems (STS) make obvious a rather simple concept: in the design of work, the social system and the technical system should be considered in tandem. Very often, people are forced to adapt to the rigidities of machinery and technical requirements in ways that are deleterious to their work lives and to the performance of their organization. At the other extreme are the human relations schools of management, which put too much emphasis on the individual worker. The sociotechnical approach attempts to synthesize the two concerns. T. G. Cummings defines the two central principles of STS analysis:

> The first is the joint operation of two independent but correlative systems: a social system composed of human beings who are the required actors in the performance of work and a technological system made up of the tools, techniques and methods of doing that are employed in task accomplishment. . . . The second concept is that a socio-technical system continually interacts with an environment which both influences and is influenced by the work system.[14]

The sociotechnical approach is heavily influenced by the concepts of joint optimization and open systems theory.[15] Roles change dramatically when work is looked at as an open system rather than a closed system. In closed systems, managers spend most of their time attempting to counter entropy—or the disintegration of order into chaos—by controlling and pushing the various members of the system—that is, employees and departments. In an open system, the manager's primary role is interacting with the boundary between the external environment—that is, customers and resources—and the internal structure. The manager draws energy from the surrounding system so as to produce desired outcomes. The union also shifts from combatting control to shared concern for boundaries. STS draws on a fundamental belief in the utility of "equifinality," the premise that a system can reach the same end state starting from different places and by getting there in different ways. There is no one

way to achieve organizational success, and lasting, internal success cannot be derived through a canned approach; there must be a dynamic
interchange of energy and information between an organization's internal and external environments.

Albert Cherns, a leading authority on sociotechnical systems, listed
nine principles of sociotechnical design. They are as follows:[16]

1. "The process of design must be compatible with its objectives." If
    the final result is meant to be inclusive, then all the major parties
    should have input into its construction. To achieve a participatory
    outcome, there must be participatory design.
2. "Minimal critical specification . . . the negative simply states that
    no more should be specified than is absolutely necessary; the posi-
    tive requires that we identify what is essential." The STS approach
    provides latitude for decision making to those who do the job.
    There are more shared principles than mandated rules.
3. "Variances, if they cannot be eliminated, must be controlled as
    near to their point of origin as possible." "Variance," which is any
    unprogrammed event, is a key concept in sociotechnical design.
    Identifying and anticipating variances reduces the overall inci-
    dence of problems as well as the time and communications steps
    required to correct them.
4. "The principle of multi-functionality" suggests that there are di-
    verse responses to changes in the environment. Treated like a
    simple machine, a work organization gets stuck when a situation
    does not exactly fit predefined expectations. When organically
    created, an organization is adaptive and creative in responding to
    the new demands of the environment. This principle leads to the
    emphasis in sociotechnical design on multiskilling. By building in
    redundancy of function rather than people, flexibility of re-
    sponse can be maintained.
5. Boundaries between groups should be as contiguous as possible
    in terms of technology, territory, and time. Management should
    manage the boundary conditions and serve as a "resource" to the
    work team.
6. "Information systems should be designed to provide information
    in the first place to the point where action on the basis of it will
    be needed." Instead of filtering information to the shop floor
    through higher levels of management, information should be sup-
    plied directly. This empowers those at the place where the
    information is provided, reduces the time needed for communica-
    tion, and minimizes distortions in communications caused by it
    having to pass through multiple layers.

7. "The systems of social support should be designed so as to reinforce the behaviors the organization's structure is designed to
elicit." Payment methods, hiring and firing, training, grievance
administration, work measurement, performance appraisal, promotion, vacation policy, hours of work, and other personnel
policies should all be congruent in their basic values and mutually
supportive of the operational system.

8. "An objective of work organization should be to provide a high
quality of work." The goal should be to mesh human desires and
values, including autonomy and discretion, opportunity for continuous learning, optimal variety, opportunity to exchange help
and respect, meaningful contribution, and a meaningful future.[17]

9. "Design is a reiterative process. The closure of options opens new
ones." The process is like a spiral and there is therefore no defi-
nite point of completion, only a rejoining of the process at
another level for continuous improvement.

Cherns addresses the role of unions in the process:

Can they [unions] be partners in design? This is a role that seldom has been
offered to, and even more rarely accepted by unions. It is not a role for which
they have prepared themselves. Yet without them the viability of the design is
in some doubt. And the design of a social support system implies designing
the functions of the shop steward if not the union official. Our first principle,
compatibility, requires that the unions be brought into the design if that is at
all possible.[18]

The role for unions in sociotechnical redesign has been thoughtfully
analyzed by Tom Rankin, a Canadian consultant who examined the design
of a new chemical plant at Shell Sarnia with Local 800 of the Energy
and Chemical Workers of Canada. The union had an extensive role in
the design of the plant as a greenfield site. But the changes were not
for management only. They also affected how the union operated, including the role of union stewards. Rankin observes: "By developing an
innovative structure the local is better able to deal with the complex
issues inherent in the collective bargaining system. As the national
representative puts it: 'you can't deal with a new management system
with an old union design. . . . If we ask management to open up their
decision making powers and let workers participate in decision making,
those members will expect the same from the union'. . . . Local 800 is
much more diverse, flexible, decentralized and participative [than traditional unions]."[19]

A joint work redesign team is frequently used in sociotechnical efforts.
Such teams cooperate in establishing the best fit between the organization,

the work team, the individual employee, and the technology. Usually an organization design task force is established. In small locations, all workers, union stewards, and supervisors can be on this task force. If the site is large, then representatives will need to be selected from the union and management.[20] To do their job adequately, the representatives should remain connected to the concerns of their constituencies, have a clear process for design, and adequate time to do a thorough job.

As a first step, the design team members are asked to "identify influential factors in the environment; to specify the organization's major inputs and outputs; to characterize the organization's major historical, social and physical features; to define the enterprise's mission or business objective; and to articulate the organization's philosophy for management of its members."[21]

In the second step, the team analyzes the technical system by noting variances that occur in converting inputs into outputs. The design team goes on

> to build a profile of the many factors in the conversion process that must be controlled through the organization's tools and procedures; to specify each step of the conversion process; to group these into unit operations; to detail what might go awry in the conversion process; that is, to identify variances; to match variances with unit operations; to pinpoint variances upstream that could interfere with steps downstream; to decide which variances need most emphasis; and to determine what information and responsibilities are required to control each key variance.[22]

Put simply, the design team maps the technological process and identifies places where it can break down. The technology of the system is far more than its machinery; it encompasses the roles, relationships, and processes used to produce a service as well as a product.

In the third step, the team analyzes the social system, including "the division of labor, mechanisms of coordination, and degree of fulfillment of psychological job requirements in the organization."[23] Ron Mitchell, a consultant who assists in team design, suggests that the design team look at organizational structure, job design, management style, roles, responsibilities and reporting relationships, skill levels, training needs, information flow, decision-making practices, pay and compensation, personnel policies and practices, organizational culture and values, job attitudes and expectations, performance measures and customer requirements as part of its analysis. The union's social system must also be considered.

In the fourth step, the team integrates the previous activities into proposals for the organization, covering the mission, organizational philosophy, major inputs and major outputs, work group organization, and need for improved technical approaches to better control variances.

A key factor is clarity about customers and the ways systems can be redesigned to meet and exceed customers' requirements. The aim is to find the best fit between the technical and social systems to meet those requirements. Given the principle of minimal critical specification, however, the final design should be as lean as possible.

Since sociotechnical systems generally involve job redesign, it is covered here, though it can be done independently of sociotechnical redesign. The major ways jobs can be changed are through job simplification, job enlargement, job rotation, and job enrichment.

Job simplification, as its name implies, streamlines or reduces the number of component tasks of a job to make the job easier to perform. *Job enlargement* and *job enrichment* do exactly the opposite. They involve horizontal or vertical loading. Horizontal loading increases the range of tasks in number and variety that an employee performs. Vertical loading adds more dimension and responsibility to a particular job, including planning and input on policy. *Job rotation* provides a way to alternate job tasks, although the nature of the tasks may not change. All of these changes have implications for collective bargaining, both for job descriptions and compensation. They also have considerable impact on selection, career paths, access to training, and fairness in assignments.

Anyone involved in job redesign efforts should pay particular attention to the critical variables of skill, autonomy, feedback, and significance. According to experts in the field, the quality of work life improves as these measures increase.[24] The less repetitive the tasks, the more a worker has the sense of working on a "whole" product; and the more the task is important to the overall production of the product or delivery of the service, the more an employee views the work experience as meaningful and the more the worker is motivated. The more independence one has, the greater one's sense of responsibility. And the more timely and helpful the feedback from co-workers, supervisors, and machinery, the better communication and responsiveness there is overall. In combination, these traits result in greater job satisfaction and higher quality. One should not assume, however, that going from screwing in one lug to two lugs or rotating to bolt insertion will make jobs wonderful. Job redesign needs to be done participatively to help workers explore and test alternatives that meet the dual criteria of increased effectiveness and increased job satisfaction.

Leaders of the Australian labor movement have developed guidelines for unions engaged in job redesign.[25] They say:

Jobs don't have to be performed as they are just because that is the way it has always been done. For the union it therefore becomes important to determine which job designs will give the members more skill, better pay and more satisfaction. Listed below are some principles which should be followed in negotiating about job design:

1. A variety of tasks. As far as possible complete tasks rather than fragments.
2. Responsibility. For example, employees can make decisions about quality, production planning, on-line maintenance. . . .
3. Adequate payment for skills.
4. A basis for working groups. As far as possible, jobs centering on a group of people rather than an individual.
5. Good social interaction between employees.
6. A healthy and safe working environment.
7. An understanding of the total system in the enterprise. Employees are familiar with the interconnections between all tasks and operations.
8. Constant learning. Employees are involved in constant learning of new skills and knowledge.
9. Adequate information to enable people to make all the relevant decisions.
10. A product or service that is useful and environmentally sound.
11. Equal opportunity for all to include training in literacy and numeracy where required.
12. An integration with other jobs so as to provide career opportunities.

The sociotechnical framework provides a comprehensive and systematic way to rethink work organizations as whole systems that interact dynamically with their environments. As such, the sociotechnical framework provides an excellent opportunity for workplace partners to engage in a broad review of how they work and what they can accomplish together. William A. Pasmore, who has written a text on sociotechnical redesign, makes clear that its breadth can be its greatest challenge. "Because it is so complex, sociotechnical systems redesign calls for careful planning, widespread involvement, adequate resources, strong management support and skillful facilitation."[26] The STS approach provides a framework in which unions and management can reconsider the ways jobs are designed, the architecture of subsystems, and how the organization interacts with its larger environment.

Self-Directed Work Teams and Autonomous Work Groups

Whereas the first part of the 1980s saw a fascination in America with quality circles, the latter half ushered in a similar attachment to self-directed work teams. In many cases, they illustrate how quality circles have moved from engaging in part-time to full-time problem solving. In some instances, teams facilitate the implementation of new technology or increase commitment to quality systems. In other cases, however, they become a new fad with little real commitment to new systems or changing management styles to support self-directed approaches. Too often the teams are ill defined, poorly trained, and left to flounder. Clothed in the rhetoric of self-management, the teams are asked to solve problems managers can't manage. Managers in effect say "We'll manage when we want to manage, and you manage when we don't." Run well, however, self-directed work teams and autonomous work groups have the potential to bring about dramatic shifts in how work is done.

The notion of self-directed work groups is not new. They were developed formally in the 1960s in Europe but only recently have had broad application. They represent an application of sociotechnical systems at the shop-floor level whereby small teams of employees take responsibility for all or most of the functions in their area. These include tasks normally handled by supervisors and some middle managers. The group plans and carries out the distribution of work tasks, the pace of production, training of co-workers, scheduling, quality control, maintenance, and other activities necessary to work performance. The group thus becomes a system unto itself, subject to outcome criteria or resource constraints imposed from outside their team. Sometimes groups are called self-managing teams or composite work groups.

An autonomous work group is defined as one in which the group members select their own group leader. When management selects the leader, it is referred to as a semiautonomous work group. Being self-directed is not an all-or-nothing matter; frequently groups evolve into greater degrees of self-management. One of the challenges in evolving self-directed work groups is to protect against their becoming too independent and ignoring possible synergies with other groups, as well as co-managing common and boundary issues with other groups, organizations, and individuals.

Since a fundamental of the autonomous or self-directed work group is multiskilling, ongoing training is critical. Each member of the group should be trained in all (or many) of the functions involved in the work unit. This means that competencies and learning requirements need to be carefully and fully defined. As new skills are learned and the competencies demonstrated, wages are generally increased. All fully trained members are paid the top of the scale. Although this broad training can be time-consuming and expensive, the investment in human resources is necessary for the flexibility desired in the group. The investment also provides the basis for the flow of information and ensures the group has the experience necessary to formulate value-added improvements in workplace operations. Although everyone can perform all or most of the functions, the group decides on the specific allocation of tasks. Members of the team take turns at different jobs, including being team leader. Special provisions need to be made for the fullest possible inclusion of workers with disabilities.

There is a practical limit to multiskilling so that many companies have pulled back from the notion that everyone has to do everything. It makes more sense to think of families of skills that complement each other. There is a danger of becoming a Jack (or Jill) of all things and master of none. This is especially true in skilled trades. Having a plumber-electrician-millwright in most cases makes little sense. Having a much broader awareness and use of a range of skills, however, can be useful. Having broad skills within sensible skill categories can enhance flexibility in ways that are more likely to be used. They may also increase workers' employment security both with their current employer and with other possible employers.

Autonomous work groups have been used successfully around the world. Among the most famous include workers at Volvo and Saab in Sweden who are members of the Swedish Metal Workers' Union. They have also been used successfully on ships and in other workplaces in Norway. Some of the earliest experiments with work groups were conducted in the mines in England, aided by Eric Trist of the Tavistock Institute. The Volvo plant in Uddevalla, Sweden, is an extremely interesting recent example:

> There is no standard production line. Instead, work teams consisting of groups of multi-skilled workers capable of handling all operations will work within U-shaped production bays. Flat hierarchies, job rotation, integrated materials handling and work stations will provide the organizational framework for assembly. High levels of quality assurance and zero rejection rates will be a common objective of workforce, management and unions. . . . Each factory will have four teams consisting of between eight and twelve workers *who will build complete cars.*[27]

In the United States, autonomous work teams have been formed extensively in the paper and petrochemical industries. Increasingly, they are being introduced in the automotive industry, as at the General Motors Delco-Remy plant in northern Georgia. During the 1970s an attempt was made to form work teams at the Rushton Mining Corporation in Johnstown, Pennsylvania. Although the operational results and health and safety benefits were very good, the effort collapsed because the teams failed to overcome internal union problems caused by differential treatment of workers in the pilot areas.[28]

In the late 1980s, team-based systems became more broad-based. Union-management versions formed the foundation for the Saturn plant in Tennessee and for the new LS-Electrogalvanizing mill in Cleveland.

Substantial labor relations problems can surface with this form of work organization. Although a great deal of the experience with team-based systems has been in nonunion settings, such as at the General Foods plant in Topeka,[29] autonomous work teams have been used successfully in unionized settings in North America, Europe, India, and Japan. Clearly, multiskilling has an impact on job classifications and compresses them into one or very few categories. Negotiation is required over the rates of pay, the specific competencies defined, career paths, and other traditional union concerns.

Seniority rights in bidding between teams are often demanded by unions, especially in North America. When the teams cannot agree to other criteria, then seniority should be the ultimate basis for decisions on the allocation of tasks. Seniority is important as a means to protect job security and avoid arbitrary management assignment. Since specific seniority systems vary between organizations, the precise approach to achieving the goals of seniority should be reconsidered. Sometimes, rigid attachment to past practice runs counter to the very interests the practice was designed to protect.

Another thorny issue is changes in classification, especially as they affect distinctions between production and maintenance work. Again, the parties need to protect their fundamental interests of employment security and competitive operation of the plant. Industrial elitism, which denies production workers higher pay and increased ability to use their skills, has no place in the work force of the future. Nonetheless, because of safety concerns or the complexity of a task, jobs may need to be designated as skilled trades. In-plant, skilled trades workers would do well to focus on reducing the need for outside contractors and performing more capital work as ways to ensure their employment. In nonunion locations, hiring and discipline are often tasks of a team. Sometimes teams can also initiate termination proceedings. In unionized locations, the individual union member still needs the right to grieve to enforce the contract, but whom to grieve against becomes muddled when the team is making hiring, termination, and discipline decisions. In hiring, firing, and discipline, although management may consult with the group, ultimate responsibility must clearly remain with management. To prevent thorny union conflicts, supporters of self-directed teams suggest that management "include unions in discussions of work teams from the very start, regardless of the time and effort."[30]

Autonomous work groups are difficult to implement. They require considerable thought to operate effectively; they require consistent attention; they require orientation of senior-level management to work with the groups; and they require supervision so members can learn new skills and new ways of operating. Not least, they require an unusual level of trust in and willingness to delegate responsibility to workers. Many managers have difficulty with the concept. They think the person "best" for the job should be doing it most of the time, not rotating it to workers who may be less able. Further, the notion of training workers in all functions runs counter to the prevailing practice of training employees in just the skills they need to know and use frequently. Employees with reserve skills represent unused potential (or idle capital in human capital theory). The underlying principles of autonomous work groups run exactly counter to the principles of the scientific management school followed by most industrial engineers and taught to most managers.

Those most affected by self-directed work teams are supervisors. With the spread of team practices, there will be a need for far fewer super-visors, and those who remain will supervise a much larger work force. The new role for supervisors, as trainer, coach, and leader, will be empowering and exciting for some and feel like a breach of contract to others.[31] No longer will supervisors be straw bosses who tell workers what to do but employees who work with them as customers and identify ways to facilitate getting their jobs done both through developing and transfer-ring skills and running interference with the outside world.

Unions also have great difficulty adjusting to the concept since the recent memory of many unionists is that they negotiate job classifications and clear work rules. Some union leaders and members see team ap-proaches as eroding work force solidarity and union affiliation. They wonder whether an approach used so successfully for union avoidance is by nature antiunion. Critics brand the process "management by stress."[32] In actuality, team-based work more closely resembles union craft work than it does routinized industrial practices. A craftsperson was known for performing high-skill, high-quality, high-wage work and for having wide latitude for decision making and variety in the work. A supervisor described a desired result and trusted in the craft workers to organize themselves to get the work done well. Today's version of craft work is more inclusive in its definition of the kinds of workers allowed to do craft work in terms of race and gender and the range of work craftspersons do. It might be helpful for unionists to view team-based work as the reinven-tion of craft. The problem for most unions in North America has been that they usually react to management's proposals rather than propose a work design that makes sense from union values.

The basic goal of autonomous work groups is to overcome alienation caused by the increasing segmentation of work into smaller and smaller bits. Involvement in the group gives the individual employee a chance to look at the entire work process from start to finish. It also provides a social support network that most traditional workplaces lack. There are, of course, some dangers. In one General Motors location, young male work team members decided that they did not want any older female workers in their group because they allegedly slowed them down. This points to the need to ensure that majority rule does not impinge on minority rights, especially those related to equal opportunity. Further, the group has to be aware of the dangers of group tyranny to avoid being more vindictive and coercive than the worst supervisor.

In general, the greatest benefit of autonomous work groups is they lead to increased flexibility and skills levels. Gains in productivity as measured by output per person hour have not always resulted; however, substantial bottom-line improvements are made by reducing absenteeism and turnover and replacement costs and improving the speed with which changes are implemented. Generally, workers like being part of these groups and develop strong attachments to them.

The industrial relations and union perspectives on self-directed and autonomous work groups have been explored more in the abstract than specifically. In Germany, unions, through works councils, are pushing for more group work. Lowell Turner, who has examined firsthand the developments in Germany, comments:

> Both sides at Wolfsburg [VW plant] recognize that new forms of teamwork are coming in one form or another; both sides appear to agree that the works council has now taken the primary initiative in this regard (so that management is now negotiating changes in the union–works council plan as opposed to vice versa); and both sides claim to be optimistic that a settlement will be found, based on overlapping interests and a joint learning process as pilot projects are examined.[33]

IG Metall, the largest union in the world, has developed twelve guidelines for group work:

1. Shared work tasks and responsibilities must utilize the full range of workers abilities and skills; allow for control and autonomy; provide task variety and a high skill level and allow for optimal group size of 5–12 workers.
2. Real responsibilities and control over rotation, sequence and methods of work; quality of group product; tools, equipment, etc.; group process meetings; and qualification of group members.
3. Flatter organizational structure and more decentralized decision making including ensuring that work groups are self-regulating; plan, control and execute their work and other management structures are designed to facilitate group work.
4. Comprehensible technology and flexible organization where work groups areas are "independent" of each other and of "outside" experts as much as possible; technology is matched to worker qualification and technology is open to worker intervention.

5. Solidarity as the basis of group relationships though while qualifications may differ all must benefit. Working conditions must
foster help and sharing and the employer must provide training
and sufficient workers.

6. Continuous learning and upgrading of individual and group
qualifications through permanent personal and occupational development; learning built into group work activities; building
blocks of formal training; and open, semi-annual evaluation, discussion and planning of training and development.

7. Regular frequent group meetings of one hour minimum per
week involving planning and administration and problem solving.

8. Representation in overall production organization through
group representatives or shop stewards but participation in
those roles should be rotated.

9. Uniform compensation principle based on shared tasks and uniform qualifications that minimize number of pay levels.

10. Voluntary participation in group work so that no one is forced to
participate; non-participants get traditional work and no sanctions against non-participants.

11. Step by step introduction to develop concepts by means of and
learn from pilot projects.

12. Worker and union participation in concept development
through a steering committee with full participation of the
union on steering committee whose role is to encourage, evaluate,
further develop group work concepts; make decisions about projects and make sure training and other resources are available.

In the American context the strongest union endorsement of new work
systems has come from the American Federation of Grain Millers. In a
policy statement, the union argues that anything less than a radical
revision of workplaces that changes structure and power at the shop-floor
level is a wolf in sheep's clothing. Among the characteristics of this new
work system are the following:[34]

- fewer levels of management;
- autonomy and responsibility distributed throughout the
  organization;
- self-managing work teams;
- open communications;
- pay-for-skills compensation; and
- bonus or gainsharing programs.

The policy statement notes, in discussing the role of the union in this
new work system, that "replacing a traditional contract with a briefer

document that emphasizes trust does not mean that the relationship is simpler or easier. There are new skills needed and new demands of time and resources. . . . A union should be skilled, competent, pro-active, and an equal partner in decision making and problem solving." Key new roles are emphasizing problem prevention and joint problem solving and using formal grievances only as necessary. The union still retains its role as the "conscience of the organization" and defender of minority points of view.

When approached seriously, new work teams offer room for the union and management alike to look outside the Taylorist principles that have dominated the world of work for the last seventy years. Teams, with the proper design and safeguards, can create new communities at work in which each person feels supported, challenged, and rewarded. Work teams are best approached as one element of a larger process of quality improvement and union-management cooperation.

World-Class Manufacturing

Under the banner of world-class manufacturing, there have been dramatic changes over the last decade in the ways factories are organized and run and more changes are sure to come. These changes have tremendous ramifications for the employment security of those in the manufacturing industry and for how they work. Changes in the marketplace, technology, and transportation have resulted in shifts in manufacturing from long runs of a standard product for local markets to product diversity and high-quality to meet global demands. Work arrangements well suited to a stable environment do not work as well in this changed world.

Stripped of the jingoism of international competition, world-class manufacturing introduces new concepts such as "just-in-time" inventory systems and cellular manufacturing, which can significantly change the shape of a manufacturing facility. Each change also has major implications for union-management relationships. To meet world-class manufacturing goals, these are deployed in conjunction with total quality management, self-directed work teams, and other approaches covered in other parts of this book, along with new design, marketing, and accounting principles.

Just-in-time (JIT) systems are much more important as a way to make organizational bottlenecks apparent than as a way to reduce inventory. Having large buffer stocks provided a way to cover up organizational inefficiencies. "Since JIT requires minute to minute coordination at the interfaces between units in the work flow, the system cannot be managed effectively from above. The operators themselves must make decisions about their own operations. This shifting of responsibility to operators must be supported with a flow of accurate information so that they can monitor their own performance."[35] As William Foote Whyte observes, in this shift in the flow of work from a top-down command and control system to a horizontal system based on the sequence of work, the need for union consultation and employee involvement becomes more intense. Union critics of just-in-time systems point out that the reduction in slack time and buffers increases the pressure on workers. Paradoxically, a just-in-time system increases union leverage since even minor disruptions in the system have broad impact on production. Managers who introduce JIT without strong labor-management relations are at risk.

Another major innovation is the introduction of manufacturing cells on the shop floor. As Richard J. Schonberger says: "Cells create responsibility centers where none existed before. A single supervisor or cell leader is in charge of matters that used to be fragmented among several shop managers. The leader and the work group may be charged with improvements in quality, cost, delays, flexibility, worker skills, lead time, inventory performance, scrap, equipment 'uptime', and a host of other factors that distinguish the world class manufacturer."[36] Cells are particularly popular at manufacturing sites with large numbers of similar parts. Frequently, they are established as self-directed work teams with a large component of multiskilling. Cellular manufacturing structures are often set up in conjunction with software, robotics, and design flexibility to facilitate adjustment to changing specifications and products. Access to programming capability is a major test of the degree of trust in workers within a cellular arrangement. For unions, the lack of predictability in the skills needed, what people will work on, career paths, and who will be responsible for monitoring quality all pose difficult questions.

For management, rethinking work flow and who does what can lead to substantial gains in productivity, quality, and customer responsiveness. For unions, cells can be established jointly in ways that increase skill development, raise income, improve health and safety, including ergonomic factors, reduce boredom on the job, and empower workers on the floor. They also have been used to speed up work and increase managerial control. The choices in new manufacturing shop-floor design and associated technology offer new ways to assemble work other than the old assembly line.

Quality of Work Life Programs

The term *quality of work life* is sometimes used generically to describe union-management cooperation or workplace participation generally. An example of this use is the definition put forward by the American Society for Training and Development, which describes QWL as "a process for work organizations which enables its members at all levels to actively participate in shaping the organization's environment, methods and outcomes. This value based process is aimed at the twin goals of enhanced effectiveness for the organization and improved quality of life at work for employees."[37]

There is wide disagreement on a more specific definition of QWL,[38] and in the early 1990s the concept fell out of favor in the United States. QWL is viewed as squishy soft on employee issues and has been superseded by the more rational and business-oriented quality approach, and some joint union-management QWL processes have been shoved aside by unilateral quality programs. QWL's approval rating is once again related to the attempt to shoot the label when practice is shoddy. The goal of QWL to build organizational change by placing the employee at the centerpiece of the change process has been replaced by the central role given to the external customer. This change ignores the fact that most QWL programs were customer and operationally focused and that most quality programs recognize the critical role of employee empowerment. Curiously, QWL has become the new banner in Japan and was adopted as the theme of the Asian Productivity Organization's 1991 Productivity Congress.

Some would argue that QWL is any one of the approaches described in part II of this book. To some, it connotes industrial democracy and new power relationships in the enterprise. To others (and they were some of the earliest proponents of the phrase), it describes sociotechnical activities. To still others, its focus is ergonomic concerns and strictly quality of work life issues, not productivity or organizational performance. A more specific definition of the term is used here, to describe multitiered efforts at organizational change that use a variety of specific techniques to accomplish broad objectives. The QWL program provides an umbrella for generating, sanctioning, and maintaining these efforts. The dominant characteristics of QWL are its open-ended agenda and broad application.

In unionized work organizations, QWL programs signal a reorienting of the union-management relationship toward a more cooperative approach and usually result from an agreement by the top leaders on both sides. Almost all programs explicitly avoid collective bargaining issues and the grievance procedure. Most tend to focus on operational issues. An exception is the New York State QWL program, in which day care, employee assistance, flextime, and other quality of work life issues are addressed.

The QWL approach can be attractive because it invites greater cooperation, flexibility, and information sharing between the union and management. A massive QWL effort is in place in the telephone industry between AT&T and its spin-off companies and the Communications Workers of America and the International Brotherhood of Electrical Workers. We worked with Pantry Pride, Inc., and the United Food and Commercial Workers International Union to develop a QWL program that included labor-management committees, union-management task forces, store-level problem-solving groups, and a department-level customer service program. Many other unions and managements have employed their own approaches.

One major example of a QWL program resulted from the 1973 agreement between General Motors and the UAW. The program employed top-level labor-management committees, autonomous work groups, business teams, and shop-floor employee participation groups among other techniques. In general, the program has been very successful in improving performance.

> The plant is organized into six business teams, each consisting of the necessary production activities and support elements: engineering, scheduling, material handling, quality control, maintenance and accounting. The system has made support employees an integral part of the plant's operations. The quality control circle concept, which has flourished in Japan and is being introduced by a growing number of firms in this country, has been incorporated into the business-team structure.[39]

The union and management have worked on a large number of issues, from new plant design to product bidding to greater employee involvement.

In the 1970s, a major quality of work life issue was working-time arrangements. Today, the debate is largely over whether new working-time patterns should be considered. Some QWL programs have looked at *flextime* as a way to improve performance and the quality of work life. Flextime arrangements allow employees to arrive and leave within a band of time so long as they work a certain number of hours. This enables them to accommodate personal schedules, traffic patterns, and family commitments better, thus giving them a greater sense of control over their lives. For the employer, flextime reduces greatly the amount of discipline over tardiness and increases productivity since employees tend to show up when they are most needed.

Flextime is very difficult to implement in assembly-line manufacturing, but it is well suited to most service industries and custom and batch production facilities. In the federal sector and in many state and local governments, flextime has been successfully introduced. Although they were initially wary, government workers and their unions have become adamant supporters of the concept. To work well, attention must be paid to getting the work force involved in understanding production or service requirements and joining together to make sure that basic work needs are met.

Other working-time alternatives considered by QWL programs are staggered hours and compressed workweeks of, for example, four nine- to ten-hour days. Time may be a major issue considered within a QWL program. These issues fall into the realm of mandatory subjects for bargaining. The union needs to be involved in the design and setup of any new working-time arrangements.[40]

One must temper enthusiasm about QWL with a sober look at the record.[41] Most of the experiments of the 1970s fell by the wayside after a few years. Neither internal cohesion nor productivity has always increased.[42] Further, union and management politics have flared over QWL initiatives. In large measure, we believe this is because of confusion that broad mandates mean vague implementation. Too many programs have been cut off at the knees because of poor attention to implementation and too great a reliance on emotional halos. Run well, however, a QWL program provides an opportunity to apply broad theoretical vision and wide-ranging technical application to the resolution of common issues and possibilities.

Conclusion

The introduction of new organizational structures generates opportunities for invention and a fresh review of how organizations should be structured. Quality circles and other forms of employee problem-solving groups can be a means of better involving shop-floor employees in the resolution of organizational problems, with important results. Introducing parallel structures, matrix organization, and/or union-management task forces encourages greater flexibility and responsiveness in dealing with organizational change. Sociotechnical systems and new manufacturing configurations require a fundamental reexamination of the technological and organizational assumptions and foundations of an organization. New team structures, including self-directed teams, provide opportunities for adaptation to change and for employee empowerment. And, finally, the quality of work life approach serves as an umbrella for joint organizational revitalization.

7. Creating New Opportunities: Cooperation on Marketing, Service, and Product Development

There are two sides to a financial statement—expenses and income.[1] For the most part, employee involvement and quality of work life efforts have dealt exclusively with one side of the ledger—costs. But a healthy organization has to pay attention to the balance of the balance sheet. Workplaces need to be run efficiently and to produce in a high-quality manner to compete. The use of employee involvement and cooperation for cost containment is thus a legitimate and important initiative. Employees have an incredible number of ideas about ways operations can be improved, and it is poor management not to take advantage of those ideas. Unions are correct to get involved, if only to intensify the focus on nonemployment-related areas for cost improvement.

Yet such a focus is only half a loaf. Too many management strategies accept the status quo. More so, far too many organizations have focused solely on how to manage their decline. They fail to apply the vision necessary for growth. Healthy and vital organizations center on growth. Meanwhile, in many companies, a great reservoir of talent and ideas remains dormant in their organizations. Their employees could generate ideas for new markets and products and a renewed entrepreneurial spirit. Front-line employees often have the most contact with customers and thereby generate critical information about what customers need.

128

Researchers at Texas A&M University, under the auspices of the Marketing Sciences Institute, have documented that employees are much more
closely aligned with customer needs and satisfaction than higher management is.[2] Producers of a product develop intimate knowledge of
current resources. These employees can be creative in the reconfiguration of these resources to produce new products at lower startup costs.
Employees also have a clear and vested interest in seeing that their
employer succeeds and therefore can be its best promoters. All of this
motivation and knowledge can be used to help employers grow.

All enterprises start with a product or service and a market. Even a
public sector agency has products, services, and markets. The organization then organizes itself to meet the demand for what it offers. Product
and market are in fact more important than cost structure. It is far too
easy to mistake the good fortune of a good market for good management.
Many companies and agencies have gotten by even with bloated costs if
they were fortunate to have a large unmet demand. Likewise, companies
whose expenses are cut to the bone cannot compensate for lack of market
demand. If the company is making an excellent product and no one
knows about it, or if the distribution networks are not intact, it will fail,
even if its pricing and cost structures are very low. Yet access to markets
may not be enough. An apt example is the situation of the buggy whip
makers at the turn of the century, after the introduction of the automobile. They could have had the best quality circle program in the world,
but it would not have made up for the lack of demand for buggy whips. In
short, the first effort a company must make in seeking to grow is to
expand the market for its products. Next, it must realistically assess the
demand for and lifespan of its products and diversify prudently as
product demand shifts.

How these ideas apply to the public sector may not be apparent;
however, agencies are also created to meet perceived public needs. The
stronger the perceived need, the better position the agency is in to
command adequate resources. Legislatures are less convinced by the
efficiency of an operation than by the nature of the public demand and
the manner in which an agency services those demands. More than one
inefficient agency has been saved by public outcry for need in the areas it
serves. Again, "market" takes precedence. Public needs do shift, and
intelligent agency management requires staying abreast of changing
demands and redeploying resources and energy to the areas of greatest
concern. If there is no longer the need for a public service, adequate plans
should be made to shift resources and people to emerging areas of need
or to help employees make a transition during the program's sunset.

For unions, involvement in the growth side of labor-management
cooperation emerges out of the inefficiency-unemployment dilemma.

In traditional employee involvement programs, employees often worry whether they are working themselves out of jobs. If the market or product base remains static, efforts that improve efficiency will of necessity lead to loss of jobs. The problem is that maintaining inefficient or sloppy procedures in a competitive environment will also lead eventually to being priced out of the market or losing market share—and losing jobs. The classic solutions are to avoid competition or to hope for natural market forces to expand the pie. The first solution leads to market distortions, and the second is based on prayer.

For employees and their unions, there can be another answer. They can consciously get involved in expanding the markets for the products or services they provide and in revising the product or service base to deal with obsolescence and shifting demand. In addition to the obvious impact on job security, expanded markets and growth make collective bargaining easier. With more cash and a larger pie, more can be shared with the bargaining unit. Employers projecting growth are more likely to reach favorable agreements than ones characterized by decline or stagnation.

A complete approach to union-management cooperation includes joint efforts not only to manage the enterprise effectively but also to promote growth and development. This view goes beyond cost containment concepts of participation and recognizes labor as a stakeholder in the enterprise's future. Labor can then be used to strategic advantage to position the enterprise for growth. In turn, labor can use its position as a partner to protect and expand the availability and quality of jobs.

When labor is viewed as a stakeholder, labor issues are not simply matters of cost reduction but of asset maximization. Instead of being a drag on profits, labor becomes a generator of profit potential. The company's human and technical resources are not obstacles to growth but assets and when configured in appropriate ways can lead to operational improvement, innovation, and increased revenues. In a rudimentary sense, this has always been true. Large organizations are built on the premise that employing additional people adds to their overall net worth. The theory is that by adding employees, products or services can be provided less expensively per unit and more reliably, and/or markets can be better served. Unfortunately, the fit between theory and practice is not always snug. Most personnel planners ask how fewer people can be used to meet fixed targets. When labor is a stakeholder, planners ask how people can be used to accomplish broader organizational goals. Targets are raised to accommodate market potential and internal asset capability, as in the highly successful Mondragón cooperative system in Spain.[3] Overall, growth is obtained through market retention, improving the yield from current customers and increasing market share, product diversification, and capital investment.

Joint Customer Service Improvement Programs

Every organization and every function within it has a customer. The customer is the reason a unit produces a product or delivers a service. Customers pay for or justify the work that is done. In the public sector, the customer is the taxpayer or the user of the service. Inside an organization, there are many units whose function it is to serve other parts of the organization, their "customers." Not only does attention to customer service maintain current relationships, but it also provides the venue for increased revenue by increasing the number of customers and how much they buy. It is a sign of trouble in any organization when the customer loses the primary position.

Customer service is not just a function of *what is* provided but also the *manner* in which it is delivered and the way the system adjusts to problems experienced by the customer or meets or exceeds customer requirements. Employees are critical to this process. One area on which management and the union often agree is the need for improved customer service. Again, this applies equally well in the private sector, where workers have contact with paying customers, and in the public sector, where they interface with patrons. Most customer service programs consist of two parts: lofty statements about the importance of customer service and general rules about how employees should serve customers. Too often, these rules are communicated in a top-down fashion and have very limited effectiveness.

In conjunction with a supermarket chain and its union, we developed a participatory customer service program to test a joint union-management approach to bottom-up customer service improvement. In retail food, customer service is the lifeblood of the industry. Working as a team, union, management, and the QWL staff implemented the program. First, a brainstorming session in each department in the store was conducted to determine six specific actions that could be done in each work area to improve customer service. Second, the ideas, uncensored, were posted on a checklist in the work areas, and employees made a commitment to themselves and the employer to carry out these ideas. Third, and finally, the checklists were updated about every three months to reflect changing conditions and to reinforce a long-term commitment to serving customers.

The checklists clearly helped improve the delivery of service to customers and gave employees a voice in their work. In addition, their use aided the supermarket chain by providing valuable data to management and the union on what employees at each location thought about customer service. The checklists thus became a way to orient new employees about working in each store. Most important, in a concrete, clear, and simple fashion, the checklists demonstrated joint union-management concern and action on customer service.

In this case, problems of customer service were also addressed in more comprehensive ways by other joint problem-solving groups, including surveying and interviewing customers to learn their reactions and suggestions.

We have since applied this concept in a variety of industries in the private and public sectors. Each time the process provides a testimony to the commitment and imagination of those who work and a demonstration of the desire to please the customer shared by management and the union. The advantage of this process is that it can be used with a geographically and occupationally diverse work force in a short period of time. It whets the appetite of employees for further involvement in customer service. The chain of customers concept has been included in this process at the stage in which groups identify and then brainstorm ways to improve service to external customers *and* to internal customers. Defining the people one works with as internal customers and finding ways to improve one's relationship improves the overall quality of service and the quality of work life.

In any organization, a variety of forums and mechanisms can be created for going beyond rhetoric and fingerpointing to improving customer service. In a sales environment, if customers are more satisfied, they are more likely to buy more and more often. New customers will be attracted. This is money in the bank. In a public service environment, stronger support is likely to develop and a larger percentage of the client population will use the service if its "customers" are well treated.

Joint Union-Management Marketing Promotions

Customer service techniques focus on ways to improve performance with people who already do business with the enterprise. Marketing is critical in helping to generate new customers. Management has a clear interest in marketing since it often results in economies of scale and additional profits. Labor sees marketing as important to maintain and expand jobs. Unions have a long-standing interest in marketing and have employed several traditional approaches. Advertisements imploring consumers to "look for the union label" are one way to market union-made products. In addition, the AFL-CIO's Union Label Department puts on an annual trade show to showcase products made with union labor, and it publishes a directory of these products. The Union Privilege Benefits Program is another major marketing effort. It provides union members with discounts for products and services. Unions and employers have also "marketed" together by jointly lobbying Congress and government bodies for contracts.

Other marketing approaches are possible. Making joint union-management calls on sales prospects helps in some industries. For example, as part of the Labor-Management Action Group of the Milwaukee Road Railroad, teams of marketing representatives and labor officials called on potential shippers several times a month. The company marketer took the lead in the discussions, but was backed up by the union representative. Having the backing of the union in a heavily unionized industry like the railroads provided important assurance to the shipper about reliability and quality. Likewise, contact with the customers provided the union with insight into the difficulties of obtaining customers and of meeting their needs. The process also helped the marketing department learn about operations from those who actually perform the service. Invariably, the customer was positively surprised by the call and the fact it involved a union-management team often made a strong impression. Opening up communications between the sales office and the union also led to ideas about marketing possibilities being channeled from the work force into the sales office. In general, the Milwaukee Road experience was very positive and contributed significantly to new sales and new jobs for railroad workers and to maintaining the railroad before its sale to the Soo Line. The Union Pacific Railroad and its unions conducted a similar program for short-line sales promotion.

In many major markets the construction industry is heavily unionized and the ability to bid on jobs in competitive markets is critical. The Building and Construction Trades Department (AFL-CIO) and the National Construction Employers Council as well as other national contractor associations have developed national labor-management committees and agreements to promote cooperation in attracting new work, especially in areas where union market share has dropped considerably. Throughout the country there are an increasing number of local multicraft labor-management construction councils, such as PRIDE in St. Louis, Union Jack in Denver, CISCO in Chicago, and Operation MOST in Columbus. Beginning during the 1980s in St. Louis, one of the most heavily unionized and least expensive housing markets in the country, the building trades provided not only capital for residential construction and purchases built 100 percent union but also a full labor guarantee for the work. In Philadelphia, the BUILT-RITE process brings together owners, contractors, and union at one level and then cascades throughout the project to improve performance through tool-box meetings, steward-foreman partnerships on quality and safety, and project and citywide joint problem solving. Such efforts have been credited with winning many millions of dollars of business for union contractors. They have hammered out prejob agreements to reduce or eliminate jurisdictional battles and have improved the quality, timeliness, and safety records of unionized construction work. This has helped create a better image of the unionized sector, thus reinforcing the notion that union construction is of high quality and value.

Certain crafts in the construction industry also conduct their own marketing efforts. One model is provided by the International Masonry Institute (IMI), a joint program of the International Union of Bricklayers and Allied Craftsmen (BAC) and their union contractors' association. Getting people to use brick, stone, and block is the goal of the effort. Through the IMI, a number of joint programs are promoted. The IMI also works closely with local and regional joint promotion programs in the United States and Canada. Materials are provided for their use, including a newsletter, slide show, videos, educational material, publicity releases, and advertising reprints. The union is clear about the employment possibilities generated by moving market share up the ladder, especially in residential construction. The impact of market growth can equal or exceed growth through organizing; a 1 percent growth in market share can add up to fifty thousand new jobs in the industry.

A central facet of the IMI marketing effort is providing information to civil engineers and architects as well as to other construction specifiers and designers on the benefits of masonry construction and on how to use masonry materials. Seminars are also conducted for building owners and public sector facilities managers. The IMI also developed computer software to assess the contribution of passive solar approaches to heating needs in one- and two-story structures. Generating positive publicity about the industry and keeping an eye on developments in building codes are other ways that markets are protected and expanded. Currently, the institute targets more than three hundred large national firms.

Joint marketing efforts can involve union-management teams and sophisticated advertising and promotion campaigns or focus on employees with customer contact. In a few cases, workers affected by slowdowns have been retrained to become salespersons. When the demand increases, they return to production. In retail, employees can engage in "suggestive selling," and delivery people and repairers can actively promote new products. Some union-management partners have used advertisements on television, on billboards, and in the print media to improve their market picture. Others have used jointly designed "gainsharing" programs that compensate employees for fruitful sales leads.

New Product Development and Intrapreneurship

Few products, whether manufactured goods or services, have eternal life spans. Current product lines may not be sufficient to generate the revenues necessary for bottom-line improvement. As such, looking at profitable new products and ideas is critical.

Union-management cooperation is helpful in two regards. First, it can speed up the introduction of new approaches, especially in the production phase. Speed is critical to profitability and market presence. Second, the union membership represents a valuable component of an ongoing product evaluation and renewal strategy. Most industrial innovations are not the result of dramatic breakthroughs but represent incremental improvements in a product or some variation in or combination of existing products. In production facilities, workers have an intimate knowledge of the production process involved. They often have ideas about how to create permutations of the current product. In addition, because of their knowledge of the existing machinery, they can often think of products that could be developed using essentially the same technology. Often, product planners are not aware of the range of product possibilities inherent in the current process and tend to consider more expensive options than those the internal work force might propose.

The Combined Shop Stewards Committee at Lucas Aerospace in England, which was concerned about declining employment caused by declining demand for its military aircraft, worked with local technology experts to develop more than 150 ideas for alternative, socially responsible products that could be made using essentially the same technology and workers in the plant.[4] The approach graphically demonstrated the alternative possibilities in the facility and the imagination of the workers. The plan failed to gain the support of management, however, illustrating also that unilateral plans by labor are unlikely to be realized when management holds all the cards. In this case, a political power struggle ensued that prevented anything from getting accomplished.

New products can also emerge out of product research. Because of the prevalence of small contractors, research in masonry has been minimal, especially in comparison with other building materials. In 1979, the Masonry Research Foundation was founded as a joint effort of four industry groups, two labor unions, and the IMI. Its first task was to assess what research was being done in the industry and to set an agenda for future research. Subsequently, research was conducted on the bonding qualities of mortar and masonry units. Other topics included the water penetration of walls, compatibility of materials, comparative costs, seismic properties, new wall systems, new lifting devices, and prefabricated stone panels.

The IMI has also been involved with market research. The particulars are of less interest to those outside the industry than the process by which its efforts came about and how they are managed. Included on the review committees for each research project are rank-and-file craftspersons, local business agents, and local contractors as well as others with a national scope. An effort is made to ensure that the research is useful and understandable to those who are likely to use it. Through this process, those with hands-on experience are brought into contact with skilled researchers in the field.

The union took a strong role in the development of the Masonry Research Foundation. John Joyce, president of the BAC, says:

> What happens in the area of promotion and research will go a long way toward determining job opportunities in masonry for our members. This is the arena of industry-level, or strategic decision making. We're affected which means we have a *reason to* be involved. We're concerned about decisions management has made in the past about these subjects, and so we *need to* be involved. We don't like the fact that when management made the masonry industry's promotion and research decisions on a unilateral basis, it decided to spend so little on these activities that we've lost markets and jobs. That's why we've gotten involved and plan to stay involved.[5]

Additional joint product development mechanisms are possible. For example, a joint union-management committee could review a proposed new product idea with a sample of the work force to find out workers' reactions to its feasibility and design. It could also examine market areas and explore new product concepts. Such a committee could also sponsor a competition to identify new product ideas among the work force and develop subcommittees to work on the more promising suggestions. Alternatively, joint union-management teams could meet with customers to find out what product innovations would be helpful. Or employees with customer contact could be trained to solicit information. A survey could also be conducted with noncustomers to find out what product innovations they would be inclined to buy. In organizations with product development groups, these efforts can be integrated with their efforts. In organizations without this specific function, those involved in the union-management effort could help catalyze and implement this activity.

Union-Management Cooperation to Plan New Facilities

Producing new products or services or expanding to meet rising sales opens the possibility of cooperation on new facilities and ventures. In the past few years there has been an increase in joint activity in these areas, especially in the auto and metals industries. For unions, involvement is attractive because it provides new jobs for current and prospective members and initial input on the work environment. For management, the workers' perspective can be a valuable asset in thinking through the new project. In new locations (that is, greenfield sites), worker involvement helps avoid costly union-avoidance battles and may provide opportunities to test new procedures that could be used in existing unionized locations. In existing plants, union-management cooperation can be used to help plan and review changes in plant layout. In the auto industry, for example, cooperation is being sought in changing models. In some plants, redesign teams have been established, and in others blueprints have been posted for all to see and comment on. The Volvo Uddevalla plant, characterized by very innovative teamwork design in production, also used a joint approach to planning the workplace, including team zones and networked workshops.[6] The new LTV Electrogalvanizing plant in Cleveland engaged in a joint design process with the United Steelworkers to build a high-performance steel mill.

At the Carborundum Corporation's refractories in Falconer, New York:

> Plant management was acutely aware of the need to redesign the old facility as a means of improving working conditions and productivity simultaneously. The proposal was put before the plant labor-management committee, and a subcommittee comprised of both union and management was formed to direct the project. Department foremen called on employees to identify problems in plant layout and make suggestions on how redesign could benefit their work, quality of working life and working conditions. One hundred sixty-seven responses were received, ranging from the relocation of a machine to the complete redesigning of a departmental layout.[7]

In Sarnia, Ontario, Shell Canada was considering the construction of a new chemicals plant and decided to invite the Energy and Chemical Workers of Canada (then the Oil, Chemical and Atomic Workers) into the design process.[8] The union's involvement worked out well for management, the union, and the membership. It also resulted in an innovative collective agreement that maximizes flexibility in operations and calls for full union involvement in all aspects of the operation of the plant. In describing the process, two of the principals reported:

> The Union accepted with two stipulations 1) that it be a full partner in the design process and 2) that it would maintain a high profile. This was quickly accepted. The participation of union representatives provided the means for capturing and utilizing organizational learning at the shop floor level. Initial concerns were quickly forgotten as the high quality of union contribution unfolded and managers congratulated themselves for their statesmanship.[9]

In the auto industry, joint planning is taking place at General Motors' Saturn plant, at Ford with the Alpha project, and at Chrysler on the Liberty car. In each case, the UAW is working in partnership to develop new ventures and facilities. The Saturn Division of General Motors, the first new GM division in sixty-six years, provides the best view of the process. It represents an exciting break with the past in manufacturing and industrial relations. The dimensions of the project are staggering. The research costs were about $1 billion and startup, billions more. GM is banking on this project to make the company competitive again in the medium-sized car market.

The UAW has been a significant player in the Saturn project. Fifty-two auto workers and union officials worked with thirty-nine salaried GM managers in seven subcommittees to develop the plan for the plant. They worked for about a year on the design and initial plan, which were submitted to the board of GM and the top leadership of the UAW. The subcommittees examined technical and human systems innovations in North America and elsewhere, including Japan, Sweden, and West Germany. Their input went far beyond how the labor relations system should be constituted and touched on every technical and operational area. The group put more then fifty thousand hours of work into this phase, and many of these hours were taken up with intense discussions among labor and management on the pros and cons of various alternatives. The final agreement proposed a wide range of innovations in automotive design, marketing, factory design, and labor relations. The UAW is involved in *every* aspect of the operation.

Since its startup, the Saturn plant has proved capable of producing a high-quality car with high customer satisfaction. Startup was not as smooth or as spectacular as its initial hype, but the focus on labor-management cooperation helped retain the emphasis on quality and contributed to working out the initial bugs that an undertaking of the magnitude of Saturn inevitably has. The involvement of the union as a partner from the shop-floor level to strategic decision making has made a significant contribution to Saturn's success.

The architectural and engineering design of workplaces has not received the same attention as work groups or career or organizational structure. Usually design is believed to be the domain of design and architectural experts. Some architects and building engineers, however, are beginning to recognize the impact that a participative design can have. Colin Clipson, director of the Architectural Research Laboratory at the University of Michigan, worked with union-management teams to design the interior and lighting of the Saturn plant to ensure that the physical design and environment supported the business and organizational style. He notes: "Planning teams addressed a series of design projects ranging from the location of team centers and workstations around the plant, to simulating novel and untested work procedures in new spatial configurations, to studying the impact of various types of lighting on interior work settings and exterior entrance ways; these teams also had involvement in the choice of work clothing."[10] The teams worked with the designers in a collaborative way through conception to testing models to design recommendations.

The implications of new workplace arrangements need to be part of the total joint planning process. Franklin Becker of Cornell University's School of Human Ecology describes three elements that make up the concept of the "total workplace." "One is the idea of integrating decisions often considered in isolation by individual departments: human resources, information technology, design and construction, and buildings operation and management. The second meaning of the total workplace concept is that the workplace is more than one's own personal office or workstation. It is the entire workplace (site, amenities, commons areas, project rooms, support areas), a series of loosely coupled settings. The third is the idea that the processes used for planning, designing, and managing the workplace are as much a part of the building's quality as are its physical characteristics."[11] Labor and management can work together on facilities issues as one area for joint cooperation. They can also rethink facilities as a way to support and drive organizational change toward the achievement of more collaborative workplaces.

Labor Representation on Boards of Directors

Though still far and away the exception, labor representation on boards of directors is increasing in the United States. In the last decade, union representatives or directors selected by unions have been seated on several corporate boards. Primarily this has occurred in distressed companies in return for wage and work-rule concessions. In some cases, such as at Eastern Airlines, the board was an arena for combat as the economic and labor-management situation deteriorated. At Weirton Steel, by contrast, the experience of having representatives of the Independent Steelworkers Union has been positive for both economic performance and the participative culture.

In 1980, the Chrysler Corporation appointed Douglas Fraser, then president of the United Auto Workers, to its board. Fraser says: "Generally speaking, I think the members of the board would agree with my assessment that my membership on the Chrysler board was a constructive one. There is, I understand, a consensus that I brought to the board a knowledge of industry but, more important than that, a perspective that nobody else could provide. . . . I am firmly convinced that, as time passes, more unions will be seeking membership on corporate boards and other means of democratizing the work place."[12] Chrysler stated at the time that the seat was not a labor seat and subsequently removed the next president of the UAW when it reduced the size of the board. This change brought a great deal of criticism.

Employee representation on boards of directors is common under the codetermination systems of Europe, where the major issue in some countries such as Germany and Sweden has been joint control of enterprises. The European experience with board-level representation has been positive, however, not only because it increased labor's voice but also because it was good for management. In Norway, one-third of the board members of most enterprises with more than two hundred employees are workers. In smaller firms, worker representation is optional. A survey in 1975 reported that in enterprises with fifty to two hundred employees, 54 percent had board-level representation by workers: "According to another survey carried out at the same time, more than half of the heads of Norwegian companies thought that the worker members of boards made a useful contribution to meetings, while 48% thought it neither positive or negative and only 1% thought it negative. Among the respondents, 78% thought that the workers' representatives had shown as much concern for the profitability of the undertaking as the other members of the board."[13] Similar data are reported for other countries with employee representation on boards.

In many cases in the United States, if a union leader is on a board of directors, he or she may exempt him- or herself from discussions of collective bargaining agreements to minimize the conflicts inherent in their roles.[14] Such conflicts are not new, however. Representatives of banks and major investors are frequently included on boards. Like union leaders, they have an interest in the success of the enterprise but often have other loyalties that may influence their decisions on resource allocation, divestment, new investments, and other matters. That members of boards of directors are objective and have singular concerns is a myth.

Board-level representation can be an opportunity for union-employer cooperation and joint decision-making at the very highest level of the corporation. Representation can be oversold, however, like the benefits of employee ownership. Board representation does not necessarily imply that the quality of work life of the average employee will be better in ways that he or she will readily perceive. In the day-to-day lives of employees, many decisions other than those determined by the board are equally critical if not more so. Further, representation does not mean that difficult and painful decisions about resource allocation and employment will not have to be made. As always, joint participation guarantees voice in the decisions but not the specific outcomes.

Joint Investment Decision Making

The allocation of capital affects both corporate health and jobs. For the most part, investment decisions are made unilaterally. There are, however, two examples of union-management cooperation on investments that demand attention.

The first example involves pension and welfare funds. Found in a number of industries, though most frequently in building and construction, union pension funds represent more than a trillion dollars in assets, making them the largest source of investment capital in the United States. By law, union pension funds must be jointly trusteed. But unions and unionized employers are asking whether the investments of some of these funds are being used in ways that undercut the investors' long-term viability. They are examining ways to use these funds prudently to provide support for unionized jobs for the workers who pay in to these funds. The AFL-CIO has developed a Housing Investment Trust to pool union resources to generate affordable housing and union jobs. It makes a lot of sense to consider this area as long as the funds are accountable and used wisely from an investment perspective. Joint trusteeship of pensions then provides a forum for cooperation and an avenue for funneling dollars into socially desirable and job-reinforcing investments.

The second joint investment program was started as a result of the 1984 GM-UAW contract. A much smaller initiative than the pension fund programs, it may provide the framework for experimentation with joint labor-management approaches to investment and job creation. GM designated $100 million as a potential capital pool for a New Business Ventures Development Group. This is administered by a negotiated Growth and Opportunity Committee with equal membership from the company and the union. According to the *UAW-GM Report,* "The bold, new program marks the first time a major corporation and union will have an ongoing activity to develop and mutually direct ventures into new, nontraditional business areas—financed entirely by corporate funds, but providing full input by the union." The new companies will, within the boundaries of labor law, recognize the UAW as the bargaining agent.

The latitude for the program is broad. Ideas for the use of the funds will in large part be generated from local job security committees, which are empowered under the GM-UAW contract to make recommendations to the General Motors National Growth and Development Committee and to develop, according to the report, "employee participation toward bringing about new, competitive business." This fund, combined with $30 million negotiated in the Ford agreement, provides a large bank of funds for joint investments in new enterprises.

Implementation of the program has been difficult. What the group looks at in assessing investment proposals includes the market for the product, equipment costs, plant modernization costs, availability of technology, characteristics of the business, nature of the bargaining agreements, and expected return on investment. The focus is on growing jobs that can competitively replace nonunion or foreign suppliers, though other possibilities can be considered. Finding the right mixture of products that build on the interests of General Motors has been elusive. Concerns about possible competition with other UAW-represented facilities and the location of the proposed sites have led to more rejections than approvals. In General Motors, the contract provision was not used until 1991, when 135 jobs were created in the B-O-C Lansing Automotive Division through a $6.5 million investment for engine remanufacturing and in Bristol, Connecticut, when 66 jobs were created to produce ball screws for antilock brakes with a $7.5 million contribution. "I never would have dreamed of working so closely with management in this corporation," said Dave Cleveland, a machinist who has been with GM for twenty-seven years in Lansing, Michigan. "We've really started to make things happen. We have the facilities, the technology and the labor that will put people back to work."[15] In the Ford program, a $460,000 investment was made at the Cleveland Engine Plant to rehabilitate equipment for work previously done by outside contractors. Though the results in the auto industry are limited, the principle of joint involvement in investing is large indeed.

Conclusion

Participants in employee involvement and labor-management cooperation efforts should seriously consider the potential for growth from collaboration. Not considering growth results in a reactive approach to the future and squanders talents and possibilities of potentially great importance.

A task force or committee can be established at the highest levels of the organization to guide and spearhead efforts at growth and development. Subordinate activities can be spun off, focused on various aspects of service or marketing, or on different product or service ideas. Under the labor-management umbrella, training in union-management cooperation and the content areas of service, marketing, and/or product development can be carried out. Where the activities go from here is limited only by the imagination of the partners.

A wide range of options can be pursued:

1. *Integration of tasks.* Jobs can be redesigned to include marketing and service as integral functions. Separate job categories such as marketers or customer service representatives can be incorporated into job descriptions. Drivers for a package service, for example, might also promote the company's services and look for extra loads.

2. *Alternation of tasks.* By switching off tasks according to need, employees can be involved in marketing and production. In Japan, some factories have retrained production workers and send them out as door-to-door salespersons when demand is slow. When demand picks up, they

go back to the line. United Airlines had a program to promote its express package service that used laid-off pilots as spokespersons. Many automakers have rotated employees through customer contact programs either to visit or call customers to check on satisfaction. Imagine if American auto workers, instead of getting unemployment and supplementary unemployment benefits, which amount to practically their entire paychecks, could market American cars.

3. *Parallel activities.* The railroad marketing example illustrates how parallel activities involving joint labor-management teams can supplement traditional marketing efforts. Use of a parallel approach does not result in changes in basic responsibilities but adds an additional structure to complement basic responsibilities. A parallel approach might also include a suggestion or reward system for product or market growth ideas.

4. *Strategic approach.* A strategic program would adopt marketing, product development, and/or customer service issues as a goal. Then, through a joint task force or committee, a comprehensive strategy would be developed for joint efforts and market improvement. The distinction of the strategic approach is its clear and broad focus on revenue and the attempt to use internal resources as much as possible. The Saturn and Alpha projects at GM and Ford are good examples.

5. *Joint contracting.* The International Masonry Institute is an excellent example of an organization that uses the joint contracting approach. Labor and management agree on important marketing and research objectives. Experts, generally from the outside, are contracted to perform the work, which is reviewed by the labor-management partners.

Each company and union presents a unique set of internal resources and aspirations and external market conditions and constraints. Factors such as the size of the enterprise, capital base, distribution networks, level of customer contact, location, skills levels of employees, degree of technological flexibility, and the like need to be considered. As employee involvement and union-management cooperation evolve and the pressures of competition increase, there will be greater movement into the revenue and growth side of union-management cooperation. The approaches described in this chapter should enable the parties to develop a foundation for a positive union-management relationship.

8. Achieving Quality: A Joint Union-Management Commitment

Q uality is a powerful organizing principle for effecting workplace change and transforming an organization as a whole. In unionized workplaces, a unilateral quality improvement effort diminishes its potential and is counter to the quality principles of organizational alignment and empowerment. The joint pursuit of quality leads to the highest quality and most effective effort. True union-management cooperation can, in the jargon of quality, delight the customer, facilitate system change and alignment, and empower employees at all levels.

The pursuit of quality has recently assumed many different forms in unionized workplaces and means different things to different people. For some union and management partners, a joint quality effort is an overall strategy for improving their competitiveness. For others, quality efforts are perceived as a way for management to extend its power at the expense of the union and its members. This chapter describes the common contours of joint quality efforts and the issues and opportunities inherent in these efforts.

Creating a Shared Vision of Quality

Ideally, union and management partners in a joint quality effort develop a shared vision that spells out what quality is and means for their organization. There is a real danger in adopting too narrow or limited a vision. Many visions incorporate the following elements:

Central focus on customer satisfaction. Meeting and then exceeding customer needs, expectations, and requirements is at the core of quality. Customers are both external to the organization (i.e., outside consumers of the goods or services produced) and internal to the organization (i.e., other employees and work units). Satisfying external customers can be a win-win opportunity for the union and management in that it leads to growth, employment stability, and individual satisfaction in jobs well done. A true understanding of quality leads to the recognition that satisfying internal customers is critical to how well an organization is able to satisfy its external customers. This connection between internal and external customer satisfaction reinforces the importance of cooperation and teamwork throughout the organization.

This focus on customer satisfaction is the foundation for measuring quality. Well-constructed quality measurement systems measure both internal and external customer satisfaction. They are not traditional measurement systems focused on work tasks and activities. The impact of the quality effort on employees is also measured. Some partners use survey research techniques to determine customers' assessments of the quality effort and employees' opinions on what the impact of the effort has been.

Employee involvement and empowerment. Empowered employees are best at delivering products and services that satisfy both internal and external customers. Thus, decision making is pushed down to "the lowest possible or practical level," based on the assumption that the employees who actually make the products or deliver the services are the most "expert" at how to do their work best. The labor organization has always been an empowerment vehicle. Many union partners in joint efforts are thus drawn to the quality approach by the potential to empower their members in new ways. Employees almost universally insist that if they were allowed to do their work as they see fit they could do it better. Unfortunately, employee empowerment is often oversold because it is such a powerful draw for employees. Too often the quality effort is vague or selective about who will be empowered, how, and to what extent. If the quality effort cannot deliver on high expectations for employee empowerment, it is probably doomed to failure.

Systems orientation. The term *systems orientation* has several different meanings in the quality arena. To establishes a clear common direction for a quality effort, this term must be defined in the joint vision statement. At a minimum, quality efforts address problems relating to the operation of one or more workplace subsystems, such as production, marketing, waste removal, or transportation. A focus on improving various processes rather than on addressing problems in isolation indicates a broader systems orientation. In this case, the aim is to bring all the processes and subsystems into alignment by seeking synergy.

A systems orientation leads to a focus on the entire workplace as a whole, as in total quality management (TQM) or total quality organizations (TQO). Looking at the whole system includes linking internal and external customers and suppliers in ways that reflect the dynamism of the organizational environment. Whole-system thinking leads to opportunities for collaboration and improvement that segmented or isolated analysis blocks. Important or systemic problems are addressed, not tangential or peripheral problems.

Structured approach to problem solving. Using one or more structured problem-solving processes to resolve problems is standard operating procedure in a quality effort. Many problem-solving processes vary in the number of steps and in the names or titles used for those steps. A six-step version is employed by Xerox and the Amalgamated Clothing and Textile Workers Union (ACTWU). When a work process cannot deliver outputs that meet customer requirements, then the barriers or problems preventing customer satisfaction are identified and solved using this six-step process. Union-management partners need to select problem-solving processes based on what will work in their particular situations. In the absence of a structured problem-solving process, people jump from identifying the problem to pursuing solutions. This trial-and-error method creates as many problems as it solves.

Data-based or fact-based decision making. Using organized sets of data to make decisions and involving employees directly in generating data for decision making leads to better results. It is more analytical and systematic than traditional "shoot-from-the-hip" decision making done by one key person. The data-based system involves employees in generating the data to make their decisions. They then have a better understanding of the decision and are more willing and able to assist in its implementation. Data-based decision making provides the basis for measuring the true impact or results of decisions. It also signals a commitment by the union and management to open communication and information sharing.

Continuous improvement. Finally there is a constant and routine search for ways to improve any and all aspects of the workplace. This reflects an organizationally approved restlessness that encourages dissatisfaction with the status quo. Quality partners move from an attitude of "if it ain't broke, don't fix it" to an attitude of "if it ain't broke, fix it anyway." Continuous improvement involves broad initiatives, including improving the ways customers are served, how the company operates, daily work life, and employees' financial well-being.

Partners involved in continuous improvement recognize the costs of quality. Designing quality into products and processes up front is the smartest mode of operation. It is less costly to correct problems during the design of products or processes than later during production or, later still, after the products or services have been delivered to customers.

Ensuring continuous improvement may be one of the most challenging elements of a shared quality effort. It requires that all employees regularly call into question all aspects of the organization through an overarching focus on the customer and quality. If a fairly narrow scope for quality has been established, pursuing continuous improvement soon pushes at its boundaries. It is virtually impossible to declare something off limits for improvement without undercutting the pursuit of continuous improvement. Quality programs commonly take ongoing aim at identifying and eliminating "nonvalue-added" steps. Most employees welcome this attempt to eliminate wasted activity, but those affected must be part of the overall process of analysis and action.

Unfortunately, too often union and management partners adopt the rhetoric of continuous improvement without understanding all of its implications. When employees hear continuous improvement, they think of significant change. Employees are often disappointed by the limited change some quality efforts deliver. They need to learn how to make change a positive and ongoing part of their work lives.

No matter where a joint quality effort is on the development path, the union-management partners can create a shared definition or vision of quality. Then specific goals and objectives can be established for the quality effort itself. By squarely and completely addressing these goals and objectives, the organization moves toward its shared quality vision.

Cooperation and Quality

Cooperation and quality are not new to unionized workplaces or unions. Beginning with the early shop committees during World War I, union-management cooperation and quality initiatives have formed a powerful strategy for improving the workplace. The B & O Plan, initiated in 1924 at the Glenwood shops near Pittsburgh, focused on improving operations and day-to-day work through a network of work unit and system-level committees. Ultimately, many North American railroads and transit companies adopted this plan as a way to improve quality and competitiveness.

William Green, president of the American Federation of Labor, wrote in an editorial in the AFL's journal, *The Federationist*, in the late 1920s: "Through a reciprocal relationship, the common problems of industry

can be solved, efficiency in service promoted, and economies in production introduced."[1]

During this same period, scientific management, the Taylorist school
of workplace design, was sweeping American industry and bringing with
it significant workplace change. The AFL, the Taylor Society, and the
American Society of Mechanical Engineers had ongoing dialogue about
the value of scientific management and organized labor's interest in it. In
1921, the Cleveland-area textile employers and the International Ladies'
Garment Workers' Union (ILGWU) signed a landmark agreement specifying joint involvement in the development of labor standards and union
assistance in helping to improve the overall process of manufacture. In
1927, the AFL sponsored a conference on the elimination of waste. Thus,
leaders of the day saw industrial science and due process as strengthening
one another. Union involvement brought greater commitment to the
standards and more reliable data, and scientific management brought
objectivity and order to the workplace.

At the same time, the International Printing Pressmen and Assistants
Union initiated a unique quality assurance process. Daily they reviewed
five hundred newspapers from around the country. If there were defects
in the appearance or workmanship, the newspaper was notified of both
the problems and ways to correct them. If the defect continued, the union
dispatched an engineer to work with the paper to correct the problem.
The union also helped in the design of new printing plants and in the
installation and repair of machinery. This service, provided by the union
at no cost, was one of the benefits to publishers of having a work force
represented by a labor organization that was committed to quality. Many
labor organizations continue to have industrial engineers and other
technical resources available to their members and employers for the sole
purpose of establishing and maintaining production processes that foster
competitiveness and fairness.

World War II was another catalyst for significant cooperation around
quality. Approximately fifty thousand joint production committees were
established during the war years, covering more than seven million
workers. The primary targets of these efforts were the conservation of
materials, transportation, absenteeism, care of tools and equipment,
productivity, quality control, and training.

The attitude of unions and their members during the war was aptly
captured by Clinton Golden and Harold Ruttenberg of the Steel Workers
Organizing Committee, who stated in 1942: "Workers have a passion for
efficiency, detest needless waste, and love to work in an orderly shop, mill
or mine where production flows smoothly. Where these conditions do not
prevail, workers are full of ideas and practical suggestions on how they can
be brought about, or where they do prevail, how they can be improved."[2]

During the 1950s, the labor-management climate in the United States polarized as unions and companies marked off the boundaries in their relationships and in their agreements. Little attention was paid to areas of common ground. Ironically, Americans involved in rebuilding the war-torn economies of Japan and Germany pioneered the use of cooperation and quality approaches influential today. In Germany, codetermination systems were developed, positioning companies and unions in formal partnerships. In Japan, joint consultation systems were established, and W. Edwards Deming worked with the Japanese Union of Scientists and Engineers to spread his concept of statistical quality control.[3] Joseph M. Juran also advised industrial leaders in Japan about quality control processes.

During the first half of the 1970s, Japan's use of quality control circles was attracting the attention of American leaders of industry, and quality circles were established in a handful of American manufacturing companies. By 1977, the International Association of Quality Circles (IAQC) was founded in the United States, indicating the enormous growth of and interest in quality circles as a vehicle for employee involvement in solving workplace problems. About half the member organizations of IAQC are unionized, a far higher percentage than the percentage of unionized organizations in the American economy as a whole. Eventually, by the mid-1980s, tens of thousands of public and private sector organizations were successfully using quality circles or had at least experimented with them somewhere within their operations. This paralleled the growth of QWL activities and union-management efforts to develop employee participation groups at General Motors, employee involvement in Ford, labor-management participation teams in steel, and QWL teams in the telephone industry.

Many organizations found that quality circles by themselves were an insufficient mechanism for effecting large-scale organizational improvement. Too often they were successful for working on problems and opportunities within the immediate control of their work unit but could not bridge to other parts of the organization or could not solve larger organizational problems. For just as many organizations, however, quality circles did achieve at least three very significant accomplishments:

1. They brought problem solving and to some extent decision making down to the operating levels of organizations.
2. Union and management partners learned in a very practical way how best to work together.
3. Tools and techniques for solving problems, conducting meetings, and managing group work overall were introduced broadly throughout the organizations.

Many of today's quality gurus and quality practitioners deny or dismiss the role of quality circles in the renewed interest in quality. But the lessons learned by management and union partners from their quality circle experiences should not be ignored. Embedded in these experiences—positive and negative—is valuable guidance on how quality can be pursued successfully together.

Today, quality programs are found throughout the world. The ISO 9000, Malcolm Baldrige Award, and other national and local awards are testimony to the broad interest in quality. Unfortunately, current applications are not always at the highest level. Indeed, a study by McKinsey and Company documented that two-thirds of the quality programs recently instituted "have fallen far short of yielding real improvements."[4] The sophisticated analysis and broad organizational span of effective quality programs also sow the seeds for their demise in organizations where management and union leaders are not willing to do the hard work of learning from the past and adequately addressing future challenges.

Though the connection is not always made, there is a clear parallel between the historical development of scientific management and of today's quality programs. Each in its own way was an attempt to impose greater rationality, systematic thinking, and scientific certainty on the workplace. Each placed a great emphasis on reexamining work processes to see what made sense and on using data-based measures to identify wasted efforts and then track improvements. In each case there was a semireligious fervor in the beginning, and each held the promise of providing everlasting progress in industry. Each started with the premise that it was management's responsibility to run the program and that the outcome would be good for workers. Like today's quality gurus, Frederick Taylor had little patience with union resistance or questions and disdained managers who would not adopt his system. Adherents of both approaches believed they created a neutral playing field, a set of fair rules, and an unbiased language. But, as advocates of Taylorism and quality improvement learned, fervent faith was not enough to make a system work in real workplaces. The challenge was not to convince employees of the rationale of the new system but to engage them as active partners in its development. The perspectives that unions brought and due process in spreading the new work approaches added real value. As these systems were developed, their advocates came to embrace the fact that employee involvement and union participation make the positive promise inherent in workplace change more possible. There are real and significant differences between scientific management and today's quality processes, but on these points they have much in common.

Too often quality is viewed as an ahistorical phenomenon or choice in American industry. In fact, it is an outgrowth of a long line of industrial engineering, organizational development, and industrial relations principles and practices. Many union-management partners recognize that quality is a long-term goal that has been pursued successfully but has been inadequately sustained. What is new is the more comprehensive view of quality and the stronger commitment to make it happen.

For unions, a focus on quality is nothing new either. Unions have always favored a high-quality strategy because it leads to higher skills, higher wages, and better working conditions. By being associated with and assisting quality-oriented employers, unions have differentiated themselves in the marketplace. Efforts such as the union label campaign make their appeal to quality. Some employers have always made their reputations based on quality, but changes in the market have made this imperative for more and more employers. Given the overlapping interests of unions and employers, quality is currently a major arena for union-management partnerships.

Initiating a Joint Quality Effort

There seem to be two starting points for a joint quality effort: evolutionary and unilateral. Efforts that evolve from previous joint activities have significant advantages in that the partners are experienced in operating cooperatively and can draw lessons from their experiences. Their relationship has usually matured significantly as well, providing a solid foundation for future efforts.

Unfortunately, some managers overlook or dismiss the value of having a solid foundation. They assert that preexisting joint employee involvement programs, quality circles, or quality of work life efforts are not as important as the quality effort they now want to pursue. Often, employees see, however, that many of the tools and techniques, much of the associated philosophy, and many of the principles of a quality effort are essentially the same as those of earlier ventures. This destructive competition between preexisting joint activities and the new quality effort ultimately has no winners. It damages both preexisting joint activities and the new effort as well, and, in the end, employees are likely to become ever more discouraged about seeing true, meaningful, and lasting change in their workplaces. Union and management partners need to assess carefully whether they foster such destructive attitudes. When the quality effort is viewed as evolutionary, initiation of the new program is more easily and effectively managed.

In a unilateral quality effort, management does not initially consider the union a partner. Sometimes, the union must insist that if management wants to involve bargaining unit employees in "their" effort, they must bargain with the union over the terms and conditions of the employees' involvement. The frequency with which unions have to insist on their rightful role in a quality effort within a unionized workplace indicates two things: the limited understanding some quality gurus and quality consultants have of the legal union-management relationship and their surface understanding of the positive contribution the union can make.

When a quality effort is begun unilaterally, it faces very serious challenges. Managers at all levels may strongly resist sharing control and leadership of "their" quality effort with the union. Some managers may continue to perceive the union as their adversary. It is difficult for such managers to acknowledge the quality arena as common ground when it is perceived as a traditional area of management's rights and responsibilities. A unilateral approach at the beginning makes conflict a self-fulfilling prophecy and the union becomes the adversary. Retrofitting cooperation into an existing unilateral quality program is very difficult.

Even when managers recognize that cooperation with the union is required, the partners must still learn to work cooperatively while implementing their effort. Usually their focus is initially on implementing the quality technology or a methodology. But eventually difficult issues and problems relating to operating jointly are likely to surface. Thus, the union and management should learn not only how to implement the quality technology or methodology but how to operate cooperatively as well. Focusing on a shared vision and on the quality of the effort, not on who initiated it, helps to broaden ownership and the impact of the program.

Development Path for Joint Quality Efforts

As more and more union and management partners pursue quality, a common development path seems to be emerging. This path is illustrated in figure 8.1. Many efforts begin by applying one or more common quality approaches, tools, or techniques, such as statistical process control (SPC), pareto analysis, or root cause analysis. Usually bargaining unit employees and supervisory and management personnel are taught the technique and urged to apply it in doing day-to-day work in their areas.

The use of quality improvement teams or groups is the next step. These groups, usually at the first-line supervisor and rank-and-file level, are organized for the purpose of solving systemic problems and/or to identify opportunities for improvement in their work areas. Very often, these groups are chartered and supported by a higher-level joint governing body that is providing the overall leadership for the joint quality effort. Typically, the groups move from applying a multistep problem-solving

Figure 8.1. Path of Joint Quality Effort

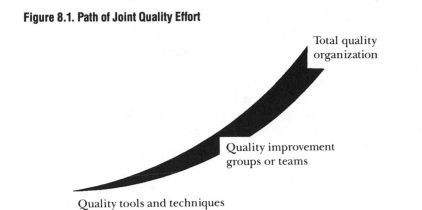

Total quality
organization

Quality improvement
groups or teams

Quality tools and techniques

process to single issues to applying a process improvement approach in which they define customers needs and requirements and explore how well current work processes deliver products and/or services to meet those needs. This shift from problem solving alone to problem solving and process improvement seems to occur naturally as organizations search for more significant results.

Finally, the union and management partners pursue total quality management or seek to make their operations total quality organizations. The U.S. Office of Management and Budget (OMB) defines TQM in the federal sector as "a total organizational approach for meeting customer needs and expectations that involves all managers and employees in using quantitative methods to improve continuously the organization's processes, products, and services." This definition is applicable to both public and private sector organizations. The OMB went on to explain TQM as:

> a comprehensive way to achieve high performance and improve quality by examining the way work gets done in a systematic, consistent, organization-wide perspective. This focus is on increasing value to the customer by ensuring that all work processes are able to provide the service that customers want. Inherent in quality improvement is:
> a) The avoidance of rework due to errors, unclear procedures, or other causes;
> b) Continuous improvement in reducing cycle time; and
> c) The elimination of non-value added work.[5]

As union-management partners move along the development path, at least four changes occur in the work organization.

The levels and extent of organizational involvement in the quality effort increase as the scope of the effort broadens. As the emphasis shifts from adopting basic quality tools and techniques to establishing quality improvement groups and finally to TQM or TQO, more parts of the organization become involved in quality efforts and unite behind a shared quality vision.

The degree of organizational change increases. Very often as a joint effort develops, the union-management partners shift from pursuing incremental change to pursuing transformational change. Richard Beckhard, one of the pioneers of organizational change and development, defines transformational change as

1. changes in what drives the organization toward goals such as customer satisfaction or the pursuit of world-class quality;
2. changes in the relationships between and among organizational parts through cooperation and partnership among and between internal and external customers and suppliers;
3. changes in how work is done so that work is organized around service streams or key work processes in which employees work in various groups and teams; and
4. changes in the organizational culture, including norms, values, and reward systems, using employee empowerment, consensus decision making, continuous improvement, and new pay systems.[6]

As TQM is introduced and a wider range of organizational subsystems are included, the complexity and impact of the changes increase. The contribution of each subsystem to and alignment with the quality vision, organizational direction, and culture becomes part of the total process of transformation.

The extent and consistency of employee involvement increase. As more employees become involved in the quality effort, improvement becomes a way of life, "standard operating procedure." Involvement moves from a part-time to a full-time responsibility for all employees. This often signals the formation of a team-based organization.

The strategic focus of the quality effort becomes clearer, more specific, and more refined. Quality eventually is positioned as the vehicle for achieving the desired direction of the organization. The products and services, work processes and procedures, technology, and human resources together form a unified whole.

Usually, joint quality techniques used early in the effort are incorporated and/or integrated into the techniques used later. When the partners recognize and feel greatly hampered by the limitations of an earlier approach, they try another approach they believe will overcome their limitations. Pursuing joint quality this way is thus based on the belief that quality will improve when individuals and groups apply quality approaches in the routine pursuit of their work. The focus is on improving what already is. There is little or no exploration of whether decidedly different production or service processes should be substituted. This smoothes out some of the bugs and snags in a system, but the impact is not usually felt in the overall organization. The adoption of quality approaches, tools, and techniques can be a sound first step; however, its limitations as the primary approach to quality soon become evident.

Relying on quality improvement groups or teams has similar limitations. They are not really an advance over quality circles when they are the primary strategy used to achieve quality. Rarely will they transform the organization. The assumption that good things spread because they are good is only that: an assumption. Structural and system changes ingrain change; a few good examples do not. In many workplaces, quality teams have been a starting point for joint quality efforts, but often larger, more powerful forces work against the quality improvement group or team, such as the need to cross over organizational boundaries to implement their solution or strategy. Using a problem-solving approach also has limitations because it has limited impact on day-to-day behavior. For example, problem solving alone does not address the need to align the work process with customer needs and requirements. Many organizations begin with a problem-solving approach but add a process improvement approach later.

Even when a combination of a problem-solving and a process improvement approach is used, the union and management partners may feel that a more comprehensive quality model is needed, especially if they want to make all of their workplace systems, including compensation, performance appraisal, and labor relations, targets of their quality effort. In this case, it may well be necessary to pursue total quality management or to become a total quality organization.

In the process of development, a joint quality effort may become linked to two other workplace innovations: new work systems and alternative compensation systems. As process or systems analysis is applied to work processes, exactly how work is performed is analyzed. This analysis can lead to job redesign or a restructuring of the production or service delivery process. Such a redesign redefines how employees are organized and enabled to produce the product or deliver the service. For the redesign phase, the union and management partners may want to consider using natural work teams or semiautonomous or autonomous work groups. New work systems, discussed in chapter 6, are often a natural development of a joint quality effort.

Similarly, the joint quality effort may become linked to alternative pay or reward systems. Providing effective recognition is critical to the success of any quality effort. As the quality partners search for ways to provide recognition and reward, they often reexamine their current reward and recognition systems. They are likely to consider small group–based incentive systems, gainsharing, pay for performance, and/or pay for knowledge. Union and management partners should learn about new work systems and alternative pay or reward systems as their joint quality effort progresses to determine whether these innovations would be valuable additions to their quality efforts.

Experiences with Joint Quality Efforts

The first winner of the Malcolm Baldrige National Quality Award in 1989 was the Xerox Corporation's Business Products and Systems Division, whose union partner was the Amalgamated Clothing and Textile Workers. Together, the company and the union engaged in a long-term change and improvement endeavor that began in the late 1970s with a joint exploration of employee participation options. In 1980, they agreed to experiment with a quality of work life effort. Together, they created a joint governing structure and introduced a six-step problem-solving process within employee problem-solving groups. Their 1983 contract adopted a no-layoff provision and required cost study teams to be formed when outsourcing was being considered.

Also in 1983, Xerox's quality effort, Leadership through Quality (LTQ), introduced a nine-step quality improvement process. This process incorporates planning, organizing, and monitoring for quality. Initially, LTQ was a unilateral, management-driven program. Many inside Xerox perceived that destructive competition and possible conflict was brewing between those involved in the joint QWL effort and those involved in LTQ. Ultimately, the union became part of LTQ. Addressing quality training for union members marked a transition in the effort toward the establishment of common ground.

By 1987, a team-centered reward and recognition program, Team Excellence, was implemented. Two years later, a gainsharing program was established that focused on common goals and customer satisfaction.[7]

Since winning the Baldrige Award, the union and management have concentrated on making Xerox a total quality company. According to David Kearns, chairman of the board of Xerox, this reflects an evolution in the shared definition of quality: "When we first set out, quality was often nothing more than another way of doing better. But today we have graduated. Our highest corporate priority is customer satisfaction. The way we achieve customer satisfaction is through quality, which we define as fully meeting customer requirements." Xerox's quality intensification effort, 10 × Improvement, examines work processes, identifies opportunities to improve these processes, and uses quality tools and techniques to achieve improvement by a factor of ten. Emphasized is the need for all employees to use their quality tools; to clarify corporate goals and bring them down to departmental and individual levels; to implement standardized work processes for data collection; to determine customer requirements; to use data to achieve customer satisfaction; and to prevent as many defects as possible.[8] Xerox's increasing market share is testimony to the success of the effort.

The union and management at Xerox have actively evolved as partners in pursuing quality. Frank J. Wayno, Jr., at Cornell University examined Xerox's long-term process of renewal. The study reached the following conclusions on how to pursue quality together:

1. Develop a vision to guide renewal.
2. Assign a high-level person to facilitate organizational learning and use that information in the development of a vision.
3. Use high-level champions to unfreeze the culture by identifying needed changes and advocating for the new quality approach.
4. Encourage union involvement in all phases of transformation. As a matter of record, David Kearns, Xerox's chairman of the board, said the exclusion of the union initially from LTQ was one of the worst mistakes he made.[9]
5. Create a cadre of dedicated internal change agents.
6. Create mechanisms for information sharing, learning, and catharsis.
7. Create opportunities for people with different "world views" to interact.
8. Recognize that structural change can facilitate cultural change.
9. Create multiple mechanisms for participation.
10. Develop a detailed strategy for change and give it symbolic weight.
11. Recognize that a quality program involves a fundamental re-design of managerial work.
12. Provide specific descriptions of desired behavior when roles are redefined.
13. Recognize that change is facilitated and focused when strategic concepts are expressed as tools. For this endeavor, both the problem-solving process and the quality improvement process (QIP) provide much needed practical definitions of what quality is day-to-day.
14. Cultural change is facilitated by a rigorous process of training. This follows the four-step cascading model for training: learn, use, teach, and inspect (LUTI). Beginning at the very top of the corporation, executives and managers learn quality tools and techniques, apply them in doing their work, then teach

them to subordinates. Subsequently, they inspect and coach their subordinates as they apply the principles to their work. Thus, LTQ is implemented throughout the organization.

15. Create mechanisms to celebrate success.
16. Top-down change is required when the organizational culture must be transformed.
17. Human resource strategy must be an integral part of an overall change strategy.[10]

The experience of the Internal Revenue Service (IRS) and the National Treasury Employees Union (NTEU) provides additional lessons on joint quality efforts from the public sector. In 1987, these two partners signed a Joint Quality Improvement Process (JQIP) agreement, signaling the initiation of the largest public sector joint quality effort, involving more than 100,000 employees nationwide in nearly one thousand locations. The previous year, IRS management had initiated a unilateral quality process via a national quality council. At that time, management had articulated five principles of quality:

- Establish a quality climate where quality is first among equals with schedule and cost;
- Emphasize product and service quality by eliminating systemic flaws during planning, implementation, and operational processes;
- Improve responsiveness to the public and other service components;
- Install a quality improvement process in every field and national office organization, and
- Develop evaluating systems consistent with and reflective of quality principles.

The historic national union-management agreement maintained these principles and provided more specific direction through six joint quality improvement process goals:

1. Develop techniques for problem identification, diagnosis, and resolution.
2. Improve the quality of internal and external work products.
3. Improve the quality of work life.
4. Improve communication among and between management, supervisors, and employees.
5. Enhance the management-employee relationship.
6. Create a process consistent with the Principles of Quality.

A Joint National Quality Council was established to guide and govern the JQIP. Similarly, joint quality councils (JQCs) were established nationwide in every IRS office, replacing any preexisting management-only quality councils. The JQCs chartered quality improvement process teams to address significant problems within each office, using a problem-solving process similar to Xerox's.

The dual challenge of working cooperatively and providing joint leadership of the quality effort proved to be very demanding. The formal transition from a unilateral to a joint effort had literally taken place overnight. The newly constituted joint quality councils inherited QIP teams chartered by their predecessors, the unilateral quality councils. In some locations they also inherited hard feelings about management's attempts to involve bargaining unit employees in the quality effort without involving the union. A massive, systemwide education and training effort was initiated as a major way to support the transition and to further the JQIP. Joint trainers provided training to the joint quality councils and to union and management facilitators of the process.

At different paces, all of the joint quality councils got on track and chartered QIP teams and educated the employee population more broadly about quality. As the entire organization became informed about quality and more committed to it, an interesting challenge to the two partners developed. As managers tried to enhance the pursuit of quality, they developed a variety of quality activities outside those of the formal joint quality improvement process. This prompted questions about the relationship of these activities to the JQIP and how bargaining unit employees could or should participate. Ultimately, an addendum to the agreement defined the boundaries of the two efforts and spelled out procedures for notification and communication about management-initiated quality efforts.

Several IRS units won the President's Quality Improvement Prototype Award. In announcing the award, James C. Miller III, director of the U.S. Office of Management and Budget, in 1988 stated: "A prototype organization demonstrates an extraordinary commitment to quality improvement, focuses attention on satisfying its customers, and establishes high standards of quality, timeliness, and efficiency. This kind of organization also serves as a model for the rest of government—showing how a commitment to quality leads to better and more efficient services and products for its customers."[11]

Since its initiation, the joint quality improvement process has evolved. More quality tools and techniques are now used by the QIP teams and JQCs, and variations of the classic or traditional QIP teams are used. Process analysis is used to understand the IRS's many work processes. The increasingly widespread use of process analysis signaled a need to improve quality systems within the IRS significantly. This led the IRS and the NTEU to examine the value of becoming a total quality organization.

Ultimately, a TQO agreement was signed in 1992, marking the next developmental stage for these partners.

The IRS-NTEU Joint Quality Improvement Process fosters innovative uses of technology to support their effort. A Quality Improvement Information System, established early in their effort, tracks and analyzes all QIP team projects nationwide. The system provides the IRS and the NTEU at all levels around the nation with data on exactly what is occurring. The Manhattan IRS office has participated in an experiment in using computer-based group decision support systems (GDSS). QIP team members use computer terminals in a special meeting room during team meetings to solve problems, prompted by the computer software. The research focuses on how GDSS can be used to facilitate team meetings and a team's work.[12]

Recently, natural work teams have been introduced throughout the IRS. Many see them as a natural outgrowth of the joint experiences with quality improvement and its focus on empowerment. Others see the teams as a prelude to the IRS's becoming a total quality organization. What is amazing and encouraging about all the innovations is that they are nurtured within an extremely large and complex bureaucracy.

Both the Xerox-ACTWU and the IRS-NTEU joint quality efforts are recognized as successes within and outside their organizations. At the same time, both continue to encounter challenges requiring creative and innovative solutions. Union and management leaders acknowledge the need to improve their efforts continually.

Strategic Positioning of Quality

Successful joint quality efforts meet both the union's and management's needs. Unfortunately, some managers expect the union to adopt automatically their views on the business value of quality yet are unwilling to see and respect the union's interests in meeting its members' needs. The union deserves a partnership that allows it to meet its "customer" requirements as well. When quality is properly strategically positioned, union and management leaders can create an imaginative and effective joint effort.

Once union and management leaders establish the importance of quality to both parties, it is essential that they communicate this importance to their constituencies: their employees or members, customers, and suppliers. Employees want to know why quality is important to their union and to their employer and how the quality effort will affect and benefit them. Communicating the strategic needs the quality effort will address is one way to answer why the organization is doing this. Communicating realistic, expected benefits will address why an individual should be involved.

When a joint quality effort is strategically positioned, it can avoid some of the weaknesses encountered in earlier employee participation and/or QWL efforts. Many of these efforts were not framed to meet specific future problems, challenges, or opportunities. They were reactive, not proactive. Even worse, they often operated without a clear direction articulated in long-term goals and specific objectives. As a consequence, many employees did not want to go on these journeys without roadmaps. Further, because there were no objectives or targets, it was impossible to measure accomplishments. These characteristics made these efforts vulnerable to attacks on their usefulness and made it difficult if not impossible to explain their value. An excellent quality effort has compelling reasons for its existence and measurable results provide evidence that it made a difference.

Challenges of Integrating Quality Systems

Management and the union must connect quality efforts with other unilateral or joint change and improvement activities and efforts already under way. Rushing to get an effort going and ignoring other parallel efforts can result in various problems:

1. The joint quality effort may end up competing for scarce organizational resources with other change and improvement efforts.
2. Employees may become confused about what connection, if any, there is between these efforts. This is especially true if some aspects seem similar.
3. In more extreme situations, employees may feel that they have to choose from among competing change and improvement efforts. When the union is excluded from certain efforts, loyalty is tested and strained all the way around.

These problems can be avoided by first assessing the integration potential of the various change and improvement efforts under way. A comprehensive integration assessment will identify and analyze perceived, substantive, and potential overlaps. Next, the union and management partners should explore the options for integration. In most situations, there are at least four such options:

1. Assigning coordination and collaboration of the different efforts, including leadership, guidance, and governance, to one top-level body or network.

2. Consolidating the strategic framework for all the efforts by compiling and using one description of the critical problems, challenges, and opportunities the workplace is facing, as well as its overarching vision and goals. This process aligns the direction of change and improvement efforts for the entire workplace.
3. Integrating as many processes and techniques as possible by deploying generic tools, techniques, and approaches in all the change and improvement efforts. This is not usually very difficult because many of the same tools and techniques are likely to be used already in several efforts. In some situations, this leads to using common training curricula and instructors. Fostering commonality of techniques and processes drives out redundancy and waste and helps maintain a unified organizational focus.
4. Integrating the change and improvement efforts themselves by developing a broad vision of continuous improvement or total quality management. Connecting all of the efforts around a central mission to serve the customer can lead to new perspectives, synergies, and initiatives and revitalize efforts that have plateaued.

At a minimum, the partners in a joint quality effort need to recognize the existence of the other change and improvement efforts and devise a strategy for managing the interfaces or boundaries between them. Ideally, the partners will make a long-range commitment to ensuring that the various efforts work in concert.

Applying Quality Principles to Collective Bargaining

The process of collective bargaining, the relationship on which it is based, and its primary tool, the labor agreement, are part of an organization's labor relations system. Joint quality partners often overlook this important system when applying quality approaches, tools, and techniques. They declare collective bargaining off limits to, a hindrance to, or an enemy of the quality process. At best, this ignores the fundamental quality principle that all subsystems are aligned. At worst, this is an offensive dismissal of the union-management relationship that only increases resistance. When quality approaches are applied to the labor relations system, value is added to the organization, and labor relations and collective bargaining are strengthened.

Benchmarking the labor relations practices of outstanding work organizations can provide management and the union with significant insights into their own labor relations. The union and management partners search for the "best-in-class" labor relations processes and compare them with their own. Through this process, the partners identify improved or superior labor relations practices to adopt.

Quality approaches can also be used to improve the contract administration system. To put it in quality language, if the contract is the standard, grievances identify variances in the system, which can be clues to quality problems in the system itself. The goal is to use grievances as a way to learn how to do things right the first time. The variances can be analyzed, using quality techniques, in several ways:

1. *By topic.* Topical analysis sorts grievances according to the relevant clauses in the contract. A pareto analysis of the number of grievances by topic or contract clause can be used to uncover the most problematic topics or clauses. Cause-and-effect analysis could then be used to determine the causes of the grievances. When a union and management at a major paper mill did this, they discovered that almost 80 percent of all the grievances were generated as a result of an extra procedure within the scheduling system. They further determined that this situation was worsened by the existence of department-specific versions of the procedure that added complexity and confusion to the situation. Together, management and the union concluded that adopting a simplified, mill-wide procedure might reduce the number of grievances and conflict on the shop floor and improve the effectiveness and efficiency of the employee work-scheduling system.

2. *By work unit generating the grievances.* Grievances can be an indication of larger, more systemic problems in the labor-management relationship. Once again, application of pareto analysis can uncover those few work units generating the majority of grievances. From here, the joint quality partners can analyze what is happening in those units. Root cause analysis can be done to determine why so many conflicts in these units are not being resolved.

3. *By percentage of grievances resolved at the different levels of the system.* Analyzing grievance resolution by levels is another way to analyze the performance of the labor relations system and to identify systemic problems. Ideally, both the union and management have a strong interest in resolving grievances at the lowest possible level, (i.e., before or at the first level). Relatively few grievances should move to the third or fourth level for resolution. Sadly, in some workplaces, a high percentage of grievances routinely move to these levels. Worse yet, the parties involved believe that the third or fourth level is the only arena for grievance resolution.

4. *By the time it takes for resolution to be achieved.* Analyzing the time it takes to handle grievances can also lead to new insights. Doing this analysis may uncover opportunities to reduce the time in the cycle and speed up the resolution process. Quality improvement teams or groups

can analyze more deeply problems and improvement opportunities within the grievance handling process. As a result, the "customers" of the process, the grievants, will have speedier, more complete resolution of their concerns.

Analysis of the grievance handling process can also uncover opportunities to apply quality approaches to the contract administration system. When high percentages of grievances go beyond the first level for resolution, it may indicate that neither supervisors nor union stewards are empowered to resolve grievances. Supervisors and stewards are supposed to have the authority to take action on grievances and, if possible, to resolve them. As contracts become more complex or the union-management relationship deteriorates, companies and unions too often decide formally or informally that supervisors and stewards should not resolve grievances themselves. This approach to contract administration flies in the face of the basic quality principle that the people closest to a problem should solve it. Empowering first-level managers and union representatives to resolve grievances and to address problems at their level in the union-management relationship can result in significant improvements in contract administration.

Initiating this empowerment process can be a simple two-step process. First, supervisors and stewards may need additional knowledge and skills relating to problem solving, communications, and leadership. Joint supervisor-steward training can be designed for this purpose. Second, supervisors and stewards need to develop a common understanding of the current labor contract, company policies, and union policies. Joint orientation sessions can be given for this purpose. Such sessions are especially effective if they are led by managers and union leaders who model the kind of collaborative and cooperative behavior they would like to see stewards and supervisors demonstrate daily in their work. Managers, union leaders, supervisors, and stewards can agree to use continuous analysis of the grievance handling procedure to measure the impact of this empowerment process.

Labor relations professionals from both parties should be encouraged to support joint quality efforts from the beginning. Too often, after declaring collective bargaining and contract administration off limits to the effort, they are excluded from direct involvement. As a result, they continue to work from very traditional, adversarial models of union-management relations. At best, they are perceived as out of sync with the changes occurring. At worst, they may reinforce behaviors that are damaging or work at cross purposes to the quality effort. These behaviors include limiting communication and the flow of information to enhance tactical advantage; approaching shared problems with a win-lose attitude; attacking people, not problems; and slowing grievance resolution processes to gain tactical advantages. Union leaders will begin to feel whipsawed as they ricochet back and forth between the joint quality arena, where they are valued stakeholders, and the traditional labor relations arena, where they are too often the disreputable enemy.

Ideally, both the union and the company will recognize the need for a new model of labor-management relations. Often this recognition comes only after problems have flared between participants in the joint quality effort and people in labor relations. Labor relations professionals from both parties need to understand what is occurring in the joint quality arena and its rationale. They should be involved in determining how to support both the labor relations system and the joint quality effort. If the joint quality effort evolves to a point where new work systems and/or alternative compensation systems are being considered, these professionals can add significant value by contributing their expertise in the areas of work design and compensation. If they have been isolated from the joint quality effort or, worse yet, are perceived as its enemies, they will not be ready or ever given the chance to assist in the transition to new work systems and/or alternative compensation systems.

Collective bargaining is probably the oldest union-management problem-solving process in existence. Many lessons can be learned from a careful examination of the process. These lessons can add value to a joint quality effort. Strategic bargaining can be used to encourage alignment of the goals and processes of labor relations with an organization's commitment to quality. Conversely, quality approaches can be applied to the collective bargaining process and labor relations, and significantly improve them as a result. Opportunities to strengthen the collective bargaining process and its integrity should not be overlooked by any serious union-management partners pursuing quality.

Conclusion

A quality effort can be an excellent way to showcase how union-management cooperation contributes to competitiveness and customer satisfaction. It can provide a broad, cohesive vision for change and a systemic reconfiguration of structures, people, and the work culture that is truly enabling and empowering. The union and management should both be vigilant, however, when pursuing quality efforts. There are real hazards, risks, and potential losses associated with them. Too often, quality gurus and their converts are so taken with quality that they are blinded to its demands and dangers.[13] Some go so far as to assert that other important workplace goals, such as equal opportunity, safety and health, community support and involvement, and cultural diversity, are secondary to a passionate commitment to quality. This singular focus is dangerous and antidemocratic. At the same time, perversions of quality should not be a barrier to considering the value of joint quality approaches. The key to success is to position quality efforts solidly within the collective bargaining relationship on a foundation of union-management cooperation.

Part III. The Design of Effective Union-Management Cooperative Efforts

9. First Steps: Deciding Whether to Cooperate and Getting Started

T he first steps in developing a cooperative program are the hardest. The initial steps of conducting a feasibility assessment, building strong commitment and involvement, setting motivating goals and objectives, making deliberate choices on whether to proceed, and developing a clear design are often rushed through or never done. Later, these omissions and oversights cause serious problems. Lasting change rarely occurs overnight. Good cooperative programs follow a process that unfolds deliberately and systematically (figure 9.1) to ensure that all the steps are thoughtfully and adequately addressed. The steps in the process of getting started are identified in figure 9.2. Most importantly, the partners should not let a crisis or anxiousness to see results lead to shortcuts in the process. A knee-jerk approach to management or union leadership may well be what got the organization into its current fix. More of the same is unlikely to make it better.

There is only one precondition to examining joint programs: respect. If management wishes to decertify the union or the union is out to oust management, there is little point in proceeding; cooperation is not possible. The parties do not need to like each other or even trust each other to get started. They need to want change.

Figure 9.1. Cycle of Labor-Management Program Success

Exploring the Motivation for Change

Typically, something or a set of circumstances motivates one or both parties to look at cooperative approaches. Rarely do organizations anticipate the need for cooperation, although this is preferable. More often than not, some crisis precipitates one or both parties to suggest a cooperative approach.

A frank understanding of the forces motivating the suggestion to cooperate is helpful and should inform the selection of goals and objectives. The range of possible motivations is infinite. If the problem is an imminent cutback or shutdown, one set of strategies may be necessary. If market conditions or customer demands for quality are changing, other approaches may be called for. Sometimes the issues are bad morale and communication. If the motivation is a desire to be in on the latest fad, then trouble is ahead.

A perceived need to change is an important element of successful union-management cooperation. Without a clear understanding of the need to change—either by taking advantage of new opportunities or recognizing common challenges—the parties will falter in or fake joint

Figure 9.2. Getting Started

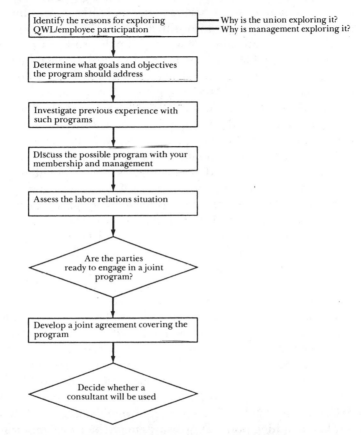

activities. Jointly understanding the motivations of the other party and its perceptions of the need for change opens up dialogue and cooperative possibilities. Too often the parties have incomplete or wrong assumptions about the motivations of the other party; both then have difficulty seeing their common forest as they hide behind their own trees. Until there is a common understanding of the need for change, building commitment is difficult at best. Without this understanding, the parties can't answer the key question "why"?

Determining Mutual Goals and Objectives

Union-management cooperative programs should do something worthwhile or not be done at all. If a cooperative program is entered into only to appease or solely to get along, the parties will soon have to answer uncomfortable questions about lack of enthusiasm and participation.

The closer the goals and objectives are to the central goals and objectives of the union and management partners, the more likely the joint effort will be maintained and result in positive accomplishments. Tangential issues dealing with the amenities of work or simple problems will not get the time and attention that central issues receive. Even if tangential issues are pursued "successfully," many do not care about the results. Some argue that cooperation should be built by first accomplishing something easy. Generally, this does not work. All this proves is that cooperative efforts can be used to tackle unimportant or facile issues; it does not breed respect for the process or a desire to use it. At the same time, the goals for initial consideration should be manageable and within the span of control of the parties involved. For example, a local steel mill may want to address unfair trade competition. The local union and management can be part of a response fashioned by an industry group or national union, but the issue is unlikely to be resolved locally. The goals should be both important and attainable. Programs should be tailored to meet real organizational needs; goals should not be squished into the confines of the particular technique being presented.

Some of the important objectives management might have are an improved financial or market picture, better quality and reliability, and/ or improved customer service. Management has a legitimate obligation to suggest that cooperative strategies be employed for cost reduction and productivity enhancement; that is part of management's job. Other objectives might be improved supervision, communications, skills development, teamwork, and flexibility to meet changing conditions. Improved profitability is often an important management goal in the private sector. Meeting legislated or departmental mandates more fully and effectively and handling political pressures might be more important in the public sector.

The union will also have many objectives. These might be giving workers a greater say in the workplace and employing their minds as well as their bodies. Other objectives might be improved health and safety, reduced problems with supervision, increased job satisfaction, increased access to information, and better union-management relations. A desire to help expand production or service in order to generate new jobs or to take a hard look at contracted-out services to see which can be provided better inside are other possible union objectives. The union might want to take a larger role in handling the over 90 percent of union members' problems that are not clearly addressed through grievances in the contract. Improving job security, working conditions, and the size of the pie available for bargaining often form the core objectives for the union.

To get started, the union and management need to have only one objective in common. With adjustments for complexity, the scope of cooperation is a function of the range of common goals and objectives. The parties do not have to agree on all of one another's objectives and goals. They can agree to disagree respectfully. At the least, at this initial stage, management should agree that working on objective X is in its interest and the union should agree that working on objective X is in its interest. They then agree to work on objective X together.

There is no more critical element for a successful joint union-management effort than having a definition of the common goals and objectives. Without this, cooperation is impossible. Goals describe in general terms what the partners want to accomplish; the objectives describe the specific targets of the effort. A common framework is to develop SMART objectives: ones that are specific, measurable, actionable, realistic, and time limited. Grandiose and florid statements may sound marvelous, but they mean little in the long run. Without shared specific goals and objectives, one party will expect certain things to be done while the other has different expectations. Real conflict between the union and management can develop. The more vague or unstated the goals, the greater the potential for confusion in management and union ranks. Further, rivals in either party can seize on the general or vague statements to undercut accomplishments or credit.

To determine joint goals, management and the union should each outline its goals. They then exchange lists and look for overlap. In some cases, the lists will be similar and can be fused. Sometimes items on one party's list will be acceptable or even welcome to the other party. There will probably also be items on which they do not agree. In the future, they may agree on some of these goals—or they may never agree. It is not worth aborting the process over areas of disagreement. Next, they prioritize the items that are agreed on and develop specific objectives to describe how these goals can become actionable.

Many parties use a process in which they develop goals together. Though we understand the motivation for this as a display of jointness, as a matter of practice it results in conflict avoidance, doubts about the real goals of the other party, and wishy-washy goals.

Over the past few years there has been considerable discussion of vision and mission as important elements of organizational success. Goals are viewed as strategic or tactical. We discuss elsewhere in greater depth how to develop strategic goals and participatory vision. As a rule, the more strategic the goal setting, the better. Thus, joint goals should be rooted in a broad understanding of the business, the union, the market, and the community. Vision and mission statements artfully crafted by labor and management off-site rarely have the same power when communicated to other workers and managers back home. Hence, it is important to link the vision, mission, and goals clearly to the language and concerns voiced normally by the parties and to involve the work force broadly in defining and understanding joint statements of purpose.

Not developing specific objectives is often a way to avoid working through the conflict necessary to arrive at specific and mutually agreeable objectives. The temptation to leave objectives ambiguous almost always comes back like a boomerang and hits the parties in the head. Without specific goals and objectives, they cannot adequately design and plan, develop effective training, communicate clearly, and monitor and evaluate effectively. In short, they cannot do well what it takes to make a joint program work well.

Examining the Organizational Climate

A clear assessment of the organizational climate is useful in deciding what kinds of cooperation, if any, are possible. Often called a *feasibility assessment* or an *organizational diagnosis*, it can be conducted internally and/or with outside help, separately and/or jointly by management and the union. In settings with multiple unions, each union may engage in its own analysis, but the various unions should coordinate as much as possible. A feasibility assessment lets the parties know whether or not they have a chance of success. Rarely is there *no* chance; the assessment informs the parties of the areas on which they are most likely to succeed. An organizational diagnosis focuses on critical problems or opportunities and the resources and constraints affecting any effort. Information for an assessment or diagnosis can be gathered through structured interviews, questionnaires, and/or a review of such organizational sources as profit and loss statements or summaries of grievance reports and safety records. An outside assessment cannot provide expert answers to all that is wrong in an organization, but it can assist insiders in the development of direction and insight.

We have conducted structured interviews with equal numbers of people from both management and unions and have found the following areas helpful to consider: possible goals and objectives; areas that need improvement and areas going well; the labor-management relationship; the current level of cooperation and innovation; how a cooperative program might be structured, governed, and managed; existing training and training needs; communications patterns; and both the forces working in favor of and against the success of a program.

Open discussion of all the issues is necessary on both sides of the table. Managers should seek the counsel of other managers at all levels on the possible nature of a joint effort. It is important that *all* the power brokers in management have some say in the initial decision and design of any cooperative program. The union should discuss it with its membership and key leadership. Unions may want to hold special sessions to get input from the membership. The more open the process, the less long-term resistance to the program there will be on either side. Sometimes, seeking information from a diagonal slice through the organization chart is used to obtain varied and sufficient employee input.

Timing is important. New top executives need time to become acclimated to their new positions, so that just after their arrival may not be a good time to initiate a cooperative program. Likewise, just before a union election is generally a bad time. Nor should the issue generally be broached at the end of the contract period. There are always excuses for why *now* is a bad time to initiate cooperative efforts. These reasons, some valid and some not, must be recognized as potential barriers and addressed seriously. The present is the moment to begin getting better, and since there is never a perfect time to begin, you might as well start as soon as possible.

The more open-minded the parties and the more data-based the readiness process, the better everyone will be at answering common questions, and all parties will have a solid basis for making decisions. Organizations of every stripe and with all manner of labor-management relations have engaged in cooperative programs—some successfully and some not. The feasibility or readiness assessment helps improve the likelihood of success by making the parties aware of circumstances or past situations that will require increased thought and attention.

Analyzing the Union-Management Relationship

There are two types of workplaces where employee involvement and cooperation programs seem to be most concentrated—those with very bad labor relations and those with very good labor relations. There have been remarkable success stories of cooperative programs at workplaces with very bad labor relations. If the relationship is poor, this must be recognized, and one of the objectives for the program has to be the improvement of the relationship. Under these circumstances, it may take a while to build a respectful relationship and get started.

Over the years, we have increasingly seen the critical importance of focusing upfront on the union-management relationship. When communication is bad and the relationship frayed, it is difficult to hear information clearly or to see in an unrefracted manner what needs to be done. A good relationship is not an end in itself, but accomplishing tasks is more difficult and sometimes impossible when the relationship is bad. Some parties hide from relationship problems, assuming that doing things together will resolve all their problems. It rarely works that way.

In other situations, the relationship is generally good. In these work-places, cooperative efforts are generally viewed as a way both to involve the union and the membership more fully and to enhance organizational performance. An assumption is frequently made that what worked well in the past will work well for the new program and the necessary training and structures are watered down. This is a big mistake; new skills and new structures are often necessary for a new program to succeed *even in the best of circumstances*.

Sometimes there is an expectation on the part of one party that before a cooperative program can be started there has to be sainthood in the collective bargaining setting. This is absolutely unrealistic. Cooperative and adversarial labor relations can and will occur simultaneously. The hope is that, over time, the collective bargaining relationship will im-prove, but this is too much to expect from the start. The reason for engaging in joint activity is not to get the other party to act a certain way but to cooperate to enhance both party's interests, including one's own. Cooperation doesn't promise perfection, just a common commitment to achieving significant improvement.

Reviewing Previous Cooperative Efforts

Past is prologue. Too often, lessons from the past are not assimilated into plans for the future. Vexingly, with each new program the same problems tend to recur time and again. Amnesia sets in, and to avoid painful memories and recriminations, the disasters of the past are not analyzed. Often proponents of a program are at a loss to explain specifi-cally why their program is "not like all of those other programs that failed in the past." It's no wonder that the lack of clear differentiation between current ideas and past failed programs leads many to be skeptical.

Previous and ongoing cooperative efforts must be examined to deter-mine what outcomes or consequences occurred and whether they were desirable or undesirable. For example, an organization considering a total quality program may previously have had a joint health and safety committee or quality circles. Or an organization considering estab-lishing a labor-management committee may previously have worked on a community fund drive for the United Way. The parties should learn if the programs had the desired effects. A simple technique is to have the parties make a list of each program and discuss what went well and what went poorly.

In addition to looking at the results of previous programs, the parties should review the process of doing each program—the startup, design process, governance, program management, training, communications, monitoring, and evaluation—to see what was done correctly and incorrectly. Make a list identifying the critical areas for each program and again identify and discuss what went well and what could have been improved. Identify the lessons gained from these experiences.

Mistakes and failures of the past should not be so disturbing as to be barriers to starting a new program. Situations may have changed. The biggest mistake, however, is not to learn from mistakes. What each party learns can be used to plan and implement a better program that meets current specified goals and objectives.

Looking at the Experiences of Others

Though each organization is unique and may come up with a unique design, it is important to learn from others. There are generally two groups to seek out—those in other parts of one's own organization and those in other organizations. Other units in one's own company, government department, or union may have engaged in similar cooperative activities. It is worth consulting with both their managements and unions to find out how they went about their activities, what went well, and what they would change if they did the activities again. In some large organizations, there are basic guidelines for labor-management cooperation and employee participation that must be followed, and these should be reviewed and discussed.

Other companies, agencies, or unions in the area may have engaged in similar cooperative efforts. Many are probably open to visits and sharing their experiences. Such groups can be found through directories of programs published by the U.S. Department of Labor and through Canada Labour. In North America, national groups such as the Association for Quality and Participation have data bases and information clearinghouses. In addition, many states, provinces, and cities have associations dedicated to the development of labor-management programs. A union can contact its international headquarters or regional staff for information on other locals and unions that have engaged in cooperative programs. In addition, college programs of labor studies or industrial relations may have individuals who are knowledgeable about such programs.

Visiting other sites can be a good way to learn about cooperative programs. Management and labor representatives can go together but may want to reserve some time to be alone with their counterparts. Visits are a favorite activity at the beginning of new efforts, although there are significant issues to consider. Taking a large number of people is often expensive, and the return does not always justify the cost. It can also send a message that labor and management are "cozy," which can fuel rumors among those who are distrustful of cooperation. Further, most program participants put on their best face, and often the visitors don't have enough experience yet to ask questions or to understand the answers that are most critical. Visiting high-quality programs well prepared with questions is the best approach.

In the absence of a visit, a telephone interview and written case studies can be helpful, as can videos or teleconferences. After reviewing such materials, the group is better able to decide whether to invest in an on-site meeting.

Regardless of what approach is used, write down the questions the union and management want answered and check out how the other organization progressed through the various phases of its program. Copycat programs rarely work. Learn from the experiences of others, but avoid mimicry. That another organization succeeded but omitted an important element, for example, may not speak to the value of the step but local politics, lack of awareness of its relevance, or just luck. Not every group has the same problems. Successes may not be the same either.

Gauging Commitment

Determining the depth of commitment on both sides is very difficult. It comes down to weighing whether there is enough respect between the two parties to proceed and assessing the importance of the issues. There are some tangible signs to look for, however. First, there should be top-level sanction and involvement on both sides. Its absence points to limited commitment and a much more difficult process of implementing changes.

Second, adequate resources should be available. A program run on the cheap will wind up with tinsel outcomes. Extravagance is not necessary, but the employer must be willing to pay for the time involved and the training needed to run an effective program. The program is a way of meeting important business or operational objectives. Paid work time should be available. Implementing some ideas is going to cost money. Management must be willing to give those ideas full consideration.

Assessing the Risks and Benefits

No situation is risk-free. If all that is seen is the potential gains of cooperation, then everyone is wearing rose-colored glasses. There are always risks in any new enterprise, especially sensitive initiatives like cooperative programs. Yet if all that anyone sees are possible problems, then everyone is being too pessimistic and adopting too narrow a perspective. It is essential, however, that the parties assess both the benefits and the risks. Don't just subtract the number of risks from the number of the benefits before deciding whether to proceed. The risks and benefits may carry different weight based on their importance. For example, in assessing a team work proposal, the risk of accidents while learning new skills may be more important than the risk that timecards will not be gathered correctly at the beginning of the program. The parties have an obligation to see what can be done to maximize the benefits and minimize the risks. It may be possible to put safeguards into an agreement to reduce the risks.

The process of risk and benefit assessment involves each party listing all the potential risks for them *and* for the other party. All the worries and concerns should be laid out on the table. Look at worst-case scenarios. Who would be taking which risks? Then list all the potential benefits. Who would receive which benefits? You can develop a group census on the relative strengths of the risks and benefits by rating each one on a scale of 1 to 10. Talk about why people feel that their scores reflect potential reality. You may not have been aware of certain dangers or have thought of certain safeguards; be open to changing your opinion. As a group, divide the list into three categories: major, possible, and minor. Think hard about how to minimize the major and possible risks and reap the benefits. It is often a good idea to share your lists to learn of the concerns of the other party. Frequently, they are similar or mirror images. The other party might also have creative solutions that you didn't consider. Remember that the key question is not how much of a benefit the other party will get but whether your return is worthwhile.

When all the information is in, a "go" or "no-go" decision must be made. If the parties have engaged in the previous steps, they will be able to make a considered judgment. The process of reaching that decision will inform everything the parties wish to do in the future. If the decision is to proceed, each needs to accept responsibility for the decision and make the process work. Shortcutting the necessary steps to a decision leads to lower levels of commitment and less informed choices. From here on, we make the assumption that the parties have decided to proceed, while recognizing that some may choose to bow out at this time.

Arriving at a Written Agreement

If the program is worth doing, it is worth putting the basic understanding and safeguards in writing. Union-management partners have long known the value of having written agreements. Without them, programs depend precariously on personalities. Inequalities in power can wreak havoc. Vague verbal exchanges make it more difficult to maintain long-term commitment and access to resources.

The first part of the agreement should be an expression of the willingness of the two parties to work jointly and equally on all aspects of the program. The second section should specify the goals and objectives of the effort. Frequently this section also covers the guiding principles and values of the effort. The third section should contain clear statements on basic safeguards built into the program. Often included are prohibitions against violations of the grievance procedure, loss of employment, downgrading of positions, or increased worker stress caused by the program. In some cases, the agreement specifies whether the program is an experiment for a limited time period or considered permanent. Some agreements also contain an exit clause specifying how the parties can get out of the program should they decide to do so.

Considering a Consultant

Consultants are not always necessary for the development of a cooperative project. Whether one is needed has to do with the complexity of the program and the labor-management situation. If the relationship between labor and management is bad, a mutually trusted third party might be helpful. If the skills needed to accomplish a program are not resident in the employer or the union, a consultant can help fill the gap.

Jointly interview potential consultants to determine their perspective, experience, and approach. Beware of consultants who will do everything for you and have quick and easy solutions. Following canned approaches leads to dependence on the consultant and simplistic analysis. The consultant should be knowledgeable about collective bargaining and understand how to handle constructive conflict. Too often human resources or organizational development consultants have little understanding of unions or the collective bargaining process and have a Pollyannalike perspective on conflict. These consultants may be personally endearing but believe that unions are necessary only because there is bad management. For them, unions are not integral to the success or operation of an organization.

Seek consultants who are evenhanded and able to deal well with both parties. Check out their references with both management and labor at places where they have worked. The consultant should be agreeable to both parties and perceive both as equal clients even if management is picking up the tab. Sometimes union-busting consultants work in unionized workplaces and try to portray themselves as friendly to unions. Their activities can blow a program apart and cast aspersions on the real motivations for the effort. More importantly, they don't really believe in union-management cooperation. Consultants who can see only the union perspective should also be avoided.

Remember when hiring a consultant that the program must remain controlled by the labor-management partners, not by the consultant.

Good consultants will have a clear plan of how they will work with you and work themselves out of a job at your location. They will help build skills at your location to maintain the effort in a high-quality way. As clients, the union and management should have a clear idea of what they want the consultant to do, thereby being cost-effective and directed. The greater the clarity of the contract between the consultant and the labor-management partners, the better the working relationship.

Conclusion

Good union-management cooperative efforts stem from a realistic understanding of the motivations for working together and from mutually acceptable goals and objectives. Setting important and realistic goals and objectives provides the centerpiece for the effort. The decision to proceed should take into consideration the current organizational climate, the labor-management relationship, previous cooperative efforts, the experience of others, and the level of internal commitment. All of these factors should be reviewed to determine the risks and benefits to the employer and the union. The parties should seriously consider ways to minimize the risks and maximize the benefits before making a go or no-go decision. Finally, they should write an agreement setting out the directions, understandings, and safeguards of the effort. In some cases, consultants will be used to help aid the process.

Adopting these first steps before entering a program will inform the entire process. Firm foundations have been set and a sturdy framework has been erected. Those who stop at this stage know what the barriers to cooperation are. Those who proceed beyond this stage are firmly grounded and ready to undertake a serious and important joint effort.

10. Setting Clear Direction: Designing and Planning an Effective Union-Management Cooperative Program

H aving decided to proceed with a cooperative effort, it is now time to turn the common goals into reality. The first step in this process is to design the program.

The program design describes the particular approach to cooperation the union and management partners will use. It also describes the specific techniques to be used in the program, such as quality improvement groups, labor-management committees, autonomous work teams, task forces, bargaining study teams, and the like. One can think of the program design as the program's blueprint. It lays out the broad framework for the program. It should present both "elevations," to show the different layers of the program, and the details of each "room" or aspect of the overall approach. The design process ensures that there is the closest fit possible between all the organizations involved and their desired goals.

The highest level of the management and union concerned with the issues to be addressed in the program should be involved in its design. These are usually the people who formulated the agreement to go forward. Other management and union representatives can also participate in this phase. Too often top leaders are not engaged in the design process and then chop out necessary elements when a design is presented. Delegation reduces commitment and ownership by the key players.

Figure 10.1. Designing a Program

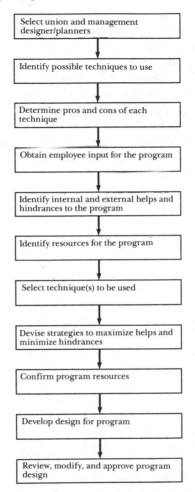

Both union and management designers should be directly and equally involved in every step of formulating the design of the program (see fig. 10.1). Typically, the designers work together in small committees and/or in union-management pairs. Management should not do the design alone. An internal or external consultant may assist the designers, but the program design should not be put together solely by a consultant. He or she should be strictly a technical resource. It is the internal parties' program, and it must fit their own situation.

Exactly how long the design phase will take will vary from location to location, depending on the range of common objectives and the scale of the cooperative agreement, as well as the particular characteristics of the employer and the union. For a simple program, the design should not take long; for a more complex one, it will take longer. Careful design of a cooperative program is an essential and critical step in a successful program. Adequate time must be set aside to do the design well.

Too often, the design step is rushed through or skipped over in favor of accepting a prefabricated design. This is usually done for understandable reasons. The parties do not trust their own knowledge of how to design a program and want to get things moving quickly. The premise of a union-management activity, however, is that experience and knowledge inside the organization can be drawn on for decision making. This knowledge, which even the best outsider cannot have, is critical to designing a program. One can learn much from others, but rushing into a program or not making proper adjustments for the local environment can cause long-term delays, muted performance, or outright failures.

Most joint programs teach a problem-solving technique for examining alternative solutions. The design process presented here models and mirrors that deliberate analytical approach to organizational change.

Over the years, we have seen that a common, if not universal, problem of cooperative programs is the assumption that there is one best approach forever. Often the parties arrive at fairly ambitious goals and objectives and then limit their thinking about alternative approaches and techniques. For ongoing programs, there is an assumption that they have to ride the one horse they hopped on in the beginning until the bitter end. In fact, we often encounter anger at the suggestion that the parties reexamine their approach. In some cases, no one even remembers why or how it was chosen. Such tunnel vision limits the potential for success. Both initially and later on, an open-minded approach to examining alternatives serves the parties well.

Being able to justify design decisions based on solid data and analysis provides a great start to a process aimed at creating more systematic thinking in the organization. Make your entire design process as data-based as possible. Link it clearly to goals, key criteria, and data about your organization. Use the data generated from employees as a way to make the design process a dialogue with them. This shows respect for employees and leads to better outcomes.

The design process works best if the steps outlined below are followed:

1. *Use the goals and objectives for the program as the basis for the design.* The design is meant to show how goals and objectives will be accomplished. The statement of goals and objectives should provide a reference point for *every* part of the development of a joint program. The design process is the first time they are put to use.

2. *Develop criteria for examining various options for participation.* Ideally, you will develop no more than six to eight such criteria. Critical areas to

consider include the level of the organization where the program will operate, the necessary level of sanction, kinds and numbers of employees who are or can be involved, resources needed, issues addressed, time commitments, training requirements, success and failure records, results generally obtained, impact on collective bargaining, staffing requirements, length of the problem-solving process, potential use with different kinds of employees in the organization, costs, impact on employment, and effect on personnel allocation and compensation. For example, continuous improvement processes often require a longer and more regular problem-solving strategy than labor-management committees. It is simplest to create a chart with the techniques along one axis and the key factors in evaluating them along the other. This will facilitate comparisons. Criteria screening can also be done by creating numerical scores for how well each technique will accomplish your goal(s) or fit your situation. When analyzing across factors, you can establish a weighting factor to account for the relative importance of the different criteria.

3. *Identify all the cooperative and participative techniques that could be used to meet all or part of the goals and objectives.* Examine at least three approaches. Stopping at two backs the group into either/or decisions. Many of these techniques and approaches are discussed in part II of this book. Table 10.1 lists objectives and problem areas and possible approaches. You may want to divide into subgroups to gather information. Not all the approaches will work in every organization, and some may need to be linked to other approaches. Exercise imagination in looking at the possibilities, and be open to combining features of several techniques or making modifications.

You may need to do additional research on some techniques. Information may be available from books and articles in an in-house library at work or the union, from libraries at a local college or in the community, or through on-line databases. Other information may be available through local, state, provincial, and regional productivity and quality of work life centers; professional associations, such as the Association for Quality and Participation; labor studies centers, industrial relations programs, or business schools; union or corporate headquarters; consulting firms specializing in this area; and/or federal sources such as the U.S. Labor or Commerce departments, and Canada Labour. You may need to contact several of these sources to get complete information. By the end of the research stage, each member of the design team should have complete information on each technique.

4. *Determine in detail the pros and cons of each technique* relative to your goals and objectives, how they would work at your organization, and how they mesh with the benefits and risks you examined earlier. The designers should discuss how the technique will aid or block the achievement

Table 10.1. Union-Management Cooperative Approaches to Use
Depending on Problem or Objective

ORGANIZATIONAL PROBLEMS	
Problem Area	*Possible Approaches*
Market	Labor-management promotion institutes
	Labor-management marketing teams
	Joint advertising programs
	Construction market recovery programs
	Customer supplier partnership
	Customer service programs
	Joint seminars for customers
	New product development
	Union label campaign
Financial	Gainsharing
	Profit sharing
	Employee stock ownership plans (ESOPs)
	Alternative compensation systems
	Healthcare cost containment
Investment	Joint investment funds
	Pension fund investments
	ESOPs
Adapting to change	Strategic collective bargaining
	Labor-management committees
	Sociotechnical redesign
	Work redesign
	Joint visioning
	Strategic scanning
	Search conferences
	Joint benchmarking
Community contribution/image	Joint promotion campaigns
	Customer service programs
	Joint United Way campaigns
	Joint volunteer efforts
	Adopt a school/educational partnering
Labor-management relations	Strategic collective bargaining
	Integrative collective bargaining
	Union-management conflict resolution
	General labor-management committees
	Supervisor-steward leadership development
	Joint relationship building process
	Relations by objectives
	Problem-solving grievance handling
	Grievance mediation

OPERATIONAL PROBLEMS	
Problem Area	*Possible Approaches*
Facilities	New plant design task forces
	Joint facility redesign committees
	Sociotechnical redesign
	Work redesign
	Ergonomics

Technology	New technology joint committees
	Union-management task forces
	Sociotechnical redesign
	Cellular manufacturing
	Self-directed work groups
	Joint meetings with vendors
	New product development
	Total productivity maintenance
Productivity	Individual and group incentives
	Productivity gainsharing programs
	New technology committees
	Labor-management committees
	Flextime/alternative shift arrangements
	Quality circles
	Total quality management
	Total productivity maintenance
	Work redesign
Quality	Total quality management/organization
	Union-management task forces
	Quality circles
	Sociotechnical redesign
	New technology committees
	Quality improvement projects
	Statistical quality control
	Quality function deployment
Resource use	Joint conservation/environment committees
	Union-management task forces
	Work redesign
	New technology committees
	Labor/management/community environmental committees
	Process and environmental audits
	Joint recycling efforts

EMPLOYEE PROBLEMS

Problem Area	*Possible Approaches*
Employment security	Strategic collective bargaining
	Contracting in task forces
	Joint marketing efforts
	New product development
	Joint training and employee development
	Board-level representation
	Joint investment activities
	Joint job placement
	Joint diversity activities
	Job banks
Working conditions	Strategic collective bargaining
	Integrative collective bargaining
	Problem-solving grievance handling
	General labor-management committees
	Health and safety committees
	Quality circles
	QWL programs

Work redesign
Flextime/alternative shift arrangements
Sociotechnical redesign
Ergonomics of facilities and technology
Process safety audits
Work redesign

Career development

Joint orientation sessions
Apprenticeship committees
Training committees
Self-directed work groups
Pay for knowledge/performance
Preretirement training
Joint layoff preparation
Plant closing assistance
Employee educational counseling
Tuition assistance

Communications

Board-level representation
Labor-management committees
Union-management task forces
Joint video network
Joint newsletters
Joint employee meetings

Personal and family concerns

Employee assistance programs
Problem-solving grievance handling
On-site day/elder care
Wellness programs
Drug and alcohol counseling
Joint family support efforts
Attendance programs
Literacy programs

of your overall objectives. What are the pros and cons of each for the employer, union, *and* employees? Usually the union as an organization is left out of consideration. The team should have a full understanding of how each technique works, what it can accomplish, and what it cannot usually accomplish.

For example, if one of the goals is to promote interdepartmental cooperation, quality circles would not be an appropriate technique since they are by definition used in one work area. But they would be useful if a goal is product quality improvement or the development of internal teamwork. If an objective is increased communication with hourly employees, for example, labor-management committees may be one way to spread information via the union to the membership. Before-work meetings or a joint newsletter might also be used to achieve the same end. If the issue is quality, quality function deployment and process analysis might be useful. In one company where we worked, the major common concern was customer service. The issue was addressed by middle-level problem-solving groups of managers and union business agents, by store committees with employees from every department, and, under the leadership of the union and management, directly with each employee who was working with other members of his or her department. The employees felt that using only one technique would not have been sufficient. As this example illustrates, several approaches are usually necessary to solve major problems.

5. *Obtain input from others throughout the organization.* The designers, based on their discussions, should develop hypotheses about the best approaches and techniques for meeting the joint objectives. These should be listed in priority order or grouped in ways that seem the most effective. Solicit the opinions of managers and employees at all levels about whether these are effective ways to achieve the stated objectives in their particular locations. Resistance to an approach does not mean it cannot work, just that implementation will require attention to the reasons for the resistance. In some cases, employee resistance may stem from not knowing about particular techniques. The more radical the change, the less comfortable employees may be—but radical change may still be necessary.

There are several ways to obtain input from employees at all levels. Begin by reviewing the input gathered during the feasibility stage. Often employees consulted at that time suggested what a cooperative program should look like. Another way to gather employee information is through information-giving and information-getting sessions. One program we worked with held such meetings with every fifth person on the seniority roster, thereby ensuring a fair and accurate distribution of opinions. Management and union designers explained what had been decided about the program thus far, such as the goals and objectives, boundaries, and safeguards. Similar efforts were described to give the employees a basic idea of the program's possibilities. The group's opinions were then solicited on key items of importance to the designers. Small focus groups could also be used for this purpose.

Another method to obtain input is via traditional management and union channels. Management can use its usual forums, such as staff meetings and memos. The union can bring up issues at a union meeting or solicit information through the union newspaper.

6. *Next generate a list of the driving and restraining forces that may affect the implementation of the joint program.* Based on the data from employees and other opinions and information available to the designers, list the internal and external helps and hindrances to implementation. An internal support might be funds already earmarked for improving operations; a hindrance might be lack of a specific budget for implementation.

In identifying the hindrances, think of everything that could go wrong or get in the way of using a particular approach. Finding the negatives is often easier than finding ways that help make the approach work. It requires real concentration to identify the helps fully. In both cases, consider resources, internal and external pressures, market conditions, suppliers, legal requirements, forthcoming events, timing, finances, the size of work units, organizational structure, seasonal adjustments, reporting relationships, shift work, geographic location of employees, customer needs, attitudes of employees, and other essential factors. Looking at both sides should provide a realistic assessment of forces working in favor and against the workability of a proposed alternative. This assessment is called a *force field analysis*. Too many programs assume that goodwill and determination will result in success. A realistic understanding of the forces involved helps avoid the shoals and catch the waves.

7. *Identify potential resources*. The designers should examine such areas as the availability of training professionals at the work site or in the union, space for meetings, skilled internal employees who have worked on similar programs, and/or funding sources. Compare the resources that are available and the resources that are needed to use any particular technique. Maximum use should be made of internal resources. Pursue cost-effective approaches to model desired behavior in the organization. This doesn't mean doing the program on the cheap. But if two techniques will achieve the same objectives, choose the one with the lower cost and/ or the more streamlined design.

8. *Consider all of the above information in deciding which strategy or set of techniques to pursue*. By this point, you should have identified at least one technique to help you accomplish each goal. You may also be able to use one approach to achieve several goals. The designers should also consider techniques used in previous programs inside the organization that affected the process and outcomes positively. Finally, the experiences of other organizations may provide key clues in selecting design features. Before making a final decision, you may need to factor in guidelines established by corporate, union, or departmental authorities. In many cases, the final result of the design phase will be a hybrid version of several approaches to cooperation and participation. Don't necessarily expect the "correct" approach to jump out at you. You have to think through and envision how each approach would work in your own situation.

9. *Brainstorm and select design features so as to maximize the internal and external helps and minimize the hindrances*. It is too time-consuming and unnecessary to conduct this analysis for every single technique, which is why we suggest doing it after the initial cut has been made. If there is a relatively close call between options, however, this analysis can be done earlier. The design group may decide, for example, that a new term should be used in response to resistance to the terms *quality of work life* and *cooperation*. Or it may be aware of a changeover in a key position and develop ways to get the new person involved.

Some hindrances cannot be completely removed or circumvented. In this case, the designers should determine what can be done to minimize them most effectively. Other hindrances will reflect areas over which there is little control and great uncertainty. For example, if the availability of workers is weather-related, there may need to be backup people and alternative times for activities. Or there may be uncertainty on funding in various parts of an organization because of legislative inquiries or the possibility of a buyout or downsizing. Clarification and flexibility may be necessary. Using a technique that has been tested successfully in an organization and already has existing supporting materials may be a help and consequently speed progress.

10. *Confirm what resources are needed.* Check to determine the extent to which resources can be counted on. In addition, prepare a list of needed resources and cost them out as much as possible. In most union-management cooperative programs, the most precious commodity is time. Supplies and consultants usually are a minor cost compared with the time employees spend on the activities of their problem-solving groups.

11. *Prepare and deliver a design report* to the entire group of top union-management decision makers about the recommended approach. The report should cover the techniques to be used, the structures to be established, including responsibilities and authority for decision making, the management and staffing of the project, the location of the initial activities, training, communications, monitoring, evaluation, and resource requirements. How the design connects to the goals and objectives and fits with the organization's culture and characteristics should be apparent.

The report should provide the decision makers with a clear idea of what the alternatives are and why the options chosen best address the primary goals and concerns of the program. It should lay out realistically what supports the program will need and what hindrances may get in the way, as well as strategies to manage contingencies. At the same time, the plan doesn't need to squeeze out invention and risk-taking so long as you have a clear idea where you are going. An accounting of the resources available and the resources needed completes the picture. Getting approval from key decision makers allows the program designers to proceed to planning, confident that a common understanding of the fundamental design has been reached.

Planning the Program

After the initial design phase, success hinges on proper planning (see fig. 10.2). Planning is absolutely critical to the success of a union-management cooperative program. Overwhelmingly, the reason a program does not succeed is that it lacked adequate planning. Conversely, a well-planned program has clear direction and participants are secure in the knowledge of what will be done. Plans are used as a way to conceptualize the entire joint process, as a way to identify needed steps not initially apparent, as an orientation tool to let others know what is being done, as goals to spur the process, and as a means to identify implications if changes are necessary.

Some program developers loathe planning. They prefer to let things happen as the process unfolds. They avoid planning in order not to look bad or off schedule. Their reasoning is that if no one knows what should have happened, it is difficult to criticize when "something" doesn't occur. Frankly, people are rarely fooled by this ruse. Paradoxically, people who do not plan often make more mistakes and vary more from perceived schedules. Sometimes people don't plan in their rush to get things done. Yet poor planning usually results in more rather than less time being needed to complete a task.

Labor and management also don't plan so as to avoid conflicts. But, in fact, the process of planning deepens their relationship and prevents conflicts later over diverging unstated agendas and approaches. Planning is critical in a labor-management project because it reflects notions of competence and power. When the union is excluded or opts out of planning, management fills the power vacuum. It takes a lot more effort to get people to change existing plans than to work though the issues jointly in the beginning. Too often in labor-management projects in which new processes are the focus, the parties rebel against the perceived rigidity of planning. A free-form approach is emotionally appealing but remains disastrous in the face of organizational politics. If there is an "emergent design," the party with the most power and resources will control what emerges—and this is usually not the union.

Most unionists and many managers have limited experience with structured planning. At best, they have "to-do lists." A list is not a plan. It isn't comprehensive enough. It does not include essential elements or provide a sequence for action.

The plan for a program should detail exactly how it will be done. In general, the plan should do three things: specify exactly what needs to be done, define the process for reaching those goals, and identify strategies and techniques to accomplish the effort. For example, it should specify how the program will be started, how it will be maintained over time, and how it will be evaluated. The basic program design is the skeleton for the program; the plan adds flesh to the skeleton in the form of descriptive detail. The plan brings to life what was only a concept.

The plan should answer several questions: who is to do what, when, where, for what purpose(s), and with what resources? For large-scale joint efforts, it may be best to devise an initial eighteen-month plan covering a

Figure 10.2. Planning a Program

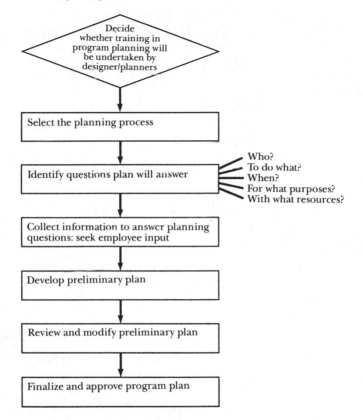

six-month startup and a one-year operating period. At the very least, the plan should cover one year. It is very important to plan later stages clearly and to provide an opportunity to review and revise major design features as necessary.

All plans change with changing circumstances. The parties should learn from miscalculations or unanticipated events to ensure more realistic planning in the future. That plans change over time should not deter the parties from planning; plans are meant to be dynamic documents that help program participants respond to changing conditions.

Developing the Plan

The management and the union designers should plan the joint effort, using the steps outlined below. As they did for the program design, the planners should draw on input from all levels of the organization. Much information useful for planning will already have been obtained; however, a clear process for getting additional input from employees is helpful. Key items to consider again are timing and resource issues.

Specificity increases the probability of successful planning. Statements like "I know what I mean but can't put it down in writing" or "don't worry about it now" signal trouble ahead.

The overall process for planning a joint union-management program is as follows:

1. *Set out the major categories that need to be planned.* These may include the selection of groups, meeting locations and times, completion of governing documents and plans, startup, training, recognition, communications and publicity, monitoring, and evaluation. Each group should have its own plan that is integrated into a master plan. Staff for the program should also plan their communications, backup contingencies, supplies, coordination with governing bodies, and other logistics. Each problem-solving group should have a plan for developing, carrying out, and tracking the problem-solving projects for which it is responsible. The governing body monitoring the groups should be able to tell at any point where each group is in its process. Prepare separate sets of plans for each level of the program—top, middle, and shop or office level. Planning should be built into the problem solving itself, including plans for data collection and the implementation of solutions.

2. *For each of these plans, collect information to answer six planning questions.*

- *Why?* Specify the statement or purpose of the effort, the need the effort is supposed to meet, and the goals and objectives that it helps meet. If there is no clear answer to these questions, then the task has to be clarified. Responding with fuzzy or no answers should lead to reconsidering whether to do the activity.
- *What?* What exactly are the tasks and activities to be accomplished?
- *Who?* Identify the people involved in the effort and what role each person plays.
- *When?* Over what period of time will activities occur, and when will planned activities begin and end?
- *Where?* Where in the organization will activities be located, and what physical space will be used?
- *How?* What processes, procedures, methods, and techniques will be used to accomplish tasks, and what additional resources will be necessary?

3. *Develop a preliminary plan.* Carefully look over the plan to see if groups can move smoothly from step to step. Review it particularly to locate illogical or unnecessary activities and periods when too many activities are scheduled at the same time. The plan should reflect what will actually

occur and describe each step to be taken. Sometimes the answers are very obvious. Such answers should be included if they address critical questions. The plan should be evaluated to determine if time and resources will be used efficiently, it promotes effective performance of the tasks, and it meets the overall goals and objectives of the joint initiative.

The pacing of the program should be brisk. Too rapid or too languorous a pace will harm the development of the program.

Someone unfamiliar with the program should be able to understand it from the plan with little difficulty. Use simple language or an outline. Don't overcomplicate the issues. Strive for comprehensiveness, not complexity.

As much as possible, the means used to accomplish tasks should mirror the values inherent in the overall effort. This means that a participation program should be participative throughout and that a joint union-management initiative should mirror jointness and equality in all its processes.

Use a common format to outline the plan. A form we have used successfully is the *action plan log*, which has columns down the page in which you list critical planning elements (see fig. 10.3). The first column is the "item" category, which lists "what" and "why." The next column is "action," in which you describe how the item will be done by noting all the tasks and subtasks necessary for completion. For each action, an entry is made under the "who" column, indicating who will be responsible and who will be involved. In the "Resources needed" column, you specify materials, equipment, or funds needed to accomplish the task. A final set of entries indicates "when." Specific dates can be entered into three subcategories: "startup," "target," and "actual."

4. *Share the plan with the top union and management decision makers involved in the effort.* Sharing it should generate additional information and input, leading to approval by top decision makers. The plan serves as an agreement about what will be done, by whom, when, and with what resources. If difficulties arise in the future, it can also serve as the basis for reserving resources and maintaining commitments. Sanction by top-level decision makers means they will help ensure close adherence to the plan. The document should also be shared with others interested and involved in the effort.

5. *Use and review the plan.* Plans have no value if they are just filed away. They must be reviewed on a regular basis. Each committee, problem-solving group, and staff person associated with a cooperative program should review its plans at least once a month. When changes are necessary, they should be discussed and agreed to by both the union and management. Keep a record of the dates of the updates to ensure that everyone is using the most recent plan. Communicate any changes to

Figure 10.3. Action Plan Log

Group Name _____

Project Number/Name _____ Page Number _____   **Action Plan Log**

Item	Action	Resources Needed	Who	When		
				Startup	Target	Actual

those affected and to the governing committees to whom groups report. Also record when parts of the plan are accomplished. Express appreciation to those who made it possible and celebrate and publicize major milestones. This will generate a sense of accomplishment along the way to completion of other major tasks or activities. If the date targeted for completion of an activity is frequently different from when it is accomplished, then future planning needs to be more realistic. It may also signal that other problems need to be addressed.

Plans are worthwhile in guiding the process of cooperation and making sure that *all* parties live up to their obligations. They should describe not only intentions but obligations. That is why it is critical to get involvement and buy-in while establishing them. Concurrence makes it easier to insist that all participants live up to their obligations. Sometimes parties have different ideas of what it is that they were supposed to do, forget, or have other more current projects on their minds. Having a written plan will prevent fingerpointing and miscommunication.

Training the Joint Designers and Planners

A number of planning processes can be used to develop a program plan, including action plan logs, PERT (program evaluation and review technique) diagrams, and critical path analysis. The union or management may have little experience with structured planning of this type. Generally, the precise techniques used are less important than the fact that there was a conscious and systematic effort to plan jointly.

Often, both union and management planners will need training in program planning processes and skills. Such training can take the form of a workshop conducted on-site for the planners by an internal or external consultant/trainer. Regardless of who conducts the training, all of the union and management planners should participate.

Useful training mixes theories of planning and application to the tasks at hand. The training should be sensitive to the various information sources and experience bases of the union and management. The parties should come away confident that they can plan their program together. Such training not only benefits the joint program but enhances the capabilities of the employer and the union in their separate responsibilities. We have seen many occasions in which unions began to use planning in their normal union responsibilities and management's planning skills were enhanced as a result.

Conclusion

The design and plan for a union-management program give it form and direction. The design tailors the program to the actual organization involved. By using a joint approach to designing the program, the first steps are taken in actualizing the union-management commitment to cooperation made earlier. A new process, skills level, and spirit are engendered.

The plan anchors the program in concrete actions. It sets specific directions and clear expectations. It describes how ideas will become reality and sets specific targets for implementing the overall goals of the program. Working together on establishing direction uncovers important questions and answers them. Later on, the plan will be an important tool for training participants, communicating about the program, monitoring progress, and evaluating results. The plan is a vital, living document in which both parties should take pride and to which they both should be committed.

11. Taking Charge: Governing and Managing a Union-Management Cooperative Program

U nion-management programs work best when both parties work together equally. Think of a rowboat. If only one oar is in the water, it is more difficult to advance quickly and to steer effectively. If there are two oars and they go in opposite ways, the boat comes to a standstill or revolves dizzily in circles. But if both oars are in the water and pull together, then the boat moves more quickly and directly. Similarly, a program in which both the union and management pull equally is more effective since it draws on the strengths and resources of both parties. They have a clearer sense of direction and usually can accomplish tasks more quickly than if they were operating alone.

Unfortunately, too many programs are undertaken unilaterally by management or with only token union involvement. Sometimes management blocks the union's involvement, and sometimes the union refuses to participate. These tend to be weaker efforts. When management and labor work well together, they provide complementary perspectives. If either side is having difficulty because of organizational pressure, they help one another out. Not only is co-management much better practically, it also recognizes the institutional responsibilities of management and the union to exercise leadership and oversight. The best way to manage a joint project aimed at mutual gains is jointly and equally. This process is shown in figure 11.1.

Figure 11.1. Governing and Managing a Program

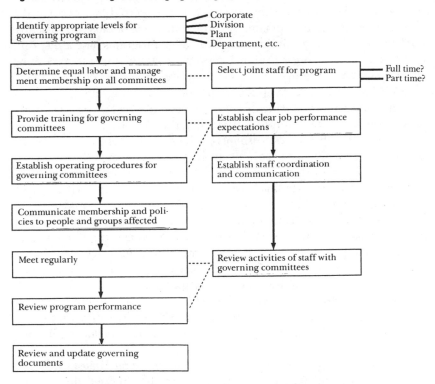

Role of Governing Bodies or Steering Committees

Whatever the size or structure of the governing body of a joint program, its primary roles are to enable change and participation to take place in the organization and to model ways of working together. The structure of the governing body depends on the kind of cooperation the program design calls for, the size of the organization, and the location of the work force. If an organization is large and/or hierarchical, having several levels of governing committees may work best. This structure links the joint activities to traditional sources of power and authority. If an organization is very spread out, having several governing bodies may work. Of course, the nature of the program is the central variable. If the program works through a labor-management committee or is focused on a way to conduct bargaining, then the governance will be different than it will be for a total quality program or employee involvement program at the shop-floor or office level.

All co-managed programs that involve the activities of more than a few small groups require effective, formalized governance to guide and nurture the effort. Informal agreements or laissez-faire approaches simply do not work beyond the short term. Too many programs become the domain of consultants or personalities on either side because no structure has been established to run the programs. Such programs have a very thin or tenuous base of organizational support and guidance. If something should happen to the prime shakers, then the program collapses. Good governing structures shore up the framework of the program.

Frequently, a joint steering or governing committee oversees a cooperative program. The committee supports the various problem-solving groups, sets guidelines, troubleshoots problems, monitors activities, visits periodically, recognizes accomplishments, and evaluates the program. The steering committee selects program facilitators and staff and then provides constructive feedback, reviews their plans, monitors their activities, and evaluates their performance. The committee should interact with management to ensure open communication, encourage technical assistance, squelch rumors, and ensure that adequate time is being allowed for the program's activities. The steering committee also should maintain open communication with local labor, address rumors, and ensure compliance with the collective bargaining contract. The committee has an obligation to try to work together as a team, to hold effective meetings, to plan for the activities in its area of jurisdiction, and to monitor and evaluate all activities under its purview, including its own functioning.

Members of the governing body rarely make good facilitators for small group activities and should not interfere directly, although they can be useful in fostering the development of small problem-solving groups in their areas. By avoiding interference and encouraging self-management, governing bodies help groups they are responsible for grow.

In most cases, steering committees do not make final decisions on recommendations for operational changes in the organization when, normally, such decisions are made by management. This is important both to maintain respect for management's decision-making authority and to contain union liability questions. In some cases, there may be joint decision-making authority. Since membership on the steering committee is not a full-time responsibility, the group needs to manage itself in a way that enables members to balance committee activities with other duties.

Top-Level Involvement

All levels of an organization have to be involved in a comprehensive joint project. This is especially true of the top level of management and the union. An executive or top-level committee provides the view from the higher rungs of the organization's ladder. Employees throughout the organization look to those at this level to determine their degree of sanction and whether they "walk their talk." Those at the top level of the program should establish the overall guidelines for the effort, provide guidance and leadership, demonstrate support, establish and ratify the overall plan, and monitor and evaluate progress. Ideally, those at the top are also engaged in joint problem solving on issues and concerns at their level of the organization.

Efforts to avoid the top levels of management and the union rarely succeed in the long term. Top-level involvement means involvement by the people with clout. It does no good to have a committee that keeps looking elsewhere for decisions. The deliberations in the committee will not be meaningful.

The players will change at the top and provisions have to be made for maintaining the policy of cooperation through transitions. Written agreements about the process, and plans for orientation and integration of new participants, are keys to such continuity. In the absence of such a plan, much of the activity at other levels of the organization stops or slows down, waiting for senior-level decisions during personnel changes.

To say that the top level has to be involved does not mean that everyone must be 100 percent committed or involved all the time. But people at the top must fully understand what is going on, sanction the process, and be willing to give it a fair chance. On some occasions, these people may have to step in and use their formal power to make sure people whom they supervise are giving the program their full support. Performance reviews provide an opportunity to reinforce support for the joint effort.

Top-level participants are often reluctant to engage in training, to attack specific problem areas, or to use structured problem-solving methods to reach conclusions. Although they are impressed with the impact of this approach in other parts of the organization, they exempt themselves. This is viewed as hypocrisy since they are allowed to shoot from the hip but others shouldn't. This attitude unfortunately prevents the spread of new skills and the resolution of problems at higher levels. The problem solving at the top level can be adjusted to the time constraints and responsibilities of the participants, but a consistent program models cooperation and thoughtful problem solving at all levels.

Middle-Level Involvement

The biggest stumbling block in many cooperative and participative programs is middle-level resistance. Several important reasons underscore why middle-level managers should be actively involved. First, they usually have a tremendous amount of knowledge about and expertise in the problems under consideration and therefore add problem-solving capabilities. Second, they are likely to be involved in approving and putting into place changes and therefore would be critical to successful implementation. Third, no one likes to have his or her position eroded, and sometimes there is the impression that cooperative programs aim to show up the mistakes of the people in the middle and circumvent their authority.

Middle-level managers and unionists can be involved in several ways. In large organizations one, two, or even more layers of governing groups may oversee the program's application in various parts of the organization. These groups, composed of middle-level labor and management members, can help monitor and adapt the program to local conditions. The aim of these groups is not to bureaucratize the process but to assist in the successful introduction, maintenance, and growth of joint activities. Unfortunately, many such groups do no more than monitor their subordinates' activities. Middle-level managers and union leaders can also form problem-solving groups in their own right and address significant issues at their level. They can also head up task forces that draw people from various parts of the organization, thereby adding real substance and respect to middle-level involvement. Middle-level managers and union leaders can also be effective in helping first-line supervisors and stewards learn new roles that aid in the transformation of the organization, thus recognizing and developing leadership.

In larger organizations, the middle level may include various levels of the union hierarchy. For example, in auto plants, zone committee persons work with higher levels in the plant; in railroads, local union chairpersons handle a location. Too often, only the top elected union official is involved.

In both small and large locations, consideration must be given to how to involve stewards. They can be members of shop-floor-level problem-solving committees or co-chair them to provide union visibility and involvement. Building communication and teamwork among supervisors and stewards can go a long way toward helping to improve a workplace.

Finally, support staff and technical experts at the middle level need to be encouraged to participate. Their expertise can be used by making them part of task forces and other problem-solving teams.

Selecting Participants

Some argue strongly that all cooperative programs need to be based on voluntary participation. We dissent from that opinion. We agree that if the members are willing participants, it makes things easier. But easier is not always what is necessary. Organizations have hierarchies and power structures. These need to be respected and used. Groups composed of top-level participants from management and the union need to acknowledge that they represent positions in their organizations. If they were to die or leave, someone would be hired to fulfill their roles (if not, then maybe the position shouldn't be there in the first place!).

People become involved in participative programs not as individuals but as parts of an organization, and their interactions occur within the context of their organizational affiliations. Programs based on personalities suffer from mood swings, but programs meshed with the organizational structure stand firm. This is not to deny the importance and desirability of good interpersonal relations but to emphasize that it is important not to confuse goodwill with good policy.

The agreement to proceed with a joint program has the force of any other policy decision. Members of the organization are expected to adhere to the policy. If cooperation and participation are ways of doing business, then managers should be required to implement this policy faithfully. If the union has agreed to cooperate in certain areas, then members must live up to this agreement. If there can be a choice of participants, it is best to take the most willing. When there can be no choice, however, as in total system change activities, then everyone should be expected to contribute and the performance of all participants should be monitored. Doubters can become great contributors when given the opportunity.

Members of governing committees should be drawn equally from labor and management. Too often, there is tokenism in union representation whereby the union is treated as a participating department of management and not as a co-equal force in the organization. In some cases equal representation may not be possible, as on the railroads, where there may be twenty different local unions at a location. But even if there is inequality in membership, there should be consensus.

Although some locations have a separate governing committee for each union, the preference is for there to be cooperation between committees. Almost never does total separation work out well for unions or management. There may be separate problem-solving groups for subsections of the program represented by different unions, but there should still be a common governing body. Whatever the composition, governing bodies should aim for consensus on decisions. In the absence of total consensus, they should agree on a fair way to make decisions that doesn't play one side off against the other and that builds the broadest agreement.

Both parties should discuss the criteria for the selection of participants. The employer should select representatives for any part of the program calling for management since delegation of tasks is a normal management responsibility. The union should select any representatives of the employees. Selection in this way makes for a stronger program. Being on the outs with influential leaders can cause disaster or gridlock. Linking to them reinforces the notion that union-management cooperation is important and central to the missions of both parties but should not lead to cronyism. Leadership should look for diverse input and participation. Sometimes the best help can come from unexpected quarters.

In a few programs, members of committees have been elected. At the Minneapolis *Star-Tribune*, the union representatives for the Newspaper Guild were elected. In general, this is unnecessary since union officials are already elected; electing committee members splits the union into two groups of elected officials: the cooperators and the confronters. This bifurcation of the union is disastrous politically and slows progress over the long term.

In programs with quality circles, employee involvement groups, or other shop- or office-level groups, leaders are designated. Traditionally, these are first-line supervisors. There is a good reason to do this. The program generally teaches new skills that enhance their abilities and standing, and, since good supervision is critical to a successful enterprise, this opportunity for skills development should not be overlooked.

In most groups, the leader's role is to ensure that the proper process is followed and not to interfere with the content. Segregating the role in this way helps prevent the supervisor from dominating the group. Some programs, such as the Labor-Management Participation Teams in the steel industry, insist on having groups co-chaired by a supervisor and a union designate, usually a steward. So long as teamwork is demonstrated, this can work well. Some programs have elected rank-and-file group leaders. We think this is a bad idea since it undercuts the role of the first-line supervisor as a problem solver and sets up political rivalries in the union by creating a competing elected office with that of the steward.

Large and complex programs do not just happen. They require people to help make them work and to take care of day-to-day tasks. The principle of each side choosing its own also holds true for the selection of coordinators and facilitators to staff the project. These staff are accountable to the governing body and the party that selected them. There may be some joint interviewing, but the final choice should be up to each party. One criterion that should be used is the ability of the people to work as part of a team. Staff should be able to work well with people, to collect and analyze data, to understand collective bargaining, and to adjust to many different situations. They should also have planning, monitoring, and other program management skills. Often many people in the union and management have the natural skills or training to perform these jobs well. Open up the possibility of serving in these roles to as broad a group as possible, including employees with various levels of seniority. Participation is an excellent career development opportunity for both future managers and future union leaders. Union representatives should recognize, however, that using their position as a political springboard against an incumbent in an election can be very risky both to their role and the program.

When there are more shop-floor employees than openings for participants in a program, selection should be as fair as possible to avoid favoritism. One successful technique is to have all who want to volunteer put their names in a hat. Participants as well as alternates are then determined by the luck of the draw. In every company we have worked with, some of the most effective participants, to the surprise of the local handicappers, turned out to be people who because of their reputations would not have been appointed. Often the more negative people become among the best participants because the program gives them a positive outlet to express their frustrations and energy.

In the development of work teams, consideration needs to be given to seniority to ensure fair access to the groups. Sometimes teams will identify appropriate questions and interview possible participants. Others test potential team members for job-related skills. When testing is used, it is important to help more senior employees feel comfortable with the testing procedures, to acknowledge their experience, and to ensure that training is available to help them compete for the jobs on a fair footing. When another system cannot be agreed upon, selections should be based on seniority.

Developing Governing Documents

Clarity in a program about its aims, the way it should work, and the areas it will avoid provides essential guidance to the participants. Too often, these issues are left unsaid. This mistakes vagueness for flexibility and inserts confusion where the parties thought they had trust. Each level of the governing structure should have a clear document outlining its policies. In general, these documents fall into three categories in a top-to-bottom joint participation program: project principles statements, policies and procedures statements, and codes of conduct. The primary objective of these documents is to encourage and support the program. They should thus be enabling documents, not naysaying instruments, and copies should be distributed to all members of the program. It is best if the committee that developed the documents presents them in person and explains them to the groups they cover. These documents can also be used to orient other employees who are not yet involved with the program.

The top level of an organization must clearly establish its support and understanding of any employee involvement program if the program is to succeed. A *project principles* statement provides guidance and leadership to the governing committee and to other levels of the organization involved in the program. It articulates the basic principles of the program while demonstrating in black and white that the union and management are working together cooperatively.

The first section sets out the basic goals and objectives of the program by listing what labor and management want to occur. It may also identify the basic motivations of the two parties to participate in the program, as well as their mission and values. The second section describes the basic structure of the program, including the various levels and activities and the responsibilities and authority of each level. The third section defines the basic boundaries, such as the program's relationship to collective bargaining and whether the program supplants management and union responsibilities. This section may also include a statement that exempts the union from liability for management decisions made by the program or that restricts problem-solving groups to addressing issues within their areas of responsibility. The fourth section lays out the safeguards for the program (discussed below). The fifth and final section puts forth the general expectations of labor and management, including a good-faith pledge to make the program successful, to devote adequate time to the effort, and to provide complete and prompt information. The top-level governing body should also develop clear operating procedures for undertaking its tasks of governance, management, and problem solving.

At the next level, a *policies and procedures* statement is created so that general principles can be adapted to activities at specific locations. This statement helps mold the program to local objectives, structures, practices, barriers, and language. It is important that it not conflict with the project principles statement. The following sections are generally included: purpose of the document; specific objectives of the group; organization of the governing body, including purpose, composition, and meetings within their area; information and publicity; recognition; procedures for handling recommendations; and monitoring and evaluation.

At the shop-floor or office level, problem-solving groups often develop *codes of conduct*, also called group guidelines or norms. Though these may sound restrictive, in practice they are not. These codes set the ground rules for behavior within the group and establish the framework for the group to manage itself and enforce its own rules. These must be consistent with the other governing documents.

It is very important that each group develop its own guidelines. Our review showed clearly that borrowed documents are much less effective. Internally generated norms and rules have much greater impact and are much more likely to be followed. When writing these documents, small subgroups of the governing body could be used to draft sections. The groups should aim for comprehensiveness, not length or complexity. An outline format is easiest to work with. In each case, the entire group has to agree to the overall document before it takes force. It can be amended later as new concerns arise.

Building Safeguards into the Programs

Basic safeguards are a necessary ingredient of a union-management cooperative program. These help establish the boundaries of the program and remove some of the worries people have about participation. With this clarity, more participation can take place. Often covered are such areas as protection of collective bargaining and management rights, job security and wages, and prohibitions against character assassination and retaliation, downgrading of classifications, and increases in worker stress.

In most programs, setting down in writing that the program will not violate collective bargaining rights is important. This protects the rights of both parties to bring any issue to the bargaining table. The bargaining route can be taken by either party and hence any issue removed from the cooperative program setting. The grievance procedure and the right to redress concerns through that process also remain untouched. This protects the union from duty of fair representation suits. If they wish, however, the parties may elect to make their program directly connected to the collective bargaining process.

Ensuring that there is no character assassination of management or labor at any level focuses the cooperative process on issues. One group we worked with saw the process as one of "fixing problems, not blame." Too often, groups dissect problems by psychoanalyzing personalities without looking at the group's behaviors and what can be changed. Amateur psychiatry is a poor way to solve problems. Further, a commitment to nonretaliation helps reduce the fear among subordinates that they will be punished for speaking honestly. Too often, the messenger of problems is shot instead of taking aim at the problem itself. If employees are punished for what they say in the cooperative context, then trust is lost and the overall program is sabotaged. Setting expectations that there won't be character assassination can't eliminate the practice, but it can make it clear that the practice is unacceptable.

Employment security is one of the most difficult issues. No worker should be asked to participate in a program that threatens his or her living. There needs to be some overall protection against loss of employment as a result of recommendations that emerge from the program. This does not mean that workers will necessarily have to do the same tasks forever. Jobs will probably change as a result of a successful program, one hopes for the better. And protection from job loss as a result of a cooperative program doesn't preclude unemployment because of general economic conditions or unrelated management decisions. Unfortunately, cooperative programs are rarely in themselves failsafe protections against job loss. But hoping that there will be more employment security without the union's involvement or in the context of generally poor performance is a fantasy.

It is in the interests of both parties to consider carefully the language concerning employment security. Union members will be unreceptive to a program that threatens employment, and union leaders will probably not be reelected if they promote a job-cutting program. Management can achieve excellent returns on investment without layoffs. The fear of job loss leads workers to be less open with their ideas for change, whereas a job security pledge often pays off for management in the quantity and quality of the workers' ideas. Such a clause should not lead to featherbedding, however. Considerable thought has to be given to how to use the time freed up as a result of improvements for activities that will benefit the employer in the short and long term. Opportunities may exist to make changes in market development, product and service development, preventive maintenance, and community service. In one General Motors location in Flint, Michigan, workers adversely affected by changes were placed in nontraditional jobs in the community until openings for useful work were found inside the plant. This project became a model for the Job Security Bank provision in the 1984 automotive industry contracts, which ensures workers community-oriented jobs if internal positions are not available. Many programs also wind up recommending new cost-effective positions. At the very least, the gains and losses of jobs should balance out, and no one should be fired as a result of a program. Sometimes downsizing can occur through attrition or early retirements.

People in cooperative programs want their working conditions or "stress" levels to improve as a result of the program. Some unions object when the goal of productivity improvement or efficiency seems to lead to speedups and reduced job satisfaction. Unions should not object to productivity improvement per se. In some cases, poor productivity makes a job less safe and more aggravating and demanding. Unions need to assess the impact of productivity on jobs, pay rates, safety, and job satisfaction. These issues can be addressed without taking broad aim at productivity as a concept. An unproductive workplace will all too soon work to the disadvantage of those employed there. It is important to remember that only through productivity increases will capital be available without inflation or large borrowing costs for improvements in wages or expansion of the business or the agency.

Fear of job loss and of worse working conditions are the biggest worries of the workers involved in cooperative programs. Other concerns include the loss of wages, especially if there is a reassignment of personnel. Ensuring that there will be no downgrading of classifications for current employees and building in training and skill enhancement address many of these concerns. Flexibility on the part of workers has to be married with willingness by the organization to imagine new opportunities and to pursue them aggressively. The goal of a union-management cooperative program is to find win-win solutions. Adequate safeguards help make that possible.

Joint Management of Cooperative Programs

Just as a cooperative program needs to be governed jointly, so too it needs to be managed jointly. The more extensive and complicated the process, the more people need to manage the process to ensure that tasks are being performed well. In a truly joint program, management is also conducted in a joint manner. We don't assume there has to be a program; the criterion is effective administration of the joint agreements. Ask how much time it will take to do what you want to do well, whether full or part time.

The union and management co-chairs of a labor-management committee can be its "staff," or other management and union people can be assigned to manage its activities. In larger programs, there is often a need for *coordinators* to administer the program. In many programs, one coordinator is selected by management and one by labor. They administer the program jointly and report to the top-level governing body. Whether they are full or part time depends on how much work there is to do.

Many cooperative programs have *facilitators* who work with problem-solving groups, monitoring their activities and aiding them in overcoming obstacles. In some programs, coordinators are called facilitators. Whatever the nomenclature, these people should be drawn as equally as possible from labor and management to demonstrate balance and to provide complementary orientations.

Regardless of whether they are management or union, coordinators or facilitators should be accountable to the governing body. In their staff roles, they bring different perspectives, but they should strive to be mutually supportive. Too often, staff take over the leadership of the program or too much decision-making authority is delegated to them. In many programs, a "cooprocracy" develops of union and management staff who mistake the program as theirs alone, thus creating problems with the work force and the governing body. The governing body should remain firmly in charge of a program and the staff serve in a support role. Program staff have an obligation to manage their activities as models for the rest of the organization. Demonstrating best practice establishes their right to make recommendations for the organization as a whole.

The governing committee should determine the organizational resources staff need to do their job well. These resources may include supplies, office space and equipment, clerical support, consultants, and training.

Staff need to be paid for their time. A bone of contention in some programs is the salary gap between management and union co-coordinators doing equal work. It is difficult reconciling the desire to pay equal pay for equal work and the danger of paying the labor coordinator at a level that will make him or her reluctant to take risks and that might possibly create jealousies that separate him or her from other rank-and-file members.

Setting Performance Standards and Monitoring Staff

Being clear about what staff people are to do is often overlooked but is essential to a smooth-running cooperative program. Good business practice involves setting realistic performance standards and measuring performance against those standards.

We have successfully used a participatory approach for setting performance standards and monitoring staff. At the outset, staff members collectively draft a job description and list of what they will do, called a behavioral checklist. These should include such items as the ways they will support problem-solving groups and communicate with key parties. Each behavior listed should be specific and observable in some way, such as "attend team meetings" or "order supplies." The draft of the list and job description are then shared with the governing body to whom the staff reports, modified as needed, and approved. This process ensures common understanding.

At the end of a year (or at some other time), the governing body should set up union-management teams for the purpose of reviewing the staff's performance. The teams can use a variety of techniques, such as interviewing each staff person privately, distributing performance or evaluation questionnaires to participants, and/or observing the person in action. The focus should be on how well staff people fulfilled their jobs, not on whether or not the review team likes them, and on ways to improve performance and reinforce positive behaviors and contributions. The review should be shared with and signed off by each staff person and placed in his or her personnel file if that is the normal practice.

At the end of the review process, all the staff and the governing body review the job description and behavioral checklist to see if they need modification and to update them as necessary. The review team should assess the process it used for review and learn how to do it better the next time. Since staff may come on at different times, there may be several review periods in the course of a year.

Conclusion

The governance and management of a joint project help establish the principles of joint and equal union-management cooperation. The particular needs for governance depend on the cooperative techniques being used. Governing committees should be designed based on the particular size, location, and functions of the employer and unions.

The governing body serves as an enabling group to help ensure success for the cooperative effort. The top level of the organization has to be involved and model what it expects for the entire organization. Depending on the particular approach, strong roles for the middle and lower levels of the organization should be introduced with an emphasis on problem solving. The methods for selecting participants for groups should be fair but recognize institutional prerogatives. Clear governing documents such as principles statements, policies and procedures documents, and codes of conduct articulate the processes, boundaries, and safeguards of the program.

Program staff should be drawn equally from both parties. They should work cooperatively and serve as the staff of the joint governing committees. There should be clear and shared expectations of performance, which should be monitored by labor and management at least once each year. This approach to governance and management helps ensure high levels of program performance and maintains control of the process in the hands of the union and management partners, where it belongs. The approach also results in leadership and competence in guiding and managing the process, ensuring excellent implementation and success.

12. Building Skills: Developing and Delivering Training for a Union-Management Cooperative Program

Good results come from knowing what you are doing. Most union-management programs require new skills and understandings. Some people believe that cooperation is as easy as sitting down together and talking. Though this is a start, the most effective forms of joint activity require training in their content areas and cooperative processes. Specifically, training does the following for any joint union-management effort:

1. *Training explains what the program is and how it will work.* It lays out the framework for the cooperative process for all to understand, including the overall goals and structure of the joint endeavor. Without this basic background, moving forward to meet common goals is extremely difficult.

2. *Training teaches the basic principles, processes, and procedures by which the activities of the program will be run.* Training tells *how* the program will operate, including the basic safeguards and approaches to be used. The training itself models the values and underlying principles involved in the joint effort.

3. *Training enhances skills in specific areas necessary to meet the goals and objectives of the program.* Different union-management programs require different skills training. For example, if the program uses labor-

management committees for joint problem solving, the committees will need training in the processes of union-management cooperation, joint problem-solving procedures, the management of meetings, and similar topics. If the focus is on creative ways to undertake collective bargaining, skills in generating and costing out alternatives are helpful. If the focus is on product quality, training is called for on the various ways to analyze, improve, and monitor quality.

4. *Training builds support for and commitment to the program.* In some cases, training could be provided by self-paced instruction through reading or by viewing videotapes. Though such approaches may sometimes be appropriate, self-taught instruction does not further the important objective of building group involvement in and commitment to the joint process. By participating together in group-based learning activities, an intangible but necessary element of support is added to the program. People feel empowered and enriched. This positive association spreads to other activities in the program.

Although training is clearly important, it is often given short shrift. The landscape is littered with well-intentioned programs that broke down in areas in which proper training could have made a major difference. The biggest loss when there is no training, however, is that the potential of the program is diminished. If group members had a better sense of how to go about their work and ways to engage in joint problem solving, the results would often be stronger and the process more directed.

Most forms of union-management cooperation by their very nature require the development of new skills. These new skills are developed most effectively through high-quality training. People might be able to pick up some of these skills on their own, but they wouldn't do it systematically and not everyone would pick up the skills that are necessary.

Developing and delivering effective training requires time and money. Too often, program planners skimp on the time allotted or budget inadequate funds. These are serious mistakes. It is best to determine what training is needed and then how much it will cost rather than setting aside an amount for training and then figuring out how much training can be squeezed in. The training development process is shown in figure 12.1. If there is truly a budget crunch, then the goals and scope of the program should be cut back. Training can be overdone, but there are also real costs to providing poor-quality training.

In the rush to get things done, many programs take shortcuts in the training. If speed is an issue, consider techniques that can be absorbed quickly. The other manifestation of the "get-it-done-fast" approach is to cram all the training into a short period of time and overload the trainees. Training needs to be delivered when it has a reasonable chance

Figure 12.1. Developing Program Training

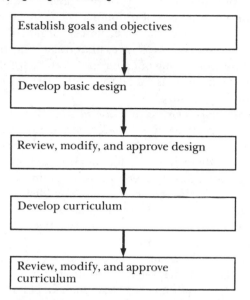

of being used. The trainees need to have a chance to absorb it and use it. Prudent pacing is a wise investment.

Establishing Joint Training Goals and Objectives

The union-management governing body establishes the goals and objectives for the training. It also specifies what training is to be offered and how it will be given. Although third-party experts or internal staff can help by providing options, decisions should be made by the union-management partners.

The general goals and objectives of the training should parallel the goals and objectives of the overall program. Those aspects of the overall objectives and goals of the program in which participants require additional understanding, skills, or commitment should be incorporated into the training. Think of what the participants should be able to do and what attitudes they should exhibit. These provide critical clues to the training needed. It is through reference to the joint program goals and objectives that the training program takes shape.

After the overall learning objectives are identified, each item should be reviewed to determine if there are subobjectives that need to be met. For example, if a general objective is to learn how to function as a member of a steering committee, there could be a range of subobjectives, including learning how to conduct meetings effectively; to identify the range of roles and responsibilities of the group; to plan, monitor, and evaluate activities in the group's area; to work well in a small group; to discern the relationship between collective bargaining and the cooperative program; and similar specific objectives. As much as possible, the objectives should describe behaviors people will learn to do.

Write out the general and specific objectives and share them with those designing, delivering, and evaluating the training program. They should also be shared with the trainees to give them a clear idea of what they will be expected to learn.

Developing the Basic Design for Training

Not every participant in every training program needs to know the same things. Some goals apply more to some groups than others. The union and management designers/planners should be clear about which training goals and objectives are directed toward which audiences. Some goals apply to all and some only to parts of the group. The design provides the framework of who is going to teach what to whom and under what conditions.

The designers/planners should then explore training methodologies. The options include group training, one-on-one coaching, self-paced instruction, films, attendance at external seminars or classes, videotapes and audiocassettes, and opportunities to observe people who have the skills they are learning. The choices will be influenced by the available resources, training needed, and background of the potential trainees. Training for the initial group may be different from training for employees who join the process later. In geographically or occupationally diverse work forces, innovative delivery solutions may be necessary.

The next order of business is to outline the topics to be covered. Many people jump first to a list of topics to be taught. The better way is to ensure that the topics flow from the objectives and audiences. Eventually, time frames for the topics and a list of who will deliver the training should be clearly specified.

Finally, the designers lay out a sequence for the delivery of the training. For example, in quality circles training, the steering committee would be trained first, facilitators second, leaders of the circles third, and the circle members fourth and last. Dates are added to the training schedule, after checking participants' and resource availability. Program training may have several cycles or phases as the program progresses; each cycle should be clearly planned.

All information pertaining to training should be brought to the governing body for review. Members should be encouraged to ask for clarification, challenge sections, make suggestions, and modify the plan as necessary. With this body's involvement and approval, it will be easier to develop a training curriculum and to implement it effectively.

Developing an Effective Training Curriculum

Developing a training curriculum tailored to a specific program takes considerable thought. The particular training needed is a function of the gap between what the group needs to know or be able to do and what *all of them* already know or can do. In some cases, materials are already available to help build the curriculum. For example, the project principles statement and the policies and procedures document outline the program and explain what it intends to do. There will be other generic topics, such as problem solving, motivation, listening, group dynamics, consensus decision making, facilitation, planning, organizational change, and conflict resolution, for which preexisting exercises, lecturettes, films, and other learning aids will be available. Carefully review them to make sure that they fit into the particular program. There may be elements that are on target, but other parts may need to be scrapped or reshaped.

The union-management relationship poses special challenges to curriculum developers. Most of the materials and exercises for teaching the skills of problem solving or organizational development do not fully or realistically incorporate union concerns. Those drawing up the curriculum must pay particular attention to make sure that the training supports and strengthens the union's involvement in the training and the union's legitimate role in the workplace. Although most of the training should be done jointly, there may be times when the union or management will want to have separate sessions. Even if participation is limited, the content and objectives of such sessions should be known to the other party.

A corollary issue is how to address the topic of collective bargaining. Usually, the issue is handled as sex education was fifty years ago: the trainers are told to avoid it, making the subject taboo. Openly discussing collective bargaining and its relationship to the joint effort is the best approach. Trainees thereby develop a common base of understanding about the nature of collective bargaining and contract administration at their location that respects its contribution. They should learn about labor relations from both the employer's and the union's perspectives. This provides common knowledge for working on the collective bargaining situation if the program is focused on it or staying clear of it if that is the objective. Knowing how contract negotiation, grievance handling, and discipline operate ensures that joint activities avoid unwanted interferences from the union or management. A process for resolving quickly and fully areas in which there may be interference should be presented and agreed to as a group.

Another major area of curriculum concern is the problem-solving process. Though there are many variations, any approach should increase trainees' facility with problem identification, problem selection, problem analysis, solution development and analysis, and preparation of a recommended solution and implementation plan. The training should also include a process for evaluating the efficacy of the solutions. The analysis section of the problem-solving process requires strong attention. Findings on the success of employee involvement groups and quality circles show that those who collect and use data well are much more successful than those who put little emphasis on data. Even more important than identifying the problem is the clarification of the issue at hand through data-based descriptions of its dimensions. This learning found a broader home in the quality movement, which broadened data collection and analysis skills such as statistical quality control.

Because there is never just one solution to a problem, it is important to examine alternative solutions. Alternative solutions need to be double-screened to make sure they are both workable and desirable from a cost-benefit perspective. Quick and dirty problem solving, while attractive sometimes, is almost always less effective than well-researched and well-analyzed solutions. The kind of problem-solving process used by a labor-management committee may differ in depth from that of a task force or employee involvement group.

In an attempt to tailor a program to a local situation, the broad perspective should not be neglected. Nor should focusing on their own opportunities for cooperation blind participants to the problems other groups face or have fought in the past. Knowing about the history of union-management cooperation and cooperative programs at other locations provides important insights for all trainees. Understanding what others have done can generate innovative approaches at one's own location.

The curriculum should be as rooted in reality as possible. Adults seek learning in hopes of making an impact on their working and living conditions. Though training should be enjoyable, an overreliance on games, simulations, and hypotheticals should be avoided. If there is a possibility to link learning to real situations at work or in the program, then this approach should be taken. If this is impossible, then fictionalized situations can be used. Likewise, training should not be psychotherapeutic. The focus of joint programs is on behavior, on what union members and managers can do, not on their psyches and feelings. In some programs, workers are asked to "bare their souls" as part of the process of building trust. Information divulged in this way can be misused, and the process shows a basic lack of respect for the privacy and feelings of working people. Psychological analysis should be done by competent professionals. Behavior and relationships pertaining to work can be explored, but the line should be drawn when it comes to issues that do not pertain to the workplace or at psychologically manipulative techniques.

The curriculum should be expressed in a training agenda whose relationship to the objectives and design of the joint program is straightforward. Topics, time frames, and methodologies should be clearly laid out. The trainers should be able to present backup documentation on the materials and content of the training. The curriculum, agendas, and backup material should be reviewed and approved by the union and management partners before they are used.

Selecting and Preparing Trainers

Once the training curriculum is identified, the training must be delivered well. (The steps are outlined in figure 12.2.) Trainers should be drawn from the union, supervision, and management as much as possible. In this way, the trainers provide a model of union-management cooperation. Most of the trainers will need to be specially trained, and for most, training will be a part-time responsibility they will perform on an as-needed basis. Ideally, they will work in union-management teams when conducting the training. As they gain skill and comfort, they will be able to train others.

The trainers should be selected by each party after consultation with one another and should be confirmed by the governing body or committee. Management and the union should consult with one another to check for compatibility and the opinions of the other group.

Selecting the first group of trainers is the most difficult because the organization may have little or no experience with cooperative programs or the training to be presented. Prior experience with training is helpful, but "know-it-alls" should be avoided. Trainers should be able to speak clearly and distinctly, respond well to a group, take pride in seeing others learn (and not strut their own expertise), and be credible within the workplace. An important criterion in selecting trainers is the willingness to learn. Good trainers learn from their training environment, examine new ways of presenting the material, and are open to new experiences and new ideas. Training is hard work and requires attention, preparation, and a willingness to listen to feedback. Great care should be exercised in the selection process.

Large organizations may have on-site trainers who are familiar with

Figure 12.2. Delivering Program Training

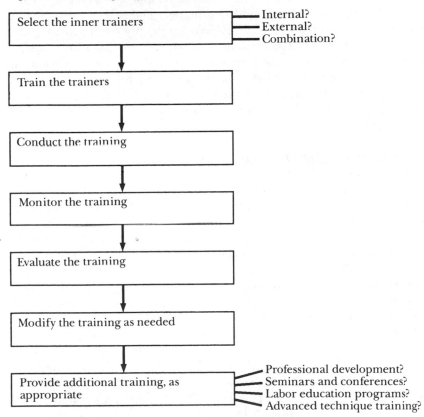

many of the necessary topics. If possible, their expertise should be used. They can be excellent consultants during development of training materials. It is important to determine their credibility with the union because their primary responsibility may be in management development. Despite their alliance with the employer, they should still abide by the process described here, which places training under the review of the union and management partners.

For the initial stages of training or for one-time training events, outside trainers can be retained. They can provide specific training that requires particular expertise not currently available in the organization. They can also help train on-site trainers. For many professional trainers, working with a union will be a new experience. The best outside trainers are ones who understand the needs of a joint program and are responsive to both management and the union.

Outside trainers should be carefully monitored to make sure they are working out well. It is especially important to make sure they are teaching in ways that meet the internally developed goals and objectives of the program and that they do not have agendas that conflict with the firm's or agency's mission. Except for highly technical subjects, they should present the governing body with a clear plan for transferring their knowledge to the internal union and management trainers. Though their help can be welcome initially, their role should diminish over time. Quality checks to make sure that the internal and external trainers are maintaining a high level of delivery and effectiveness will be necessary.

Conducting Effective Training

There are some basic principles to keep in mind when conducting training for joint union-management programs. First, modeling joint participation in the training can be just as important as the content of the training itself. The training should thus be given as much as possible to joint audiences and should provide a model of union-management cooperation. Though there may be some times when the parties are addressed separately, this should not be overdone. Having teams teach also makes it easier to manage the training sessions and makes it more interesting for the participants.

Second, broad and open participation in training is vital. Training should thus be given not only to the people directly participating in the cooperative program but also to a broad cross-section of other employees, supervisors, managers, and/or union officials on what the effort is to accomplish and how. The mix will maximize understanding of, support for, and commitment to the program. Training should not be used to reward favorites or to pay back personal or organizational debts. This damages the credibility of the program.

Third, the training must adhere to the principles of adult learning. It should recognize that the trainees are not empty receptacles waiting to be filled. They bring experiences, ideas, knowledge, and opinions to the training, all of which can be valuable learning tools. Rather than a passive lecture style, the training should use participative and experiential methods. Adult learners also require direct feedback on their performance. Clear and constructive feedback on whether they are grasping the knowledge, skills, and values being taught is essential. If they have difficulty, additional attention or new strategies are needed.

Fourth, training is best done in small, "digestible" chunks or segments. People have a limited tolerance for learning new things. When that tolerance level is passed, even the best-presented material will not be absorbed. Breaking the training into segments will not only make learning easier for the trainees but will also make the program easier to manage and conduct. Further, it will provide opportunities for application and observation in the workplace. With some time between segments, adjustments can be made to the training to make it more effective. The use of segments also minimizes the degree to which participants' normal work is disrupted.

Fifth, there must be adequate time to conduct each segment of the training. Rushing through items so that there is not sufficient time for coverage, comprehension, and integration is a total waste. In general, adult workers learn best when they are told what they are going to learn, have a chance to learn the skills and apply them in a safe setting, and are able to then reflect on the experience to develop general principles and understanding. Simply saying something once and expecting it to be remembered is a pipe dream. Use visual cues to assist retention. More is not necessarily better, however. Training should be maximally efficient and effective. This can be achieved by setting and adhering to realistic time frames.

Sixth, trainees often come from many different educational, age, and cultural backgrounds. They may have a wide range of skills and abilities. Trainers should therefore be prepared to work empathetically and respectfully with participants whose reading and writing skills are limited or who are worried about not having been in a class in many years. Extensive reading and writing assignments and fancy jargon should be avoided. Handing out basic notes about each topic removes stress, enables the trainees to concentrate, and provides a reference for later review. Language barriers may not be indicative of intelligence but rather the inability of the instructor to speak the trainees' native language. In multicultural environments special attention must be paid to respecting the diversity of cultures and ensuring access to employees of various backgrounds. Similarly, trainers should avoid using sexist language and stereotypes to ensure equal respect of men and women.

Seventh, the trainers should aim for a smooth presentation. The keys are early planning, preparation, and flexibility. Training rooms need to be up to the challenge of creating a good learning environment. Having conducted training in frozen rail yards and next to noisy machinery, we've seen the problems created by poor environments. A training room works best when it is convenient for the trainees, free from distraction and noise, and fairly comfortable. Finding such locations is not always easy, since it is best to be in or near the workplace. Trainers should be proficient in using various training tools and equipment, such as flip charts, overhead projectors, and videotapes. Sufficient training materials and handouts should be prepared and ready for distribution with a minimum of fuss. And there should always be extra supplies in case of shortages or equipment breakdowns.

Monitoring and Evaluating the Training

The union-management governing bodies at the various levels of the organization should monitor the training as it is given. Specifically, they need to assess how well the training is meeting its goals and objectives. Monitoring can be done through direct observations of the training and/or by asking trainees for their reactions. At the conclusion of each segment of the training, the trainees should be asked to anonymously complete evaluation forms on how well the training met its objectives, the usefulness of each part of the agenda, and the overall proficiency of the trainers, as well as additional comments. The trainers should also lead a discussion with the group at the end of the training period about what went well and what could be improved. The results should then be analyzed by the trainers and governing body to make sure that the training is as on target as possible. If there are problems, adjustments should be discussed and if possible implemented. This process is called a "reaction evaluation."

Sometimes good reactions are mistaken for good training. To conduct a "use evaluation," which assesses the impact and relevance of training after it has been put into practice, use the methodology described in chapter 14. The parties will need to determine relevant questions, identify indicators, select methods of data collection, analyze the data, and draw conclusions about effectiveness. Impact can be assessed by asking the participants later on about their training, asking the facilitators in their areas how well it has been applied, or checking records to see whether areas covered in training are being done well or not. The use evaluation should assess how well the training worked and determine issues that need further attention. A training or evaluation professional can help in the framing and discussion of the questions, but it is essential that the union-management partners analyze the information themselves and draw their own conclusions.

Training as an Ongoing Function

Training should not occur only at the beginning of a program. It should be ongoing. New people will become involved in the program and need to be trained. Or the parties may decide to expand the program to cover new topics or new locations and need training with a new focus and/or for new participants. As basic techniques for problem solving or addressing the content areas designated in the effort are learned, more advanced techniques can be taught, such as more sophisticated forms of statistical analysis.

Ongoing employee problem-solving groups often need a brief course that includes some advanced skills training and a review of what they should know. Program facilitators and coordinators may want to schedule ongoing continuing education into their responsibilities. Participants in the program may want to attend college classes, seminars, or conferences to broaden their perspectives. Labor studies programs and industrial relations departments may have appropriate offerings. Circulating new literature or creating a book discussion group are other ways to keep participants fresh and up-to-date.

Conclusion

Joint training is critical to the success of a joint program. It provides participants with the skills to implement the goals and objectives of the program. It creates a setting for personal and organizational growth. It serves as a forum for the explanation and resolution of key points in the program. It offers participants valuable skills that can result in overall improvements in the performance of management and the union. Finally, joint training models a basic value of cooperative efforts, that learning together helps empower the members of an organization to address its problems and identify opportunities in creative, effective, ongoing ways.

13. Creating Awareness: Communications and Publicity in a Union-Management Cooperative Program

On one level, the whole idea of union-management cooperation and employee participation is to improve communication and awareness. Cooperation opens up the avenues of communication and creativity within and between labor and management. Consequently, the less effective the communication, the less effective the cooperative program. Improving awareness about what is going on in the organization and the possibilities for improvement is equally important. Awareness leads to inclusion of a broader range of people, ideas, and data to help resolve problems.

Communication is a two-way process. Each side must share information and ideas with the other and listen to what the other party has to say. There must be clear communication about the program to employees who are not participating directly and to and among its various active participants. The key elements of this process are presented in figure 13.1. When nonparticipants are kept in the dark, conflict can erupt or misunderstandings occur. Similarly, lack of communication with those in the program creates confusion, wastes time and energy, and reduces the cross-fertilization of experience and ideas.

Rumors occur in all workplaces. In a cooperative program, they can be fatal. The goal is to maintain communication on as open a basis as

Figure 13.1. Communicating about and Publicizing a Program

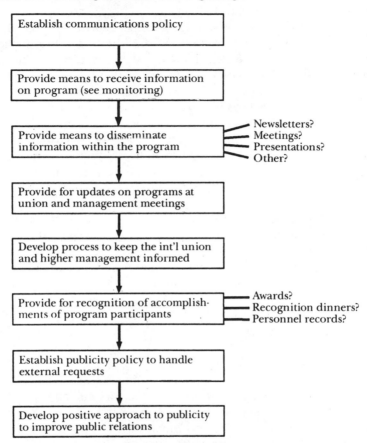

possible to help contain potentially damaging rumors and to demonstrate trust and the sense that everyone is welcome. The foundation of a union-management cooperative effort is inclusiveness, not exclusivity.

Establishing a Communications Policy and Plan

Establishing effective communications in a joint program takes forethought and follow-through. The governing body should ensure that communication occurs within and about the effort. The goal is to establish open, multidirectional communications channels so that everyone has a voice, thereby linking and listening to the whole organization. Open communications exist in organizations and situations involving mature, effective relationships with mutual respect. When poor communications are a frequent complaint, it is more frequently a symptom of a poor relationship than of poor technique.

Inventory the existing communications mechanisms generated by the employer and the union to determine what can be used to further the joint program. Determine their frequency of communication, whom they reach, and how to work with them. Begin by identifying how to dovetail with current communications channels. Sometimes this may involve helping to improve the existing channels. In some cases, current mechanisms are insufficient or not trusted and additional routes must be used. Some joint programs have their own newsletters, videos, and posters. Others hold meetings in various parts of the organization on a periodic basis to keep people informed. In any case, the parties should retain the option of communicating to their constituencies unilaterally.

During the start-up phase of a program, inaccurate assumptions are frequently made about the effectiveness of communications channels. Techniques become stale, thereby losing their effectiveness. It is therefore important to check regularly to see whether information is flowing freely and whether your audience got the messages you sent and responded as you hoped. Adjust or vary your communications channels as your program matures, and don't assume that one approach is sufficient or that communications that seem right to those inside a program are effective and motivating to others.

Keeping Participants Informed about Progress

Cooperative union-management programs thrive when there is a continuous flow of information in a continuous loop, especially with the immediate of participants. Several mechanisms can be used to keep program participants well informed. One is to schedule regular meetings with key groups involved in the program. If there is a TQM or quality circle program, facilitators should meet on a regular basis to share their experiences. This is particularly important when peer facilitators are used. They can learn from each other what does and doesn't work. These meetings provide an outlet for discussing feelings and frustrations that may not be appropriate to share with the groups they facilitate. Similarly, leaders or co-leaders of shop-floor groups should get together. A popular event is to get together all the participants in the groups once a year to present awards and review the highlights of the program. If there are labor-management committees, it is helpful for the co-chairs to meet and discuss common concerns. The frequency of the meetings will depend on the needs of the groups involved.

Some programs jointly publish newsletters to keep people informed and to acknowledge and recognize achievements. Issued on a quarterly basis or at some other interval, they give updates on program activities and accomplishments. These newsletters can be handled by the coordinators of the joint effort or by a special committee.

Minutes should be taken at every meeting of a cooperative program. They should record who attended and what was done, including major decisions and findings that were shared with the group. They should not be editorial instruments of the recorder or used to embarrass members for what was said. Having good minutes helps ensure that accurate perceptions are reported and that goals are met. Minutes of meetings can thus be critical instruments for communicating about a program. Some programs develop lists of people inside and outside the program who should be sent minutes.

Other means of communication include bulletin boards, both in work areas and on computers, journals or diaries, correspondence, targeted-issue newsletters, and end-of-year reports itemizing goals, activities, and outcomes.

Keeping Employees Who Are Not Directly Involved Informed

It is important to keep personnel who are not directly involved informed of program developments. The mechanisms used to maintain internal communications can also be used to communicate with these employees. Either at special meetings or as parts of regularly scheduled events, updates and explanations of what is going on at regular meetings should be provided for both management and labor. The union should have on its fixed agenda at regular union meetings an update on the joint efforts. If the joint activity is part of the union's basic mission, then these updates should be a routine part of the union meeting and members should have an opportunity to challenge how well the joint program is going. Newsletters can be distributed to the general work force or to a broad range of people in the workplace, or a column about the program can be included in regular internal publications. When groups are composed of part of a work unit, minutes of the groups' meetings should be posted for all employees in the area to see. Posters and banners can also be used to raise awareness and illustrate key points, or videos can be used to show what is going on.

Inviting visitors to joint activities is an excellent way to enhance understanding. In one company we worked with, at the end of each meeting program participants would decide whom to invite to the meeting the next week. They first invited the more skeptical workers. In addition, visitors from outside the company sat in at meetings. The only restrictions were that visitors had to let the co-leaders know in advance that they were coming and they had to respect the rules of the group. Such firsthand exposure can be very effective.

Keeping Management Informed

Particularly in large organizations, it is important to keep higher-level managers informed of the cooperative program and the results being recorded. Too often, senior managers are involved in the early stages of a program but are left out later on. After the startup stage, they move on to other projects and their potential contribution is lost to the program. They should be given an ongoing, balanced view of both the accomplishments and problems. Overly rosy pictures are out of place. High-level management sanction and involvement contribute to success. Continuing involvement also allows access to the authority of higher management when problems develop for which their status or expertise is necessary. Honest and periodic updates help ensure their assistance will be available when needed. Visits to program activities also enhance their understanding and support.

There are two principles to follow to ensure that the management hierarchy is respected. First, projects should not be end runs from lower in the organization around the formal organizational structure, especially the middle, as a means to avoid certain decision makers or to undercut their authority. If you don't want them making decisions, change the locus of decision making or change the personnel. Second, projects should not be end runs from the top to get around middle managers directly to workers. By keeping everyone in the management chain of command informed about what is going on, broader involvement and sanction are developed.

In large corporations or agencies that have a variety of cooperative activities or many locations, it is very important to share information about local activities. Developments should be reported regularly to higher-level liaisons who can then disperse the information throughout the system. Good ideas are thus shared and common problems that may call for solutions or additional resources are identified. Some companies we have worked with have held annual meetings for representatives of programs at different sites. If there is a steering committee at the corporate level, it is important to give them firsthand exposure to the people and processes at local sites.

Keeping the Local Union Leadership Informed

Not every union officer is involved in every cooperative program or in all phases. It is therefore very important to make sure all of them are kept informed about what is going on. In a few instances when only a limited number of union leaders were privy to information about a cooperative program, they were later ousted in union elections. The union should review the progress of activities with its executive committee, bargaining committee, or board. In addition, as the union's communications net- work, stewards should be included in information sharing. Stewards and union officers are key links to union members and are likely to learn of their concerns and dissatisfactions with the effort. It is better to learn about them early on and deal with these problems before they escalate.

In recent years, a dissident movement has aimed to discredit joint programs as sellouts. Some union leaders who have agreed to joint efforts have excluded these dissidents from the information loop to avoid con- flict at union meetings. To the degree that their concerns are legitimate, they need to be addressed head-on by presenting the facts and linking the affirmation of joint programs to union goals and interests, not manage- ment accommodation. Union leaders need to be careful not to encourage ideological opponents who do not reflect the broad concerns of the membership, yet they must ensure that all perspectives are fully repre- sented. Rather than ignore critics, try to involve them in the process and deal honestly with their legitimate concerns.

Keeping the International Union Informed

Just as those in the corporate or departmental chain of command need to be kept informed, so too does the international union for several important reasons. Other parts of the union may have tried similar approaches or encountered the same problems. Sharing information may lead to new ideas on how to handle issues in one's own setting. Those in other parts of the union will also be concerned about establishing precedents that could affect other locals in the union. These issues need to be worked through.

Communication is particularly important with the international rep- resentatives who service the locals and with the regional officers of the union. There is a tendency not to share information about cooperative programs with these officials. Since a large part of the public image of union leaders emphasizes conflict, the cooperation that takes place is often ignored. Further, since higher-level representatives cover a large area and unions are understaffed, they generally spend most of their time putting out fires and dealing with conflicts. Finally, there is some- times a fear at the local level that those in the union hierarchy will step in and squelch the effort. To be sure, many representatives got where they are because they are good at managing conflict and they may not be familiar with the particular cooperative approach being used. Careful explanations and a collegial attitude are often necessary. A well-planned program with clear union goals will not worry the international union. The same is true of international officers. They can be a tremendous asset if they are informed and involved. They will be embarrassed, however, if they hear about a local cooperative program in their area from the international office or through sources other than the local union. We have seen many international representatives provide positive leadership.

The international office also needs to hear about what is going on at the local level. Other locals may be involved in similar activities and need to know how (and if) the local overcame its difficulties and the good ideas and approaches that were used. Further, patterns may not be evident at the local level. Usually the research department or education department of the union keeps tabs on such patterns and trends. Local unions should be forewarned that the international may not have answers to particular questions since other locals may not have shared the necessary information.

International unions need to take a stronger role in publicizing the activities of their local unions. Such publicity provides a better image of the union among potential members and offers a positive alternative to the image presented by employers. A few unions, such as the National Association of Letter Carriers, have regular columns in their national magazines or newspapers covering joint efforts. There is also a need to network about joint programs at educational conferences and conventions sponsored by the international union.

Handling Information Sharing and Proprietary Information

Organizations that do not share important information about their performance or upcoming changes breed rumors and foster distrust among the work force. One of the great opportunities of union-management cooperative programs and increased employee participation is that they increase information sharing. The primary purpose of general labor-management meetings, for example, is to share information. Any form of cooperation provides an opportunity for this sharing to take place. In organizations with high levels of cooperation, there is a great willingness to share information. Management keeps the union and the work force abreast of developments and key indicators of organizational performance. Some organizations have made it a matter of practice to answer all requests for information from inside and to be forthcoming in volunteering important information. Each side can decide on the limits to information sharing, but the greater the cooperation, the greater the sharing of information that generally takes place.

One organization we worked with built information sharing into the agenda of every union-management meeting. Management reported on what had taken place since the group last met and what was planned for the future. The union shared information on what it was doing and what it had heard from the work force. Personal information, such as retirements, weddings, births, and other events, was also shared. This mixture of institutional and personal information was well received, and participants found these sessions useful and looked forward to them. In some groups sharing is done at the beginning of the meeting and the group never gets to its other agenda items. We therefore suggest that such sharing be at the end of the meeting and sufficient time allotted.

It is very important for both sides to exercise restraint and discretion in sharing proprietary or very sensitive information. The union should pledge that proprietary information will not be shared with outside parties. Violating this principle on either side undercuts the trust and respect the parties need to work with one another.

Getting accurate and timely information to problem-solving groups is absolutely essential to success. For example, if major changes in budget, personnel, equipment, or policies are planned, the problem-solving groups should be advised. Information delays can substantially slow their progress. There has to be a clear understanding that information will be supplied promptly, fully, and accurately to all groups so they can meet their goals.

Building Recognition into Joint Programs

The contributions of employees who participate in joint efforts need to be recognized and nourished. Some regard this as unnecessary if joint activities are part of business as usual; however, the normal conduct of work should also include appreciation, personal contact, and acknowledgment. Work life improvements, savings, and increased customer satisfaction as a result of joint efforts should all be recognized. Contributing to the betterment of the workplace and taking risks to make changes also deserve sincere recognition. Placing a letter in the personnel file of each participant in the joint effort is one way to express recognition. Some companies hang plaques with the names of the participants engraved on them. Pins, jackets, caps, and other small gifts and promotional materials can be distributed or certificates awarded on the completion of training. Recognition breakfasts, lunches, or dinners are another way to honor participants. Pictures of the groups can be placed in program newsletters and/or other internal employer and union publications. Finally, governing committee members should go to joint activities within their jurisdiction and offer words of praise.

A few words of caution are necessary on the use of recognition devices. They should not consume so much time that they hurt the performance of the program. Fancy recognition programs cannot hide deficiencies in a program's design or performance. Also, competitions or special privileges should be avoided, as well as ostentatious gifts, which may cause jealousy. The greatest recognition should be the increased awareness among workers of the positive impact of the program on the workplace.

Handling External Requests for Information and the Press

Good news travels fast. Employers and unions in your local area or even from far away may want to come and learn about your program. First, there should be a clear policy about such requests. Often participants can learn from the visitors, but make sure the visits are acceptable to both parties. Some unions have objected to visits from representatives of nonunion employers. Similarly, allowing representatives of a company on the AFL-CIO boycott list could cause serious problems with the union. Second, a limitation should be set on how many groups will be allowed to visit. It is flattering to get requests to visit, but internal responsibilities should come first and external requests should be handled as time allows. If there are many requests, then an information packet can be put together and sent out. Some companies, such as Corning, have scheduled times for visits and a limited number of slots. Those interested sign up at the convenience of the employer and the union. The same principles apply to presenting at conferences and meetings on union-management cooperation. In moderation, these forums can be very helpful but they should not obscure the primary responsibility to maintain the program.

It is not uncommon for a local newspaper to want to do a story on a cooperative program. This may be welcomed so long as both parties are agreeable to the idea of publicity and both discuss their perspectives with the reporter. It is very damaging to the program to have it described from the vantage point of only one side. The same is true of papers by academics and students. In all cases, the writers should be minimally intrusive and hear all sides.

It is a good idea to limit publicity in the early stages of a program. Premature publicity may lead to an inundation of requests for more information. There are other more pressing issues that need to be addressed, and the shakedown period is hardly the time for the glare of the public eye. Besides, later on there will be more to report.

Using Union-Management Cooperation as a Marketing Tool

A successful union-management cooperative program is a source of pride. Television commercials such as the Ford advertisement that said "Quality Is Job One" and the General Motors promotion that "GM Is People" are examples of how cooperative programs can be used to get positive publicity. Wheeling Pittsburgh took out print ads to tout its new union-management relationship with the United Steelworkers after a widely publicized strike. In the educational setting, site-based decision making can demonstrate teachers' and administrators' commitment to excellence in education and school reform. Publicity can show there is teamwork and dedication in an organization and that everyone is working together to produce high-quality products or services. Touting a cooperative program can also help improve the public image of an organization whose image needs improving. Many such promotions mention the union by name, thereby improving the union's public image as well.

One task of an established joint union-management effort could be to consider strategies to create positive publicity about the effort for marketing purposes, to enhance the image within the organization of the units involved, or to increase community awareness and approval. Publicity could take the form of advertisements or presentations. People prefer to deal with responsive and reliable organizations. Showing that an organization has a commitment to being responsive and reliable can help a lot. We cover marketing issues in chapter 7. Using a cooperative program to enhance market success and to send a message to legislative authorities is a legitimate use of joint programs. The first step is to determine the key audiences for the publicity. External audiences include radio and television broadcasters, newspapers, business groups, trade associations, university faculty, human resource associations, local labor councils, legislators, and public officials. Some labor-management teams have gone to community groups and schools to explain their programs.

When communicating with outside groups, be sure to summarize the cooperative effort in a succinct format, free of jargon. Encourage people in the news media to interview participants in roundtable discussions or to observe problem-solving meetings or presentations or to talk to people at the shop-floor or office level. Set up photo opportunities. Be advised, however, that media people are looking for simple clear stories and will rarely capture the full dimensions and complexity of the effort. Respect that and provide them with clear summaries of the accomplishments.

Conclusion

Communications undergirds an effort to achieve union-management cooperation. Awareness between and among the partners creates the best conditions for success. Information and concerns therefore need to be regularly and systematically shared by all the participants in the program. All levels of the management and the union hierarchy should be included in the information loop, not just those who are directly participating. Information sharing between the union and management is a critical component of cooperative programs, but it sometimes involves matters of a sensitive or proprietary nature. These issues must be handled with discretion. Getting timely and accurate information necessary to solve problems helps improve the results of joint problem solving. Finally, the need for recognition of effort and accomplishments should be part of the fabric of a program.

How to handle publicity should be addressed while planning a program. Attention from the press, academic world, or other employers and unions may be welcomed so long as both parties agree to its value and it does not divert necessary attention from the program itself. Positive use can be made of the joint program to help improve the marketability of the firm's or agency's product or service and/or the community image of the employer and union.

14. Keeping Tabs: Monitoring and Evaluating Union-Management Cooperative Programs

S etting up a program is one thing. Keeping it going and making sure it is doing what it is supposed to do is quite another. All of the hard work at the beginning would be for naught if the program bogged down during implementation. To keep tabs on how the program is working, effective mechanisms for monitoring and evaluating it need to be designed and deployed. Monitoring applies directed attention to the process to keep it running smoothly. Without ongoing attention, there is the danger of conflict and bad habits developing without anyone knowing it.

Some programs suffer the doldrums after the initial excitement of their introduction. Adequate monitoring and evaluation help revitalize the process so the catalyst for review won't be a crisis. They help ensure that the outcomes of the program are visible and measurable, and that the program makes a real difference in the operation of the organizations involved and in the lives of the people in them.

Establishing Joint Monitoring Policies and Procedures

Monitoring simply means keeping tabs in a purposeful, systematic, and periodic manner. A variety of mechanisms can be used to ensure that the program is proceeding according to plan or to determine when it is off track (see figure 14.1). As a starting point, the governing body

Figure 14.1. Monitoring a Program

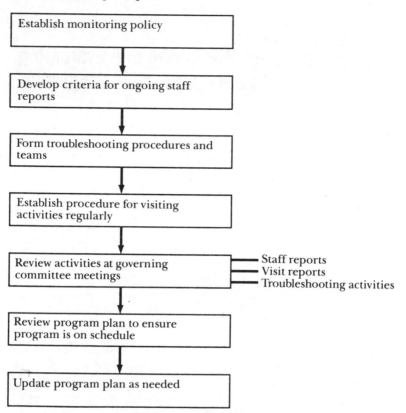

should establish a clear policy for monitoring and include a commitment to monitoring in its governing document.

Monitoring can function like a radar system. When it is in place and operating, it can alert you to problems when they are still manageable. Monitoring can also alert you to nurture successes. Monitoring involves four related tasks:

1. determining what you want to track;
2. collecting information;
3. using the information to measure progress against plans and expectations; and
4. providing feedback on progress.

The governing body should take the lead in identifying that it wants to track, by what methods, and with what frequency. It then should communicate to the participants in the program its intentions and methods. Key messages to communicate are that monitoring helps a joint program keep track of what is occurring and live up to its promises; that the governing body is open to feedback on whether the monitoring is check-ing the right things in the right ways; and that the information gathered will not be used in a punitive way but rather to support and enhance the joint effort. Letting people know what will be checked—and then checking—is the best form of problem and conflict prevention for joint union-management programs.

Monitoring Techniques

Monitoring checklists are an excellent tool that indicate what the parties want to check on a regular basis. Frequently, governing bodies are enjoined to monitor what is going on. Usually the whats and how are not specified. By brainstorming and agreeing on a monitoring checklist, the group will be clear on what it wants—and doesn't want—to review. The more specific these lists are, the better. Clues to what should be included are found in the governing documents of the group, its goals, and its plans. Items to include are such topics as where the groups are in the problem-solving process, attendance, the energy level of the groups, potential conflicts with the traditional collective bargaining contract, resistance and/or reaction to the program in the organization, specific direct or indirect accomplishments, degree of change (positive or nega-tive), costs, and progress against goals and plans.

Reports by the staff of the program, whether they are coordinators or facilitators, provide critical information on how the groups are function-ing and what is planned. The staff should primarily address the items on the monitoring checklist. If there are other items of burning importance, then they can be addressed as well, but long, boring reports on issues of little interest to the governing body should be avoided. They also shouldn't tattle on what has been said by whom in the groups. At the same time, the staff should be candid about the problems groups are facing. Difficulties will boomerang when the problems finally surface. In some programs with a large staff, a schedule is developed for staff reports from various locations.

Another very important way to monitor the activities of a cooperative program is to *make visits*. All the members of the governing body should have a chance to sit in on problem-solving groups within their jurisdic-tion. There is no need to be at all their meetings, but periodic visits demonstrate interest and provide firsthand impressions. It is best when the group knows about the visitors ahead of time and visitors stay for the duration of the meeting. By doing this, the problem-solving group will feel genuinely supported rather than spied on. Visits have two-way bene-fits. They increase the commitment of the visitors, and they increase the morale of those visited by opening up communications between them and their visitors.

Another method is to *share important documents* such as charts, plans, minutes, and surveys of the various components of the program with those who need to know what is going on. The content tackled by the groups is just as important as their adherence to the process. Sharing such information can generate information that could help the problem-solving process. The governing body must not preempt or undercut the efforts of a problem-solving group, and it should not prejudge preliminary data or draft documents. Instead, it should review documents to see whether it can assist in any way and assess whether the group is on target.

An area of particular importance in monitoring is how well problem-solving techniques are being used. Early intervention to correct mistakes, oversights, and useless tangents can save an incredible amount of time and aggravation later on. Many experts advocate quality-control intervention before the end of an assembly line so that quality defects can be caught and corrected early. Likewise, high quality standards need to be maintained in joint programs. Ongoing and early assessment of the problem-solving process and adherence to the governing documents improve the quality of the final results and help avoid failures and blowouts.

Using Joint Troubleshooting Procedures and Activities

In every program's life a little rain must fall. Inevitably, difficulties arise, and there is no way to anticipate all of them. The aim should be to manage these difficulties as early as possible, at the lowest level possible, and with the least disruption to the program and organizations involved. Joint troubleshooting is a way to ensure that the governing bodies truly steer the program.

Several counterproductive strategies are often used. Some program staff do ostrich imitations when trouble looms, and stick their heads in the sand. One major part of the anatomy remains exposed, however, with this approach! In other locations, shotguns are drawn to shoot at minor issues. Top-level people are sucked in to solve petty problems that could have been resolved at lower levels. Senior managers and unionists generally resent this intrusion on their time, especially if it occurs with any frequency. Typically, practitioners of this approach have a favorite troubleshooter and call on him or her all the time. These "favorites" tire quickly of this role. When a big gun is brought in immediately, particularly to confront middle management, there is a residue of resentment left over that carries long-term negative consequences. In some cases, program staff are nervous nellies and call meetings of the governing bodies for every little thing. Such meetings are unnecessary and a waste of time for the group.

Forming joint labor-management troubleshooting teams, designated on a rotating basis by the governing body, is one way to avoid the traps discussed above. The governing committee designates the team, of one management and one union representative from the committee, and it is on call for a specified time period, usually one to three months. Any member of the program may call on the team to examine a problem and help solve it. Both team members consult together on possible solutions. If it is a labor problem, the union person is given first crack at solving it. If it is a management problem, the manager tries first.

Sometimes a group refuses to go forward with problem solving because of the slow processing or unfavorable outcome of a grievance. This situation is often referred to as "hostage taking," that is, holding the cooperative activities hostage to try to get something in the traditional collective bargaining arena. Although hostage taking does not happen repeatedly, it can and does occur. The union should inform the group of the separate processes for cooperative problem solving and grievance resolution, the different agreements that pertain to them, and the fact that not all grievances can be won despite the union's best efforts. An effective approach when a group is having difficulties is to try to get accurate information from employees about the real situation.

Similarly, middle managers sometimes put up roadblocks to the accomplishment of a task, forbid or discourage attendance at group meetings, or have frequent "emergencies" that just happen to occur at the same time as scheduled meetings. The management member of the troubleshooting team should inform the resisting managers of the overall commitment of management to the program and counsel them to desist. Usually a word to the wise will be sufficient, but sometimes intervention from a superior is necessary.

From time to time, problems occur because of delays from technical support groups that provide information to the problem-solving groups. Their slowness is generally due to their unfamiliarity with requests from nonmanagerial employees. A friendly reminder from the troubleshooting team is usually sufficient to remedy this problem.

If a troubleshooting team feels it cannot resolve a problem, it should be handled by the full governing committee, preferably in a regular session, although a special meeting may be necessary. If the full committee can't resolve it, the issue should be bumped up the ladder to the next highest level in the program for resolution. In some cases, the issues may not be clear-cut and the appropriate level of governing body may need to establish or clarify policy on the matter in question. In our experience, troubleshooting teams can settle most issues themselves.

A discussion of troubleshooting leads to the issue of authority. As much as possible, good sense should be used in a cooperative program. Unfortunately, in some situations it is not enough. Individual players cannot be allowed to sabotage an institutional policy of cooperation. If a manager is undercutting the agreed-upon policy, then traditional hierarchical authority will need to be enforced. On the labor side, individuals may have legitimate reservations, but the membership should abide by any agreements the union has made. Selective application of agreements by labor opens the door for the other side to do the same. The enforcement mechanism is generally stronger on the management side—an employee's job. If union-management cooperation is a way of doing business, it should be enforced like any other basic policy of the organization.

In some programs too much emphasis is placed on the voluntary nature of the process. Managers cannot volunteer not to produce their employer's product or service or make up ways of operating that are fundamentally counter to the policy of the employer. They go along with policy or leave. The same principle should apply to joint programs. Too many programs have gotten the image of being pushover efforts shielded from the reality of the work world. Sabotaging behavior should not be tolerated. It demonstrates nothing but lack of concern. Such behavior can corrode and erode commitment to the program. As part of their performance appraisals, some organizations review managers' participation in the joint process. Cooperation is then highlighted as a standard operating procedure and rewarded. Education and counseling are first-level strategies to prevent sabotage, but, if necessary, agreements must be enforced.

Using Program Plans to Measure Progress

The various plans developed throughout the program are the critical instruments for monitoring progress. Without them, the criteria for monitoring can shift from moment to moment, there is little sense of a comprehensive review, and there are no clear-cut measures of changes. The plans for the entire program, the work of the staff, and the activities of the problem-solving groups provide the basis for the review. Inadequate monitoring is likely to be interpreted as a lack of commitment or interest in these plans, not as freedom to be innovative. In hopes of not appearing to hover, no one knows about problems when they first occur. When plans aren't monitored, the pace begins to lag, and as it lags energy and interest in the program drop off as well. Without reference back to the plans, individuals and groups make up their own plans or go their separate ways. Sometimes these tangents are helpful, but usually groups get so caught up in tangents that it is difficult to bring them back on board and the whole program ends up in a morass.

At each meeting of the governing body, plans should be reviewed to see whether planned activities are being implemented, whether they are occurring on time, and what the next steps should be. If there is a difference between the plan and what is taking place, this should be discussed. The mere fact that a plan is not being followed is not a problem. Not knowing why and what to do about it is.

In most cases, monitoring helps flag problems early and clearly. If there is consistently a lag between the plan and the accomplishments, either the planning was unrealistic or there are barriers impeding progress. If planning skills are lacking, the group should learn from its mistakes, perhaps get some training, and try to plan more realistically. Often, deviations from a plan are symptomatic of problems in the group. Fingers are usually pointed at outside influences first, but in reviewing groups that are behind schedule, a careful look at their internal functioning is in order. There may be problems in accomplishing tasks or in group dynamics. Sometimes the problem is that the group leaders and members lack adequate training. The plan should be clearly communicated to all members of the group so that all can aim for clearly understood goals. A troubleshooting team should be used if a group has significant problems accomplishing its plans.

Accomplishing tasks in a carefully devised plan is an important milestone for any group. Monitoring should include praise for those who plan and accomplish tasks as well as recognition of problem areas when progress does not keep pace. Used effectively, plans provide a source of pride and accomplishment for a group.

Establishing a Joint Evaluation Process

For many people, evaluation is a scary word. To some, it sounds academic; to others, it conjures up painful memories of bad report cards. Managers may see evaluations as preludes to major changes, harassment, delays, or punishment. But evaluations don't have to be all that bad.

Evaluations are absolutely essential to the long-term success of cooperative union-management programs. Without knowing what the program's results are or what went right or wrong in implementing it, people can keep marching in the wrong direction. Organizations that do not evaluate what they are doing are like people walking down blind alleys. They might get where they want—but then again, they might not!

The governing bodies have to make a clear commitment to evaluation at all levels of the program—and carry it out. They should assess the particular solutions being implemented, each element of the program's process, and the overall results. Evaluations too often fall by the wayside as programs get under way and get lost in the shuffle of institutional priorities. When those affected learn that no one is evaluating the program or their participation, the quality of performance suffers.

The goals of an evaluation are really very simple. It should measure both the process for introducing and maintaining a project and the specific results—including those anticipated in the goals and objectives set out at the beginning. It assesses whether the program is doing what it set out to do and if it is doing it in an acceptable manner, how what has been done well can be done even better, and how aspects that are not going well can be corrected. Sometimes parties are tempted just to look at the results and bypass the process. This limits the value of the evaluation and leaves them in the dark about how to strengthen the results.

A good evaluation will provide important answers to questions about the program's progress, but, even more important, it will provide clues to where the effort should go in the future. In addition, by adopting a joint union-management approach to evaluation, understanding and teamwork are strengthened. We have seen previously reluctant internal union and management evaluators increase their awareness of the program significantly. The usual end result is a stronger commitment from both parties to make their program even better and a pride in their accomplishments.

Conducting a Joint Evaluation

Most formal evaluations are done by outside evaluators in order to preserve "objectivity." Although this is understandable for academic papers and formal comparisons, the objective of an evaluation of a union-management project is different. The people inside want to know in terms they can understand what has gone on. We have tested the approach outlined in figure 14.2 and it has been shown to provide the kinds of answers that can be used to help strengthen a program. Joint development of the evaluation design models the bilateral nature of the partnership on which the cooperative program is based. The data-based design reinforces the credibility of the evaluation. You may want to have outside evaluations done to supplement this process. Further, it can be supplemented or incorporate information from employee or customer surveys.

The union-management partners should do as much of the evaluation as possible. Although external assistance can be helpful, the union and management principals should maintain control over the process. The magic of this approach is in the relationship of the internal parties to the learning, not in the degree of statistical reliability.

Who should evaluate whom and what should be reviewed must be clearly understood at the outset. Every group in a program should

Figure 14.2. Evaluating a Program

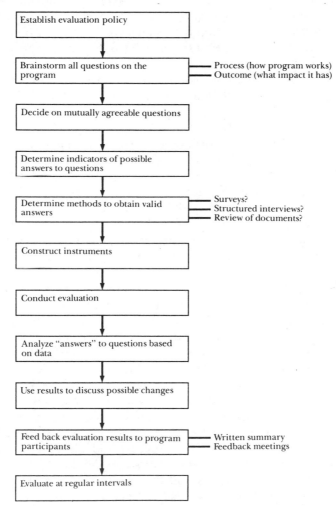

evaluate itself and its subordinate groups, and these various evaluations should be integrated into an overall plan for evaluation. All the groups should work together to ensure that they are in sync in terms of timing, areas of investigation, and methodology. For example, in a program with three tiers, those at the top level should evaluate their own functioning and the performance of the program overall as well as that of top-level staff. Those at the middle level should review their own activities and subordinate groups and reporting staff. Those at the base level should review their own performance. To avoid duplication, the evaluation can flow upward so that those at the next higher level use the results of those at the previous level as a starting point, then examine additional questions that seem important, and incorporate them into their self-assessment. In some cases, however, the group may want to review similar questions to those addressed at other levels, especially when the answers are subjective rather than data-based.

When conducting reviews of cooperative programs, the impact on and role of the union is usually ignored. Balance the picture by looking at organizational roles and results that include the union as a respected partner worthy of examination.

The first step is to brainstorm questions the union and management partners have about the process of their effort. Although these questions should be internally developed, it may be helpful to look at other evaluations of joint projects. These aids should supplement rather than replace the group's own questions. Examples of process questions are "Did the groups follow the problem-solving process?" "How frequently did the governing body visit the problem-solving groups?" and "What training was provided to what groups, and how effective was the training?"

These questions refer to the way the program was established, or the *how* of the program. General process questions might be included on the overall design process, management of the project, relationship to non-direct participants, development of program staff, development of the governing bodies, communications, implementation and development of shop-floor or office-level groups, and/or the use of consultants. Preferably, the group determines the major categories of program implementation and then brainstorms questions within these categories.

The second step is to brainstorm questions about outcomes. This is when the results are addressed, or the *what* of the program. The primary necessity is to measure whether the goals and objectives set by the governing committee have been met. Questions should address a balance of areas that affect operations and the work force. In addition, there should be an accounting of the results of the various groups associated with the program, such as top- and middle-level committees, task forces, shop-floor problem-solving groups, and other joint mechanisms. The evaluation can capture information on accomplishments not originally targeted, but be careful not to take undue credit.

The third step is to review the list of questions and determine those that are agreeable to both parties. A surprisingly large number of questions may have emerged during brainstorming. Asking all of them is neither necessary nor efficient. Setting a minimum number of votes each question needs in order to be included will help determine priorities. At the end of this step, you should have a list of the most important questions for the evaluation.

The fourth step is to figure out how to determine answers that will be accurate and complete, or "indicators." The group should not jump ahead to answers at this time. For example, indicators of the program impact on organizational performance could be unit profit and loss statements, production records, or quality scoresheets. An indicator of customer satisfaction might be the level of customer complaints. Indicators of the labor-management relationship might be the number of grievances and when they were settled. An indicator of the level of interest of employees in participating in the program might be attendance at meetings. Indicators should be listed under each question. The aim should be to look for hard-data indicators before relying on composites of opinions.

The fifth step is to determine the methods for collecting the information. Examine each question and its indicators and see whether a review of documents, surveys, structured interviews, and/or observations would be the best way to answer the question. An obvious and important way to get information is to review records and documents available within the organization. These include production records, summary grievance reports, productivity assessments, minutes of meetings, attendance logs, and similar documentation. Use these sources first.

Surveys and structured interviews may be necessary to get additional information. Surveys are a good way to get information confidentially from a large number of people. The questions included should be clear about the options provided. Too many open-ended questions make analysis difficult. It is wise to consult texts or experts on the construction of surveys to minimize bias and to ensure that the information generated in fact provides the information needed by the group.

A structured interview is a way to elicit open-ended reactions and assessments. A structured interview is not a general conversation or rap session, but a carefully prepared series of questions. Similar kinds of interviewees should be asked the same set of questions, however, and the interviewer should be careful not to lead the person being interviewed or to interject his or her own opinions. It is not a good idea to have immediate supervisors or subordinates do the interviewing.

The sixth and final step is to construct the appropriate instruments for gathering the data. Check sheets may need to be developed for reviewing organizational documents or gathering information. Surveys and structured interviews need to be prepared and tested to make sure they will accomplish their intended tasks. If an instrument doesn't work, it is best to eliminate the bugs before everyone uses it.

After all this preparation, it is time to conduct the evaluation. If a sample is being used, be careful that it is representative of the whole group or set of documents. You might want to assign labor and management teams to work with particular groups, kinds of data, or evaluation questions.

Guaranteeing confidentiality is essential to ensure accuracy when conducting surveys and structured interviews. By using identification codes, no one except the interviewer will know who filled out which response sheet.

When the data are collected, the answers need to be summarized and analyzed. You may want to assign subgroups of union and management evaluators to summarize the interviews or the data from surveys and/or to work on particular evaluation questions. Your analysis of the data may reveal a variety of patterns, observations, and conclusions. The hope is that management and the union will interpret the data similarly, but there may be differences and these should be respected. Next, the evaluation material is brought together and each one of the overall questions is answered based on the data collected. Some questions will have simple answers. Others will require more analysis and/or a comparison of data from different sources. Some will require judgment calls.

Finally, you're ready to write an evaluation report, based on the questions and the answers. If methodology is a concern, an explanation of the approach and the instruments can also be included. The report should be a highly readable document that can be understood by program participants.

An evaluation does not end when the results are tabulated and reported. The most important part of the evaluation is to use the results to learn how to do the program better. The evaluators and the entire governing body need to review carefully what has been uncovered and collected to determine what improvements are needed. Consider using a problem-solving process similar to one used in the joint program to review problems and alternative solutions. Improvements should be stated as action items, and there should be a clear plan for timely implementation. The next evaluation will determine how well these improvements have been applied.

The evaluation process itself should be evaluated to see what went well and what could be improved. Use the following criteria in conducting such an assessment.

Accuracy. Did the evaluation reveal and convey adequate information about important features of the joint effort?

Feasibility. Were the evaluation procedures practical, diplomatic, and efficient?

Usefulness. Did the evaluation serve the practical information needs of the participants and other stakeholders?

Propriety. Was the evaluation conducted legally, ethically, and with due regard for the welfare of those involved with the evaluation as well as those affected by the results?

Cooperation. To what degree did the evaluation reinforce and model cooperation and the building of skills in labor and management?

The results of the evaluation should be reported in some form to the participants in the evaluation and made available to others who would like to review them. One way to do this is through a summary report listing the major findings. Some firms have meetings for the problem-solving groups within the jurisdiction of the study to let everyone know the findings and what is planned based on the results. The groups evaluated should be complimented on their achievements as well as told areas needing improvement. This step should be a two-way process in which those who were subjects of the evaluation are encouraged to ask additional questions about the results.

This evaluation process may seem long and involved, but it need not take major amounts of time if it is managed well. Further, the benefits go well beyond the specific answers that are derived. The process teaches leaders in the union and management how to do systematic evaluations, which will have positive effects on their work. And the teamwork that emerges helps build a stronger commitment to the joint process. Union and management participants understand much more about the program than they would if the evaluation were contracted to another group or outside evaluator. Finally, the subjects of the study are constantly reminded that it is important because they see important people in the organization involved.

Evaluations should not be one-time events; they should be done regularly. Subsequent evaluations should be easier to manage than the initial review. Many questions will already have been established as important and can be updated, bugs in the methodology will have been worked out, and the members of the governing body will be more experienced. Usually, a thorough evaluation should be done once a year, but this will vary depending on the program.

Program Renewal

An evaluation can provide a catalyst for program renewal. For a joint program, a thorough evaluation that examines all its activities and accomplishments is a way to reinvigorate the effort. In other cases, there may be a unilateral program in which management wants the union to participate. In this case, a thorough joint evaluation enables both parties to learn how to proceed together. The process will educate the union about the current program and encourage management to rethink and improve its activities.

After a program evaluation, the parties should review their current goals and objectives and determine the extent to which they have been achieved. A strategic scan (or an update of a previous one) can help identify new goals and renew the sense of purpose. Jointly identify any goals that need to be changed either because they were accomplished or are no longer necessary or because new challenges have presented themselves. One party can't drop a goal based on a whim or for spite. Eliminating a goal requires joint agreement. Sometimes there has been a turnover in the personnel who developed the original goals. Make sure you understand why goals were originally on the list and seek to incorporate goals important to new members. Employee and governing body understanding of what is possible may have changed over time. For this reason, goal statements written in the renewal stage may be more realistic and helpful than those initially postulated. Sometimes the overall goals remain the same but the parties shift the specific objectives to reflect accomplishments or new circumstances. After this review, develop a strategy for communicating to the work force the newly revised goals and why the changes were made.

The risks and benefits of the program also may have changed. These should be reviewed by the governing body to determine what should be done. The governing body may need to reexamine its strategies and techniques to minimize risks and maximize benefits and to see whether they need to be revised. A new design will require new plans and may signal the need for new training. Regardless of whether there are new goals or not, there is always room for improvement. Reflect on the current design and practices, including communications channels, and see what can be done to make them better. As always, communicate the changes broadly and effectively. And be prepared to make reviewing the program an ongoing process to improve the quality, magnitude, and significance of the results.

Conclusion

Planning, monitoring, and evaluating are key elements in successful joint union-management programs. They are linked because each requires careful thought, agreement between the partners, and reflection on what should or did happen. Initially, the partners plan together; as the program evolves they monitor their progress; and periodically they systematically evaluate their progress. Evaluation leads to new goals and plans for continuing what has been done well and to necessary improvements. The entire process outlined in this section leads not only to more secure representation of the interests of the union and management but a stronger program. This process may also positively influence performance in other areas of management's and the union's responsibility.

It may seem like a formidable task to do all the things discussed in this part. In many ways it is. But unless all the areas of program development discussed are covered, there will be significant long-term costs in the form of aggravating problems for both the union and management, diminished potential for the program, and increased possibility of fail-ure. It is worthwhile to expend the extra energy it takes to engage in a complete approach to cooperation. A new and stronger creative energy will be unleashed as a result. The reason the union and management entered into a joint effort is because they have important goals and objectives in common. This joint systematic and pragmatic approach gives them the best chance for realization of these goals and objectives.

Part IV. The Financial Side of Cooperation

15. Sharing the Pie: Alternative Reward Systems, Collective Bargaining, and Profit Sharing

Cooperating in the area of finances appeals to two basic human needs: self-interest and the desire for a common purpose. Companies engage in this form of cooperation when it helps meet their basic goals for successful financial performance. Similarly, employees are motivated to support new compensation and participation systems when there is a clear monetary benefit. Together, employees and companies can cooperate to their mutual financial benefit by expanding the pie and improving performance.

Union and management partners are naturally linked in a basic cooperative relationship in the area of finances. Management must manage employees so that operations are maximally effective to enhance and secure organizational finances. The union must represent employees so that they obtain the best compensation for their contribution to the organization. Traditionally, the union and management divide up the financial pie at the bargaining table by setting basic compensation rates. Recently, however, many union and management partners have begun examining more closely profit sharing and employee stock ownership plans. Union and management partners also are assessing cooperation in the area of overall employee compensation through gainsharing, pay for knowledge, and pay for performance.

Traditionally, hourly employees receive time-based pay. Furthermore, employers commonly adjust time-based pay on an annual basis. In the last ten years, employers have been exploring various additions and alternatives to this arrangement. These alternatives are collectively described as alternative reward systems (ARS), alternative pay systems, or compensation at risk. Employers are examining exactly what they want their compensation policies and systems to accomplish. At a minimum, employers want compensation to reward desired employee behavior and activities and to serve to attract, retain, and motivate employees. Because of significant market and business pressures, many employers want to link desired employee behavior more directly to business goals and objectives and business performance. To go beyond paying employees solely for their time, employers are looking to pay employees for their contributions to the business. Finally, employers want to move to more variable employee pay systems. They want to make compensation costs variable in the way that some of the other costs of doing business are. These work organizations establish employees as stakeholders who are directly involved in and committed to their work organization. Sometimes employees assume some of the risks in the business via their variable pay.

Unions and companies must grapple with three very significant challenges as they consider alternative reward systems:

1. How to modify the compensation system successfully, especially since many alternative pay systems have limited track records and there is even more limited research on their application.

2. The new basis or bases for compensation; time is relatively easy to measure. Measuring performance, skill, knowledge, or contribution to productivity or whether other business objectives have been met is not as easy.

3. How to structure the transition to a new and different compensation system. In any workplace, undertaking a new pay system is a very significant organizational change. Many union and management partners have discovered that managing this change is much harder than deciding what the change will be.

This part examines employee participation in various financial aspects of organizations and the less traditional forms of employee compensation. The four chapters describe ways management and unions can work together to increase the financial return to employees and employers in both the public and private sectors.

How Are Financial Gains Traditionally Shared?

Traditionally, employees share the financial gains of their organizations through pay and benefits. In unionized workplaces, these are among the key items addressed at the bargaining table. Additionally, various bonuses are devised to reward employees for extra effort, and raises acknowledge employee tenure, skills, or performance. With few exceptions, financial gains have been shared on the "trickle-down theory." The organization gains through increased profits or a higher budget and employees eventually get their share of these profits as they work their way down from the top of the organization. The union wants to obtain more for its members, and management wants more for its own compensation, dividends, investments, and growth.

Recently, this search for more has been conducted in the context of declining profits or organizational budgets and the declining strength of the labor movement. Organizations haven't had greater financial resources to be shared and have been less willing to cut into their shares. Further, corporate financial performance is harder to predict. Historically, the search for more has concentrated on getting a greater share of the existing pie rather than on increasing the size of the pie. Employee involvement in less traditional forms of employee compensation often contributes to increasing the size of the pie. Employees focus on improving the financial performance of the business and thereby build up both the employer's and the employees' financial resources. The result is that the financial pie becomes larger, more stable, and/or more flexible.

How Is Participation Linked to Financial Incentives?

A 1982 survey by the New York Stock Exchange found that the main reason a majority of companies use financial incentives is to improve overall company performance and/or productivity. The rationale is that employees participate in the company more intensely, especially through their job performance, when participation is tied to a financial reward. In 1987, a Hay Group survey revealed that 87 percent of the largest American companies use some non–base pay incentives or alternative pay system. The most common forms in use were profit sharing (37 percent), group incentives (16 percent), and gainsharing (16 percent).[1] Group-based forms of incentives are on the increase, while individually based forms are declining.

Initially, many employee participation and quality of work life programs were not involved in issues of employee compensation or financial incentives. Now these programs are linked either to compensation or other financial incentives or at least peacefully co-exist with nontraditional compensation and/or financial incentive programs. This connection is worth pursuing for union and management partners whose constituencies are asking "What's in it for me in cooperation?" Without changing organizational practices, improvements in organizational performance are difficult to sustain and gains in compensation are often diminished or lost. Without employee participation, it is very difficult to change organizational practices.

A Framework for Alternative Reward Systems

Alternative reward systems can be organized into five categories according to the aspect of the organization to which the employee's compensation becomes linked. First, profit sharing links compensation to the organization's overall profitability. Second, some systems link compensation to organizational productivity. Individual financial incentive programs emphasize personal productivity. Gainsharing programs emphasize organizational or group productivity. Third, pay for performance or merit pay programs provide employees with incentives to raise their individual and in some cases group performance. Fourth, pay for knowledge programs engage individual employees and groups of employees in human resource management and planning. In this case, the company seeks to increase its worth by enhancing the knowledge and skills of its human assets. Fifth, through employee stock ownership plans and employee buyouts, employees in private sector organizations participate in capital formation. All of the chapters in this part describe how employees can invest in their companies and how the value of their investment will fluctuate.

Changes in participation regarding finances are usually part of larger organizational changes. Alternative reward systems can be a vehicle for initiating large-scale change or for reinforcing changes already under way. Whether the change leads to or lags behind larger changes, the transition to nontraditional financial participation has very significant implementation costs, including feasibility studies, employee attitude surveys, communications and education packages, as well as administrative expenses. Too often the union-management partners do not recognize that there are psychological and social costs to employees as well. Employees often perceive that they are trading in their traditional compensation system for an uncertain or at least unknown system. When the popular term compensation at risk is used, it only reinforces employee fears that their base pay will erode over time. Popular wisdom suggests that when their base pay is at or above market level, employees perceive alternative pay systems as additive and not necessarily threatening. Conversely, when their base pay is below market level, employees worry that the alternative system will reduce their base pay over time.

Within the decade various pay options will be offered, just as various benefits options are now commonplace. An employee's compensation will be a veritable layer cake that includes traditional or base compensation as well as one or more layers based on alternative reward systems. Union-management partners must learn how to evaluate the potential value of the various financial participation schemes and what they can do for them.

Collective Bargaining as a Financial Gainsharing Mechanism

Collective bargaining is the most common mechanism for sharing the results of improved financial conditions. Monetary items or items affecting employee compensation by far comprise the bulk of the items addressed through collective bargaining. It is a very effective way for the union and management to reach agreement about how to divide up the financial pie.

Collective bargaining has a much longer and broader track record as a mechanism for joint decision making about financial issues than any of the other less traditional systems. And when other less traditional mechanisms are adopted in unionized workplaces, they are often introduced at the bargaining table. In other cases, union-management partners explore alternative systems as part of a joint effort and later incorporate a new system into the collective bargaining agreement.

Collective bargaining has two distinct advantages over other mechanisms for employee involvement in the financial area. First, collective bargaining has overall equity and fairness as guiding principles. Financial benefits are shared fairly by all the workers in the bargaining unit. Collective bargaining recognizes that each employee makes a unique contribution to the organization and that employees as a group make a contribution greater than their individual contributions. For this reason, unions advocate dividing financial benefits among workers on an objective, fair, and equitable basis. Supervisory and middle-management compensation packages are usually adjusted by management to keep pace with the financial benefits obtained by agreement-covered employees working under them. If anything, union insistence on equity and fairness through collective bargaining has had the effect of supporting teamwork and has mitigated against the "every man for himself" attitude that some less traditional mechanisms for employee involvement in organizational finances can foster.

Second, collective bargaining is a process by which management and the union examine the total organizational picture. Financial resources and gains are divided up with an eye to this total picture. Many of the other financial mechanisms identified in this book are not based on such a broad, inclusive perspective. Most of them zero in on one or more measures of financial success. Using this narrower, less comprehensive perspective has real limitations. For management, sharing gains through collective bargaining provides predictability and an opportunity to weigh different factors and to cost out different options. Tying financial gains to one factor such as productivity, however, can be risky and possibly undesirable if, for example, productivity is enhanced but revenues decline. Or the skills and knowledge of employees could increase through pay for knowledge, thereby resulting in higher labor costs, while the revenues remained the same or declined. Depending on which reward system is used and which measures are used to determine rewards, a company could be paying out financial rewards in addition to base pay when it was not profitable or had overall poor performance.

Collective bargaining is the best process whereby management and the union can divide up the organization's financial resources equitably and fairly based on an analysis of the total picture of the organization. Despite a popular belief that collective bargaining hurts economic performance and productivity, there is a growing body of evidence to the contrary. When wages can be varied to compensate for overall performance, there is less pressure for productivity growth. But with union demands to maintain higher wages, productivity growth can spur overall performance. Union compensation structures can indeed be a driver helping to promote productivity. Unions and collective bargaining are positive forces for encouraging productivity, skill development, employee retention, and technological innovation.[2]

What Is Profit Sharing?

Profit sharing is an arrangement whereby a company shares its profits with its employees. As of 1981, more than 350,000 firms in the United States had profit-sharing plans.[3] In 1989, the Bureau of Labor Statistics conducted a survey on employee benefits in medium and large firms. The survey revealed that 16 percent of the employees had profit sharing available to them. Procter & Gamble pioneered the use of profit sharing by establishing a plan in 1887. Other major companies, such as Kodak, Sears, Johnson Wax, and Harris Trust, established plans in the 1920s. In 1939, Congress passed a law allowing tax deferments for companies with qualified profit-sharing plans. More than 90 percent of today's plans began as a result of this provision.[4]

Under profit sharing, the company contributes to the plan once a year. The amount contributed may be a fixed percentage of before-tax profits, a discretionary amount decided upon by the board of directors, or a combination of a fixed and a discretionary amount. Bonuses are then credited to all employees participating in profit sharing. Usually the amount is based on compensation or years of service.

Most profit-sharing plans defer actual payment of an employee's share of the profits until retirement, death, disability, or termination. In this way employees gain investment earnings. When the employee retires or leaves, he or she receives both the profits allocated to the account and the investment earnings on those profits. Some plans distribute all or part of the employee's share as cash once a year. Other plans allow employees to add to their accounts as soon as the share of profits is calculated. Some combination plans pay part of the employee's share as a cash award and defer the remainder until the employee terminates employment.

From a tax standpoint, everyone in the company benefits from profit sharing. The company can deduct its contributions to the plan, and costs for the trust that handles the plan are tax-exempt. Employees do not pay taxes on the funds in their accounts until they actually receive them. Most employees obtain their profit-sharing bonuses upon retirement, when most are in a lower tax bracket.

Most profit-sharing plans provide for no real, direct employee participation in the management of the company. As a result, the employees' share of the profits is affected by decisions over which employees have little or no say. Some plans encourage employee participation through such channels as suggestion systems. Others communicate regularly with employees about the financial status of the company but communication is primarily one way. Many plans co-exist alongside employee participation programs but there is no direct connection between them.

How Effective Is Profit Sharing as a Motivator?

Profit-sharing plans sometimes give employees the feeling that they have a stake in their company and its success. In this way they can indirectly have a positive impact on employee productivity and morale. Employees are usually aware, however, that company profits are influenced by many internal and external conditions, most of which are divorced from their control or influence. These conditions include changing commodity prices, political upheavals, currency fluctuations, liability losses, and the like. Because profits can decline because of factors outside their control, it is not wise to try to convince employees that by improving their performance they will necessarily gain a financial reward through profit sharing. Employees will be dissatisfied and disillusioned when there is no profit sharing. Financial rewards from profit sharing may be too unstable or insubstantial to be positively motivating to either employees or the organization. Bad experiences with profit sharing can poison the workplace atmosphere and block the introduction of other alternative reward systems.

For any incentive to be motivating, the reward must be distributed as close as possible to the time period in which it was earned. Insofar as a majority of profit-sharing plans defer payment until retirement or termination, the financial rewards are very removed from day-to-day work and performance. Even if cash is distributed, it is awarded annually, after the year in which the profits were earned. These circumstances can make profit-sharing incentives too remote to be strong motivators.

Nonetheless, there are valid reasons that a union and management may wish to engage in profit sharing. It is very common in small to medium-sized firms where an individual's performance would seem to count for more in the company's overall performance, although in and of itself it may not be an effective motivator.

Profit sharing provides mutual financial gains but with certain limitations. It provides more—and welcome—income for employees by linking employee compensation to the macro or corporate business picture. Increasingly, profit sharing is implemented with other alternative reward systems or gainsharing, which then connect overall employee compensation to the picture at the local organization or site.

16. More for More: Individual Incentive Plans, Small Group Incentives, Pay for Performance, and Pay for Knowledge

T he wage incentive systems discussed in this chapter—individual incentives, small group incentives, pay for performance or merit pay, and pay for knowledge—have all been examined, negotiated, and implemented by unionized organizations to improve organizational performance and share financial benefits with employees. In all four systems, an employee's wages or compensation are structured so as to provide stronger financial incentives for him or her to perform and develop on the job. Individual incentive systems focus on individual output or productivity. Small group incentive systems focus on the out put or productivity of one department, one work unit, or one work team. Pay for performance systems focus primarily on individual effectiveness or performance. Pay for knowledge systems focus on individual skills and knowledge. In all four cases, individual employees can obtain more by personally doing more.

What Are Individual Incentive Plans?

Piecework is probably the most well-known form of individual incentive plan. In a piecework plan, an employee is paid according to his or her individual output. A price or piece rate is paid for each unit completed or processed. Piecework is effective only when employee output is easily measured on an individual basis and when production is standardized and stable so that the piece rates or prices are relatively stable over time.

Standard hour plans or 100 percent incentive plans are examples of other individual incentive plans.[1] First, a methods study is done to ensure that a job is being performed in the most efficient fashion. Then a time study is done to set the standard.[2] For each 1 percent performance over the standard, the employee is awarded 1 percent over base wage. Base wage is guaranteed, and the employee receives 100 percent of the gains made.[3] Standard hour plans are used in production operations where piecework is not an option.

In both piecework and standard hour plans, time and motion studies are used to establish standard output and thus to set wages. These studies also identify methods employees can use to improve their output and obtain financial bonuses. Union and management partners considering either piecework or standard hour plans must agree on both the methodology and the industrial engineer(s) to be used in the time and motion studies. Through joint training on industrial engineering methods, the partners can learn to analyze the situation competently and reach agreement on the methodology and specialists to be used.

To link successfully wage incentives and labor standards established by time and motion studies, it is important to develop the best practical method for doing the work or performing the job; train the workers to use the best method; measure accurately both manual and machine times; have employees participate in making changes affecting their jobs; and follow up after the standards are issued to ensure their proper application.[4] Though piecework and standard hour plans may seem simple and therefore appealing, there is more to applying them successfully than first meets the eye.

A third less common individual incentive system uses leisure time incentives. Time off or leisure time is given in lieu of extra wages or financial bonuses. In parts of the transportation industry, for example, time off is allowed if a run is completed more quickly than the standard established for it. This is called an "early quit." In other industries, time off is earned when a certain level of production is reached. Other names for this arrangement are stint work, task work, or sunshine bonus systems.[5]

In one of the early joint quality of work life experiments, leisure time incentives were a major part of the program. At the Harmon Industries–United Auto Workers project at the Bolivar, Tennessee, plant, one of the ways productivity gains were shared was through earned idle time (EIT). As part of a one-year experiment, individuals or groups had the choice of going home or continuing to produce after production goals were met. Employees could leave early with a full day's pay; earn extra pay for extra work based on group performance; or earn bonus hours in which they could do whatever they wanted in the plant.[6] Groups of employees in the EIT experiment increased their productivity and changed their work methods. Eventually, EIT was expanded plantwide and a free, in-plant education program was begun to provide courses requested by the workers that they could attend during "earned idle time."

Giving time off though very appealing may send the wrong message to the work force. Many union-management partners are trying to transform control-based workplaces to commitment-based workplaces where workers identify strongly as stakeholders. Rewarding high performance at work by providing opportunities to leave work may send a confusing message or a message that is seemingly inconsistent with the commitment orientation. At the same time, employees who earn time off value the arrangement. It would be difficult and probably very time-consuming to measure precisely the true cost of this incentive. Shortening the workweek for all employees as many of our world trading partners have done might increase productivity overall.

Probably the greatest controversy surrounding individual incentives is how much of an incentive is needed to be motivating. Experts suggest that workers must be paid 15 to 35 percent more than their hourly base rate for an incentive to be motivating.[7] As experimentation with various incentive systems continues, more precise calculations of the levels at which incentives are truly motivating will probably be necessary.

Issues Surrounding Individual Incentive Plans

Individual incentive plans bring to the fore many difficult issues. Employees are often expected to change their production or output directly. Yet machine- or computer-paced operations control that output. Further, regardless of machine pacing, jobs have different potentials for applying improved work methods or production shortcuts. Such differentials seriously challenge the equity and fairness of individual incentive systems. In effect, different employees have different opportunities for improving their output and obtaining gains, which can cause jealousy and division among employees. Not surprisingly, unions worry that individual systems reduce union solidarity.

Industrial engineering, which sets the standards for incentives, is not a precise science. Nor has giving industrial engineering a key role in American production over the past forty years necessarily resulted in the highest-quality products or the most effective production processes, although industrial engineering has made many significant contributions to American industry. Management and the union often have very different levels of belief in the competence residing in and the credibility of industrial engineering. Employees often have negative opinions of industrial engineering as a source of assistance in doing their jobs well. Employees may question not only whether the standards are properly set but also whether the production processes themselves were properly designed and engineered.

Workers can manipulate individual incentive systems in a variety of ways: by restricting output to convince management to revise the standards downward or by keeping production at a level above the standard and no higher so that the standard will not be revised upward. Initially, incentive rates can be motivating. Standards can become outdated, however, and sometimes they become obsolete because of changes in production processes. Because employees resist changes to their standards and individual incentive system, updating the system is not always easy. Alternatively, raising the standards too high or condoning under-the-table shortcuts can lead to safety hazards.

Individual incentives can also become counterproductive at some point. For example, an individual incentive system can be a barrier to achieving higher levels of cooperation and engaging in teamwork. For this reason, many union-management partners are considering group-based gainsharing efforts.

A successful incentive plan requires accurate record keeping and bookkeeping, good supervision, and excellent communications. In some situations these requirements can't be met because the organization does not have the information management systems and/or capabilities. Management misjudgments, incompetence, and failures can so adversely affect operations that employees' chances of meeting the standards and obtaining the bonuses are reduced or eliminated. This can be a real area of conflict for union and management partners in an incentive program. In this case, the union probably would demand a role in setting the standards, but reaching agreement on the standard-setting process and the standards themselves can be a serious challenge for management and the union.

Despite these issues, individual incentive programs can result in greater daily output. Improved work methods resulting from time and motion studies often enable workers to produce more with the same effort. And employees try to eliminate wasted time so that they can exceed the standard and obtain a bonus. Most qualified workers can easily meet reasonable work standards and thus are encouraged to increase their speed and turn out more work. The average output of a group of qualified workers operating under an incentive program normally exceeds the standard by 14 to 45 percent.[8]

An outstanding example of how a union and management can successfully cooperate to institute an individual incentive program is the

Productivity Incentive Plan, undertaken in 1980 by the International Brotherhood of Teamsters and the Certified Grocers of California. The union and management jointly established work standards after hiring an outside company to do the necessary time measurements and analyses. Performance standards were devised for individuals and crews. The average worker now performs at 139 percent of the standard. At the same time, employees who perform at only 90 percent of the standard still have their jobs because their lower performance is balanced by the higher performance of others on their crew. Time off or cash is given for exceeding the standards. Standards for both individuals and crews were developed jointly to ensure that all employees would be given fair treatment. Both the union and management are satisfied with the program.

At one time individual incentive systems were the premier innovation in pay systems. Today, they are but one option among a growing array of individual, small group, and organization-based incentive arrangements. Given all the technological and cultural changes occurring in most unionized workplaces, it is unclear what the future of individual incentive systems will be.

Small Group Incentives

Scientifically established individual incentive systems and organizational gainsharing systems have been in existence for more than fifty years. Small group incentives, focusing on individual departments, work units, or teams, have been developed more recently. Basically, these plans apply gainsharing principles and practices at lower organizational levels and within the framework of one unit rather than the work site as a whole. Small group incentives are viewed as alternatives to large group gainsharing in situations in which the nature of the work performed by various departments, work units, and/or work teams is so different that it would be difficult to establish a meaningful overall gainsharing measurement formula.[9]

Small group incentives are most useful when fostering teamwork in work groups is the primary focus rather than a sense of stakeholdership and collaboration within the work site or organization as a whole. This point also suggests two of the serious shortcomings of small group incentives: First, departments, work units, or work teams often end up competing in ways that reduce overall teamwork and collaboration. The long-term success of any work site depends to a large extent on cooperation among and between the work units within it. Second, the solidarity of the bargaining unit as a whole could be threatened because members of the bargaining unit have different and unequal opportunities for obtaining additional compensation. This occurs because small group incentives contribute little if anything to a unified sense of stakeholdership in the work organization as a whole.

Performance improvement programs (PIPs) are one way companies reward performance improvements made by work teams. The focus of PIPs is on achieving specific performance targets and thereby earning award vouchers that can be applied toward the purchase of merchandise. The incentives are meant to be temporary, probably lasting no longer than two years, in recognition of their limited motivational effect. Non-direct teams can also participate, by improving the support and assistance they provide to work teams, and thereby receive a fixed proration of the awards earned by the teams they support. Managers and supervisors help their teams to improve their performance, monitor team progress, and track results. An outside consultant computes the earnings of each team and provides the award vouchers earned.[10]

Another example of a small group incentive plan is the team suggestion program (TSP), which can be useful if organizations want to increase revenues or reduce costs in the very near term (i.e., ten to sixteen weeks). As in PIPs, achievement is rewarded with vouchers used to purchase merchandise. TSPs are also temporary, usually lasting for only several months. Teams of five to seven employees are organized to meet one hour per week to develop suggestions, and an evaluation committee of middle managers accepts or rejects the suggestion within ten to twenty days. Suggestions worth at least $500 are awarded points based on the expected yield in the first year after full implementation. Once again, management oversees the TSP and a consultant provides a system for tracking the suggestions through an evaluation and implementation process.[11]

Both PIPs and TSPs require significant organizational attention during the time frame in which they are operating. It is easy to see why employees often view them as short-term quick fixes or cheerleading efforts that do not capture their attention. Although both PIPs and TSPs have had respectable immediate results, the results drop off quickly and steadily when the programs end.[12]

Union and management partners should approach small group incentive plans with a great deal of caution. These approaches probably will not deliver long-term change and improvement. Further, they can have seriously negative effects, including reducing bargaining unit solidarity, reducing stakeholdership throughout the organization, and possibly poisoning the organizational climate for other financial participation arrangements. Even worse, in situations in which concessionary or stagnant bargaining has occurred, employees may perceive that they have traded real compensation for unneeded merchandise and trinkets and that management is attempting to buy employee loyalty and effort while reducing the solidarity of the bargaining unit.

Pay Systems and Organizational Change

Pay systems are a significant force in any organization and are an important organizational cost. In manufacturing, payroll costs are estimated to be as high as 40 percent in many cases. In service organizations, payroll costs can be as high as 70 percent of total organizational costs.[13] Pay systems are also significant because they are tied to other major aspects of the organization, such as the organizational structure, superior-subordinate relations, job design, organizational climate, management philosophy or style, information and control systems, management training and development, and performance appraisal. Pay affects pricing structure and competitiveness. From the union perspective, pay determines the degree of wage competition in an industry and its relative status. The pay system affects the entire organization and involves everyone within it.

The union and management should consider the relationship of the pay system to any organizational change effort. In many cases it is the primary system wherein change is concentrated initially. There are some compelling arguments in favor of this approach:

1. Pay is important to all employees and affects all.
2. By beginning with the pay system, the organization demonstrates its commitment to real change.
3. Most organizations have problems with their pay systems, such as perceptions of inequity, rewards that are not contingent on performance, and overall inadequate administration.
4. Dealing successfully with the pay system can lead to measurable differences in individual performance and organizational effectiveness.
5. Beginning with the pay system can provide a model of how to deal with other significant problems and can lead to the identification of those problems through the connection of the pay system to other major organizational systems.[14]

In any case, compensation issues are bound to arise in a long-term organizational change effort. The pay system can hinder that effort if it does not reward the behaviors necessary to make the required changes. Pay for performance and pay for knowledge are increasingly being adopted as part of overall organizational change efforts.

What Is Pay for Performance?

Pay for performance, or merit pay, is a compensation arrangement whereby some portion of an employee's compensation is dependent on his or her individual performance. A 1984 study of pay for performance in U.S. industry conducted by the Conference Board revealed that of five hundred firms surveyed 95 percent had pay for performance programs for their exempt (nonhourly) employees. Eighty-two percent considered their programs to be successful.[15]

Pay for performance plans vary along three dimensions: whose performance is rewarded, how performance is measured, and what form the reward or pay takes. Pay for performance plans can cover individual employees, groups of employees, or entire organizations but most commonly cover individuals. Performance can be measured by productivity, cost effectiveness, or a superior's evaluation. The reward can take the form of a salary increase or a cash bonus.

The general rationale for pay for performance is that by linking compensation to performance, performance and satisfaction are enhanced. Social psychological theories support the concept. The expectancy theory maintains that an employee is motivated to perform based on three perceptions: "expectancy," the perception that a certain level of effort will lead to a certain level of performance; "instrumentality," the perception that a certain level of performance will produce certain outcomes; and "valance," the attractiveness of the outcomes. The stronger these perceptions, the more motivated the employee should be.[16] Pay for performance has been most widely used among supervisors and managers, but it is increasingly being applied to hourly employees.

How Does Pay for Performance Work?

The key element in a pay for performance system is how performance is measured. In most cases, measurement is through an appraisal process in which the employee's performance is appraised by his or her superior and in some cases by peers. The ratings on the various elements of the appraisal produce an overall rating, which determines the actual amount of merit pay the employee will receive. Most organizations rely primarily on subjective ratings. They are easy to gather, don't require an elaborate and expensive management information system, and can be an inclusive measure of all the significant behaviors an employee needs to perform to do his or her job effectively.[17] A subjective performance appraisal process requires a high degree of trust, however, to ensure credibility and effectiveness. The union and management partners must recognize that an effective performance appraisal process is the key to a pay for performance system and that trust is the foundation on which this process must be based. The union and management can cooperate or clash over the elements and conduct of the appraisal.

Experts in performance appraisal have identified several organizational conditions that are necessary for a performance appraisal process to be effective:

1. An emphasis on behavior and objectives;
2. use of a predetermined set of goals and/or job functions;
3. an opportunity for subordinates to have input into the evaluation process;
4. a regularly scheduled appraisal cycle that fits with the nature of the jobs being appraised;
5. different meetings to discuss performance, pay, and career development;
6. a due process that includes an appeals procedure at which a subordinate may discuss an allegedly unfair appraisal; and
7. evaluations of how well managers carry out appraisals.[18]

Managers and union leaders in the federal sector probably have the most experience in negotiating performance standards for bargaining unit employees. They have found that this process can be an opportunity to think about how work should be done together or a venue for niggling and conflict. Recently, alternative or nontraditional performance appraisal processes have been developed that include peer appraisals and appraisals of one's supervisor as well. Supervisors are retrained to view employees as customers, and their "customers" conduct periodic reviews of their performance.

The size of the merit increase is another element of pay for performance plans. Employees should be able to obtain a substantial increase if their performance has truly improved. At least a 3 percent increase is needed to be motivational. During periods of high inflation, increases have to be higher than 3 percent in real terms.[19]

Another element of pay for performance plans is the frequency of the payout. The payout period should be short enough to be maximally motivating but long enough to allow for useful, accurate performance appraisals or other performance measurements. Further, the pay increases should be large enough to be motivating but frequent enough that employees connect them to their day-to-day performance. Most merit pay systems evaluate employee performance and award increases or bonuses annually. Unfortunately, the size and frequency of the payout can lead to some tradeoffs. If a longer payout period is used, higher payouts may be necessary.

The final element of a pay for performance system is whether employees participate in its design. Employees should definitely participate in new plants where employee participation is built into the overall operation and in existing plants where the pay system is linked to the development of a more participative management style.[20] The GM-UAW Saturn Project is a good example in this regard. In this case, union-management committees designed the pay for performance system. The incentive pay system negotiated by the National Treasury Employees Union and the Internal Revenue Service is an even older example of a system that not only is employee-designed but also employee-maintained. Employees involved in designing a system will be more committed and more knowledgeable about it, will have more control over how it is implemented and operated, and will trust the system. Creating a joint union-management study team to design the system helps ensure that the interests of both the union and management are represented.

What Makes Pay for Performance Effective?

Research on the effectiveness of pay for performance offers two primary conclusions: (1) managers like their pay to be based on performance, and (2) merit pay has the greatest effect on performance and motivation when the pay for performance link is clearly perceived and understood by employees. Beyond this, experts don't agree on what determines how effective pay for performance is. Some suggest that merit pay has less impact on motivation when there is high inflation. Others assert that satisfaction with pay for performance depends on the increase and the demographic characteristics of the recipients.[21] Others maintain that merit pay increases must be larger for employees with higher earnings than for employees with lower earnings for the same level of performance. For this reason, pay for performance programs calculate the increases as a percentage of base pay. This assertion seems to be no more than a restatement of one of the key givens of traditional compensation systems: those who get more initially get still more. This given can limit the motivation of those who earn less but work just as hard if not more so. In response to this inequity, lump-sum incentives based on earnings levels have been replacing traditional merit systems that adjust base pay.[22]

Pay systems expert Edward Lawler III rated the effectiveness of pay for performance programs as follows:

1. Programs that evaluate and reward individuals are most effective, followed by group and then organizational programs.
2. Programs that reward with a bonus rather than a salary increase are more effective. Bonuses offer greater flexibility in responding to changes in performance. Salary increases tend to become permanent and less mutable.
3. Group and organizationally based programs are more effective in promoting cooperation than individually based programs.

4. Employees are least accepting of individually based programs, fearing favoritism.[23]

Other organizational conditions affect program effectiveness as well.

1. The organization must measure performance accurately and consistently. All relevant job behaviors and employee contributions must be taken into account. Furthermore, objective evaluative criteria should be established for all jobs.
2. The budget for pay for performance should be large enough to finance adequately merit pay increases significant enough to be motivating and to administer the system properly. Sometimes merit pay is cut when economic times are tough. Employees then doubt the sincerity and reliability of merit pay.
3. Employees must be able to affect the evaluative criteria and believe that their performance is being measured accurately. When favoritism enters the picture, it erodes support for performance-based pay considerably.
4. The work organization should provide education and training opportunities to enable all employees to improve their performance.
5. Employees must be willing to participate in the pay for performance system and want the increases available to them.

These five conditions represent a checklist for management and union partners establishing a pay for performance system.

Benefits of Pay for Performance

The most obvious benefit of pay for performance is that employees are motivated to improve their performance on the job. People are attracted to and more easily retained by organizations that reward them for their high performance. Pay for performance requires clarification of roles and measures. Further, it requires clear, structured feedback on specified performance measures. This process can strengthen relationships between supervisors and subordinates and the organization. Finally, employees may be more satisfied with their jobs because they see a clear link between what they do on the job—their performance—and at least part of what they get out of their job—their pay.

Issues and Problems with Pay for Performance

The first concern is the amount of money available for the increases and bonuses. Many plans have a bonus pool but allocate rewards on an individual basis. The size of the bonus pool determines the amount of the increase or bonus and also may determine who gets rewarded.

The second concern is who will participate in what plan and how many plans there will be. Traditionally, managers have had pay for performance. Some organizations now have pay for performance systems that cover all levels of the organization and/or vertical slice performance units. Corning, for example, eliminated its separate management and hourly bonuses and adopted one pay for performance formula.

The third issue is whether to use bonuses or pay increases. Many plans use both, although bonuses are currently the trend. Pay increases can come to be viewed as a permanent rather than a variable portion of compensation and therefore may be less useful as a reward over time.

An overriding question is how motivating pay for performance is. A merit pay system may put too great an emphasis on money as a motivator to the exclusion of other motivators. This may diminish the importance of the job itself, which has also been demonstrated to be a very powerful motivator. There are many other unanswered questions about pay for performance: How much can on-the-job performance be improved over a specified period of time? What happens once a person is performing optimally? How does one continue to motivate a high performer?

There are two other potentially serious problems in a pay for performance system: the costs and the impact on teamwork. An effective pay for performance system can be very costly. There are no conclusive data available on the potential returns on investment. Individually based pay for performance systems may also work against group cooperation and teamwork. Too often pay for performance systems foster significant resentment among employees who have not received an increase or who have received small increases. These employees feel very alienated from the work organization and devalued and cheated by it. This is particularly true if they feel that the merit increases were gained through favoritism or "sweetheart deals." Employees may feel that their performance was negatively affected by extenuating circumstances, such as health problems or a family crisis, in which case they may perceive their employer to be unsympathetic and even punishing. In this way, a pay for performance system can defeat its own purpose.

What Is Pay for Knowledge?

Pay for knowledge is a wage incentive system that pays employees for the range of jobs they can perform. It rewards increased human resource potential in an organization rather than operational outcomes. The American Compensation Association asserts that skill-based pay or pay for knowledge is the second most frequent alternative reward system. It describes pay for knowledge as a means of enhancing a company's ability to deploy its work force in a timely, efficient, and effective manner. From this perspective, the system provides flexibility along two dimensions: in capability and in attitude about what the job is and is not.[24] Recently, unions and management have been looking at pay for knowledge systems as one approach to reorganizing work and the workplace. Pay for knowledge is not a new concept, however. The garment industry has used it for years.[25] The public education system has also built professional development into its compensation system.

There are three kinds of pay for knowledge systems: multiskill-based systems, increased knowledge-based systems, and combination systems. In multiskill-based systems, pay is linked to the number of different skills an employee learns and performs. An employee increases his or her earning power by learning and demonstrating competency in all the jobs in a work area, or through horizontal skills building. Increased knowledge-based systems link an employee's pay to increased knowledge and skill within the same general job category. An employee increases earning power through vertical skill building by learning all there is to know up and down within the job category. Usually multiskill-based pay systems are applied to production employees, and increased knowledge-based pay systems are applied to mechanics and other workers in skilled trades.[26] The third kind of pay for knowledge system combines both vertical and horizontal skills building.

How Does Pay for Knowledge Work?

In multiskill-based pay systems, employees must demonstrate mastery of one job before learning another. How such a program works is illustrated by the program at the GM Delco-Remy battery plant in Fitzgerald, Georgia. There, hourly employees increase their wages by increasing their knowledge of the jobs within their teams until they reach the top level, level 4. The first two levels through which an employee advances after hiring are tied to seniority as well as task accomplishment based on the UAW contract. After level 4, an employee can move to another team and begin to learn the jobs there. He or she gets an increase in his or her rate of pay and can progress up to level 6 in that team. Level 6 certifies that an employee knows all the jobs in two different teams.

In GM's program one concern was that different teams had jobs requiring different technical skills because of the higher or lower technology involved. To address this problem, a level 6 or plant rate was established. An employee probably takes longer to advance on teams working with higher technology and advances faster on teams working with lower technology. An employee assigned initially to a higher technology team can now transfer to a lower technology team and "catch up" while working toward the plant rate. This pay for knowledge system is tied to self-managing autonomous operating teams supported by technical and administrative teams.[27]

The increased knowledge or vertical skill building pay system works in a similar fashion. There are also different levels with different rates, but these levels are all within a particular job category. The employee is not learning new and different jobs but is learning everything there is to know about her or his job.

What Makes Pay for Knowledge Effective?

Pay for knowledge is a relatively new phenomenon in unionized workplaces. Other than in teaching, most applications have been in manufacturing. Manufacturers with batch processing technologies are the most common users. Usually the system is established as part of the overall startup of the plant. The local work culture values work itself and personal growth and development.[28] How pay for knowledge will be applied in nonmanufacturing environments in both the public and private sectors is yet to be determined.

Pay for knowledge is most effective when certain organizational conditions exist. Management must value employee growth, worth, and quality of work life and be wholeheartedly committed to pay for knowledge. Required support mechanisms include effective employee selection, a job design that facilitates job rotation, training and development activities complementary to the pay for knowledge system, effective performance appraisals modified for use in pay for knowledge, and clear and open communications overall.[29] The union should be open to experimenting with the pay for knowledge concept, and employees should be receptive to being involved in the system and in designing it. Finally, pay for knowledge works best under favorable economic conditions.

The union and management partners should jointly specify competencies and knowledge requirements clearly linked to job performance, develop appropriate training curricula, and deliver the needed training to ensure maximum opportunities for all employees to learn and advance. Both rank-and-file employees and supervisors should participate in specifying the competencies. Finally, the partners will have to bargain over the pay levels and advancement requirements. In Australia, the leadership of the ACTU has linked a broad-based goal of career development and higher incomes to competency-based skills development and pay.

As more and more union-management partners deploy cross-functional teams in the workplace, the need for pay for knowledge will be reinforced and additional arenas will emerge in which to use newly acquired skills. Union and management partners who pursue continuous improvement are basically pursuing continuous skill development. Pay for knowledge will both reinforce and be reinforced by the move into continuous improvement.

Benefits of Pay for Knowledge

The advantages to the employer of pay for knowledge are quite significant: increased flexibility within the work force, higher quality of output, greater long-term productivity, leaner staffing, and lower absenteeism and turnover because of the increase in job satisfaction. There are related advantages for employees: increased motivation, greater feelings of self-worth, more job security, and greater commitment and loyalty to the company.[30] Employees have the potential to acquire many more job skills and more money at the same time. Having broader skills can be useful in an uncertain economy, when employees may have to change not only employers but also careers. With pay for knowledge, narrow job classifications are broken down and employers have greater flexibility in using their human resources. This benefit was expressed well by Peter J. Pestillo, vice president for labor relations at Ford Motor Company: " 'I think pay for knowledge will ultimately do more to break down the burden of narrow classifications than anything else.' "[31] For some unions, pay for knowledge is attractive because it enables workers to make higher earnings while minimizing the disparity in wages between workers.

Pay for knowledge can also have financial benefits. At the GM Delco-Remy plant, the cost of producing car and truck alternators has fallen by 6 percent, attributed to the pay for knowledge system. Volume has increased, and quality has improved. The plant hasn't had to hire additional hourly workers, and the salaried work force has shrunk by 18 percent.[32] Comparable pay for knowledge systems have had similar results.

Issues and Problems with Pay for Knowledge

The major questions surrounding pay for knowledge concern which employees and which jobs will be involved. Production jobs are better suited to pay for knowledge programs because they are often well defined and relatively stable. Also, performance depends more heavily on teamwork and coordination in these jobs. It is not clear how this concept would be applied to service jobs at a comparable level. Also unclear is how many jobs can be learned and retained and how much rotation can occur. In a typical pay for knowledge program, employees learn four to eight jobs and rotate among them.[33]

There are also concerns about when and how the learning and training should take place. In most pay for knowledge programs, the bulk of the learning and training takes place on the job. Some programs, however, require that employees study on their own, which raises several thorny issues. Many employees do not have enough personal time to study because of family, union, or community commitments or other job or educational obligations. In particular, working mothers, single heads of households, dual job holders, and people pursuing an education may not have the requisite time in their "off hours" to devote to studying.

There is also the potential for serious discrimination. To advance in the pay for knowledge system, employees usually have to have good study skills and be able to read reasonably well. Ample statistics confirm, however, that many of America's working adults are functionally illiterate. Furthermore, because of limited educational opportunities or discrimination by educational institutions, many working adults do not have good study skills. Who is responsible for ensuring that the participants in pay for knowledge programs have the requisite reading abilities and study skills? Does pay for knowledge result in two classes of workers: those who are fairly well educated to begin with and can take full advantage of the program and those who are educationally disadvantaged and whose advancement through the pay for knowledge system is limited on that basis? Given the legacy of unequal educational opportunities based on racial differences, pay for knowledge may create a new excuse for racial discrimination. The record keeping required to support pay for knowledge will document this or any other discriminatory pattern that develops. Companies could be open to lawsuits on this basis unless they address this potential for discrimination upfront.

These are several serious questions union and management partners should consider before adopting a pay for knowledge program. The partners should consider providing remedial education and study skills training to ensure equal opportunity to participants. Further, the job training and study should be on company time and be designed so that all employees acquire sufficient skills and knowledge to advance, regardless of their backgrounds.

There are three additional problems for employees: holdups, maxing out, and supervisor dissatisfaction. Holdups occur when an employee is ready to move to a new job but can't because there are no vacancies. Some programs have a special holdup rate to compensate employees held back by the system. Maxing out occurs when an employee has learned all the jobs he or she can.[34] He or she has no way to obtain additional compensation. In some organizations, merit or cost-of-living increases are given from that point. In others, multiskill-based and increased knowledge-based systems are combined to ensure that maxing out takes a very long time to occur or is eliminated for all practical purposes. These two problems can reduce individual and group morale and diminish confidence in the pay for knowledge system.

The third problem occurs when supervisors feel threatened by pay for knowledge. They may become very unhappy as the pay, knowledge, and skills of their subordinates increase. The gap between their pay and their subordinates' may narrow or disappear entirely. Further, the perception that only the supervisor really knows the jobs and the work in the area is seriously challenged as the roles of supervisor and subordinate are radically changed. Some adjustment may be needed in the terms and conditions under which supervisors work to help them promote and support the pay for knowledge program. In organizations attempting to redesign the supervisor's role and job, this may not be a problem. In these cases, the pay for knowledge system will seem to be a natural part of employee training.

Organizational problems can also arise with pay for knowledge. Supervisors may be the only stable or permanent employees in a department as other employees rotate in and out as part of the pay for knowledge program. It is thus more difficult to build teamwork, making the supervisor's job more taxing. Some organizations have developed assistant supervisor positions or team leader positions to provide more stability.[35]

Usually, some employees in an organization, often clerical or administrative workers, do not participate in the pay for knowledge program. They may feel dead-ended in their jobs and become demoralized as they see employees in other jobs rotating and advancing. In organizations with other incentive-based bonus systems, employees may even come to view pay for knowledge as adversely affecting their productivity and/or performance. Such employees may value the rewards they receive through other competing systems more than they value the rewards of pay for knowledge, resulting in their resisting pay for knowledge or just marking time in the program.

The costs of a pay for knowledge system can be substantial. Hourly labor costs are usually higher than in traditional wage plans. Further, overall wages are often higher than in comparable jobs at traditional workplaces. The training costs are also significant, and productivity may suffer from the constant use of "trainees." The ratio of the length of time spent learning a job and the length of time spent doing it can be very high. Because employees are motivated to learn and move on as quickly as possible, some organizations have set time requirements for how long a worker must perform a job. Despite these drawbacks, pay for knowledge is often promoted as a way to reduce labor costs and especially as an alternative to concessions.[36]

Tracking the costs of a pay for knowledge program can also be significant. There is much more record keeping than in a traditional workplace with conventional job assignments and a traditional wage system.[37]

Finally, the adoption of a pay for knowledge system may lead to labor conflicts. A fair grievance system must be in place to ensure that disputes about the process and over assessments of qualifications are resolved fairly. This is particularly true in situations in which the issues and problems described above have not been addressed before the adoption of the program. Although General Motors has had great success with its pay for knowledge program at its Delco-Remy plant, there was a strike at its Missouri plant in January 1985 over use of the system. Further, at its Orion Township plant in Michigan, the pay for knowledge system was the UAW's number-one bargaining issue during the 1984 negotiations there. The compromise reached allowed workers to opt out of the program.[38]

A serious problem can arise when there is a major shift in technology or process. What happens to the pay of employees who have mastered the previous competencies but who now must work in a new set of requirements? Do they "go back to go," or do they work at a higher rate next to new employees who are learning the current system of competencies?

For the union and management partners in a pay for knowledge program to be successful, the union and management must jointly determine how to handle all these issues and problems.

Conclusion

Wage incentive systems hold real potential for improving organizational performance. In particular, pay for performance and pay for knowledge systems have been closely scrutinized by unions and management as avenues for changing organizations and addressing a range of workplace concerns. Both are complex systems requiring favorable organizational conditions for their success. Union and management partners should proceed carefully before implementing either of these systems.

17. Gainsharing: Scanlon, Rucker, Improshare, and Customized Plans

R ecently, American industry has been avidly pursuing gainsharing programs. One study indicates that 73 percent of the current gain-sharing programs have been adopted since 1980.[1] Union and management partners come to gainsharing for a variety of reasons. Some want more viable and/or successful organizational performance. Others use gainsharing to reward new and different behaviors and to reinforce teamwork and cooperation. Some unions look to gainsharing to improve their stagnated compensation levels and/or to redress concessionary bargaining losses. Some companies want to build more flexibility into their compensation system. According to a 1987 nationwide survey, "People, Pay, and Performance," conducted by the American Productivity and Quality Center, 92 percent of respondents cited productivity improvement as the primary reason to implement gainsharing; 73 percent cited quality improvement as the primary reason; and 65 percent better employee relations.[2]

In the past, manufacturing organizations pursued gainsharing, through standard programs such as Scanlon, Rucker, and Improshare. Recently, all kinds of work organizations have been pursuing gainsharing, very often by creating customized programs themselves. The survey "People, Pay, and Performance" indicated that most companies now use customized programs.[3]

What Is Gainsharing?

Gainsharing refers to efforts to make "gains" over past and/or targeted organizational performance and then to share the financial benefits from these gains between the employees and the organization. Four basic characteristics distinguish a gainsharing from an individual incentive system:

1. Benefit sharing is productivity-based.
2. The program covers employees as a group rather than as individuals.
3. Teamwork and cooperation are emphasized.
4. Measurements of productivity are based on the total group involved.[4]

Gainsharing is a self-funding system in which the financial gains generated are used to "pay" for the effort.

Gainsharing has been successfully established in both older organizations and new plants. It can be adapted to virtually any private sector environment but traditionally has been used primarily in small to medium-sized manufacturing facilities. There have also been some applications of gainsharing in the public sector.

Many older plants with individual productivity incentive plans are converting to group-based gainsharing plans. In Holland, Michigan, the Hart and Cooley metal stamping plant, affiliated with International Association of Machinists Lodge 1418, provides a good example. It previously had a forty-year-old individual incentive plan covering five hundred workers. Bonuses under this plan ranged from 130 to 250 percent of base pay. Nonetheless, the plant had many serious problems, including high rework rates, high grievance rates, low productivity, high absenteeism, and high accident rates. Updating the old plan would have been costly and may not have corrected many of the problems. Instead, a gainsharing plan was installed with significant positive results: a 30 percent increase in productivity and a 9 percent reduction in the hourly labor costs with exactly the same work force. Furthermore, 65 percent of the employees are earning more under the gainsharing plan than under the individual incentive plan. Hourly base pay was also upscaled and usually is at a level twice that of the previous base. The union and management partners are basically satisfied with the new program.[5]

Many new plants institute gainsharing programs early in their operations as part of a total participative management system. A new plant should operate for some time, however, before undertaking a gainsharing program to debug and stabilize operations. By then, a history of operating results will be available to use in setting base performance levels. There are two key questions for union-management partners considering gainsharing: (1) Is this the right strategy for your situation, and (2) If so, what should the design of the gainsharing effort be?

Employee participation plays a central role in gainsharing since employee expertise is used to solve operational problems and increase productivity. Sometimes unions and management focus solely on the dollar benefits to be obtained from gainsharing and not on the employee involvement needed to effect the improvements that lead to the gains. This is one of the most serious and common mistakes made by union-management partners in developing a gainsharing effort.

Gainsharing combines two very powerful workplace forces—employee participation and financial incentives—that in combination draw unions and management to it.

How Gainsharing Works

First, the goals and objectives of the gainsharing effort are defined. Usually, the overall goal is linked to strategic organizational goals. There are usually other more specific objectives as well, such as quality improvement or improved teamwork. These should be clear and manageable sets of drivers.

Second, the parties determine who will participate. Gainsharing plans vary widely in this regard. In Scanlon plans, all employees, including executives, usually participate. In Rucker plans, hourly workers and sometimes supervisors, professional employees, technical employees, and administrative employees participate. In Improshare plans, only hourly employees participate.[6] Who participates should reflect primarily who helps foster teamwork that leads to improved organizational performance. In most cases, the entire work force at a plant or work site should be included. More recently, plans have been offered at the department or work unit level. We think that to support organizationwide teamwork involvement of the total work site is essential. (Small group-based financial incentives are addressed in chapter 16 along with individual incentives.)

Third, a formula is developed for measuring whether performance improvement has occurred. The goals and objectives of the plan should help define the indicators to be incorporated into this formula. The standard gainsharing programs have measures built in. Customized programs use a variety of single and multiple measures, and many use a family of measures to reflect the multiple outcomes desired. The most desirable measures answer the question, "How do we know that real performance improvement has occurred?" To optimize the motivational power of the measures, they should be performance levers employees can control. The more complicated the measures used, the harder they are to communicate to employees, the more difficult it is to build employee understanding and acceptance of them, and the more costly it is to obtain and use the data necessary to calculate gains. There are also more technical accounting considerations to be addressed in developing a measurement formula. For example, if measures focus on production levels or output, then the formula should consider work in progress, inventory, returns, and rework.

Fourth, a performance baseline or payout threshold is established. Later, performance will be measured and compared to this base. Traditionally, there have been three ways to establish a performance or productivity base: the history of the operations; standards developed by engineering formulas, work measurements, or other mathematical techniques; and financial plans. Ideally, bases are established when prices, wages, and profits are at reasonably competitive levels. The standard programs have predetermined methods for establishing a base. Customized programs use a variety of methods. Recently, many have been using baselines that are higher than previous or past performance levels, especially when past performance was unacceptable. Also, it is increasingly common to use performance baselines that vary, called rising or ratcheting baselines. As higher levels of performance are achieved, baselines are revised and raised.

The productivity or performance base may have to be modified when there are changes in the operation, such as new products with different labor and/or material content, major capital investments that affect other inputs, the elimination of products, or major changes in marketing or pricing, causing changes in the input-output ratio.[7] It is critical that great care be taken to establish the productivity or performance base and that accurate, complete data be gathered to compare current performance against the base. The credibility of a gainsharing effort rests on this foundation.

Fifth, a performance period must be established. It should be long enough for data to be compared with the base. At the same time, for bonuses to be motivating, they shouldn't be given too long after the performance they reward. This would support setting a relatively short performance period or bonus reward period. Some experts suggest that bonuses obtained through gainsharing are a form of feedback from the organization to employees. They recommend regular, frequent feedback, usually on a monthly basis.[8] A recent innovation is to use different payout periods for different groups of employees (i.e., monthly periods for bargaining unit employees and quarterly periods for managers). Other firms pay out only when the gains generated reach a certain level.[9] In any case, the performance period should be chosen to best suit the work force.

Sixth, how the company or organization and the participating employees will split the gains must be negotiated. Different plans use different sharing ratios. In Scanlon plans, employees receive 75 to 100 percent of labor-related productivity gains. In Rucker plans, employees receive 100 percent of these gains. In Improshare plans, the company and employees split the hours saved 50/50.

The process of determining the sharing ratio should be guided by a sense of equity and fairness. The ratio should be changed when experience shows that there is a more equitable formula for sharing the gains, when business plans change, or when economic or other external conditions dictate that a larger share should go to either the employees or the company. At the same time, constantly changing the sharing ratio may cause confusion, suspicion, and dissatisfaction with the gainsharing effort. Too often employees view a change in the ratio as a bait and switch tactic. Changes should be made only to establish or maintain fairness or equity. A recent innovation is to have varying sharing ratios, usually to reflect significant changes in performance levels. For example, as the baseline ratchets upward, employees obtain a higher percentage of the gains to reflect the greater difficulty of making those performance improvements. Likewise, when performance historically has been significantly lower than that required to be competitive, a higher percentage may go to the company until a competitive performance level has been achieved.

Historically, three different ways have been used to allocate gains among participating employees: on the basis of hours worked, as a percentage of compensation, or in equal dollar shares. There are pluses and minuses to each of these methods. Allocation based on a percentage of pay is the most common method, probably because it is easily calculated and understood and it supports the basic structure of the existing pay system. Conversely, if the base pay system is viewed as arbitrary and unfair, then gainsharing takes on that characterization as well. It must be calculated on actual compensation not base pay; otherwise it violates the Fair Labor Standards Act.

Allocation based on hours worked is probably the second most common method. It is attractive because of its fairness, but it has complicating aspects as well. To be legal, overtime hours must be counted as 1.5 hours and exempt employees who aren't paid by the hour must be credited in some fashion with hours worked. The simplest method is to use a standard number of hours above forty for each exempt employee.

Finally, there is the equal shares allocation option. The apparent simplicity and fundamental equity make this option appealing; however, there are a number of legal complications. These complications stem from the portion of the Fair Labor Standards Act that requires nonexempt employees to be paid a 50 percent premium over their base rate for all hours worked in excess of forty hours per week. Under this provision, gainsharing payouts must be considered compensation. Practically, this means that gainsharing payouts have to be added back into a nonexempt employee's base pay and overtime pay then recalculated. In many cases, a gainsharing payout would result in more overtime paid retroactively. To be lawful, the equal shares option is not a simple allocation scheme.[10]

The size of the bonus or payout is an additional consideration. Theoretically, the bonus is a measure of improvement, not a goal in and of itself. Some experts suggest that the size of the bonus is not as important as it may seem if gainsharing results in better management, effective employee participation, and improved job security. The motivational power of the size of the bonus needs to be balanced against the motivational power of the frequency of the bonus discussed earlier. Most organizations use a separate check to emphasize that gainsharing bonuses are not routine compensation. Taxes and social security must be deducted because the bonus is still compensation. Generally, the bonus is not used in calculating other income-based benefits. This is one reason many companies are pursuing gainsharing. It is a way to increase compensation without increasing the cost of benefits, especially pension contributions. Nevertheless, as a general rule, bonuses must average approximately 10 percent of compensation to be significantly motivating or for employees to react positively to gainsharing.[11] The "People, Pay, and Performance" study reported that gainsharing bonuses consistently pay out 5 to 10 percent of employee base pay.[12] Some gainsharing efforts specify a minimum payment level for a bonus to be given. Often this is $25 to $50.[13]

How Scanlon Plans Work

Scanlon plans are the most common of the standard gainsharing plans. Approximately five hundred companies have used them, and there are between two hundred and three hundred plans in operation today.[14] The basics of the plan were developed in the 1930s by Joseph Scanlon, a local union president in a steel plant threatened with closing because of competition from more efficient operations. By instituting the plan with management, the plant was reopened and able to compete successfully. Initially, the basic feature of the plan was that it tied wages to plant productivity. Through discussions with Clinton Golden of the Steel Workers Organizing Committee, a suggestion committee system modeled on one used by the B&O Railroad was added to the plan.

All Scanlon plans are characterized by a philosophy and practice of cooperation, an employee involvement system designed to increase efficiency and reduce costs, and sharing of the benefits based on a productivity measurement.[15] Traditionally, a bonus is paid when there is an improvement in the ratio of the total labor costs to the sales value of production:

$$\frac{\text{Total labor costs (inputs)}}{\text{Sales or market value of production (outputs)}}$$

Labor costs include direct and indirect factory labor, all other wages and salaries, overtime premiums, vacation and holiday pay, and hospitalization and workers' compensation. Usually, salespersons' commissions, the employer's portion of social security, state and federal unemployment insurance, pension costs, and other miscellaneous employee costs are not included in the total labor costs.[16] The sales or market value of production commonly does include adjustments for fluctuations in inventories.[17] This productivity ratio is easily understood, doesn't require complicated record keeping, and allows employees to influence directly the input side of the ratio.

Not every Scanlon plan uses the traditional productivity ratio. For a productivity ratio to be useful with this plan, it should be a good performance measure over time; perceived as fair; understandable by employees; flexible enough to meet changing conditions; easily administered; useful in isolating problem areas; and designed to orient employee effort in the desired direction.[18] In any case, once the productivity formula is developed, it should be tested under actual organizational conditions before it is applied.

Several basic principles underlie the measurement of productivity in a Scanlon plan. The focus in on the group and thereby teamwork. There is a real educational value to this focus on variables of critical importance to the company. Limiting the input side of the formula to labor costs links the work force to something over which it can exert control. The productivity standard is really set by the employees themselves in that the historical performance of employees is used as the basis for setting the standard. Bonuses are paid monthly to be maximally motivating and are paid as a percentage of compensation to recognize individual skills and contributions to the organization. Measurement is an integral part of a comprehensive Scanlon program for improving productivity.[19]

Employee participation is one of the essential elements of a Scanlon plan. To foster participation directed toward organizational improvement, a two-level system of suggestion committees is established. *Production committees* are composed of a supervisor and two or three employee representatives. Employees submit suggestions for improvements to the production committee in their area. This committee is empowered to implement suggestions that don't involve other departments or areas or costs above a certain specified amount. At the next level is a *screening committee*, composed of representatives from all the production committees, senior managers, and union officials. The screening committee meets monthly to discuss and evaluate suggestions referred to it by the production committees, to analyze current performance and determine bonuses, to administer the Scanlon plan overall, and to engage in troubleshooting, as needed. The screening committee also reviews and discusses the basic economic health of the company.

In most situations, the agreement-covered participants on production committees are selected in elections held for this purpose. In this way, all employees have the opportunity to participate directly in the suggestion committee system. Also, all employees are asked to examine their work on a continuous basis in an effort to achieve quality improvement, quantity enhancement, and cost reduction.[20] Since everyone participates, teamwork is fostered by the program. The Scanlon plan is more effective the greater the percentage of employees participating in it. The only employees who are routinely excluded are summer workers, part-time workers, new hires during their probationary period, and salespersons with their own incentive plans.[21]

The financial gains from a Scanlon plan are usually shared so that 75 percent go to the employees and 25 percent to the company. The rationale is that since the productivity formula is based on labor productivity and the company gets the full benefit of the savings, the employees should get a higher percentage of the benefits from the program. In most cases, 25 percent of the gains are set aside in a reserve fund and the remainder is split 75/25 as described above. The reserve fund is used to cover future deficits in the plan. It usually builds up over the year and is closed out at year's end, when any surplus is distributed according to the 75/25 formula. A deficit in the reserve fund is covered by the company so that the plan can start each year without having to overcome the previous year's losses.[22]

There are several other major features of a Scanlon plan. Often an employee survey is used to determine employee interest before instituting the plan. Experts recommend conducting a survey annually to evaluate the impact of the plan overall. A formal meeting before installing the plan is also recommended. At this time, employees discuss the plan and vote on whether to try it out for a one-year trial period; an 80 percent acceptance rate is standard to start a plan.[23] Many organizations with Scanlon plans hold a year-end meeting to bring closure to the year's efforts and to involve employees.[24] Such meetings are an opportunity for the union and management co-sponsors of the program to demonstrate their joint leadership of it. Finally, most Scanlon plans have a memorandum of understanding between management and the union included in the labor contract. This document usually covers what the plan is, how and why it was started, the principles of the plan, how the bonus is calculated, how the committee system works, and the procedures for handling suggestions.[25]

Scanlon plans are very sound ways to motivate employees. Employees' bonuses relate to factors in the workplace that they can influence and are distributed as soon as possible after the relevant performance period. The plantwide nature of a Scanlon plan reinforces teamwork and organizational objectives. Through the suggestion committee system, employees develop an understanding of how the business can be successful and how to contribute to its success. Scanlon plans can complement overall organizational development efforts and profit-sharing programs.

Among the standard gainsharing programs, Scanlon plans have been the most widespread vehicle for union-management cooperation. They have a long-term, proven track record that union-management partners find very appealing. Union-management partners are increasingly using other measures in addition to labor productivity to reflect their broader and more refined improvement goals. These plans can be a sound and viable cooperative way to combine real participation with financial incentives.

How Rucker Plans Work

Another standard productivity-based gainsharing program, the Rucker plan, was developed by Allen Rucker in its most basic form in the 1930s. Rucker was an economist who observed that labor costs as a percentage of value added remain stable in the manufacturing sector over a long period of time. Further, this stable relationship is not affected by the peaks and valleys of the business cycle.[26] He concluded that any change in the relationship of labor costs to value added or production value is very significant and represents a change in productivity. This observation undergirds the Rucker plan.

Under the Rucker plan, productivity and bonuses are calculated as follows:

$$\frac{\text{Labor costs}}{\text{Production value (value added)}}$$

Whenever actual labor costs in relation to value added or the production value are less than the standard, a bonus is paid. Production value or value added is calculated by adding net sales and increases in inventory, then subtracting materials and supplies used. Employees receive the entire amount of the labor savings as a bonus. Bonuses are usually paid out monthly as a percentage of monthly earnings. There is an account to handle months when there is a deficit.

Approximately two hundred to three hundred Rucker plans are in operation, primarily in manufacturing. The plan is designed mostly for nonexempt employees. Its proponents suggest that excluded employees (executives, managers, supervisors, and professional staff) be paid a bonus out of the company's share from the results of the improvements. Many plans incorporate suggestion systems and committees together with an extensive communications system so as to enhance the bonus potential. Most plants have a single, plantwide committee, but there can also be a network of multilevel committees.[27] A participative management philosophy and style support the use of the Rucker plan with rank-and-file employees.

How Improshare Plans Work

Improshare (Improved Productivity through Sharing) plans were developed by Mitchell Fein in the early 1970s. The emphasis is on organizational performance and less on financial productivity than in Scanlon and Rucker plans. The goal is to produce more final products in fewer person hours and to reflect the real changes that occur in the workplace, especially in technology and the structure of work. Improshare plans are designed to reward group performance. Because of the increase in the ratio of indirect to direct workers, indirect workers are included when measuring and rewarding productivity. Improshare plans facilitate the introduction of new equipment,[28] since performance is calculated based on the base productivity factor (BPF), determined by using industrial engineering methods. The basic formula is:

$$\frac{\text{Actual time worked for all employees}}{\text{Total standard time earned for a base period}}$$

Gains are recorded as hours saved. These gains are divided 50/50 between the employees and the company. Employee bonuses are paid, usually weekly, based on the actual time worked during the performance period. The base is adjusted when new equipment or methods are introduced. Further, the company can "buy" a permanent change in the BPF and bank bonuses to cover periods of low or nonexistent gains.[29]

Improshare plans traditionally have had no formal employee participation program or tie-in to participative management approaches. Recently, in some situations, participatory elements have been added. Nevertheless, the vehicles for union-management cooperation are less well developed in Improshare plans than in Scanlon plans.

Improshare plans have several important advantages: the formula used is easily understood by employees; employees can really affect productivity as defined here; and management doesn't have to reveal significant corporate financial information as with some other gainsharing plans.[30]

Some of the results reported from Improshare have been very impressive. In one study of all known Improshare users, the median first-year productivity increase was 8 percent and the mean 12.5 percent. By the third year, the median was 17.5 percent and the mean 22 percent. After three years, a plateau was generally reached and in many plants further significant improvements did not occur. The researcher concluded that slack in the operation was taken up in the initial three years of the Improshare effort and that further improvements would require the implementation of large-scale, broader changes.[31]

What Makes Gainsharing Effective?

No one factor makes gainsharing effective, but there is a family of practices that leads to and reinforce success. Edward Lawler identified fourteen items that are critical to a successful gainsharing program:

1. The company has fewer than five hundred employees.
2. The organization is old enough and stable enough to have an adequate performance history for developing standards.
3. Product costs can be controlled by the employees.
4. The market for the organization's output is able to absorb additional production. If this is not the case, the plan could result in layoffs.
5. There is a participative management style applied in an open organizational climate with a high level of trust and open communications.
6. There is limited use of overtime, so that employees are not too dependent on it.
7. There is a high to moderate degree of work-floor interdependence.
8. The business is not seasonal.
9. Little capital investment is planned, making operations more stable and various measurements easier.
10. Few product changes are planned, which also makes measurements easier.
11. Management is technically capable, supportive of participative management, open to new ideas and suggestions, and has good communications skills.
12. The work force is interested in participation and higher compensation, technically skilled, and interested in organizational finances.
13. The union is favorable to a cooperative effort.

14. Engineering and maintenance groups are capable, willing, and able to respond to changes and improvements growing out of the gainsharing program.[32]

Probably no organization meets all of these criteria. But the union and management partners should at least consider these items before embarking on gainsharing. The innovative approaches to and features of gainsharing efforts developed in recent years make gainsharing more diverse than ever. This diversity reflects the resiliency and strength of gainsharing as a workplace strategy, but it also makes it even more difficult to generalize about what makes gainsharing effective.

More and more of the research on and practical experiences with gainsharing indicate that employee participation is a key component. Studies done by the New York Stock Exchange and the U.S. General Accounting Office in the 1980s indicated that 63 to 70 percent of all gainsharing efforts had some element of formal employee participation.[33] Conversely, employee participation is taken much more seriously and is often positioned more centrally within the organization when employee involvement pays off financially through gainsharing. Everyone wants employee participation to work so that everyone can continue to benefit from the gainsharing. Employee participation and gainsharing thus become mutually reinforcing organizational activities. To obtain gains, the organization must improve. Waiting for someone else to make changes and improvements means essentially waiting for the gains. To make real gains means that employees must be broadly and routinely involved. The central importance of employee participation to gainsharing ensures that both the union and management will work constructively and continuously together.

Having a continuous flow of information about the workplace operation also contributes to the effectiveness of gainsharing. Very often gainsharing encourages union and management partners to share information about aspects of the operation that they never discussed before. Typically, much of this information concerns the competitive position of the operation and where it needs to be. In this way, the common ground between the union and management and thus between employees and the company is reinforced. This flow of information thus serves six purposes:

1. to bring disenfranchised employees into the organizational culture and give them a personal stake in the organization;
2. to infuse a feeling of association between employees throughout the organization;
3. to enable employees to be better informed so that they can better contribute to organizational planning at all levels;

4. to ensure that employees understand when progress is slow or set-
    backs occur in the improvement arena;
5. to reduce suspicion of and resistance to change;
6. to increase the overall level of trust.[34]

Management's leadership in a gainsharing effort helps make it effective. Managers have to value participation, equity, and the partnership
between labor and management as well as model effectiveness and be
willing to organize and promote their organization. Robert J. Doyle, a
gainsharing expert, asserts that management leadership includes valuing
the union's role: "The organization that is serious about gainsharing
must state clearly the value that labor and management not only are not
adversaries but are, of necessity, partners in the enterprise."[35] Personnel
policies need to demonstrate a clear commitment to employees. Long-
range goals to guide the operation overall should be clearly communicated
and accepted by the organization. Ideally, there is a climate characterized
by open communications, effective decision making, and a belief among
employees that they have influence in the organization. Management
must show respect for and be supportive of workers and believe in and
practice teamwork.[36]

Employment security is another essential component of effective gainsharing. Basic employee security must exist or be established to realize
the full potential of gainsharing. No layoffs can result because of the
gainsharing effort. Without this protection, employees will be reluctant
to participate fully. Gainsharing efforts may lead to job (re)design,
but employment security must support the gainsharing effort over the
long haul.

Benefits of Gainsharing

A successful gainsharing program has diverse and significant benefits
including increased profits; higher returns on investment; higher rates of
on-time deliveries; improved quality; reduced product costs; improved
survivability and employment security; greater employee awareness and
understanding of what it takes to make a business successful; more
effective change management; broader teamwork, cooperation, and coordination; improved supervision as a result of changing from production pushing to production facilitating; lower turnover and a wider
selection of job applicants; reduced absenteeism; greater job satisfaction;
and a declining frequency of grievances and better, quicker handling of
those that are filed.[37] It is important to remember that such benefits occur
only when the necessary time and energy are invested in developing and
operating the gainsharing program.

More research has been done on Scanlon plans than on the other two standard gainsharing programs or the tailormade gainsharing programs. Nevertheless, the experiences with and lessons gained from Scanlon plans can be useful to union-management partners contemplating any form of gainsharing. Experts in Scanlon plans report a 90 percent acceptance of suggestions coming through the network of suggestion committees.[38] Research also demonstrates that in most cases such suggestions lead to significant improvements in productivity. In a 1958 study of ten companies with Scanlon plans, the average improvement in productivity over the two-year period studied was 23.1 percent; the minimum was 10.3 percent and the maximum was 39.2 percent. All but one of the companies involved in this study were unionized, and as a group they represented a sample of companies in manufacturing and fabricating. In 1973, Brian E. Moore and Timothy L. Goodman reviewed the literature on Scanlon plans and analyzed thirty successful experiences. They identified the following outcomes when a Scanlon plan was applied successfully:

1. Coordination, teamwork, and the sharing of knowledge were enhanced at lower levels in the organization.
2. Social needs were recognized via participation and mutually reinforcing group behavior.
3. Attention was focused on cost savings, not just quantity of production.
4. Acceptance of change caused by technology, market, and new methods was greater because higher efficiency led to bonuses.
5. Attitudinal change occurred among workers, who demanded more efficient management and better planning as a result of the plan.
6. Workers tried to reduce overtime, to work smarter not harder or faster, and to produce ideas as well as effort.
7. More flexible administration of union-management relations occurred.
8. The union was strengthened because it was responsible for a better work situation and higher pay.[40]

The company benefits by having a better return to stockholders or owners, a reduction in complaints about spoilage or imperfect work, and improvements in deliveries. Furthermore, supervisors are more likely to lead their employees and focus on managing the work.[41] Though these results could be obtained with other gainsharing programs, Scanlon plans incorporate three elements other plans may not have: the philosophy and practice of cooperation, employee involvement, and a labor-based productivity measurement as the basis for sharing gains. Plans that do not have these three powerful elements may not produce similar results.

How to Determine If Gainsharing Is Feasible

As with any union-management program, the union and management partners should determine together whether gainsharing is feasible by examining the current organizational climate as it relates to union-management cooperation in general and to gainsharing in particular, reviewing other cooperative efforts undertaken, surveying the range of options, and assessing the risks and benefits.

It is helpful to simulate the financial bonuses of all the gainsharing plans under consideration, using current data. Modeling various plans requires the active participation of the finance and accounting resources of the organization. These employees know how to assemble not only the information needed to determine the feasibility of gainsharing but also the measurement data needed to calculate the gainsharing formula and apply it over time. In some cases, they will have to make changes in management information systems or accounting processes to accommodate the gainsharing effort and to fulfill its data needs.

The union-management partners also need to decide what is most appropriate and applicable: a standard gainsharing program such as Scanlon, Rucker, or Improshare or a customized program. To do this, the three standard programs should be fully analyzed. There are organizations that specialize in each. Consultants who design tailormade programs can explain what is involved and indicate the potential of using a customized plan. The union and management partners should concentrate on deciding whether gainsharing can help achieve strategic goals and objectives and which, if any, of the available programs would work best.

The union and management partners need to plan exactly how they are going to involve employees in the gainsharing effort. At a minimum, they should seek employee input about the plan's objectives, measurements, participant groups, performance period, sharing ratio, and basis for allocating gains. Employees can be actively involved in designing a tailormade program or in designing a plan to implement a standard program.

Many union and management partners want to explore how to convert an individual incentive program into a gainsharing effort. In many unionized workplaces, individual incentive programs are obsolete because they don't reflect and support such critical workplace values as cooperation and teamwork. Further, many individual incentive programs or piecework schemes are designed around outmoded production processes. These schemes are often costly and can foster employee dissatisfaction, conflict, and safety problems.

The transition from a piecework scheme to gainsharing changes how improvements are pursued and rewards are given. In a piecework

scheme, individual workers are primarily responsible for any improvements they make to production. Under gainsharing, formal employee
participation methods are used to foster a wide range of improvements.
In a piecework scheme, some employees are usually very successful at
achieving high bonuses and others are less successful. Too often these
differences reflect differences in access to opportunities, not differences
in performance. Under gainsharing, employees have more equitable
opportunities to make gains. Therefore, to make the transition, union
and management partners need to minimize or eliminate the loss of
income some employees will experience under gainsharing. There are
three common ways to make this adjustment:

1. by permanently adjusting base pay based on some past average of
   incentive earnings;
2. with a temporary red circle (i.e., guaranteeing average incentive
   pay for a specified period and then phasing out this guarantee);
3. through an incentive buyout (i.e., lump-sum compensation to
   cover the loss of opportunity for incentive pay); usually such
   buyouts are equivalent to one year of average incentive earnings.[42]

The final consideration in making such a transition is that there will
probably be a significant decline in productivity during the transition.
This decline will not be permanent, but it may be as high as 25 percent.
Some union and management partners decide to maintain their existing
individual incentive scheme while adopting gainsharing. If the existing
scheme is well designed, well maintained, and aligned with organizational strategic goals and objectives, this may be the easiest course
to pursue. We have seen some organizations front-load gainsharing
with a large bonus against expected benefits. Unfortunately, this well-
intentioned payout sends the message that gainsharing is a gift, not the
result of working together on changing the organization.

To determine the feasibility of a gainsharing program requires the
union and management partners to commit significant time, energy, and
resources. The stakes are very high; the result can be either an effective,
successful gainsharing effort that becomes standard operating procedure
or a costly, demoralizing failure that makes the use of any financial
incentive programs unlikely if not impossible.

Critical Decisions to Make about Gainsharing

There are several critical decisions union and management partners
must make together in designing a gainsharing effort: who participates,
what the performance period for calculation of the bonus and what the
payment period will be, what input and output measures will be included

in measuring performance, how the financial gains will be divided between employees and the company or organization, whether a reserve fund will be established and, if so, what portion of the gains will be held in reserve, and what method will be used to pay the benefits.

Several other design issues must also be addressed:

Defining eligibility to obtain gains. Usually there are two special employee groups to consider when defining who will participate in gainsharing: permanent part-time employees and employees who haven't worked the full performance and/or payout period. Typically, all permanent employees including part-timers are eligible for bonuses. The second group has been addressed by establishing waiting periods for new hires or requiring that employees be on the active payroll on the first and last days of the performance period.[43]

Smoothing out the inevitable variations in the gainsharing measures. No matter how well constructed the gainsharing formula or measures are, there will probably be times when there will be significant, possibly inexplicable and unavoidable swings in the measurement data. Unions and companies use many different mechanisms for avoiding or smoothing out these variations, including deficit reserves; rolling payouts, whereby bonuses are based on the average performance of two or more periods rather than on one period; methods for reducing employee shares until lost company shares are recovered; and year-to-date payout limiters, so that the cumulative payout for the year can never exceed the employee share of year-to-date gains regardless of period calculations.[44] Once they have established their gainsharing formula or measures, union and management designers need to determine whether such mechanisms are valuable.

Adjusting for technology and other capital improvements that positively affect gainsharing. At a minimum, a company wants to obtain its return on its capital investments before it starts to generate gains for gainsharing. This is especially true of capital investments in expensive new technology. Some partners agree to adjust the baseline by whatever amount is calculated as being the effect of the capital improvement. Other partners are content to allow the adjustment to occur automatically by using a rolling or ratcheting baseline. Whatever the approach, recognize that this issue will probably need to be addressed and that it is wise to make proactive, upfront decisions about capital investment adjustments.[45]

Capping or limiting the amount of gains that can be obtained. Sometimes management fears that gainsharing bonuses will spiral ever higher. Sometimes the union is concerned that employees will become dependent on the gains and that financial hardships and a backlash against gainsharing will result when the gains are lower or nonexistent. As a consequence, some union and management partners put a cap or upper limit on possible gains. Improshare automatically caps gains at 30 percent of pay. When gains exceed the cap, they are placed in a deferral account. Funds from this account are paid out when gains are lower than 30 percent. As a result, all gains are ultimately paid out under Improshare plans. Rolling or ratcheting the baseline can serve as a limiting or capping function as well.[46] Caps are a way to limit the bonuses and thereby the company's financial exposure, but they can also limit the potential for improvement by reducing employees' motivation and commitment to gainsharing.

Concerns about Gainsharing

Even if a gainsharing effort is implemented successfully, several dilemmas can develop. When gainsharing is successful, over time a certain percentage of employees' compensation becomes variable. Both unions and companies have examined the implications of making this change in the compensation system.[47] Employees may come to depend on the money even though they know it can vary. A drop in their bonuses could precipitate financial crises for some employees. Having variable pay could thus mean having unstable pay and unstable personal finances. If there is a prolonged depressed period, the company could lose valuable employees precisely when they are needed most. The union bets on having possibly higher returns by adopting some of the company's downside risks. If it doesn't work out, the members will blame the union.

Another concern is the relationship of gainsharing to collective bargaining. Historically, wages, hours, terms, and conditions have been at the core of the collective bargaining process. Gainsharing clearly is on that list. Some gainsharing consultants suggest that the design of the gainsharing effort not be negotiated. We couldn't disagree more. Gainsharing relates to compensation and as such rightfully belongs within the collective bargaining arena. Gainsharing can be the ideal candidate for win-win bargaining or for strategic bargaining if the two parties design and develop the system together. Most unions insist that the design be put to the membership for ratification. Similarly, many management organizations present the design to the senior operating committee of the corporation or in some cases to the board of directors for approval.

The measurement formula for gainsharing efforts poses problems as well. Initially, reaching agreement about what measurement formula to use and which measures to include may be difficult. Later, questions and concerns about the accuracy of the measurements may be raised. Having accurate and complete data is necessary to obtain fair and equitable bonuses. Conflicts can occur if one or both parties want to change the formula to reflect changes in the operation or organization. Developing and maintaining a measurement system that is trusted is a continuously demanding activity.

Significant people problems can occur around the new roles a gainsharing effort presents to employees at all levels. Rank-and-file employees are asked to focus more on their jobs and the organization as a whole. Supervisors must commit to teamwork and provide clear leadership. As employees become more actively involved, they may challenge supervisors, their authority, and their actions to a greater extent than before and in new ways. Employees will perceive that supervisory and managerial decisions may adversely affect their gainsharing payout.

Managers are asked to be more attentive to planning and coordinating the work processes overall. Unfortunately, many managers are better firefighters than planners and coordinators. Because of gainsharing, employees will be taking a more critical look at managerial decisions and organizational plans and their execution. This may expose significant weaknesses with management.

A union involved in gainsharing is expected to take a regular, active part in improving the operations of the organization. Making business decisions and encouraging broad employee involvement may be new roles for the union. There is a lot of room for misunderstanding and misinterpretation of this new role. For some people in the union, these new or proactive roles are welcome; for others, they are suspect or too demanding.

The success of any gainsharing effort rests on the acceptance and support of the work force. Because gainsharing is group-based, excessive peer group pressure can develop as well as other negative group dynamics. Less skilled, handicapped, or older workers may be made to feel undesirable if other workers perceive that the less skilled workers are holding the group back. Gender and race issues can come to the forefront. Sometimes gainsharing is promoted with promises that it can't possibly keep. When employee expectations aren't fulfilled, the credibility of the program is damaged. Overreaction and disappointment on the part of employees can be deadly.

The final problem occurs when gainsharing is seen as a substitute for something else: for adequate and equitable wages and benefits, for a strong union organization, and/or for a competent management team. Gainsharing has value in and of itself as a way to drive and reward organizational change, but it cannot solve all the problems of a workplace. Nor should it be a substitute for other necessities for workplace success. The recent growth of gainsharing could result in too many people overselling the idea. The sad truth is that if gainsharing is oversold to and by the union and management, they will both be losers. Expectations, impatience, and the hunger for results will skyrocket and take energy away from addressing constructively and successfully the very real problems and opportunities gainsharing presents.

Necessary Conditions for Gainsharing to Be Successful

Gainsharing as a cooperative union-management endeavor depends for its success on the same factors that any joint effort does. There are nine factors necessary for a gainsharing effort to succeed:

1. *A long-term commitment by the union and management at all levels to the success of the gainsharing effort.* To make a shared commitment requires that both parties have a reasonably healthy and constructive union-management relationship overall. Gainsharing will not make a bad relationship better.
2. *Realistic expectations from the beginning.* Gainsharing programs are not the solution to all of an organization's problems and ills.
3. *A properly designed formula.* The gainsharing formula must be focused on organizational drivers that are easy to understand and acceptable to both the union and management and be motivating to employees.
4. *Adequate wages and benefits.* Gainsharing cannot be a substitute for inadequate wages and benefits.
5. *Proper planning from the beginning.* A joint planning process strengthens the program and gets it off to the best possible start.
6. *An effective employee education process.* Building employee commitment starts with employees being well informed about the gainsharing formula and plan and the new behaviors required in the workplace.
7. *Vital, continuous employee participation.* This is the channel for the generation of ideas and strategies for improvement that create the changes in productivity reflected in the bonus payments.
8. *An effective communications system.* Communication channels help ensure a continuous flow of information about the gainsharing effort.
9. *Accurate, accessible accounting and record keeping for the program.* A credible and responsive record-keeping system provides the feedback to employees on their contributions and a way to account for bonus payments.

Having these conditions ensures that a gainsharing program is built on a solid foundation. Applying gainsharing in a mechanistic or formulistic way can either seriously limit its success or doom it to failure when it is buffeted by other forces or currents within the larger organizational system. Gainsharing is a powerful strategy for driving organizational change. It can also be a significant component of a larger change strategy.

Conclusion

Gainsharing can be a potent mechanism leading to bottom-line improvements for both employees and employers. There are opportunities for joint action at every step in the process of developing and sustaining the effort. For union and management partners who have been pursuing employee participation together, gainsharing is an excellent opportunity to reward this participation. When the gainsharing effort is a first attempt to cooperate, the two parties have a significant opportunity both to foster and reward broad employee participation. When union and management partners act together via well-designed gainsharing, they are harnessing truly significant energy and power to their mutual benefit.

18. Taking Stock: Employee Stock Ownership Plans and Employee Ownership

I n its ideal form, employee ownership is an attractive concept. Employees share in the success of the company they work for, as well as influence the governance of the organization and all aspects of its operation. In reality, it falls far short. Voting rights are rarely provided to worker-owners, and when they are, the amount of stock owned by any one employee provides little sense of ownership and consequently little influence. The degree of ownership and the actual dollar returns are often so diluted as to have little motivational effect, much less provide any control over corporate direction. In these situations, employee ownership is valuable primarily as a corporate financing tool and not as a vehicle for union-management cooperation.

Employee ownership is a promising avenue for cooperation when five conditions prevail:

1. Sufficient stock is vested in the employees.
2. Employees can vote their stock.
3. There is employee-union representation on the board.
4. There is clear communication and solicitation of employee input into board-level decisions.

5. Steps are taken to involve employees and their unions in decision making and operational improvements.

Unfortunately, few employee stock ownership plans (ESOPs) meet these criteria. Rarely do highly profitable firms elect to become democratically employee-owned. More often, employee buyouts occur in marginal firms. Further, simply becoming employee-owned does not magically transform a loser into a winner in the marketplace. Nonetheless, an employee buyout of a marginal operation can mean the difference between failure and success. In addition, operations whose returns on investment do not satisfy corporate requirements can be converted into successful employee-owned enterprises. These firms have to grapple, however, with the issues of long-term profitability and the ability to generate capital for expansion and modernization. Of all the options in the arena of union-management cooperation around financial participation, employee ownership is the most challenging.[1]

There are two categories of worker ownership: direct ownership, in which employees actually own their shares, and beneficial ownership, in which employees own their shares through the vehicle of a trust. Direct ownership includes direct stock ownership plans through stock bonus or stock purchase plans and producer cooperatives. Beneficial ownership includes a variety of employee stock ownership plans.

There is a long history of worker ownership in the United States. Between 1791 and 1940, almost four hundred companies were established in which a large portion of the stock was directly owned by employees. Today, worker ownership is very much in the news as many organizations pursue it as a strategy for ensuring organizational survival. Currently, there are more than 8,700 ESOPs and similar plans, including stock bonus plans, covering about seven million employees.

How ESOPs Work

As of 1985, the annual growth rate for new ESOPs was 10 percent, largely because of lucrative tax incentives given to companies with ESOPs in 1984. In 1986, however, the tax credits were eliminated. Tax-credit ESOPs, or TRASOPs, were too costly in terms of lost tax revenues.[2] In 1984, 90 percent of all participants in ESOPs and 79 percent of all the assets in ESOPs were in these tax-credit ESOPs or TRASOPs. A survey conducted by Hewitt Associates in 1987 indicated, however, that only 2 percent of the companies with tax-credit ESOPs planned to convert to standard ESOPs.[3]

In the 1920s, many stock purchase and bonus plans were established as part of the welfare capitalist approach to labor-management relations as a way to link employees more closely to shareholder interests. Most of these plans were destroyed by the 1929 stock market crash and the resultant Great Depression.

Louis Kelso, an investment banker, has been promoting ESOPs as a way to equalize the distribution of wealth since the 1950s. He suggests that by broadening capital ownership through employee stock ownership, the return to capital will rise to the true competitive market level, the return to labor will drop, and labor wage incomes will be lower but workers will have a second income from their stock.

Essentially, an ESOP provides employees with a way to acquire their employer's stock without having to put up money of their own. Usually, the management gives the employees equity in the company in exchange for something else, often some other form of compensation. Technically, an ESOP is an employee benefit plan. All cash and stock contributed to the plan are allocated to individual accounts of the participating employees. These allocations are held in an employee stock ownership trust (ESOT) that oversees and invests the assets of the ESOP. The ESOT is administered by a trustee or trustee committee. Theoretically, the ESOT is a legal entity existing independently of the employer specifically for the purpose of acquiring stock for the benefit of employees.

ESOPs can be leveraged or nonleveraged. A leveraged ESOP borrows money to purchase stock in the company. The company in turn promises to contribute to the plan so that the loan will be paid off. As the loan is paid down, stock is allocated to the employees participating in the plan according to a formula. The company treats all ESOP contributions as business expenses, thereby writing off both the principal and the interest on the loan for tax purposes. The ESOP thus becomes a significant business financing tool through which the company can obtain cheap capital with few strings attached. In fact, the use of leveraged ESOPs to raise capital funds has been limited. In 1987, the Government Accounting Office (GAO) reported that only 16 percent of ESOPs used the special leveraging provisions of the tax code to raise capital funds. Of this number, only 76 percent used that capital to buy out the previous owners rather than to acquire or rehabilitate the physical plant.[4] In a non-leveraged ESOP, the company contributes stock to the ESOP or pays it cash to purchase stock. The stock is allocated to the employees according to some formula, and the company contribution is a tax-deductible business expense.

Participative or cooperative ESOPs are a form of ESOPs in which the ESOT is organized as a cooperative. Voting rights are not related to the equity value that employees have. In these ESOPs, each employee gets only one vote rather than having votes in proportion to the stock owned.

There are six variables in any ESOP: (1) the level of corporate contribution and how contributions are made, (2) the amount of stock held by the

ESOT, (3) voting rights, (4) the formula for allocation to participating employees, (5) the vesting process, and (6) the handling of dividends.

There are essentially three different methods by which corporate contributions are made to an ESOP: on a profit-sharing basis, which diverts a portion of profits; on a cost principle basis, whereby a fixed percentage of the labor costs is contributed; and on the fixed contribution principle, whereby a certain dollar amount is transferred. ESOPs vary in the amount of stock held. In closely held companies the stock holdings of the ESOT are often relatively small. In only 10 to 15 percent of all ESOPs do employees hold a majority of the stock. In ESOPs established to prevent plant shutdowns, usually the ESOT holds a majority of the stock. In 10 to 20 percent of all ESOPs, employees hold a very small percentage of the stock. In the majority, employees own between 15 and 50 percent.

Often the trustee or trust committee votes the stock according to some agreed-upon procedures and voting rights are not passed through to employees. More often than not, the real owners of the company and/or management retain control by restricting the voting rights of the employee-stockholders. In some ESOPs, nonvoting stock is held. In 85 percent of all ESOPs, the worker-owners do not have direct voting rights.[5] Voting rights are attached to the vesting of ownership interest. Vesting rules determine the rate at which employees gain ownership over their shares. Employees gain greater rights to their shares as they accumulate tenure with the company.

The vesting timetable will vary from plan to plan. In general, vesting starts at two to three years at the 20 to 30 percent level and continues until there is 100 percent vesting at ten years. Usually stock is allocated to employees based on their compensation or is equally distributed among participants. In most cases, an employee is 100 percent vested by the time he or she retires. At that time, employees can do anything they want with their stock. In some cases, the ESOP has the right of first refusal on all shares an employee owns if the employee wants to sell them. Employees pay no tax on their stock while it is in trust and pay minimal tax when they receive their stock upon retirement or termination.

Dividends are paid on stock held by the ESOT. These dividends are either allocated to the employee's account or are passed through and paid directly to the participants. There is no tax liability for the dividends held in the trust.

Although ESOPs are considered a kind of pension plan, they are exempt from many costly protections under the Employee Retirement Insurance Security Act (ERISA). ESOPs can invest primarily in the employer's securities and are not governed by the 10 percent limit on other pension plans. ESOPs are not subject to the funding requirements of other pensions and are not covered by Pension Benefit Guarantee Corporation Insurance. An ESOP is a defined contribution plan, which means that although a specified amount will be paid into the plan there is no guarantee what the benefit will be upon retirement. By comparison, pension plans are usually defined benefit plans, which means that the benefit level to be paid upon retirement is specified.[6] Clearly, ESOPs are not a good substitute for traditional pensions. ESOPs can pay off well, but they can also leave employees with limited or no financial resources upon retirement.

How ESOPs Have Been Used

ESOPs have been used in six major ways:

1. as a means of corporate financing;
2. as a form of deferred compensation, that is, as a substitute for more conventional pensions and/or to provide remuneration in place of other wages and benefits;
3. as a method for transferring ownership of companies, especially failing ones, to workers;
4. as a way to create an in-house market for the stock of a closely held company;
5. as a strategy for fighting hostile corporate takeovers; and
6. as a way to raise worker motivation and therefore positively affect profitability, productivity, and overall performance, which may in turn save jobs.

As more ESOPs are established, two uses stand out: companies use ESOPs to give employees stock ownership in exchange for wage concessions, and closely held or privately held companies use ESOPs to sell out to their employees rather than to conglomerates.

There are many clear advantages of ESOPs for employers. They provide cheap capital for refinancing because of corporate indebtedness and a new market for stock that allows the company essentially to protect itself from outside control while limiting worker control as well. ESOPs can create new stockholders who have ownership but little or no control; therefore, management increases its power relative to its stockholders. ESOPs allow a closely held company to raise capital without having to go public to do so. ESOPs can eliminate pension plan costs and reduce the pressures for upgrading pension plans and/or increasing wages.

Through ESOPs, employees can obtain stock without any initial outlay. Where employees have voting rights with their stock, they also can have important input into corporate decision making and can share in the financial gains of the company.

Often ESOPs are promoted as avenues for increasing worker motivation and thereby improving profitability, productivity, and performance. A GAO survey of ESOPs in 1986 indicated that 70 percent of those in existence at that time had been established to improve productivity. In fact, 36 percent of these ESOPs reported higher productivity and 23 percent reported improved profitability.[7] The GAO conducted research to determine whether improved profitability or improved productivity actually resulted from having ESOPs. Although there was some evidence of transitory improvements in profitability, there was no statistically significant relationship between the existence of an ESOP and improved profitability or improved productivity.[8]

The GAO also examined other factors associated with ESOPs, including the structure and extent of employee ownership and the extent of employee control over or participation in management of the firm, industry, firm size, and trading status of the firm's stock. Only employee participation in corporate decision making had an impact on improved productivity in the ESOPs. Specifically, the greater degree of employee participation in corporate decision making, the higher the rate of change in labor productivity from the pre-ESOP period to the post-ESOP period.[9] The GAO studied all the previous major studies on ESOPs and corporate performance and concluded that the evidence was inconclusive.

Some research does indicate, however, that ESOPs have these desirable effects. When the National Center for Employee Ownership studied 360 high-technology companies, it found that companies having employee ownership grew two to four times as fast as companies without employee ownership. It also studied 52 employee-owned companies throughout American industry and found that the best performers were those that made the largest stock payments to workers' ESOP accounts. These companies also gave workers a voice in decision making and had strong "ownership culture."[10] Research also shows that profitability in worker-owned firms is often higher than in traditional firms and that the greater profits are directly linked to the proportion of stock owned by workers.[11] Additional studies by the National Center for Employee Ownership concluded that publicly traded companies that were at least 10 percent employee-owned outperformed 62 to 75 percent of comparable competing companies by various performance measures.[12] Although no absolute conclusions can be drawn, it is fair to say that ESOPs may have a positive impact on worker motivation and organizational profitability, productivity, and performance.

Two examples of how American companies and unions have used ESOPs illustrate some of the features of ESOPs in unionized workplaces. In 1982, all Pan Am employees gave up 10 percent of their wages in exchange for a nonleveraged ESOP and one seat on the board of directors. The company donated 10.8 million shares, or an average of 450 shares worth less than $3 per share, for each of the twenty-four thousand participants in the plan. Plan participants were fully vested from the beginning and had full voting rights. The ESOP held 13 percent of the company's stock and operated alongside a profit-sharing plan. It was anticipated that over time the ESOP would acquire between 20 and 35 percent of Pan Am's stock. Neither the ESOP nor board representation could offset the significant market pressures within the airline industry, however, and Pan Am ultimately went bankrupt.

Chrysler Corporation's ESOP was mandated by Congress as part of a bailout of the company. Ninety-four thousand employees received more than $40 million worth of stock through the ESOP. Voting stock was allocated equally among employees, and each received sixty-six shares, worth about $441, at the beginning of the plan. As of 1984, the ESOP held approximately 15 percent of the company stock, making it the largest bloc stockholder. The ESOP board consisted of two United Auto Workers representatives and two company representatives. In 1984, the ESOP was terminated by mutual consent. The stock in the ESOP was then worth approximately $487.5 million. It paid off handsomely.

ESOPs have been used in American industry in a variety of ways to serve a number of purposes. Even without the very attractive tax credits given to PaySOPs or TRASOPs, ESOPs will continue to be actively used, though much less extensively, to improve and/or strengthen the viability of American workplaces. A 1983 survey conducted by the National Center for Employee Ownership determined that 7 percent of all ESOPs would exist even if there were no tax benefits. It is estimated that 40 percent of all ESOPs have been established primarily for tax purposes.[13]

One important fact does stand out: ESOPs are not a "free lunch." Taxpayers pay for the tax benefits ESOPs receive. Existing stockholders pay for the establishment of the ESOPs by the dilution of their stock and/ or the costs of making contributions to the ESOP. Employees pay when they accept ESOPs as substitutes for existing wages and benefits, in place of increased wages and benefits, or in place of a true pension. The important issues for union and management partners regarding ESOPs are who benefits, who pays, and how. An ESOP can be a smart investment or a necessary means to ensure jobs, but there is no guarantee of positive results.

How Employee Buyouts Work

Most employee buyouts occur when a company is in severe economic difficulty or failing. Others occur because the corporate parent wants to sell the company because it is not profitable enough or no longer fits into the overall corporate business strategy. Many closely held companies are sold off to their employees when the owner and/or major investors don't want to continue to hold it. The "new" company is usually reorganized in one of three forms: as directly employee-owned, as an ESOP, or as a producer cooperative. ESOPs are by far the most common form of employee buyout.

All three forms have advantages and disadvantages. In all cases, however, the employees agree to give up some of the financial security gained through collective bargaining to take on some of the employer's financial risk. They do this to maintain their jobs and the company. They are not giving up collective bargaining per se. Fundamentally, each employee agrees to take on the risk of his or her own investment. This may lead to conflicts among employees, which sometimes leads to conversion back to nonworker ownership.

Employee-owners often disagree over how to use the company's financial resources, such as by awarding higher wages or greater dividends in the short term versus reinvesting in the company to ensure its long-term success. This was the case at both Chicago Northwestern Transportation Company and the Vermont Asbestos Group. Or employees and their unions may be sold short if they don't have adequate control. This happened at South Bend Lathe in Indiana. In 1975, an ESOP buyout was created through negotiations. Employees were not vested until they completed three years of service. Then they could vote their allocated shares according to the following schedule: after three years, 30 percent; after four years, 40 percent; and after ten years, 100 percent. In reality, only 20 percent of the ESOP stock was vested and could be voted by employees five years after the buyout. The ESOT committee could and did vote the rest of the shares. Furthermore, the ESOT committee was appointed by the board of directors and elected the board of directors! In such a closed system, there could be no real worker control.[14] The postscript to this story is that the workers at South Bend Lathe ultimately went on strike against the company that they "owned."

Producer cooperatives can also experience problems as the value of employee-held stock increases. Retiring employees may have to sell their shares to nonemployees to obtain their market value. Younger employees may not be able to afford to purchase shares when they are hired. Nonshareholding employees and nonemployee shareholders result. Over time, this changes the firm until it is no longer worker-owned. This has happened at many of the plywood cooperatives in the Northwest. The union and management partners need to commit themselves to conducting a good economic feasibility study and to using the process outlined in part III of this book for structuring a buyout.

How Employee Buyouts Have Been Used

Often in employee buyouts control is divorced from ownership, leaving the company employee-owned but not employee-controlled, even though employees own a controlling interest of the stock. There are many examples of closely held companies that were purchased by their employees in which there was no immediate financial crisis. In larger companies, however, buyouts have often been conducted in a crisis environment so that employees literally bought their jobs. This has led to some employee buyouts of weak, disorganized, and obsolete operations. It is very difficult to construct an effective buyout when the viability of the business is in doubt. Unfortunately, for some workers, this is their only option other than unemployment. The following brief case studies of employee buyouts are not meant to be representative but descriptive and to some extent prescriptive.

Weirton Steel Company. Weirton was a division of the National Steel Company that was not making enough money to meet corporate goals. National Steel offered to sell the company to the employees in 1984. A joint study committee did a feasibility study. A leveraged ESOP was established with 100 percent employee ownership. The employees were represented by the Independent Steelworkers Union. Initially, the ESOP trustee voted the stock in the ESOP, but eventually employees will vote their shares on a one-person, one-vote basis. The union selected three of the twelve members of the board of directors. Eventually, employees will elect a majority of board members. Weirton probably has the most open communications system in the steel industry and has full-blown employee participation programs at all levels. It has become one of the most profitable integrated steelmakers in America. For the seven thousand employees who purchased this company, employee ownership has been a welcome boon for them and their community. Not only did they save their jobs but they also now own a profitable company.

Rath Packing. Rath's participative or cooperative ESOP was begun in 1979 by the local union, United Food and Commercial Workers Local 46, and the company under intense market pressure. Wage reductions and termination of the pension plan were exchanged for 60 percent of the company's stock. Union members elected the entire board of directors. Employees had control and real power as well as a system of employee participation at all levels.[15] The union had veto power over changes in the plan or termination of the agreements that created the plan. They fought hard for survival. Eventually, the union president became president of the company, but he still confronted difficulties in the union-management relationship. Rath also had a very rough time in the marketplace because of conditions the partners couldn't control. As a result, in 1983 Rath filed for bankruptcy and was reorganized into a smaller, regional packer. This example illustrates clearly that even the best ESOP cannot necessarily salvage a deteriorating company faced with serious market challenges or magically transform a difficult union-management relationship.

Hyatt-Clark. In 1981, the employees at this division of General Motors purchased their company for $53 million through a leveraged ESOP. A key element of this buyout was an agreement by GM to purchase a portion of all of its bearings from Hyatt-Clark through November 1987. This division had been unprofitable, however, for five years before the sale, had a declining product demand combined with obsolete equipment and plant layout, and had a history of poor labor relations. The employees took a 25 percent wage cut and a 50 percent reduction in benefits and accepted new work rules in exchange for 100 percent ownership.

The workers didn't have voting rights, but the union, the UAW, controlled three seats out of twelve on the board of directors. The union-management relationship under employee ownership was a rocky one, marked by conflicts over how much authority workers had over the selection and compensation of management and over how monies were to be spent. At the same time, a productivity bonus system and profit sharing were established.

In September 1985, the board of directors unanimously voted to authorize the sale of the company to someone other than the employees. Adding to their troubles, GM had refused to lend Hyatt-Clark much-needed funds for equipment and modernization. Further, Japanese bearing makers had penetrated the U.S. market, driving down the price GM had to pay for bearings purchased from Hyatt-Clark. Finally, the partners couldn't overcome their poor relationship. Corey Rosen, executive director of the National Center for Employee Ownership, explains: "Hyatt was one of the first major buyouts of a failing company and there was a lot of groping around. They did some things right and they did some things wrong, but mostly they didn't ever resolve their bad labor relations."[16] In January 1986, Hyatt filed for Chapter 11 bankruptcy. Additional financing was obtained after significant wage concessions were given.[17] This was still not enough, and in 1987 Hyatt was closed.

Throughout the 1980s there was a pattern of concessionary ESOPs (i.e., trading stock for wage and benefit investments and for commitments to change the work organization and/or improve productivity). These well-publicized examples were in steel, airlines, automobile production, trucking, meatpacking, and railroads. But concessionary ESOPs such as these represented less than 4 percent of all the employee ownership transactions at that time.[18]

Employees will probably continue to try to protect and/or save their jobs through buyouts, in whatever form they may take. In areas with high unemployment and a concentration of high-seniority employees with few other employment prospects, there may be no better alternative. Owners of closely held firms will probably continue to sell to their employees for many reasons, not the least of which is the attractive tax incentives ESOPs offer. A number of labor unions are currently examining employee buyouts as an alternative to plant shutdowns. To give buyouts the best possible chance to succeed financially, and thus provide jobs and ensure community economic vitality, it is important that the participants address the problems that have marred many buyouts in the past.

Unions and Employee-Owned Firms

Collective bargaining occurs in employee-owned firms because the employees are not the majority owners and almost always there is still a management organization. There are relatively few unionized companies in which the employees are rank-and-file employees, managers, and owners simultaneously. There are an array of collective bargaining issues relevant to employee ownership. Even in the best circumstances, there needs to be a clear articulation of employee interests to balance capital interests. Labor organizations provide that employee focus quite effectively.

Unions have been skeptical of employee ownership.[19] This skepticism has focused on whether employee ownership is feasible and whether it really serves workers' interests. In many employee ownership situations, management takes the lead in making the conversion. The union's attitudes in these cases seem to be situationally specific. Some international unions, including the Communications Workers, Teamsters, Steelworkers, and National Maritime unions, have endorsed ESOPs.[20] Unions don't consider ESOPs an acceptable substitute for conventional pension plans, however, since they lack most of the protections afforded to conventional plans and they take significant risks with workers' deferred wages. Collective bargaining is considered the proper arena to determine the detailed structure for any employee ownership opportunity. Unions are concerned that employee ownership arrangements may break down worker solidarity by pitting workers who want to maximize their short-term gains (take-home pay or current dividends) against workers who want to maximize their long-term gains (return on and value of their stock).

Several other significant issues relate to the union's role and responsibilities in employee ownership.

Duty of fair representation. In several instances union members have charged their unions with inadequately representing them in the development of ESOPs. Duty of fair representation liability exists if the union provides loans or other financial assistance to some locals and not to others. Further, there can be some liability when unions give advice about the feasibility of an ESOP. If the ESOP fails after the union presented it as a good business proposition, then some members may feel that they were not fairly represented.[21]

Union representation on boards of directors. Unions could end up representing workers on the boards of competing firms in the same industry. This may raise antitrust issues, especially around the motivation and opportunity for price fixing. Unions can limit their risks by having different people serve on competing boards and by having these representatives appointed or elected by stockholders, thereby removing them to some extent from union control and responsibility. The value to employees of being involved at the board level in critical investment decisions usually makes them willing to take these risks.

Conflicts of interest. The Landrum-Griffin Act and other antitrust regulations establish a series of situations that union officials must avoid in order to be free of conflicts of interest that are particularly touchy under worker ownership. These include accepting payments or fees paid by the employer when the union represents employees, investing union funds in employer stock, and holding employer stock.[22] The UAW presidents who served on the Chrysler Corporation Board of Directors donated the fees they received for this service to charity to try to limit the possibility of conflict of interest. If the union or union officials hold stock, this could give them a pecuniary or personal interest that would potentially conflict with union members' interests. On this basis there could be a violation of the Landrum-Griffin Act.

Maintaining the employer's duty to bargain over employee rights. All aspects of the employee ownership plan should be mandatory bargaining items. In this way the employer's duty to bargain is fully retained. Ownership does not in any way preempt the right of any employee to pursue his or her rights under the agreement through the grievance procedure.

There are real risks that unions assume by representing member-employee-owners. Union officials should assess carefully the risks in their situation. Similarly, managers need to understand how to avoid unintentionally compromising their partners. In some cases, employee ownership has been used to reduce the strength of bargaining units or to counter union organizing drives in nonunion firms. Union and management partners should make it clear that this is not their intention. Only through careful planning and honest dealing can the union and management partners strengthen their relationship while pursuing employee ownership and avoid the appearance, or the reality, of union busting.

The final issue concerns single-plant buyouts. When a single plant is bought out, it is no longer covered under the union's master contract. This sets up wage competition between the worker-owners of the newly created company and the workers of the parent company. The buyout may thus weaken the union's national contract but be the only way to maintain local jobs. This is probably one of the most serious buyout-related dilemmas a union, especially at the international level, is likely to face. A comprehensive assessment of the risks and benefits and a plan to address them are the only protections the union and management partners have against making mistakes that may later threaten not only the collective bargaining relationship but the very survival of the company.

Employee Participation in ESOPs and Employee Buyouts

Among the important indicators of employee influence in an employee-owned company are the percentage of equity owned by the workers; whether the workers have voting rights, what kind, and to what degree; and whether the workers have representation on the board of directors. By these indicators, participation is often quite limited. For example, in an overwhelming number of ESOPs, workers don't have voting rights.

Another indicator of how much employees are engaged in employee ownership is whether there are specific participation programs designed to enhance the role of rank-and-file employees as workers and share-holders. Many companies with ESOPs have no such programs. Too often it is assumed that employee ownership will lead to greater employee involvement in the running of the business. Unfortunately, this is probably the most common misconception, especially in employee buyout situations. By contrast, in producer cooperatives and participative ESOPs, employee involvement activities are a critical part of employee ownership.

In any case, the union and management partners cannot ignore what other companies know about the value of employee participation. For employee-owners to obtain the best possible return on their stock, the company has to be the best performer it can be. Employee participation provides the most direct avenue for improving organizational performance. Equally important, it gives employees the means to enhance the value of their ownership share.

Necessary Conditions for an Employee Buyout to Be Successful

Three general conditions are necessary for an employee buyout to be successful: voting rights, voting rights that are separate from equity accumulation, and an effective education and training process. Voting rights are the means by which employees exercise control over their equity. They are a key indicator of the real power employee-owners have. Separating voting rights and equity accumulation in an employee-owned firm injects a more democratic structure into the decision-making arena. Participative or cooperative ESOPs do this by applying the one-person, one-vote rule, although employees accumulate different amounts of stock. Education and training should help employees at all levels obtain the expertise necessary to function actively as employee-owners. The training should build job skills and participative skills while expanding understanding of the business. When voting rights are maximized and separated from equity accumulation and when continuous education and training occur, employees and the entity optimize their chances for success.

The National Center for Employee Ownership has conducted extensive research into what makes an ESOP successful. It determined that the company must make a significant contribution to the plan, at least 5 percent annually and preferably 10 percent of the payroll for covered employees. Companies should be strongly committed to employee ownership, treat employees as owners, and bring employees into company decision making. The Weirton Steel Company, mentioned earlier, is one of the best examples of a company in which employee participation supports and advances employee ownership. The company also must have an active communications program through which employees learn about their ESOP. The National Center also concluded that a financially successful company is in a better position to have the features that make an ESOP work well. Financially troubled firms usually cannot afford to do what it takes to make the ESOP successful unless they turn their financial situation around quickly.[23]

Pitfalls of ESOPs and Employee Buyouts

Serious organizational problems can result from employee ownership. First, it may be difficult for employee-owned firms to obtain capital, especially in buyout situations, because of biases against employee ownership.

Second, ESOPs are a risky form of pension plan and may also be an unstable form of employee compensation. Employees deserve to be adequately compensated for their efforts and paid for their long-term contribution to the company through an adequate pension plan.

Third, employee ownership in no way ensures labor-management harmony or peace. A positive union-management relationship has to be developed over time by working successfully together on cooperative activities. Employee ownership can provide opportunities and an incentive for the union and management to work together, but a structured process must be established. Too often employee ownership results in increased management power and control at the expense of stockholders and employees. Voting rights and control of the board of directors are two key areas in which employee interests should be well represented to balance management interests. Sometimes stock is sold to the ESOP at inflated prices, or management purchases stock at a much lower price than it is purchased through the ESOP for employees. Neither of these occurrences helps build the union-management relationship.

Fourth, expectations about the power or control of employee-owners, the likely stock dividends, or the profitability and survival of the company can become problems. Sometimes the positive results of employee ownership are oversold. If expectations are unmet, dissatisfaction and disillusionment can result.

Fifth and finally, those running the company may not have the entrepreneurial capacity and managerial expertise they need. Employee ownership may enhance organizational effectiveness, but it is not a guarantee that a company will be a success in the marketplace. Often outside professionals must be hired to help in critical areas when the expertise is not resident in the company.

The union and management partners need to figure out how they can avoid the pitfalls while getting the maximum benefits of employee ownership. Deborah Groban-Olson, executive director of the Michigan Center for Employee Ownership, recommends these strategies for overcoming the common pitfalls:

1. The terms of the ESOP should be a mandatory subject for collective bargaining.
2. All stock held by the ESOP trust should have full voting rights; these rights should be passed through to employees in closely held firms; an advisory committee elected by the employees should direct the voting of the stock by the ESOP trustee.
3. Diversification of ESOP trust funds should be required where there is no other pension plan.
4. If the company already has a pension plan qualified under ERISA, it should not be able to replace that plan with an ESOP.
5. Regulations should be developed to prevent ESOPs from paying inflated prices for the stock of closely held firms.
6. Vesting schedules should be shortened to provide full vesting after three years of employee participation.[24]

Conclusion

Employee ownership is one approach union and management partners can take to improve organizational effectiveness, save jobs, and enhance the quality of work life. Financial success flows from organizational success. But organizational success means that stock ownership must also include a sense of job ownership. There is a lot of rhetoric concerning employee ownership; when it is tied to majority control of the stocks, it carries with it great opportunity and great risk. The key, as with other approaches, is to pursue employee ownership jointly in a careful and organized fashion. By building in high-quality union-management cooperation at the equity, governance, managerial, and operational levels, significant success is possible.

Notes

Chapter 1. What Is Union-Management Cooperation?

1. U.S. Department of Labor, *The New Work Systems Network: A Compendium of Selected Work Innovation Cases*, BLMR 136 (Washington, D.C.: U.S. Department of Labor, Bureau of Labor-Management Relations and Cooperative Programs, 1990).

2. Asian Productivity Organization, *Labour-Management Consultation Mechanisms* (Tokyo: Asian Productivity Organization, 1984), p. 189.

3. Lowell Turner, *Democracy at Work: Changing World Markets and the Future of Labor Unions* (Ithaca, N.Y.: Cornell University Press, 1991); see chap. 2.

4. Ron Callus, Alison Morehead, Mark Cully, and John Buchanan, *Industrial Relations at Work: The Australian Workplace Industrial Relations Survey* (Canberra: Australian Government Publishing Service, 1991).

5. Janez Prasnikar, *Workers' Participation and Self-Management in Developing Countries* (San Francisco: Westview, 1991).

6. *Workers' Participation in Decisions within Undertakings* (Geneva: International Labour Office, 1981).

7. *Compensation and Working Conditions* 44 (Washington, D.C.: Bureau of Labor Statistics, 1991).

8. Frederick Harbison and John R. Coleman, *Goals and Strategy in Collective Bargaining* (New York: Harper and Brothers, 1951), p. 20.

9. Harbison and Coleman, *Goals and Strategy in Collective Bargaining*, p. 54.

10. Harbison and Coleman, *Goals and Strategy in Collective Bargaining*, p. 90.

11. Caroll E. French, "The Shop Committee in the United States," speech presented at Johns Hopkins University, 1922, p. 8.

12. William Leavitt Stoddard, *The Shop Committee* (New York: Macmillan, 1919), p. 93.

13. Report of the AFL Seventh Annual Railway Employees Conference, 1928, pp. 19–20.

14. Otto S. Beyer, *Wertheim Lectures on Industrial Relations: 1928* (Cambridge: Harvard University Press, 1929), pp. 3–4.

15. Clinton Golden and Harold Ruttenberg, *Dynamics of Industrial Democracy* (New York: Harper and Brothers, 1942), pp. xvii–xviii.

16. Charles E. Meyers, "Conclusions and Implications," in *Causes of Industrial Peace* (New York: Harper and Brothers, 1953), p. 47.

17. Irving Bluestone and Barry Bluestone, *Negotiating the Future: A Labor Perspective on American Business* (New York: Basic Books, 1993).

18. Thomas A. Kochan, Harry C. Katz, and Robert B. McKersie, *The Transformation of American Industrial Relations* (New York: Basic Books, 1986), p. 204.

19. Collective Bargaining Forum, *New Directions for Labor and Management*, BLMR 120 (Washington, D.C.: U.S. Department of Labor, Bureau of Labor-Management Relations and Cooperative Programs, 1988). The Forum also produced a document on how to implement its principles: *Labor-Management Commitment: A Compact for Change*, BLMR 141 (Washington, D.C.: U.S. Department of Labor, Bureau of Labor-Management Relations and Cooperative Programs,1991).

Chapter 2. The Union's Decision to Cooperate

1. Bureau of Labor-Management Relations and Cooperative Services, *Labor-Management Cooperation: Perspectives from the Labor Movement* (Washington, D.C.: U.S. Department of Labor, 1984).

2. Samuel Gompers, *Labor and Employers* (New York: E. P. Dutton, 1920), p. 305.

3. *AFL-CIO News* press conference, Tulsa, Okla., July 13, 1985.

4. Charles C. Heckscher, *The New Unionism: Employee Involvement in the Changing Corporation* (New York: Basic Books, 1988).

5. Hy Kornbluh, ed., "Unions, Labor Education and Worker Participation Programs," *Labor Studies Journal* 8 (Winter 1984).

6. Edward Cohen-Rosenthal, "Should Unions Participate in Quality of Work Life?" *QWL: The Canadian Scene* 4 (1981): 7–12. Also see Thomas A. Kochan, Harry Katz, and Nancy Mower, *Worker Participation and American Unions: Threat or Opportunity?* (Kalamazoo, Mich.: W. E. Upjohn Institute for Employment Research, 1984).

7. "Judy McKibbon—Workers Set the Pace," interview with Jan Mears, *Workplace Democracy* 53 (Summer 1986): 11, 24.

8. Mike Parker, *Inside the Circle: A Union Guide to QWL* (Boston: South End Press, 1985). Also see Donald Wells, *Empty Promises: Quality of Working Life Programs and the Labor Movement* (New York: Monthly Review Press, 1987).

9. Guillermo Grenier, *Inhuman Relations: Quality Circles and Anti-unionism in American Industry* (Philadelphia: Temple University Press, 1988).

10. Andy Banks and Jack Metzger, "Participating in Management: Union Organizing on a New Terrain," *Labor Research Review* 8 (Fall 1989): 1–42.

11. John Mathews, *Tools of Change: New Technology and the Democratisation of Work* (Leichhardt, New South Wales, Pluto Press, 1989), p. 2.

Chapter 3. Management's Decision to Cooperate

1. Federal Mediation and Conciliation Service, *Labor-Management Committees: Planning for Progress* (Washington, D.C.: GPO, 1977), pp. 6–7.

2. Charles G. Burck, "Working Smarter," *Fortune*, June 15, 1981, p. 73.

3. S. Andrew Carson, "Participatory Management Beefs Up the Bottom Line," *Personnel* (July 1985): 47–48.

4. Joel Cutcher-Gershenfeld, "The Impact on Economic Performance of a Transformation in Workplace Relations," *Industrial and Labor Relations Review* 44 (Jan. 1991): 241–60.

5. Maryellen R. Kelley and Bennett Harrison, "Unions, Technology, and Labor-Management Cooperation," in *Unions and Economic Competitiveness*, ed. Lawrence Mishel and Paula B. Voos (Armonk, N.Y.: M. E. Sharpe, 1992).

6. Karl Frieden, *Workplace Democracy and Productivity* (Washington, D.C.: National Center for Economic Alternatives, 1980), pp. 21–22.

7. Frieden, *Workplace Democracy*, pp. 21–22.

8. Adrienne Eaton and Paula B. Voos, "Unions and Contemporary Innovations in Work Organization, Compensation and Employee Participation," in *Unions and Economic Competitiveness*, pp. 211–14.

9. Michael Rosow and Robert Zager, "The Sharonville Story: Worker Involvement at a Ford Motor Company Plant," in *The Innovative Organization: Productivity Programs in Action*, eds. Michael Rosow and Robert Zager (New York: Pergamon Press, 1982), p. 60.

Chapter 4. Reorienting the Roots

1. David Lewin, "Collective Bargaining and the Quality of Work Life," *Organizational Dynamics* 28 (Autumn 1981): 37–52.

2. John J. Popular, "Labor Management Relationships by Objectives," in *Industrial Relations Guide Service* (Englewood Cliffs, N.J.: Prentice Hall, 1982), sec. 42, p. 184.

3. Robert R. Blake, Herbert Sheperd, and Jane S. Mouton, *Managing Intergroup Conflict in Industry* (Houston: Gulf Publishing, 1964), p. 144.

4. Robert R. Blake, Jane Srygley Mouton, and Richard L. Sloma, "The Union-Management Intergroup Laboratory: Strategy for Resolving Intergroup Conflict," *Journal of Applied Behavioral Science* 1 (1965): 31.

5. Robert R. Blake and Jane S. Mouton, "Developing a Positive Union-Management Relationship," *Personnel Administrator* 28 (June 1983): 23–32.

6. Cynthia Burton and Edward Cohen-Rosenthal, "Collective Bargaining for the Future," *Futurist* 21 (March-April 1987): 34–37.

7. This process was developed at Scott Paper Company in Mobile, Alabama, with the International Brotherhood of Electrical Workers, Local 2129. The process emerged from their setting, and they shaped and guided the process throughout.

8. Gerard H. Langeler, "The Vision Trap," *Harvard Business Review* 70 (March-April 1992): 46–55.

9. Marjorie Parker, *Creating Shared Vision* (Clarendon Hills, Ill.: Dialog International, 1990), pp. 2, 3.

10. Alastair Crombie, "The Nature and Types of Search Conferences," *International Journal of Lifelong Education* 4 (1985): 4.

11. Marvin Weisbord et al., *Discovering Common Ground* (San Francisco: Berrett-Koehler, 1992).

12. Marvin Weisbord, *Productive Workplaces* (San Francisco: Jossey-Bass, 1988), p. 285.

13. Richard Walton and Robert B. McKersie, *A Behavioral Theory of Labor Negotiations* (Ithaca, N.Y.: ILR Press, 1991), p. 11.

14. Walton and McKersie, *Behavioral Theory of Labor Negotiations*, p. 128.

15. Walton and McKersie, *Behavioral Theory of Labor Negotiations*, p. 137.

16. Walton and McKersie, *Behavioral Theory of Labor Negotiations*, p. 139.

17. Lane Tracy and Richard Peterson, "Tackling Problems through Negotiations," *Human Resource Management* 18 (Summer 1979): 23.

18. Walton and McKersie, *Behavioral Theory of Labor Negotiations*, p. 152.

19. For an excellent discussion of these issues, see James J. Healy, ed., *Creative Collective Bargaining: Meeting Today's Challenges to Labor-Management Relations* (Englewood Cliffs, N.J.: Prentice-Hall, 1965).

20. Ernest J. Savoie, "The New Ford-UAW Agreement: Its Worklife Aspects," *Work Life Review* 1 (1983): 5.

21. Roger Fisher and William Ury, *Getting to Yes: Negotiating Agreement without Giving In* (New York: Penguin, 1983). Two subsequent books elaborate on this process: Roger Fisher and Scott Brown, *Getting Together: Building a Relationship That Gets to Yes* (Boston: Houghton Mifflin, 1988) and William Ury, *Getting Past No: Negotiating with Difficult People* (New York: Bantam Books, 1991).

22. Fisher and Ury, *Getting to Yes*, p. 59.

23. Fisher and Ury, *Getting to Yes*, p. 91.

24. Arthur A. Sloane and Fred Witney, *Labor Relations* (Englewood Cliffs, N.J.: Prentice-Hall, 1977), p. 224.

25. For an analysis of the categories of grievances and their disposition, see Dan R. Walton and William D. Tudor, "Win, Lose or Draw: The Grievance Process in Practice," *Personnel Administrator* 26 (March 1981): 25–29.

26. K. L. Sovereign and Mario Bognanno, "Positive Contract Administration," in Dale Yoder and Herbert G. Heneman, eds., *Employee and Labor Relations* (Washington, D.C.: Bureau of National Affairs, 1976), pp. 7–177.

27. Stephen B. Goldberg and William P. Hobgood, *Mediating Grievances: A Cooperative Solution*, BLMR 110 (Washington, D.C.: U.S. Department of Labor, Bureau of Labor-Management Relations and Cooperative Programs, 1987), p. 1.

28. Thomas J. Quinn, Mark Rosenbaum, and Donald S. McPherson, "Grievance Mediation and Grievance Negotiation Skills: Building Collaborative Relationships," *Labor Law Journal* 41 (Nov. 1990): 762.

29. Quinn, Rosenbaum, and McPherson, "Grievance Mediation and Grievance Negotiation Skills," p. 762.

30. Suzanne Arnold, Jeanne Brock, Lowell Ledford, and Henry Richards, *Ready or Not: A Handbook for Retirement* (New York: Manpower Education Project, 1987).

31. Ivan Charner and Shirley Fox, *Union Retirees: Enriching Their Lives, Enhancing Their Contribution* (Washington, D.C.: National Institute for Work and Learning, 1990).

32. Paul Gerhart, *Saving Plants and Jobs: Union-Management Negotiations in the Context of Threatened Plant Closing* (Kalamazoo, Mich.: W. E. Upjohn Institute for Employment Research, 1987).

33. William L. Batt, Jr., "Canada's Good Example with Displaced Workers," *Harvard Business Review* 83 (July-Aug. 1983): 4–11.

34. *Plant Closing Checklist: A Guide to Best Practice* (Washington, D.C.: U.S. Department of Labor, 1985); see also Gary B. Hansen, "Ford and the UAW Have a Better Idea: A Joint Labor-Management Approach to Plant Closings and Worker Retraining," *AAPS Annals* 475 (Sept. 1984): 158–74.

Chapter 5. Building Linking Structures

1. Paul J. Champagne and Mark Lincoln Chadwin, "Joint Committees Boost Labor-Management Performance and Facilitate Change," *SAM Advanced Management Journal* (Summer 1983): 20.

2. See chaps. 2 and 3 in William Foote Whyte, Tove Helland Hammer, Christopher B. Meek, Reed Nelson, and Robert N. Stern, *Worker Participation and Ownership: Cooperative Strategies for Strengthening Local Economies* (Ithaca, N.Y.: ILR Press, 1983).

3. Robert W. Ahern, "Positive Labor Relations: Plant Labor-Management Committees and the Collective Bargaining Process," prepared by the Buffalo–Erie County Labor-Management Council, April 1976.

4. Ronald Contino, "Productivity Gains through Labor-Management Cooperation at the NYC Department of Sanitation Bureau of Motor Equipment," in *Teamwork: Joint Labor-Management Programs in America*, ed. Jerome Rosow (New York: Pergamon Press, 1986), pp. 169–86.

5. *Starting a Labor-Management Committee in Your Organization* (Washington, D. C.: National Center for Productivity and Quality of Working Life, 1978).

6. Robert P. Quinn and Graham L. Staines. "The 1977 Quality of Employment Survey" (Ann Arbor: Survey Research Center, University of Michigan, 1979), p. 178.

7. *Major Collective Bargaining Agreements: Safety and Health Provisions*, Bulletin no. 1425-16 (Washington, D.C.: Bureau of Labor Statistics, 1976).

8. *The Role of Labor-Management Committees in Safeguarding Worker Safety and Health*, BLMR 121 (Washington, D.C.: U.S. Department of Labor, Bureau of Labor-Management Relations and Cooperative Programs, 1990), p. 3.

9. Kevin Sweeney, *Building an Effective Labor-Management Safety and Health Committee* (Washington, D.C.: American Center for Quality of Work Life, 1984), p. 5.

10. American Labor Education Center, "Labor-Management Health and Safety Committees in Sweden, West Germany, Austria and Saskatchewan, Canada," draft, prepared for OSHA, June 1980, p. 4.

11. Thomas A. Kochan, Lee Dyer, and David Lipsky, *The Effectiveness of Union-Management Safety and Health Committees* (Kalamazoo, Mich.: W. E. Upjohn Institute for Employment Research, 1977), p. 83.

12. Sweeney, *Building an Effective Safety and Health Committee*, p. 6.

13. *Role of Labor-Management Committees in Safeguarding Worker Safety and Health*, p. 43.

14. Robert Karasek and Tores Theorell, *Healthy Work: Stress, Productivity, and the Reconstruction of Working Life* (New York: Basic Books, 1990), p. 2.

15. Patrick Q. McMahon, "Health Care Cost Containment: A Labor-Management Issue," *Personnel* 13 (May 1988): 66–70.

16. *Controlling Public Employee Health Care Costs through Labor-Management Committees* (Washington, D.C.: State and Local Government Labor-Management Committee, 1991), p. 1.

17. *Controlling Public Employee Health Care Costs*, p. 9.

18. Ray Marshall, *Unheard Voices: Labor and Economic Policy in a Competitive World* (New York: Basic Books, 1987), p. 84.

19. Alan Gladstone and Muneto Ozaki, eds., *Working Together: Labour-Management Cooperation in Training and in Technological and Other Changes* (Geneva: International Labour Office, 1991).

20. Louis A. Ferman, Michele Hoyman, Joel Cutcher-Gershenfeld, and Ernest J. Savoie, eds., *Joint Training Programs: A Union-Management Approach to Preparing Workers for the Future* (Ithaca, N.Y.: ILR Press, 1991), p. 4.

21. Thomas Pasco and Richard Collins, "A Program in Action," in *From Vision to Reality: The UAW and Ford Create New Directions in Employee Development and Training* (Dearborn, Mich.: UAW-Ford National Development and Training Center, 1985), p. 16.

22. "Workplace Reform, Skill Development and High Competence, Educated Workforce," policy statement, ACTU Congress, Sept. 1991, p. 3.

23. Gerald G. Gold, *Employment-Based Tuition Assistance: Decisions and Checklists for Employers, Educators and Unions* (Washington, D.C.: National Institute for Work and Learning, 1985), pp. 3, 11.

24. Barry Sheckley, Lois Lamdin, and Morris Keaton, *Employability in a High Performance Economy* (Chicago: CAEL, 1992).

25. An excellent description of union roles in literacy programs is in Anthony Sarmiento and Ann Kay, *Worker Centered Learning: A Union Guide to Workplace Literacy* (Washington, D.C.: AFL-CIO Human Resources Development Institute, 1990).

26. Anthony P. Carnevale, Leila J. Gainer, and Ann S. Meltzer, *Workplace Basics: The Skills Employers Want* (Washington, D.C.: American Society for Training and Development, 1988); also see Maurice C. Taylor, Glenda R. Lewe, and James A. Draper, *Basic Skills for the Workplace* (Toronto: Culture Concepts, 1991).

27. Anthony Sarmiento, "Do Workplace Literacy Programs Promote High Skills or Low Wages?" *Labor Notes* (July 1991): 1.

28. *America's Choice: High Skills or Low Wages!* (Rochester, N.Y.: National Center on Education and the Economy, June 1990).

29. Ellen Galinsky and Dana Friedman, *The Corporate Reference Guide to Work-Family Programs* (New York: Families and Work Institute, 1991).

30. See Wayne Weagle and Gordon Skead, *Maintaining and Enriching Your EAP: The Role of the Joint Committee* (Troy, Mich.: Performance Resource Press, 1984) and William J. Sonnenstuhl and Harrison M. Trice, *Strategies for Employee Assistance Programs: The Crucial Balance*, Key Issues no. 30, 2d ed. (Ithaca, N.Y.: ILR Press, 1990).

31. Frank P. Burger, "Ensuring a Viable Program," *EAP Digest* 10 (July-Aug. 1990): 14.

32. Sonnenstuhl and Trice, *Strategies for Employee Assistance Programs*, p. 37.

33. Edward Cohen-Rosenthal, "QWL and EAPs: Making the Connection," *EAP Digest* 5 (May-June, 1985): 42–52.

34. Robert H. Rosen, *The Healthy Company: Eight Strategies to Develop People, Productivity and Profits* (Los Angeles: Jeremy P. Tarcher, 1991).

35. Hy Kornbluh, James Crowfoot, and Edward Cohen-Rosenthal, *Worker Participation in Energy and Natural Resources Conservation: A Final Report* (Ann Arbor: University of Michigan Institute of Industrial and Labor Relations, Dec. 1984), summarized in *International Labour Review* (Nov.-Dec. 1985): 737–54.

36. Edward Cohen-Rosenthal, James E. Crowfoot, Roger Kerson, and Hy Kornbluh, "Preliminary Conference Report of U.S. Survey Data," presented at Employee Participation in Conservation: The U.S. and Japan Experience Conference, Ann Arbor, Mich., Sept. 1983.

37. Cynthia E. Burton, "Participation in Conservation: Maryland Department of Health and Mental Hygiene," in *United States Case Studies* (Ann Arbor: University of Michigan Institute of Labor and Industrial Relations, 1983), pp. 1–57.

38. Richard Grossman and Gail Daneker, *Energy, Jobs and the Economy* (Boston: Alyson Publications, 1979).

39. Art Kleiner, "What Does It Mean to be Green?" *Harvard Business Review* 69 (July-Aug. 1991): 38–47. See also Robert Seemer, "Keeping in Step with the Environment: Applying TQC to Energy Supply," *National Productivity Review* 9 (Autumn 1990): 439–55.

40. *Trade Unions and the Environment: Proposals for Action* (Brussels: International Confederation of Free Trade Unions, March 1990), p. 5.

41. Patrick Carson and Julia Moulden, *Green Is Gold: Business Talking to Business about the Environmental Revolution* (Toronto: Harper Business, 1991), p. 65, and Stephan Schmidheiny, *Changing Course: A Global Business Perspective on Development and the Environment* (Cambridge: MIT Press, 1992).

42. Dennis Chamot and Michael D. Dymmel, *Cooperation or Conflict: European Experiences with Technological Change at the Workplace* (Washington, D.C.: Department of Professional Employees, AFL-CIO, 1981); see also Steven Deutsch, "International Experiences with Technological Change," *Monthly Labor Review* 109 (March 1986): 35–40.

43. Doris B. McLaughlin, "The Impact of Unions on the Rate and Direction of Technological Change," NSF Grant no. PRA 77-15268, University of Michigan Institute of Labor and Industrial Relations, Detroit, 1979).

44. International Association of Machinists and Aerospace Workers, *Let's Rebuild America* (Washington, D.C.: IAM, 1983), pp. 189–98.

45. For an exploration of the process of labor-management technological change, see Robert J. Thomas, *What Machines Can't Do: Politics and Technology in the Industrial Enterprise* (Berkeley: University of California Press, 1992).

46. Shoshana Zuboff, *In the Age of the Smart Machine: The Future of Work and Power* (New York: Basic Books, 1988).

47. John Mathews, *Tools for Change: New Technology and the Democratisation of Work* (Leichardt, New South Wales: Pluto Press, 1989), p. 41.

48. David C. Mowery and Bruce E. Henderson, eds., *The Challenge of New Technology to Labor-Management Relations*, BLMR 135 (Washington, D.C.: U.S. Department of Labor, Bureau of Labor-Management Relations and Cooperative Programs, 1991).

49. Mathews, *Tools for Change*, p. 59.

50. Bert Painter, *Good Jobs with New Technology: How Labour and Management Can Achieve Good Jobs in an Era of Technological Change* (Vancouver: BC Research, 1991), pp. 21, 22.

51. Richard Walton, "Challenges in the Management of Technology and Labor Relations," in *HRM: Trends and Challenges*, ed. Richard Walton and Paul R. Lawrence (Boston: Harvard Business School Press, 1985), p. 215, emphasis in original.

52. Sally Klingel and Ann Martin, eds., *A Fighting Chance: New Strategies for Employment and Workplace Systems* (Ithaca, N.Y.: ILR Press, 1988).

53. Klingel and Martin, *A Fighting Chance*, p. 1.

54. Robert C. Camp, *Benchmarking: The Search for Industry Best Practices That Lead to Superior Performance* (Milwaukee: Quality Press, 1989), p. 10.

55. Jeanine Derr, *Labor and the American Red Cross* (Washington, D.C.: American National Red Cross, 1987).

56. For a discussion of labor's community resources, see part III of Arthur B. Shostak, *Robust Unionism: Innovations in the Labor Movement* (Ithaca, N.Y.: ILR Press, 1991).

57. John Auble, Jr., "Giving the United Way," *St. Louis Globe Democrat*, Sept. 16–17, 1967.

Chapter 6. Developing New Organizational Structures

1. There are a number of "cookbooks" associated with quality circles, and the prevalence of canned approaches has tended to diminish their reputation. Some of the more popular are Sud Ingle, *Quality Circles Master Guide* (Englewood Cliffs, N.J.: Prentice-Hall, 1982); Phillip C. Thompson, *Quality Circles: How to Make Them Work in America* (New York: AMACOM, 1982); and Ralph Barra, *Putting Quality Circles to Work: A Practical Strategy for Boosting Productivity and Profits* (New York: Prentice-Hall, 1983).

2. Edward E. Lawler III and Susan A. Mohrman, "Quality Circles after the Fad," *Harvard Business Review* 63 (Jan.-Feb. 1985): 65–71.

3. Kaoru Ishikawa, *QC Circle Activities* (Tokyo: Japan Union of Scientists and Engineers, 1958).

4. Mike Parker, *Inside the Circle: A Union Guide to QWL* (Boston: South End Press, 1985).

5. Robert Cole, "Some Principles Concerning Union Involvement in Quality Circles and Other Employee Involvement Programs," *Labor Studies Journal* 8 (Winter 1984): 221–29.

6. For a fuller discussion, see Cynthia Burton, "How to Do Quality Circles in a Unionized Workplace," *International Association of Quality Circles Transactions* (1983): 48–58.

7. Resolution adopted by IUE International Executive Board, Jan. 1982, and at IUE Twentieth Constitutional Convention, Sept. 1982.

8. Owen Bieber, "UAW Views Circles: Not Bad at All," *Quality Circles Journal* 5 (Aug. 1982): 6.

9. Susan Albers Mohrman and Gerald E. Ledford, Jr., "The Design and Use of Effective Employee Participation Groups: Implications for Human Resource Management," *Human Resource Management* 24 (Winter 1985): 413–28.

10. Barry A. Stein and Rosabeth Moss Kanter, "Building the Parallel Organization: Creating Mechanisms for Permanent Quality of Work Life," *Journal of Applied Behavioral Science* 16 (1980): 373.

11. Dale Zand, "Collateral Organization: A New Change Strategy," *Journal of Applied Behavioral Science* 10 (1974): 63–89.

12. Stein and Kanter, "Building the Parallel Organization," p. 384.

13. For a good discussion of task forces in general, see James P. Ware, "Making the Matrix Come Alive: Managing a Task Force," in David Cleland, *Matrix Management Systems Handbook* (New York: Van Nostrand Reinhold, 1984), pp. 112–31.

14. T. G. Cummings, "Socio-technical Systems: An Intervention Strategy," in *Sociotechnical Systems: A Sourcebook*, ed. William A. Pasmore and John J. Sherwood (San Diego: University Associates, 1978), p. 169.

15. John G. Maurer, ed., *Open System Approaches* (New York: Random House, 1971).

16. Albert Cherns, "The Principles of Socio-technical Design," *Human Relations* 29 (1976): 792–93.

17. Drawn from Fred Emery and Einar Thorsrud, *Democracy at Work* (Leiden: Martinus Nijhoff Social Sciences Division, 1976), p. 159.

18. Cherns, "Principles of Socio-technical Design," p. 792.

19. Tom Rankin, *New Forms of Work Organization: The Challenge for North American Unions* (Toronto: University of Toronto Press, 1990), p. 129.

20. Ontario Quality of Working Life Centre, "Starting Up a Redesign Project," *QWL Focus* 1 (March 1981): 7.

21. Calvin H. P. Pava, *Managing New Office Technology: An Organizational Strategy* (New York: Free Press, 1983), p. 26.

22. Pava, *Managing New Office Technology*, p. 27.

23. Pava, *Managing New Office Technology*, p. 28.

24. Randall B. Dunham, "The Design of Jobs," in Wendell French, Cecil Bell, and Robert Zawacki, *Organization Development: Theory, Research and Practice* (Plano, Tex.: Business Publications, 1983), pp. 301–14.

25. *Making Better Jobs: Guidelines for Negotiating Better Jobs in the Workplace* (Melbourne: Australian Council of Trade Unions, 1990).

26. William A. Pasmore, *Designing Effective Organizations: The Sociotechnical Systems Perspective* (New York: John Wiley, 1988), p. 109.

27. John Mathews, *Tools of Change* (Leichardt, New South Wales: Pluto Press, 1989), p. 114.

28. For an analysis of the Rushton and Topeka experience, see Paul S. Goodman, Rukmini Devedas and Terri L. Griffith Hughson, "Groups and Productivity: Analyzing the Effectiveness of Self-Managing Teams," in John P. Campbell, Richard J. Campbell, and Associates, *Productivity in Organizations* (San Francisco: Jossey-Bass, 1988), pp. 295–327.

29. Richard E. Walton, "From Hawthorne to Topeka and Kalmar," in French, Bell, and Zawacki, *Organization Development*, pp. 292–300.

30. Jack D. Orsburn, Linda Moran, Ed Musselwhite, and John H. Zenger, *Self-Directed Work Teams: The New American Challenge* (Homewood, Ill.: Business One Irwin, 1990), p. 195.

31. Two excellent resources on new supervisory roles are Janice A. Klein, *Revitalizing Manufacturing* (Homewood, Ill.: Irwin, 1990), pp. 467–79, and the set of three studies, *New Roles for Managers* (Scarsdale, N.Y.: Work in America Institute, 1990), which outlines the trainer/coach/leader approach to supervision.

32. Mike Parker and Jane Slaughter, *Choosing Sides: Unions and the Team Concept* (Boston: South End Press, 1988).

33. Lowell Turner, *Democracy at Work: Changing World Markets and the Future of Labor Unions* (Ithaca, N.Y.: Cornell University Press, 1991), p. 124.

34. *The Grain Millers' Role in Creating Labor/Management Partnerships for New Work Systems* (Minneapolis: American Federation of Grain Millers, 1991).

35. William Foote Whyte, "The New Manufacturing Organization: Problems and Opportunities for Employee Involvement and Collective Bargaining," *National Productivity Review* 9 (Summer 1990): 339.

36. Richard J. Schonberger, *World Class Manufacturing: The Lessons of Simplicity Applied* (New York: Free Press, 1986), p. 10.

37. Edward Cohen-Rosenthal, "Worker Participation in Management: A Guide for the Perplexed," in *Quality of Work Life: Perspectives for Business and the Public Sector*, ed. Daniel Skrovan (Reading, Mass.: Addison-Wesley, 1983), p. 179.

38. David A. Nadler and Edward E. Lawler III, "Quality of Work Life: Perspectives and Directions," *Organizational Dynamics* (Winter 1983): 20–30.

39. Stephen H. Fuller, "How Quality-of-Worklife Projects Work for General Motors," *Monthly Labor Review* (July 1980): 38.

40. Simcha Ronen, *Alternative Work Schedules: Selecting, Implementing, Evaluating* (Homewood, Ill.: Dow-Jones-Irwin, 1985).

41. Harry C. Katz, Thomas A. Kochan, and Mark R. Weber, "Assessing the Effects of Industrial Relations Systems and Efforts to Improve the Quality of Working Life on Organizational Effectiveness," *Academy of Management Journal* 8 (1985): 509–26.

42. Edward E. Lawler III and Gerald E. Ledford, Jr., "Productivity and Quality of Work Life," *National Productivity Review* 1 (Winter 1981–82): 23–36.

Chapter 7. Creating New Opportunities

1. This chapter is drawn extensively from Edward Cohen-Rosenthal, "Orienting Labor-Management Cooperation towards Revenue and Growth." *National Productivity Review* 4 (Autumn 1985): 385–96.

2. A. Parasuraman, V. A. Zeithami, and L. L. Berry, "A Conceptual Model of Service Quality and Its Implications for Future Research," Report 84–106, Marketing Sciences Institute, Cambridge, 1984.

3. William Foote Whyte and Kathleen King Whyte, *Making Mondragón: The Growth and Development of the Worker Cooperative Complex*, 2d ed. (Ithaca, N.Y.: ILR Press, 1991).

4. See, for discussion, Hilary Wainwright and Dave Eliot, *The Lucas Plan* (New York: Allison and Busby, 1982).

5. Interview in *IUBAC Trowel*, Winter, 1984, p. 5.

6. Jan Ake Granath, *Architecture, Technology and Human Factors: Design in a Socio-technical Context* (Göteborg, Sweden: Chalmers University of Technology, 1991.)

7. *Starting a Labor-Management Committee in Your Organization: Some Pointers for Action* (Washington, D.C.: National Center for Productivity and Quality of Working Life, 1978), p. 11.

8. Norman Halpern, "Organization Design in Canada: Shell Canada's Sarnia Chemical Plant," in *People and Organizations Interacting*, ed. A. Brakel (New York: Wiley, 1985), pp. 117–51.

9. Louis E. Davis and Charles S. Sullivan, "A Labour-Management Contract and Quality of Working Life," *Journal of Occupational Behavior* 1 (1980): 33.

10. Colin Clipson and Hy Kornbluh, "Designing and Learning: Towards a Redefinition of Participatory Design Procedures," paper delivered at Swedish Cultural Center, Paris, 1991.

11. Franklin Becker, *The Total Workplace: Facilities Management and the Elastic Organization* (New York: Van Nostrand Reinhold, 1990), p. 235.

12. Douglas Fraser, "My Years on the Chrysler Board," *Across the Board* 23 (June 1986): 43.

13. *Workers Participation in Decisions within Undertakings* (Geneva: International Labour Office, 1981), p. 96.

14. Tove H. Hammer, Steve C. Currall, and Robert N. Stern, "Worker Representation on Board of Directors: A Study in Competing Roles," *Industrial and Labor Relations Review* 44 (July 1991): 661–80.

15. "Growth and Opportunity Fund Creates New Jobs," *UAW-GM People*, Winter 1991, p. 6.

Chapter 8. Achieving Quality

1. *American Federationist*, June 1927, p. 729.

2. Clinton Golden and Harold Ruttenberg, *Dynamics of Industrial Democracy* (New York: Harper and Brothers, 1942), p. 233.

3. W. Edwards Deming, *Out of the Crisis* (Cambridge: Massachusetts Institute of Technology Center for Advanced Engineering Study, 1982).

4. Gilbert Fuchsberg, "Quality Programs Show Shoddy Results," *Wall Street Journal*, July 20, 1992.

5. U.S. Office of Management and Budget, "Draft Circular to Replace A-132," Dec. 1989, pp. 1–2.

6. Richard Beckhard, "A Model for the Executive Management of Transformational Change," in J. William Pfeiffer, ed., *1989 Annual: Developing Human Resources* (San Diego: University Associates, 1989), p. 256.

7. Frank J. Wayno, Jr., *The Road to the Baldrige Award: Human Resource Aspects of the Strategic Transformation of Xerox* (Ithaca, N.Y.: Programs for Employment and Workplace Systems, School of Industrial and Labor Relations, Cornell University, 1991), pp. viii–ix.

8. *USMG Partnership: A Guide to Work Process Improvement* (Rochester, N.Y.: Xerox Corp., 1990), p. 4.

9. Wayno, *Road to the Baldrige Award*, p. 71.

10. Wayno, *Road to the Baldrige Award*, pp. 106–32.

11. Ned Hamson, "The FQI Story: Today and Tomorrow," *Journal for Quality and Participation* 13 (July-Aug. 1990): 48.

12. Gerardine DeSanctis, Marshall Scott Poole, Howard Lewis, and George Desharnais, "Using Computing to Improve the Quality Team Process: Some Initial Observations from the IRS-Minnesota Project," *Proceedings of the Twenty-Fourth Annual Hawaii International Conference on Systems Science* (Jan. 1991): 1–16. See also Terry Campbell, "Technology Update: Group Decision Support Systems," *Journal of Accountancy* 170 (July 1990): 47–50.

13. "The Downside of Quality," *Training and Development* 46 (March 1992): 11–12.

Chapter 15. Sharing the Pie

1. Charles R. Gowen III, "Gainsharing Programs: An Overview of History and Research," *Journal of Organizational Behavior Management* 11 (1990): 83.

2. Lawrence Mishel and Paula Voos, eds., *Unions and Economic Competitiveness* (Armonk, N.Y.: M. E. Sharpe, 1992).

3. Edward E. Lawler III, *Pay and Organization Development* (Reading, Mass.: Addison-Wesley, 1981), p. 152.

4. Robert J. Doyle, *Gainsharing and Productivity: A Guide to Planning, Implementation and Development* (New York: AMACOM, 1983), p. 19.

Chapter 16. More for More

1. Ralph M. Barnes, *Motion and Time Study Design and Measurement of Work* (New York: Wiley, 1980), pp. 482–83.

2. Garth L. Mangum, *Wage Incentive Systems* (Berkeley: Institute of Industrial Relations, University of California, 1964), pp. 5–7.

3. Barnes, *Motion and Time Study Design*, pp. 482–83.

4. Barnes, *Motion and Time Study Design*, p. 629.

5. Mangum, *Wage Incentive Systems*, pp. 12–13.

6. Robert Zager and Michael P. Rosow, eds., *The Innovative Organization: Productivity Programs in Action* (New York: Pergamon Press, 1982), pp. 196–97.

7. Mangum, *Wage Incentive Systems*, p. 16.

8. Barnes, *Motion and Time Study Design*, pp. 487–88.

9. James E. Nickel and Sandra O'Neal, "Small Group Incentives: Gain Sharing in the Microcosm," *Compensation and Benefits Review* 22 (March-April 1990): 23.

10. Elizabeth M. Doherty, Walter R. Nord, and Jerry L. McAdams, "Gainsharing and Organization Development: A Productive Synergy," *Journal of Applied Behavioral Science* 25 (Nov. 1989): 213–14.

11. Doherty, Nord, and McAdams, "Gainsharing and Organization Development," pp. 212–14.

12. Doherty, Nord, and McAdams, "Gainsharing and Organization Development," p. 225.

13. Edward E. Lawler III, *Pay and Organization Development* (Reading, Mass.: Addison-Wesley, 1981), p. 4.

14. Lawler, *Pay and Organization Development*, pp. 197–98.

15. "Pay for Performance Works, Most Firms Say," *Miami Sun Sentinel*, June 12, 1984, p. 12C.

16. Robert L. Heneman, *Pay for Performance: Exploring the Merit System* (New York: Pergamon Press, 1984), pp. 4–5.

17. Lawler, *Pay and Organization Development*, p. 89.

18. Lawler, *Pay and Organization Development*, p. 131.

19. Lawler, *Pay and Organization Development*, p. 131.

20. Lawler, *Pay and Organization Development*, p. 108.

21. Heneman, *Pay for Performance*, pp. 11, 17.

22. American Compensation Association and Marc J. Wallace, Jr., "The American Compensation Association-Sponsored Study of Innovative Pay," in *Rewards and Renewal: America's Search for Competitive Advantage through Alternative Pay Strategies* (Scottsdale, Ariz.: American Compensation Association, 1990), p. 9.

23. Lawler, *Pay and Organization Development*, pp. 94–96.

24. American Compensation Association and Marc J. Wallace, Jr., "American Compensation Association-Sponsored Study," p. 21.

25. G. Douglas Jenkins, Jr., and Nina Gupta, "The Payoffs of Paying for Knowledge," *National Productivity Review* 4 (Spring 1985): 121.

26. Jenkins and Gupta, "Payoffs of Paying for Knowledge," p. 122.

27. Zager and Rosow, eds., *The Innovative Organization*, pp. 136–37, 298.

28. Jenkins and Gupta, "Payoffs of Paying for Knowledge," pp. 126–27.

29. Jenkins and Gupta, "Payoffs of Paying for Knowledge," p. 125.

30. Jenkins and Gupta, "Payoffs of Paying for Knowledge," pp. 122–23.

31. Quoted in "A Work Revolution in U.S. Industry," *Business Week*, May 16, 1983, p. 110.

32. Leonard M. Apcar, "Work Rule Programs Spread to Union Plants," *Wall Street Journal*, April 16, 1985, p. 6.

33. Jenkins and Gupta, "Payoffs of Paying for Knowledge," p. 128.

34. Jenkins and Gupta, "Payoffs of Paying for Knowledge," p. 128.

35. Jenkins and Gupta, "Payoffs of Paying for Knowledge," p. 128.

36. Jenkins and Gupta, "Payoffs of Paying for Knowledge," p. 124.

37. Jenkins and Gupta, "Payoffs of Paying for Knowledge," p. 129.

38. Apcar, "Work Rule Programs," p. 6.

Chapter 17. Gainsharing

1. Charles R. Gowen III, "Gainsharing Programs: An Overview of History and Research," *Journal of Organizational Behavior Management* 11 (1990): 77.

2. Larry Hatcher and Timothy L. Ross, "From Individual Incentives to an Organization-wide Gainsharing Plan: Effects on Teamwork and Product Quality," *Journal of Organizational Behavior* 12 (1991): 171.

3. Alan S. Blinder, ed., *Paying for Productivity: A Look at the Evidence* (Washington, D.C.: Brookings Institution, 1990), p. 23.

4. Arthur J. Ringham, "Designing a Gainsharing Program to Fit a Company's Operation," *National Productivity Review* (Spring 1984): 132.

5. Robert Kearns, "Gainsharing Tempers Wage Inequities," *Chicago Tribune*, Oct. 17, 1983, sec. 3., p. 3.

6. Robert J. Doyle, *Gainsharing and Productivity: A Guide to Planning, Implementation and Development* (New York: AMACOM, 1983), p. 123.

7. Doyle, *Gainsharing and Productivity*, p. 129.

8. Doyle, *Gainsharing and Productivity*, p. 125.

9. Doyle, *Gainsharing and Productivity*, p. 133.

10. John G. Belcher, Jr., *Gainsharing: The New Path to Profits and Productivity* (Houston: Gulf Publishing, 1991), pp. 116–20.

11. Doyle, *Gainsharing and Productivity*, p. 136.

12. Jerry McAdams, "Alternative Rewards: What's Best for Your Organization?" *Compensation and Benefits Management* (Winter 1990): 134.

13. Belcher, *Gainsharing*, pp. 146–47.

14. Doyle, *Gainsharing and Productivity*, p. 5.

15. Brian E. Moore and Timothy L. Ross, *The Scanlon Way to Improved Productivity: A Practical Guide* (New York: Wiley, 1978), p. 1.

16. Moore and Ross, *Scanlon Way to Improved Productivity*, p. 62.

17. Moore and Ross, *Scanlon Way to Improved Productivity*, p. 7.

18. Moore and Ross, *Scanlon Way to Improved Productivity*, p. 22.

19. Frederick G. Lesieur, ed., *The Scanlon Plan: A Frontier in Labor Management Cooperation* (New York: Technology Press of the Massachusetts Institute of Technology and Wiley, 1958), pp. 73–76.

20. Moore and Ross, *Scanlon Way to Improved Productivity*, p. 6.

21. Moore and Ross, *Scanlon Way to Improved Productivity*, p. 98.

22. Doyle, *Gainsharing and Productivity*, p. 9.

23. Moore and Ross, *Scanlon Way to Improved Productivity*, p. 37.

24. Moore and Ross, *Scanlon Way to Improved Productivity*, p. 132.

25. Moore and Ross, *Scanlon Way to Improved Productivity*, p. 40.

26. Doyle, *Gainsharing and Productivity*, p. 11.

27. Doyle, *Gainsharing and Productivity*, pp. 11–13.

28. Doyle, *Gainsharing and Productivity*, pp. 15–16.

29. Doyle, *Gainsharing and Productivity*, pp. 17–19.

30. Roger T. Kaufman, "The Effects of Improshare on Productivity," *Industrial and Labor Relations Review* 45 (Jan. 1992): 312.

31. Kaufman, "Effects of Improshare," p. 318.

32. Edward E. Lawler III, *Pay and Organization Development* (Reading, Mass.: Addison-Wesley, 1981), p. 144.

33. Gowen, "Gainsharing Programs," p. 84.

34. Christopher S. Miller and Michael H. Schuster, "Gainsharing Plans: A Comparative Analysis," *Organizational Dynamics* 16 (Summer 1987): 58.

35. Doyle, *Gainsharing and Productivity*, p. 57.

36. Doyle, *Gainsharing and Productivity*, pp. 57–60.
37. Doyle, *Gainsharing and Productivity*, pp. 23, 25–29,31–35.
38. Lesieur, *Scanlon Plan*, p. 49.
39. Lesieur, *Scanlon Plan*, pp. 110–11.
40. Paul S. Goodman and Brian E. Moore, "Factors Affecting Acquisition of Beliefs about a New Reward System," *Human Relations* 29 (1976): 573.
41. Slichter, Healy, and Livernash, *Impact of Collective Bargaining on Management*, pp. 875–77.
42. Belcher, *Gainsharing*, pp. 141–44.
43. Belcher, *Gainsharing*, pp. 144–47.
44. Belcher, *Gainsharing*, pp. 122–29.
45. Belcher, *Gainsharing*, pp. 132–36.
46. Belcher, *Gainsharing*, pp. 130–32.
47. For a discussion of variable or at-risk pay, see Martin L. Weitzman, *The Share Economy: Conquering Stagflation* (Cambridge: Harvard University Press, 1984).

Chapter 18. Taking Stock

1. See Frank T. Adams and Gary B. Hansen, *Putting Democracy to Work: A Practical Guide for Starting Worker-Owned Businesses*, rev. ed. (Eugene, Ore.: Hulogosi Communications, 1993), and Joseph R. Blasi, *The New Owners: The Mass Emergence of Employee Ownership in Public Corporations* (New York: HarperCollins, 1991).
2. Alan S. Blinder, ed., *Paying for Productivity: A Look at the Evidence* (Washington, D.C.: Brookings Institution, 1990), pp. 150–51.
3. *Employee Stock Ownership Plans: Little Evidence on Corporate Performance* (Washington, D.C.: U.S. General Accounting Office, Oct. 1987), pp. 35–36.
4. *Employee Stock Ownership Plans*, p. 33.
5. Elaine Hopkins, "Peoria Has ESOP: Management Has Control," *Guild Reporter*, June 7, 1985, p. 7.
6. Steven Hecker and John Hubbird, *Employee Buyouts and Job Retention: An Oregon Workers' Guide to Employee Ownership* (Eugene: University of Oregon Labor Education and Research Center, 1987), p. 8.
7. *Employee Stock Ownership Plans*, p. 10.
8. *Employee Stock Ownership Plans*, pp. 21–22.
9. *Employee Stock Ownership Plans*, pp. 26–31.
10. "ESOPS: Revolution or Ripoff?" *Business Week*, April 15, 1985, p. 94.
11. Institute for Social Research, University of Michigan, *Employee Ownership: Report to the Economic Development Administration* (Washington, D.C.: U.S. Department of Commerce, 1977), pp. 2–3.
12. Corey M. Rosen, Katherine J. Klein, and Karen M. Young, *Employee Ownership in America: The Equity Solution* (Lexington, Mass.: Lexington Books, 1986), p. 2.
13. Rosen, Klein, and Young, *Employee Ownership*, pp. 26, 46.
14. Hecker and Hubbird, *Employee Buyouts and Job Retention*, p. 11.
15. Tove H. Hammer and Robert Stern, "The Yo-Yo Model of Cooperation: Union Participation in Management at the Rath Packing Plant," *Industrial and Labor Relations Review* 39 (April 1986): 337–49.
16. Douglas R. Sease, "Worker-Owned Hyatt Clark Industries Looks for Buyer after GM Refuses Loan," *Wall Street Journal*, Sept. 10, 1985, p. 7.
17. Corey Rosen and Michael R. Dulworth, "Employee Ownership: Issues for Labor and Management," *National Productivity Review* 6 (Summer 1987): 218–21.

18. Joseph R. Blasi and Douglas L. Kruse, "Employee Ownership: Opportunities for Unions," *Workplace Topics* 2 (July 1991): 7–17.

19. *Workplace Topics* (special issue on employee ownership) 23 (July 1991).

20. Rosen, Klein, and Young, *Employee Ownership*, p. 216.

21. Deborah Groban-Olson, "Union Experiences with Worker Ownership: Legal and Practical Issues Raised by ESOPs, TRASOPs, Stock Purchases, and Cooperatives," *Wisconsin Law Review* (1982): 796–97.

22. Groban-Olson, "Union Experiences with Worker Ownership," pp. 800–803.

23. Rosen, Klein, and Young, *Employee Ownership*, pp. 138, 145.

24. Groban-Olson, "Union Experiences with Worker Ownership," pp. 772–73.

Index

International Masonry Institute (IMI), 44, 134, 135–136, 143
International Printing Pressmen and Assistants Union, 148
international union, informing of cooperative program, 229–230; *See also* unions
International Union of Bricklayers and Allied Craftsmen (BAC), 134, 136
International Union of Electronic, Electrical, Technical, Salaried and Machine Workers, quality circles policy of, 106
International Union of Operating Engineers, 85
interviews, for evaluation process, 245; *See also* evaluation
investment decision making, by union-management, 141–142; cooperative approaches to, **186**; in employee buyout, 307; *See also* decision making
ISO 9000 award, 150
Israel, union-owned business in, 8

Japan, competition from, 18; quality circles in, 105, 149; resource conservation in, 92–93; union-management relationship in, 6–7, 74, 149
JIT. *See* just-in-time systems
job descriptions, 115; in pay for knowledge systems, 273–274, 275; for staff of cooperative program, 210–211; *See also* classification systems; lay-offs
job redesign, 114–116, 142–143
job security, 64, 79, 85, 95, 118, 119, 130; cooperative approaches for, 187; cooperative safeguards for, 207–208; in gainsharing plans, 291; grievances about, 69; management planning for, 21; *See also* career development; compensation
Job Security Bank provisions, 208
Johnson Wax, 258
joint committees. *See* union-management committees
joint consultation system, contest with management-initiated schemes, 20; early experiments with, 18; union involvement with, 6; *See also* consultants
joint orientation sessions, 70; for new hires, 72–73
joint process, benefits of, 24; co-optation avoidance in, 29–32; design of, 174–175; equality required for, 30; evaluation in, 36; for grievances, 70; strengthening union politics, 26; union pitfalls in, 28–29; *See also* cooperation; union-management cooperative program

joint quality improvement process (JQIP), 158, 159
joint study teams, in steel industry, 63; in working harmony agreement, 13
joint training committees, 84–88; *See also* training
Joyce, John, 136
JQIP. *See* joint quality improvement process
Juran, Joseph M., 105, 149
just-in-time (JIT) systems, 123–124

Kanter, Rosabeth Moss, 107–108
Katz, Harry C., 21
Katzell, Ronald, 43
Kearns, David, 99, 156, 157
Kelso, Louis, 302
Kirkland, Lane, 23–24
Klingel, Sally, 98
knowledge compensation. *See* pay for knowledge
Kochan, Thomas A., 21, 81
Kodak, 258

labor education. *See* education; skills; training
Labor Notes, 30
labor-management committees. *See* union-management committees
Labor-Management Participation Teams, 204
labor-management relationship. *See* union-management relationship
laissez-faire, absence of in workplace cooperation, 5; pitfalls of in cooperative program, 200
Landrum-Griffin Act, 311
Lawler, Edward III, 270, 289
lay-offs, joint meetings for, 73–75; retraining for, 85–86; within cooperative program, 208; *See also* job security
leadership, in adversarial situations, 26; designating for cooperative programs, 204; developing for, 27–28; education for, 27–28; informational procedures for, 228–229; involving in program design, 182; by management in gainsharing program, 291; skills improvement for, 41; union, education requirements for, 27–28; visionary, 58–59; for work groups, 117, 118; *See also* executives; stewards; supervisory personnel
Leadership through Quality (LTQ) program, 156–157
Ledford, Gerald E., Jr., 107
leisure time incentives, 262–263; *See also* compensation

About the Authors

Edward Cohen-Rosenthal is a senior extension associate in the Programs for Employment and Workplace Systems in the Cornell University School of Industrial and Labor Relations, and labor director of the Institute for Collective Bargaining. He also is director of the Work and Environment Initiative at Cornell's ILR School. Previously, he served as assistant to the president of the International Union of Bricklayers and Allied Craftsmen (AFL-CIO). He has also been associate director of the American Center for the Quality of Work Life, on the faculty at the Rutgers University Labor Education Center, and project adviser for the Trade Union Study of Alternative Working Patterns in Europe. He has published and lectured extensively on new working and learning arrangements. He founded ECR Associates in 1979 and is a principal partner in the firm. He holds a master's degree in education from Harvard University and a bachelor's degree from Rutgers College.

Cynthia Burton is president of ECR Associates in Foster, Virginia. She also is a consultant to large private and public sector organizations, small businesses, and nonprofit organizations, with which she works to improve their organizational effectiveness. Before working at ECR Associates, she was program associate at the Maryland Center for Productivity and Quality of Working Life, and codirector of Strongforce, Inc., a Washington, D.C., economic development organization. She began her career in management at a major international company. In addition to publications in union-management cooperation, Burton is coauthor of a book on women and economic development and a workbook on equal education for women. Burton holds a bachelor's degree from Western Michigan University.

Cohen-Rosenthal and Burton have consulted together since 1979 for a wide variety of union, government, corporate, and educational organizations for which they conceptualize and implement joint union-management projects. They have developed programs in the areas of employee participation, QWL and productivity improvement, strategic bargaining, resource conservation, and new technology.